D0536732

THE**CLUSTERED**WORLD

Also by Michael J. Weiss
The Clustering of America
Latitudes & Attitudes

how we live, what we buy, and

 Little, Brown and Company   Boston New York London

THE**CLUSTERED**WORLD
what it all means about who we are

MICHAEL J. WEISS

FIRST EDITION

The Clustered World is based on survey-generated maps, market profiles, and demographic statistics about the United States provided by Claritas Inc. and its PRIZM cluster system. The U.S. survey data was collected by Mediamark Research Inc., NFO Research, Inc., The Polk Company, and Simmons Market Research Bureau, under an agreement with Claritas Inc. All rights reserved and used with permission.

Statistical data, maps, and information about Canada were provided by Compusearch Micromarketing Data & Systems and its PSYTE segmentation system. Material about countries outside North America was provided by Experian Micromarketing and its MOSAIC International Network and Global MOSAIC segmentation system. Used with permission.

Claritas Inc., PRIZM, and Claritas are registered trademarks of Claritas Inc. The cluster names, such as "Blue Blood Estates" and "Winner's Circle," are trademarks of Claritas Inc. Other company names and product names are trademarks of their respective companies and are hereby acknowledged.

Library of Congress Cataloging-in-Publication Data
Weiss, Michael J.
    The clustered world : how we live, what we buy, and what it all means
about who we are / by Michael J. Weiss.
        p.   cm.
    ISBN 0-316-92920-4
    1. United States — Social conditions — 1980– 2. United States — Social
life and customs — 1971– 3. Consumers' preferences — United States.
4. Postal zones — Social aspects — United States. 5. Social surveys —
United States.   I. Title.
HN59.2.W449   2000
306' .0973 — dc21   99-32831

10   9   8   7   6   5   4   3   2   1

Printed in the United States of America

For Phyllis, Elizabeth, and Jonathan — as always

CONTENTS

THE**CLUSTERED**WORLD

INTRODUCTION **CONFESSIONS** OF A **DEMOGRAPHIC DETECTIVE**

Fifteen years ago, I started writing a story that I have not been able to finish. I interviewed a social scientist turned entrepreneur named Jonathan Robbin who'd classified all Americans into forty neighborhood types, or "clusters," with catchy nicknames like Blue Blood Estates, Shotguns & Pickups, and Norma Rae-ville. Marketers quickly discovered that the clusters were a powerful tool to analyze Americans and predict what they like, which messages they respond to, how they think. People outside the business community also became enamored of the clusters for what they revealed about American lifestyles — both profound and trivial. Why do we live in raucous cities, fight the commute in the suburbs, or flee the metro areas for quieter exurban towns? What prompts some of us to eat Brie and others to devour Velveeta cheese? And where are other people who share these tastes and quirks?

As a journalist, I saw the dual potential of the clusters: as a clever way to sell soap and an insightful guide to understanding how people live. With the mass market splintering into niches of distinct populations and tastes, the clusters helped explain the new cartography of American society. Based on database-driven maps and statistical profiles, the clusters reflected the nation's diversity in all its messy glory — from the yuppie enclaves of San Francisco to the ghettos of the South Bronx to the prairie villages of western Minnesota. In both hard numbers and anecdotal portraits, the clusters showed the big picture of our peculiar social disorder. I found myself drawn to cluster information the same way others are intrigued by sex surveys: to discover who's doing what, where, and how often.

Gradually, geodemographics — as this marketing science is formally known — became my beat. In 1988, my book *The Clustering of America* introduced to general audiences the clusters of Claritas Inc., the Arlington, Virginia–based marketing information company. In 1994, I mapped the consumption patterns of everything from Twinkies to theme parks in *Latitudes & Attitudes.* I wrote articles, gave lectures, and created cluster-based maps for magazines and web sites, detailing which Americans eat chocolate, listen to talk radio, hate baseball, or worry most about the economy. I used the clusters to root out the reasons for human behavior, and talk-show hosts began introducing me as the Demographic Detective.

Over the intervening years, interest in clusters has grown as marketers continue to slice and dice consumer segments, merging and mining data to learn what people want with every shift in taste. Cluster-based marketing has gone mainstream and is now used by corporate, nonprofit, and political groups alike to target their audiences. Ad agencies search the clusters for hot buttons on the consumer psyche. Restaurants, banks, and retailers use cluster systems to identify locations in which to open new outlets or close poor performers. Direct mailers discover the best prospects from subscription lists by correlating addresses to cluster tastes and spending habits. Even health officials are using clusters to correct the bad habits of citizens, earmarking funds for prevention programs based on a community's cluster profile.

What's in a Name?

Clusters go by different names in different countries. The table below compares affluent lifestyles types in urban and suburban areas in three countries, according to their cluster name.

Socioeconomic Grouping	United States *(PRIZM)*	Canada *(PSYTE)*	Great Britain *(MOSAIC)*
Elite Suburbs	Blue Blood Estates	Suburban Executives	Clever Capitalists
	Winner's Circle	Mortgaged in Suburbia	Rising Materialists
	Executive Suites	Technocrats & Bureaucrats	Corporate Careerists
	Pools & Patios	Asian Heights	Ageing Professionals
	Kids & Cul-de-Sacs		Small Time Business
Upscale Urban Areas	Urban Gold Coast	Canadian Establishment	Bedsits & Shop Flats
	Money & Brains	The Affluentials	Studio Singles
	Young Literati	Urban Gentry	College & Communal
	American Dreams		Chattering Classes
	Bohemian Mix		

(Sources: Claritas Inc., Compusearch, Experian Micromarketing)

Today, this clustered view of society has spread throughout the world. Cluster systems have been developed for twenty-five countries, from Canada and Great Britain across Europe to South Africa, Australia, and Japan. The globalization of products and ideas is partly behind this boom in cluster systems, as corporations, eager for new consumers, charge across national borders. But the fall of Communism and the rise of the European Union is also fueling the disintegration of traditional markets. Experian Micromarketing, based in Nottingham, England, and Orange, California, has launched an international cluster system called Global MOSAIC that segments nearly 800 million people around the world into fourteen common neighborhood types. For the first time, marketers can follow their prime audience from, say, the Elite Suburbs cluster in the United States to similar cluster havens in Ireland and Germany. Or they can develop marketing campaigns mixing the global clusters with country-specific cluster systems, which have also christened their lifestyle segments with names that are often witty (like Great Britain's Chattering Classes) and sometimes wrenching (South Africa's Crammed Chaos).

So, on the eve of the millennium, I've returned to the cluster systems for a reality check, to assess the changes America has undergone over the last decade and to compare America's clustered society today with those of other nations. My research for *The Clustered World* is the most extensive ever done on the subject. I began by analyzing the cluster systems of three of the world's largest geodemographic companies: Claritas in the United States, Compusearch in Canada, and Experian throughout Europe. Next, I went to the businesses that use the data to learn how their cluster-based campaigns helped them reach their target customers. To better understand how consumers spend their time and money, I tapped the surveys of several North American research firms — Mediamark Research Inc., NFO Research, Inc., The Polk Company, and Simmons Market Research Bureau — as well as others abroad. Finally, to bring these statistical portraits to life, I hit the road, visiting seventy-five communities in four countries, following a computer-generated itinerary of neighborhoods that best represented the U.S. clusters of PRIZM, Claritas's geodemographic system, and selected clusters in Canada, England, and Spain. Although I packed my bags with an American perspective, I tried

All told, I logged nearly 80,000 miles and interviewed more than 400 people — local residents, politicians, shopkeepers, librarians, clergymen, even street people — anyone who could give voice to his or her cluster lifestyle.

to view the international lifestyles in developed and emerging countries with an open mind.

All told, I logged nearly 80,000 miles and interviewed more than 400 people — local residents, politicians, shopkeepers, librarians, clergymen, even street people — anyone who could give voice to his or her cluster lifestyle. The journey was always illuminating, though sometimes unsettling. In a cramped apartment in Atwater Village, a downscale Hispanic Mix neighborhood in Los Angeles, four children shared a single bedroom; in another unit, two slept in a closet. In Monroe, Georgia, a Norma Rae-ville town east of Atlanta, segregated social patterns are so entrenched that there are two American Legions — one for blacks and one for whites. In the Blue Blood Estates suburb of Potomac, Maryland, the Beemers and Jeeps of the high school students are far nicer than the subcompacts of their teachers.

Abroad, I discovered how American culture is seeping inexorably into lifestyles around the world. In Madrid's Retiro Park, an upscale Classic Bourgeoisie Neighbourhood cluster in the MOSAIC Iberia system, the local shopping malls look just like those in Beverly Hills, California, or Scarsdale, New York, right down to the marble floor and airy atrium surrounded by posh boutiques. In the English village of Yate, a Nestmaking Families cluster community in the British MOSAIC system, young homemakers serve Barbie brand spaghetti from a pink can emblazoned with the familiar visage of America's sweetheart doll. And though each country has a unique culture, the cluster systems show that many lifestyles are similar throughout the world. Indeed, there appears to be a universal yuppie type, Educated Cosmopolitans in the Global MOSAIC system, with a fondness for costly outdoor vacations. From Boston to Barcelona, a winter holiday means skiing in Aspen. Around the globe, the clusters indicate how many people are living in parallel universes.

One caveat: This is by no means an academic dissertation on the geodemographics industry. There are no technical comparisons of one cluster system's mapping software versus another, and little about the competitive pressures facing individual companies. Though I have always been more interested in what each company's cluster system says about people outside their offices, it's also important to quickly note what has been going on inside their boardrooms, as the industry has undergone some noteworthy changes in recent years. After a number of mergers and acqui-

sitions, two cluster companies, Claritas and Experian, now dominate the industry. Claritas, which is owned by VNU, the giant
Dutch-based publishing and information services company, has
brand-name recognition with PRIZM in the U.S., and is rapidly
pushing into Europe. Experian, a division of Britain's Great Universal Stores conglomerate, is the dominant player in Europe, and
in 1997 landed on American shores with its US MOSAIC system.
The same year, Canada's Compusearch firm was bought by The
Polk Company, the oldest consumer marketing information company in the U.S., and it soon introduced an American cluster system of its own called PSYTE USA. With only a handful of
companies in a somewhat specialized industry, it's not surprising
that the same personnel keep popping up at the different compa-

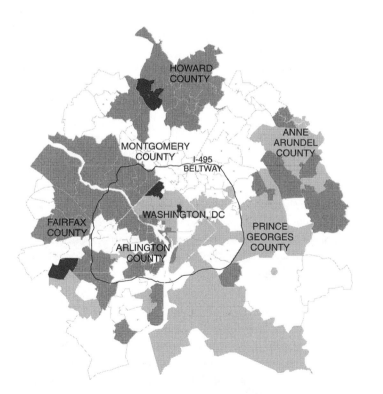

A Tale of Two Cheeses: Brie and Velveeta in Washington

Cluster-based maps are not only important for businesses trying to identify their
niche markets in a community. They also
reflect cultural differences and divisions.
In Washington, D.C., a fault line exists
between the fans of Brie cheese, who
tend to hold down executive jobs and
write the laws of government, and those
of Kraft Velveeta, who maintain the service
economy.

*High Brie and Velveeta consumption, compared to U.S.
averages, by Washington-area zip codes*

■ Both products high usage
▨ High Brie usage (>13.2%)
▨ High Velveeta usage (>15.2%)
☐ Both products lower usage

Top Brie Clusters Country Squires / Military Quarters / Blue Blood Estates / Winner's Circle / Young Literati

Top Velveeta Clusters Mid-City Mix / Urban Gold Coast / Big Sky Families / Kids & Cul-de-Sacs / Big Fish, Small Pond

(Sources: PRIZM, Claritas Inc., Simmons Market Research Bureau)

nies. But in an unusual case of corporate switch-hitting, former adman Robin Page was hired by all three companies to develop the names for all of their American clusters. He alone is responsible for appellations such as Kids & Cul-de-Sacs (PRIZM), Country Clubbers (US MOSAIC), and Gerberville (PSYTE USA) — a feat comparable to one person's naming every car model produced by Detroit's Big Three automakers.

Despite my long love affair with clusters, I cannot deny the chilly reception they're met with in some circles. Some critics object to the whole "pigeonholing" process of being tagged as bar-hopping, Volkswagen-owning, MTV-viewing members of the Bohemian Mix cluster, with predictable views on politics and the arts. Still others complain that the clusters are used by marketers — especially junk mailers and telemarketers — in increasingly intrusive campaigns that cross the lines of privacy and propriety. But after years of covering the industry, I take some comfort in the benign nature of the clusters, in the fact that they're designed to explain patterns of group behavior without the need to delve into individual households. And I recognize that the basic clustering concept, that people in the same neighborhoods tend to behave (or at least consume) the same way, goes back to cave-dweller time. The clusters simply help describe our diverse world today — the good, the bad, the dull, the outlandish.

Ultimately, by blending statistical data with on-the-street research, *The Clustered World* presents an insider's view of some of the world's quintessential lifestyles at the turn of the millennium. A window on the global village, the book highlights the demographic changes that have swept across the United States over the last decade, describes settlement patterns in other countries, and compares the lifestyles of consumers in the U.S. and abroad. Since my first introduction to the clusters, I've come to appreciate their ability to illustrate how people live in an increasingly fragmented world. And all my travels, through neighborhoods and survey data, have only convinced me of their power to divine the mysteries of how we live. "You're a busybody," one man from rural Matheson, Colorado, declared as he dismissed my request for an interview. Well, I suppose I am. But you have to be to write about life in a clustered world, where constant change makes providing a conclusion to my story virtually impossible. Just ask any marketer — or your next-door neighbor.

1 AROUND THE CLUSTERED WORLD
an overview

We read about scoundrels and politicians on Page 1, but it's all the other folk who make up most of the country.

— Charles Kuralt

The fragmenting of America

At first glance, Berwyn, Illinois, resembles many of the close-in suburbs of Chicago, a settled middle-class community of beige brick bungalows known as a gateway for immigrants. Since Berwyn's founding a century ago, waves of Czechs, Italians, Poles, and Irish have come to work in the area's foundries and patronize the ethnic bakeries and restaurants along Cermak Street. Proud of their toehold on the American Dream, homemakers in babushkas would sweep their back alleys clean enough to eat dinners of stuffed cabbage, sausage, and spaghetti off the asphalt.

But times changed, the factories closed, and Berwyn's old-world residents aged. More recently, Central and South American immigrants have discovered Berwyn, carving up the neat bungalows into overcrowded apartments and sending their children to schools where 80 percent of the students speak Spanish. Today, Berwyn is a simmering stew of foreign-born residents who work side by side at blue-collar jobs but go their separate ways after hours. Italians congregate at the Italian-American Club for dinners and boccie tournaments. Hispanics meet at new Mexican restaurants and super *mercados,* and throw noisy parties on Cinco de Mayo, Mexico's independence day. Regular proposals to unify the ethnic groups and merge a Hispanic festival with the Czechs' Houby Days parade (celebrating an old-world mushroom) inevitably fail. Relative newcomer Rana Khan, a Pakistani doctor who came to Berwyn in 1994 with her husband and three children, found an insular community. "I went to a PTA meeting, and for two hours not one person said a word to me," she recalled. "With Americans, it's always 'hi and bye.'"

In the 1990 census, Americans identified themselves as belonging to 300 races, 600 Native American tribes, 70 Hispanic groups, and 75 ethnic combinations.

Few places present a greater refutation of the American "melting pot" image than contemporary Berwyn. But cultural dissonance has developed, to some degree, in communities all around the country. On the eve of the twenty-first century, America has become a splintered society, with multi-ethnic towns like Berwyn reflecting a nation more diverse than ever. In the 1990 census, Americans identified themselves as belonging to 300 races, 600 Native American tribes, 70 Hispanic groups, and 75 ethnic combinations. Since 1970, the number of immigrants living in the U.S. has nearly tripled, increasing to 26.3 million and creating school districts in New York, Los Angeles, and Chicago where students speak more than 100 languages and take bilingual classes in everything from Armenian to Tagalog. The explosion of niche cable TV programming, on-line chat rooms, and targeted businesses like Urban Outfitters and Zany Brainy all point to a population with a classic case of multiple personality disorder. The mind plugged into the next set of Walkman headphones may be attuned to Christian rap, New Age drumming, or Deepak Chopra–style self-improvement.

For a nation that's always valued community, this breakup of the mass market into balkanized population segments is as momentous as the collapse of Communism. Forget the melting pot. America today would be better characterized as a salad bar. From the high-rises of Manhattan's Upper East Side to the trailer parks of South Texas, from the techno-elite professionals with their frequent-flier cards to the blue-collar laborers who frequent corner bars, America has fractured into distinctive lifestyles, each with its own borders. The horrors of urban living have sparked a migration of city dwellers to the countryside, creating a nation polarized between cosmopolitan cities and homogeneous exurban communities — not to mention pockets of latte-and-Lexus culture appearing amid cows and country music. At the same time, the rise of gated communities in America bespeaks a population trying to get away from children, gangs, the poor, immigrants, anyone unlike themselves.

Today, the country's new motto should be *"E pluribus pluriba"*: "Out of many, many."

Evidence of the nation's accelerated fragmentation is more than anecdotal. According to the geodemographers at Claritas, American society today is composed of sixty-two distinct lifestyle types — a 55 percent increase over the forty segments that defined the U.S. populace during the 1970s and '80s. These clusters are based on composites of age, ethnicity, wealth, urbanization, housing style, and family structure. But their boundaries have undergone dramatic shifts in recent years as economic, political, and social trends stratify Americans in new ways. Immigration, women in the workforce, delayed marriage, aging baby boomers, economic swings: All these trends have combined to increase the number of distinct lifestyles. And advances in database technology that link the clusters to marketing surveys and opinion polls are permitting more accurate portraits of how these disparate population groups behave — whether they prefer tofu or tamales, Mercedes or Mazda, legalizing pot or supporting animal rights.

In today's clustered world, America has become a nation of Executive Suites (upscale suburban couples), Big Fish, Small Pond (midscale exurban families), and Rustic Elders (downscale rural retirees). If you live in a new cluster called Young Literati, present in North Brooklyn, New York, and Hermosa Beach, California, your neighbors are likely coffee bar–addicted Generation Xers into hardback books and music videos. If you've fled the city for the country lifestyle of Graft, Vermont, or Sutter Creek, California, you more than likely inhabit New Eco-topia, where your baby-boom neighbors enjoy country music, camping, and protesting to their congresspeople over the encroachment of big business. In Mid-City Mix, a cluster of working-class African American neighborhoods, residents believe O. J. Simpson was properly acquitted of murdering his former wife and her friend. In Greenbelt Families, an upscale white enclave typically located near Mid-City Mix communities, residents almost universally believe he was guilty. When you say "oil" in Rural Industria, a blue-collar heartland cluster, residents think "Quaker State." In the family suburbs of Winner's Circle, the second most affluent lifestyle, they think "extra virgin olive."

These lifestyles represent America's modern tribes, sixty-two distinct population groups each with its own set of values, culture, and means of coping with today's problems. A generation ago, Americans thought of themselves as city dwellers, suburbanites, or country folk. But we are no longer that simple, and our neighborhoods reflect our growing complexity. Clusters, which were created to identify demographically similar zip codes around the U.S., are now used to demarcate a variety of small geographic areas, including census tracts (500–1,000 households) and zip

When you say "oil" in Rural Industria, a blue-collar heartland cluster, residents think "Quaker State." In the family suburbs of Winner's Circle, the second most affluent lifestyle, they think "extra virgin olive."

America's Clustered Lifestyles

According to Claritas's PRIZM cluster system, America consists of 62 classic lifestyle types, divided into 15 socioeconomic groupings. They are listed below with demographic descriptions.

Clusters	Demographic Snapshots	Social Groupings
Blue Blood Estates	Elite super-rich families	Elite Suburbs
Winner's Circle	Executive suburban families	
Executive Suites	Upscale white-collar couples	
Pools & Patios	Established empty-nesters	
Kids & Cul-de-Sacs	Upscale suburban families	
Urban Gold Coast	Elite urban singles and couples	Urban Uptown
Money & Brains	Sophisticated town-house couples	
Young Literati	Upscale urban singles and couples	
American Dreams	Established urban immigrant families	
Bohemian Mix	Bohemian singles and couples	
Second City Elite	Upscale executive families	Second City Society
Upward Bound	Young upscale white-collar families	
Gray Power	Affluent retirees in Sunbelt cities	
Country Squires	Elite exurban families	Landed Gentry
God's Country	Executive exurban families	
Big Fish, Small Pond	Small-town executive families	
Greenbelt Families	Young middle-class town families	
Young Influentials	Upwardly mobile singles and couples	The Affluentials
New Empty Nests	Upscale suburban fringe couples	
Boomers & Babies	Young white-collar suburban families	
Suburban Sprawl	Young suburban town-house couples	
Blue-Chip Blues	Upscale blue-collar families	
Upstarts & Seniors	Middle-income empty-nesters	Inner Suburbs
New Beginnings	Young mobile city singles	
Mobility Blues	Young blue-collar / service families	
Gray Collars	Aging couples in inner suburbs	
Urban Achievers	Midlevel white-collar urban couples	Urban Midscale
Big City Blend	Middle-income immigrant families	
Old Yankee Rows	Empty-nest middle-class families	
Mid-City Mix	African American singles and families	
Latino America	Hispanic middle-class families	

Clusters	Demographic Snapshots	Social Groupings
Middleburg Managers	Midlevel white-collar couples	Second City Centers
Boomtown Singles	Middle-income young singles	
Starter Families	Young middle-class families	
Sunset City Blues	Empty-nesters in aging industrial cities	
Towns & Gowns	College town singles	
New Homesteaders	Young middle-class families	Exurban Blues
Middle America	Midscale families in midsize towns	
Red, White & Blues	Small-town blue-collar families	
Military Quarters	GIs & surrounding off-base families	
Big Sky Families	Midscale couples, kids, and farmland	Country Families
New Eco-topia	Rural white- or blue-collar and farm families	
River City, USA	Middle-class rural families	
Shotguns & Pickups	Rural blue-collar workers and families	
Single City Blues	Ethnically mixed urban singles	Urban Cores
Hispanic Mix	Urban Hispanic singles and families	
Inner Cities	Inner-city solo-parent families	
Smalltown Downtown	Older renters and young families	Second City Blues
Hometown Retired	Low-income, older singles & couples	
Family Scramble	Low-income Hispanic families	
Southside City	African American service workers	
Golden Ponds	Retirement town seniors	Working Towns
Rural Industria	Low-income blue-collar families	
Norma Rae-ville	Young families, biracial mill towns	
Mines & Mills	Older families, mines and mill towns	
Agri-Business	Rural farm town and ranch families	The Heartlanders
Grain Belt	Farm owners and tenants	
Blue Highways	Moderate blue-collar / farm families	Rustic Living
Rustic Elders	Low-income, older, rural couples	
Back Country Folks	Remote rural / town families	
Scrub Pine Flats	Older African American farm families	
Hard Scrabble	Older families in poor, isolated areas	

(Sources: PRIZM, Claritas Inc.)

plus 4 postal codes (about ten households). Once used inter-
changeably with *neighborhood type,* however, the term *cluster*
now refers to population segments where, thanks to technological
advancements, no physical contact is required for cluster membership. The residents of Pools & Patios, a cluster of upper-
middle-class suburban couples, congregate in La Crescenta,
California, and Rockville, Maryland, but they also can be found on
one block in Spring Hill, Tennessee, and in a few households in
Portland, Maine. These residents can meet their neighbors across
a fence to borrow a cup of sugar or argue issues, or they can
schmooze on-line in the nonphysical world, debating the merits of
a vacation in Austria or Hungary. In the clustered world, geographic communities united by PTAs, political clubs, and Sunday
schools have given way to consumption communities defined by
demographics, intellect, taste, and outlook. Today's town square is
the on-line chat room.

The cluster system serves as a barometer in this changing
world, monitoring how the country is evolving in distinct geo-
graphical areas. No longer can sociologists lump "American" behavior into a single trend line. Despite what network newscasters
might have you believe, Americans are not becoming smarter or
fatter or more indebted — but particular clusters most assuredly
are. When Georgia's Division of Public Health cluster-coded the
state's entire population, it found higher rates of breast cancer
among women who lived in the factory towns classified Mines &
Mills; afterward, it targeted mammography programs to those
cluster communities. Nationwide, the poorly educated, small-town
residents of Back Country Folks are typically more overweight
than the college graduates of Urban Gold Coast, who heed the fat
and cholesterol information printed on packaged foods. Surveys
find that one in three Americans smoke, but many city-based
Money & Brains sophisticates would be hard-pressed to name a
smoker in their circle of friends and family (not counting, of
course, those men and women caught up in the recent yuppie-
stoked cigar-sucking craze). Smokers thrive in other lifestyle
types, like Grain Belt and Scrub Pine Flats, a long geographic and
demographic distance from upscale, college-educated, health-
conscious surroundings. As the "American Way" becomes more
elusive, the insights offered by the cluster system help us to appreciate who we are and where we're headed.

Sometimes, the clusters simply underscore realities already

apparent, such as the widening gap between the richest and poorest Americans. The nation's most affluent neighborhood type, Blue Blood Estates (where the heirs to "old money" fortunes reside), has been joined by other wealthy havens, such as Winner's Circle (new-money suburbs dotted with split-levels) and Country Squires (ritzy small towns like Middleburg, Virginia, characterized by horse farms and sport-utility vehicles). At the other end of the spectrum, America's poorest citizens are no longer confined to the urban ghettos of Inner Cities or the isolated settlements of Hard Scrabble, where hunting and fishing help put food on the table. For the first time, the poorest neighborhoods in America are found outside the nation's largest metros, in Southside City, a cluster of midsized city districts where blue-collar African Americans have a median income of $15,800, barely above the poverty line of $15,570 for a family of four. Between the 1980 and 1990 census, the median income of the wealthiest cluster jumped 55 percent, to $113,000 annually, while that of the poorest cluster increased only 39 percent, to $15,000. Sociologists say global competition and the cyber-revolution have widened the gap that divides the haves from the have-nots. But long-term contracts for workers in blue-collar industries are also disappearing. No longer are Americans rising and falling together, as if in one large national boat," former labor secretary Robert Reich observed. "We are, increasingly, in different, smaller boats." And not all of us are assured of life rafts.

At the same time, the American family is evolving into many different kinds of households with wildly different needs. Marketers once pitched products nationally on network TV to just a few dominant prototypes, the favorite being the white middle-class housewife wearing a sweater and fake pearls who worried herself sick over ring around the collar. Today, there's no overwhelming type of household in the United States. The most common model, married couples without children, represents 30 percent of the nation's households. Married couples with children make up about 25 percent, and about the same percentage of Americans live alone, up from less than 8 percent in 1940. One result of the continuing singles boom is the emergence of a cluster called Upstarts & Seniors, which contains both young and older singles living in modest homes and apartments often located in inner-ring suburbs. Despite their differences in age, they share a fondness for movies, health clubs, and coffee bars. In Upstarts & Seniors communities like Lakeside, Virginia, outside of Richmond,

"No longer are Americans rising and falling together, as if in one large national boat," former labor secretary Robert Reich observed. "We are, increasingly, in different, smaller boats."

a visitor can find a shopping center with a tanning salon next to a shop specializing in denture care.

If there is any successor to the traditional homemaker who dominated popular culture a generation ago, it's today's Soccer Mom, that working mother of school-aged children whom commentators celebrated as the key to the 1996 presidential election. Found in a dozen lifestyle types, Soccer Moms typically describe themselves as political moderates concerned about family values, reducing military spending, and increasing environmental programs. Although some political commentators doubted their impact on the election, the pervasiveness of their lifestyle cannot be overlooked. In Upward Bound, a midsized city cluster of new subdivisions filled with dual-income couples, Soccer Moms swarm the streets every afternoon and weekend in their GMC Suburbans and Mercury Villagers, carting kids to chess clubs, tae kwon do lessons, and, yes, soccer leagues. In the cluster community of Federal Way, Washington, south of Seattle, many women log three hundred miles a week in after-school schlepping. A local marketing survey found that more people eat meals in their cars than any other place — including the home.

Under the cluster system, the "average American" — that is, the typical citizen trumpeted by network commentators — proves to be a figment of statisticians' imaginations, since the "average" lifestyle cluster represents less than 2 percent of the population. The "middle class" now comes in variations ranging from suburban white-collar couples (New Empty Nests) to rural blue-collar families (Shotguns & Pickups). Even the most populous cluster lifestyles are too small to have much meaning. Ten years ago, the largest cluster in America was Blue-Chip Blues, a collection of blue-collar family suburbs like Ronkonkoma, New York, and Mesquite, Texas, where the lifestyle resembled an old episode of *Roseanne.* Residents liked to relax by drinking beer or going to the Elks Club, and meals included heavily processed food like Hamburger Helper, potato chips, and creamed corn. But as manufacturing jobs disappeared and the children of Blue-Chip Blues grew up and moved out, the cluster population dropped from 6 percent of U.S. households to 2 percent. And its working-class lifestyle faded. In recent years, membership in fraternal organizations has dropped, beer sales have nosedived, and *Roseanne* has disappeared, to be replaced by sitcoms like *Friends,* whose characters pursue typical Bohemian Mix lifestyles. *Roseanne* just couldn't compete, despite an abrupt story-line shift that found the blue-collar family suddenly rich beyond their imagination after hitting the lottery — one working-class version of the American Dream.

Although hip urban lifestyles may be in vogue on TV, the most populous cluster in the nation today is Kids & Cul-de-Sacs, a collection of white-collar family suburbs like Wheaton, Illinois, known for its noisy medley of bikes, boom boxes, carpooled kids, and dogs. Home to about 9 million people, this cluster is the nation's largest — eleven times larger than the smallest cluster, Urban Gold Coast. But by no means does it represent the "average American" type. Even with its sprawling families — this cluster ranks first for having families with four or more people — only 3.5 percent of all Americans live in Kids & Cul-de-Sacs. The median household income, $61,600, is 40 percent higher than the national average. And the cluster contains half as many blacks and twice as many Asians as the U.S. norm. Together, these demographics have a singular effect on consumer patterns. Kids & Cul-de-Sacs households are much more likely than the general population to eat Brie cheese, drive Infinitis, buy CD-ROM disks, and shop at Price Club. When it comes to television, *This Old House* outranks *NYPD Blue*. On the sidewalks of Wheaton, it's not unusual to see traffic jams involving strollers; the lives and crimes of the *NYPD Blue* squad just don't resonate here.

On the other hand, there's plenty of evidence that a thriving homogenized culture exists in America, with identically dressed counter people flipping identically dressed hamburgers in strip malls from coast to coast. In this slice of Anywhere, U.S.A., giants like Wal-Mart and Home Depot offer almost anything to anybody, smothering the local shops that in the past gave cities and small towns their character and charm. On local TV stations, the bland voices of anchorpeople have supplanted regional accents. Social scientists have dubbed this process "the McDonaldization of society." They could just have well have termed it the salsa-dipping, Cajun-seasoning, Carolina-barbecuing of America, as fast-food chains have watered down and dispersed these once-regional food trends throughout the nation.

Who buys what?

A journey through the clustered world reveals that such mass-appeal businesses do not reach out and touch millions. Not all Americans have equal access to McDonald's and mall outlets; indeed, there are many clusters where consumers have never sampled the tart taste of an Arch Deluxe. And the creeping sameness of malls is one reason that over the last three years, some analysts estimate, as many as 600 of the nation's 2,000 malls have experienced financial trouble. In contemporary America, different products and brands mean different things to different people. The hip city dwellers of Young Literati and Urban Gold Coast may look down on McDonald's as a déclassé purveyor of fat-laden meat and fries, counter to their lifestyle, which celebrates lean, low-cholesterol health food. In Norma Rae-ville, a cluster of mill towns concentrated in the Southeastern states, having a McDonald's in town is a sign that your community is no longer a backwater. In Monroe, Georgia, a cluster community where the closest white-tablecloth restaurants are a twenty-minute-drive away in Athens, residents were tickled when a McDonald's outlet recently arrived. On a Saturday afternoon, it's often the center of community activity, the cars lined up fifteen deep at the drive-in window. Many wish more chains would move in. As one resident observes, "I'd really feel like we made it if a Red Lobster came to town."

Of course, regional loyalties that once thrived in geographic isolation still affect values and consumer patterns. In the kitchens of the Northwest, coffee bean grinders are mandatory. Salsa has

The Wal-Marting of America

Many American communities have Wal-Marts and McDonald's, but that doesn't mean the country is completely homogenized. In today's fragmented marketplace, mainstream chains do not appeal equally to all clusters. Wal-Mart's biggest fans are middle- and working-class families in heartland clusters like Grain Belt; it's less likely to attract city dwellers, the affluent, and minorities in clusters such as Bohemian Mix.

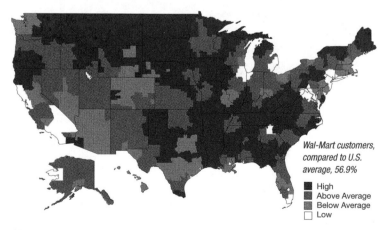

Wal-Mart customers, compared to U.S. average, 56.9%

■ High
■ Above Average
■ Below Average
□ Low

Top Clusters   Military Quarters / Hard Scrabble / Grain Belt / Red, White & Blues / Mines & Mills

Top Markets   Clarksburg-Weston, West Virginia / Bluefield–Beckley–Oak Hill, West Virginia / Ottumwa, Iowa–Kirksville, Missouri / Glendive, Montana / Jonesboro, Arkansas

(Sources: PRIZM, Claritas Inc., Mediamark Research Inc.)

outsold ketchup for years in the Southwest. "If it ain't fried, it ain't Southern" is how one resident of the Red, White & Blues town of Hiram, Georgia, describes her regional cuisine, which includes fried peach pie. Sales of grits still mimic the old boundaries of the Confederate States of America. Fashion designers have long known that logos confer different degrees of status depending on where shoppers live. When Rough Hewn clothiers slapped logos on shirts and sweaters, they became hot items in the Southeast; in the Northeast, sales plummeted.

And yet, as major corporations continually foist their uniform products and national brands on consumers across the land, regional differences are having less and less influence. Sharper distinctions of taste occur up and down the cluster ladder. Along the mean streets of Inner Cities neighborhoods in the South Bronx, some young adults will literally kill for a Starter jacket or pair of Timberland shoes, their logos prominently displayed. An hour away in the upscale Second City Elite town of Northport, some shoppers cut out the designer labels of new clothes so they won't be judged by anything so superficial. These consumers look to other products and brands — albeit with more subtle logos — to connect them to their cluster community.

More and more, Americans define their world view through a cluster lens. In Big Fish, Small Pond, an upper-middle-class lifestyle typified by Mount Juliet, Tennessee, a bedroom suburb of Nashville, an important measure of success is which college your child attends. Befitting their interest in education, residents are more likely than the general population to buy the latest books and computers. But in Lynchburg, Tennessee, a downscale rural town classified as Shotguns & Pickups, what matters is how your son or daughter performs on a basketball court or athletic field. Residents speak of the importance of athletics over academics in a community where the major employer is Jack Daniel's distillery. "The most popular kids in high school are the ones who play on the basketball team, not who get the good grades," says librarian Sara Hope, adding that patrons resist reading newsweeklies and out-of-town papers. "People here aren't looking for the latest product seen on a TV commercial," explains Clayton Knight, assistant manager at the Lynchburg Hardware and General Store. "They all know the good old products." Indeed, at the local pharmacy, shoppers can still buy liniment, lye soap, and Watkin's vanilla flavoring, as their grandparents did before them.

In an age of overwhelming consumer choices, cluster residents look to brand names and product myths as distinguishing lifestyle markers. Saturn car owners can now gather for company-sponsored "reunions" — though they've never previously met. The upscale, politically correct urban residents of Money & Brains support the Body Shop and the myth of its founder, Anita Roddick, who supposedly jets around the globe in search of ancient potions that can save the rainforests by making their plants and peoples — at last — economically viable. David Brooks, an editor at the *Weekly Standard* in Washington, D.C., noticed that many of his neighbors in the Money & Brains neighborhood of Cleveland Park liked things "rough." "Smoothness connotes slickness, glitz, the Reagan '80s," he wrote in the *Washington Post.* "Roughness connotes authenticity, naturalness, virtue. Whether it's bread, clothing, or furniture, you can never have too much texture. That's why unrefined sugar is now considered the height of refinement." While his neighbors may all agree that coffee bars like Starbucks are essential to their community, they can still realize individual self-actualization by ordering complex concoctions like a half-decaf, no-foam, double-shot skim latte with almond syrup and a dash of cinnamon.

Moving to other clusters causes people to adopt new buying patterns, but most Americans inhabit only a handful throughout the course of their lives. Mobility rates have been steadily declining even while fracturing trends have increased due to economic shifts and increasing divorce rates, among other trends. Twenty years ago, 20.1 percent of all Americans moved every year. Today that figure is 16.7 percent. "Most people move to where they've been before, either where they went to school or vacation," reports Kristin Hansen, a mobility expert at the Census Bureau. Now even laid-off workers are reluctant to move for a new job, though the cluster system may reflect a downshift in lifestyle at the same address. According to Challenger, Gray & Christmas, an international outplacement firm, only 18 percent of laid-off managers and executives were willing to relocate for a new position in 1995 — the lowest figure in a decade. "We are becoming a nation of isolates in which we are apprehensive about venturing outside of the lives in which we have become so comfortable, even after we lose a job," observed John Challenger, executive vice president of the firm. Rather than risk moving to an unfamiliar setting, workers stay put, taking comfort in what real or imagined social and emotional support their communities provide.

Twenty years ago, 20.1 percent of all Americans moved every year. Today that figure is 16.7 percent. Even laid-off workers are reluctant to move for a new job.

This process has left too many Americans alienated from each other, divided by a cultural chasm. Just how wide and deep the differences are hit home when journalist Peter A. Brown examined whether the popular press is as out of touch with mainstream America as some critics claim. Brown cluster-coded the home addresses of 3,400 editors, reporters, and columnists for publications like *USA Today,* the *Washington Post,* and the *Milwaukee Journal.* He found that the vast majority of full-time journalists live in the ten wealthiest urban and suburban neighborhood types — clusters like Urban Gold Coast, Pools & Patios, and Blue Blood Estates. By contrast, they were markedly underrepresented in forty-eight of the clusters, including suburban middle-class lifestyle types that more closely aligned with their papers' readership — clusters such as Greenbelt Families and Middleburg Managers. As Brown observed, "Most journalists are different from real Americans. And their perspective on the world is different from how most Americans live." The American experience, most often seen from the viewpoint of educated and affluent white European descendants, must now be told in different ways.

In clusters like Hispanic Mix, home to downscale, predominantly Hispanic families, you can live most of your life without needing to speak or read English. In Atwater Village, a typical cluster neighborhood in Los Angeles, residents shop at *carnicería* meat markets, watch soap opera *novellas* on TV, and sing along in

	Where Journalists Live	Index	Socioeconomic Rank
	Urban Gold Coast	948	High
	Young Literati	644	High
	Money & Brains	578	High
	Bohemian Mix	498	High
Top Clusters	Urban Achievers	277	Medium
	Pools & Patios	181	High
	Second City Elite	167	High
	Blue Blood Estates	166	High
	Single City Blues	161	Low
	Winner's Circle	144	High

An index of 100 equals the U.S. average; 144 means 44 percent above average.

Media Bias: Out of Touch?

Long before former Vice President Spiro Agnew called them "nattering nabobs of negativism," journalists were criticized for being out of touch with the concerns of everyday people. And a cluster survey reveals there's some truth to that notion. An analysis of where the editorial staff of such papers as the *Washington Post* and *USA Today* lives discovered a wide socioeconomic gap between the press and the communities it covers. Compared to the U.S. average, journalists are much more likely to live in upscale metro clusters.

(Sources: PRIZM, Claritas Inc., 1994 Peter A. Brown study of 3,334 journalists)

Spanish karaoke bars. It can be a dangerous place, with gang violence erupting over territory and drugs. But the local Chevy Chase Recreation Center serves as a sanctuary for children arriving after school to do homework, take arts classes, or play basketball. When local gang members hang out at the center's parking lot or handball court, director Sophia Pina-Cartez tries to cool hot tempers and maintain peace in the neighborhood. "I tell them, 'Don't tell me what you're up to, just don't make the children your victims,'" she says. "I just want to make this a safe haven."

Across the country in Glen Rock, New Jersey, an affluent suburb west of Manhattan classified as Money & Brains, residents faced a different sort of problem. Several years ago, the unmistakable odor of a nearby landfill wafted down their stately streets lined with solid Tudors and shady trees. People of eminently good taste and environmental sensitivity, these residents devised a solution apropos of their appreciation for the finer things in life. The local government scented the garbage dump with lemon, as if it were a huge cup of espresso. When that plan failed to clear the air, they did the next best thing. They hired a trucking outfit to haul all their garbage to another town. End of problem.

Today, the notion of a star-spangled melting pot seems quaint, of another age. Increasingly, America is a fractured landscape, its people partitioned into dozens of cultural enclaves, its ideals reflected through differing prisms of experience. And this fracturing is likely to continue as the self-concept of America shifts from a majority white–minority black nation to a pluralistic society of many ethnic and racial groups. At the close of what's been called the American Century, during which the nation emerged as the dominant world power in commerce and politics, old myths are dying hard and new ones are just being forged. In this clustered world, the national identity is changing, and most of us don't even know it.

From melting pot to salad bar

The ongoing fragmentation of America is a far cry from the experiment in democracy our forefathers envisioned, a blending of European immigrants into a unique amalgam. Many historians cite the 1782 observations of J. Hector St. John de Crèvecoeur as the early model for pluralism: "Here individuals of all nations are melted into a new race of men," he wrote in *Letters from an American Farmer.* In 1835, French politician and author Alexis de Tocqueville celebrated that pluralistic ideal in his *Democracy in America,* writing, "Imagine, my dear friend, if you can, a society formed of all the nations in the world . . . a society without roots, without memories, without prejudices, without routines, without common ideas, without a national character." Such writings created a myth of the American character even as immigrants continued to arrive. But the new nation was unable to produce an egalitarian society. Racial, economic, cultural, and religious differences were entrenched in America from its beginnings, resulting in diverse classes that remain separate and unequal to this day. Jim Crow laws exacerbated a racially divided nation. Religious discrimination created restricted neighborhoods, clubs, and schools.

But Americans have always clung to the notion of egalitarianism, and not only during times of hardship and war, when the draft united the middle class and the poor. Sociologists refer nostalgically to the 1950s as a time of cohesion, a mass market, and a common lifestyle. Following the Depression and World War II, the country entered a period of unparalleled prosperity. The GI Bill provided veterans access to higher education, opening the economic door to starter houses and cars. As men returned from the war and joined the workforce, women left the labor market to tend to home and family, creating a common realm of experience that businesses didn't ignore. Before long, a majority of Americans were reading *Life,* watching *The Ed Sullivan Show,* and driving cars made in Detroit. A 1954 nationwide poll found that Americans even agreed by a large margin on their favorite meal: fruit cup, vegetable soup, steak, French fries, peas, and apple pie à la mode.

But the '50s era of mass culture was an aberration, and it didn't last. The '60s shattered the traditional family structure. Women entered the workforce in large numbers. Divorce rates rose. The Vietnam War divided families and created a class split. And more immigrants arrived — not white Europeans, but Asians, Hispanics, and others with "alien" cultures. Soon powerful social forces added fault lines to the common ground where Americans once stood. In the 1970s, institutions like the military draft that once bridged our cultural enclaves disappeared. Others, such as public schools and labor unions, fell into disarray. By the 1980s, the two-party political system had been shredded by divisive issues — abortion, affirmative action, and welfare. Social upheavals of the current generation — suburbanization, globalization, technologies that collapse time and space — continue to dilute the notion of

A 1954 nationwide poll found that Americans even agreed by a large margin on their favorite meal: fruit cup, vegetable soup, steak, French fries, peas, and apple pie à la mode.

community based on proximity and shared concerns. Meanwhile, the diversity movement, intent on abolishing the ethnic categories on census forms, advises Americans to celebrate their differences.

As a result of these demographic and societal shifts, the mass market of the post–World War II era didn't just fade away, it shattered into niche markets. In 1974, when social-scientist-turned-marketer Jonathan Robbin founded Claritas, he identified forty "lifestyle segments" in the nation, combining zip codes with marketing research to create the PRIZM cluster system. Following the 1980 census, Claritas expanded the clusters down to the block level and adjusted the forty groups to reflect changes in demographics and product usage, dropping clusters like Ethnic Row Houses (downscale industrial areas) and Marlboro Country (midscale family farms), and picking up Gray Power (upscale retirement communities) and Black Enterprise (upper-middle-class minority neighborhoods). But experts still needed only forty clusters to accurately reflect the U.S. population profile.

That changed in 1990, following the most ambitious, far-reaching, and data-rich census ever conducted. When the Census Bureau finally released its findings, the ramifications rippled through America's political and social institutions. Congressional seats were added in eight states, including Florida, California, and Texas, and dropped in thirteen others, including New York, Ohio, and Pennsylvania. At Claritas, the demographic shifts revealed in the census enabled a finer segmentation of lifestyles and resulted in wholesale changes to the PRIZM system, which dropped thirteen clusters, redefined another seven, and added thirty-five new lifestyle types. When David Miller, Claritas's lead technician who oversaw the clustering process, completed the 1990s model, only twenty clusters from 1980 remained largely unchanged.

Creating a lifestyle cluster system is no mean feat. Geodemographic segmentation systems, mixing demographic information with small units of geography, begin with millions of raw statistics from census surveys. Next, the nation's households are classified into groups based on similarities — much as living things are divided by biologists into orders, families, and so on. When Claritas analysts first examined the 1990 U.S. census, they looked at the six hundred variables influencing settlement at the neighborhood level. They then came up with thirty-nine key factors in five categories to organize the neighborhoods into natural lifestyle clusters. Every census tract, block group, and zip plus 4 unit of microgeography — averaging a dozen households in 22 million postal areas — was assigned to one of the clusters.

But the basic clustering principle, that people of the same ilk flock together like birds of a feather, had a new wrinkle. The self-absorption of Americans, cocooned in their homes and immersed in their electronic gadgets, had exacerbated the lack of cohesion within each neighborhood. Nowadays, the characteristics and tastes of a community, from age and marital status to preferred political cause and brand of soda, may change block by block and house by house. Thus, while cluster systems can now distinguish the preferences of a yuppie couple from those of a comparatively nonmaterialistic family living next door, their power remains in classifying the lifestyle these people share at the neighborhood level. As in the beginning, cluster systems show how the residents of one neighborhood have a common identity. Their core truth can be simply expressed: *You are like your neighbors.*

Cluster evolution

With sixty-two lifestyle types, the expanded cluster system allows a more detailed portrait of the nation's diversity. The stereotype of the suburbs as a vast, homogeneous wasteland has become outdated. Fourteen different tribes now occupy the suburban landscape, some congregating outside second-tier cities like Schaumburg, Illinois, and Annapolis, Maryland, others living in new subdivisions. New data has also picked up on the continued outmigration of city dwellers to the rural landscape. The expanding suburban sprawl has created what journalist Joel Garreau calls "edge cities," with their megamalls and high-rise monoliths, and exurban boomtowns, with their enclaves of retirees and telecommuters. To capture these hybrid lifestyles, the new cluster system added a "second city" designation, a unique grouping of twelve lifestyle types that are *city* living but not *urban* living. For instance, Dallas has a central downtown area and a number of urban clusters, while Fort Worth, with very little urban core, falls into the second-city category. Similarly, an inner-city dweller from Chicago has a very different lifestyle than a resident of smaller Nashville. Second-city dwellers are more apt to buy American cars, for example, while urbanites with similar demographics tend to purchase imports. In a cluster called Second City Elite, affluent, college-educated couples tend to read *Shape,* listen to adult contemporary radio, and watch *Melrose Place.* In urban Money &

> *Nowadays, the characteristics and tastes of a community, from age and marital status to preferred political cause and brand of soda, may change block by block and house by house.*

Not Urban, But City

The migration of Americans out of the nation's cities has created fast-growing satellite cities with moderately dense population centers and self-sufficient commercial districts. In the Washington, D.C.–Baltimore metropolitan area, Annapolis, Maryland, qualifies as a "second city," with a population-density score of 71 on a 100-point scale (with 100 being the highest-density area). The in-town Washington neighborhood of Georgetown, by contrast, has a density figure of 91. Over a span of 50 miles, motorists can experience America's five different types of settlement density: urban, suburban, second city, town, and rural.

(Source: PRIZM, Claritas Inc.)

Urban
Suburban
Second City
Town
Rural

Brains, demographically similar people read *Town & Country*, listen to jazz, and watch *Wall Street Week*.

Cluster evolution during the 1980s saw five lifestyles disappear as a result of the dwindling manufacturing base and downsized blue-collar workforce. One cluster, Rank & File, vanished entirely because of declining union membership. Even new standards of political correctness worked changes into the system. The former Tobacco Roads, a downscale African American cluster whose nickname was based on Erskine Caldwell's Depression-era book, was dropped because it sounded pejorative in the 1990s. Instead, the Southern-based cluster picked up some neighborhoods from the predominantly white Share Croppers cluster and now goes by the more benign label Scrub Pine Flats. The second-wealthiest lifestyle, called Furs & Station Wagons in the 1980s, lost its moniker because animal rights groups had bullied the rich into forsaking their fur coats (or at least putting them into cold storage). Claritas staffers spent weeks debating a replacement name for these new-money suburbs, considering suggestions like Jeeps & Jewels and Spandex & Minivans. The winning name: Winner's Circle.

Behind the changing cluster names, the fragmenting of America has not been a smooth process. When communities that have been accustomed for generations to a certain way of life are invaded by newcomers or surrounded by distinctly different lifestyles, friction is bound to occur. Longtime residents often jealously protect their familiar ways, shunning other clusters that don't share their values — a finding that has broad cultural and commercial implications. When giant Arkansas-based retailer Wal-Mart set its sights in 1990 on Vermont — then the only state in the union without one of its megastores — the company encountered surprising resistance. Residents in the state's small towns simply didn't want discount palaces like "Sprawl-Mart" with their oversized shopping carts, computerized inventory control, and other trappings of outlet culture. It turns out Vermont is home to the country's largest concentration of residents classified as New Eco-topia, a cluster typified by consumers with above-average educations and a fondness for civic activism. With its population of small-town consultants, merchants, and telecommuters, New Eco-topia's consumer patterns are more typical of city dwellers' than those of their country neighbors. Residents tend to surf the Internet to stay in touch with mainstream news via web sites for CNN or ABC-TV. They're more likely than average Americans to own stock, buy health food, and write letters to editors. In Westminster, Vermont, town council meetings can go on for two days as residents debate everything from school budgets to buying the fire department volunteers new jackets. Whereas New Eco-topians make up 1 percent of the U.S. population, in Vermont they represent fully 20 percent. These are the exurban Americans — "granolas," the natives call them — who fled the city and don't want their adopted rural state to become what they left behind: a clutter of superstores and seven-acre parking lots. After years of fending off the incursion, state activists relented in 1994 and Wal-Mart got its store, but only after agreeing to build a scaled-back outlet near the downtown of Saint Johnsbury (population 8,000 New Eco-topians).

Across the nation, cluster residents announce their distinct lifestyles to the rest of the world through their purchasing power. They demand products — from cheese to jeans to minivans — tailored to reflect their changing tastes and attitudes. In the opulent 1980s, the yuppies of Young Influentials bought gold jewelry as a status symbol. Now, in a less ostentatious age, the hot new status

Whereas new Eco-topians make up 1 percent of the U.S. population, in Vermont they represent fully 20 percent.

symbol is a good job that allows time for exercise. With affluent tastes now running more toward utilitarianism and self-fulfillment, the onetime owners of BMW sedans tool around in Range Rovers with racks toting skis and bikes. In the Young Influentials community of Redmond, Washington, home of Microsoft and Nintendo, workaholic techies routinely put in long days on the job and then head for the surrounding mountains on the weekends to go hiking or biking. Arleen Hiuga, a store manager of REI, a recreational equipment company, sees a steady parade of Young Influentials who come in to be outfitted for "adrenaline sport" activities that are both physically and psychically challenging. "When your reality is sitting in front of a computer screen for eighty hours a week, you require a balance and pursue a sport for decompressing," she says. "The ultimate experience is a challenging climb uninterrupted by the sight of other nature lovers." Of course, these Young Influentials still meet those challenges with a few creature comforts. Among REI's best-selling products are global guidance systems that provide latitude and longitude lines anywhere in the wilderness and espresso makers designed to work over a campfire.

But yuppie tastes aren't just changing; America's yuppies are disappearing altogether. The Young Influentials cluster has shrunk — from 2.9 percent of U.S. households to 1.1 percent — as

Stressed-Out Americans

Nearly a third of American heads of households wish they had more time to engage in stress-reducing activities, but they're not the big-city dwellers or Soccer Moms you may have imagined. Surveys indicate that the highest concentration of people who feel the need to relax most acutely are young singles and financially strapped families from midsized towns. The downtown denizens of Urban Gold Coast and Bohemian Mix clusters actually enjoy the stress that comes with fast-paced city life.

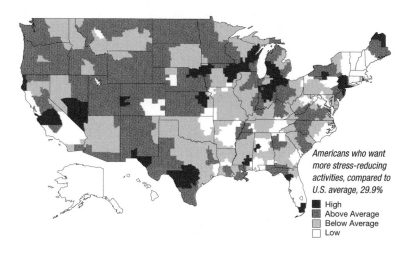

Americans who want more stress-reducing activities, compared to U.S. average, 29.9%

■ High
▨ Above Average
▧ Below Average
□ Low

Top Clusters   Old Yankee Rows / Hispanic Mix / New Beginnings / Single City Blues / Young Influentials
Top Markets   El Paso, Texas / Las Vegas, Nevada / Madison, Wisconsin / Lansing, Michigan / Presque Isle, Maine

(Sources: PRIZM, Claritas Inc., NFO Research, Inc.)

baby boomers have aged, married, left the city for the 'burbs, and begun shopping at Price Club rather than Sharper Image. Taking over their city apartments are the Generation Xers of the Bohemian Mix cluster, those twenty-something singles who never seem to leave their local coffee bars, which offer them retro music and obscure 'zines. In fact, children are becoming an endangered species in many Bohemian Mix neighborhoods. Karyn Robinson, a thirty-three-year-old writer from Dupont Circle, a Bohemian Mix section of Washington, D.C., observes that she's more likely to see a gay couple than a family with children on neighborhood streets. "The breeder culture is nonexistent around here," she says.

Likewise, advancements up the socioeconomic ladder by African Americans have resulted in cluster adjustments. The former Black Enterprise segment, typified by upwardly mobile blacks, disappeared in the 1990 cluster system as surveys showed its residents had more in common with nonblack families of similar socioeconomic status than with other blacks. As a result, the residents of zip code 30034, outside Atlanta, formerly a Black Enterprise community, are now classified Kids & Cul-de-Sacs, with higher-than-average purchases of BMWs, computers, and cell phones. Race does play a major role in some consumption patterns, particularly affecting media preferences. Surveys show that African Americans who live in integrated suburban communities still share with their inner-city brethren some of the same tastes in TV (BET), radio (gospel), and magazines (*Jet, Ebony, Essence*). When urban black radio station WVAZ in Chicago was trying to attract Citibank as one of its advertisers, the financial services firm resisted because the demographic profile showed that the station attracted a high percentage of downscale urban blacks. Yet a cluster analysis revealed that about 30 percent of the audience were upscale residents who'd assimilated into Blue Blood Estates and Young Literati areas, and the bank eventually signed on. "The issue isn't skin color," says Linda Brown, research director of Eagle Marketing in Fort Collins, Colorado. "It's attitude."

The lack of any predominantly black affluent cluster shows that the civil rights movement and anti-discrimination laws have provided the opportunity for African Americans to put down roots almost anywhere they can afford. Between 1980 and 1990, the proportion of blacks in some overwhelmingly white suburban clusters more than doubled. But two trends trouble demographers:

"The issue isn't skin color," says Linda Brown, research director of Eagle Marketing in Fort Collins, Colorado. "It's attitude."

First, few black-only communities in America are wealthy. And second, there's little sign of upscale African Americans returning to city neighborhoods to help revitalize them. Census data confirms that the gentrification of the nation's cities remains a phenomenon of young white singles. "The black middle class will never come back to the inner city," says Edward Smith, director of American Studies at American University in Washington, D.C. "People who can afford to leave the city have done so, and they're happy."

For all the progress toward integrated subdivisions, some aspects of race relations haven't changed. Socially, people tend to cling to those like themselves, a fact that helps explain why, outside of housing or employment, much of America remains a segregated society. True, blacks and whites are intermarrying at rising rates, but mixed-race families still account for less than 3 percent of all households. And there's no one cluster dominated by mixed-race residents. More common is the lifestyle of New Empty Nests, a cluster of predominantly white upscale suburbs where residents say that the races get along and relations are certainly better than they were in the past, but social divisions remain. In the cluster community of Tucker, Georgia, an Atlanta suburb surrounded by increasing numbers of African Americans, Hispanics, and Asians, one can walk into any number of restaurants and shops and almost never see any of the minorities who live nearby. And Sunday remains the most segregated day of the week in the area's racially divided churches. Reverend Michael Cash, minister of the First United Methodist Church of Tucker, attributes the voluntary segregation to historically different styles of worship. "The black singing style includes clapping and swaying, and the preaching style is longer and more rhythmic than in white churches," says Cash, a thoughtful forty-two-year-old white clergyman. "The joke we like to say is, 'God leaves the white sanctuaries at noon,' because the black churches are still going on." But Cash isn't laughing as he shares this fact. Of 1,500 members of his church, none are black.

As middle-class whites and blacks have left the nation's cities, immigrants have moved in, at some of the highest rates seen this century. Nearly one million foreign-born residents arrive now each year, mostly from Asia, South America, and the Caribbean. Asians, the fastest-growing minority group, inhabit a number of upscale

True, blacks and whites are intermarrying at rising rates, but mixed-race families still account for less than 3 percent of all households.

segments in above-average concentrations, illustrating their successful assimilation into American society. The number of predominantly Hispanic clusters increased from one to five, but, in a sign of the growing poverty among Hispanic Americans, none of these clusters is affluent. Only one is midscale suburban, and two are midscale urban. In the Mobility Blues cluster, concentrated in cities throughout the western states, the households are filled with young middle-class families who dream of sending their kids to college, read *Working Woman,* and enjoy HBO. Meanwhile, in more downscale Family Scramble, newly arrived Hispanic couples, struggling to protect their children from gangs, drugs, and violence, are more concerned about finding affordable housing and English language classes. In all, sixteen clusters have above-average concentrations of Latinos.

Today, the American Dream is no longer a single vision but depends on what you see when you look into a mirror. In Grain Belt, a cluster of tiny farm towns, the dream means having enough people to sustain a community. In the small middle-class cities of Starter Families, it's finding a good job and being able to buy a home. In a new cluster called American Dreams, composed of cities filled with first- and second-generation Americans, one can find varied hopes within these remnants of the melting pot. In Buena Park, California, a cluster community in the Los Angeles sprawl, the descendants of Japanese, Dutch, and Hispanic immigrants have achieved the traditional signs of status: comfortable homes, well-paying jobs, and college educations for their children. Yet even in this enviable setting, cross-cultural mixing is limited. Older Dutch-descended residents attend their own parties, and the newer Hispanic residents keep to their own stores. Tom Shozi, the sixty-nine-year-old son of Japanese immigrants, was born in Colorado, interred in California concentration camps as a teenager, and today calls himself "an all-American," with his cowboy boots, Chevy pickup, and country music tapes. But when not working on his strawberry farm, he and his wife attend a Japanese church, watch Japanese soap operas on cable, and socialize at dinner parties with Japanese friends. In his bicultural home, Shozi takes off his shoes at the door and sits down to a typical dinner of meat loaf and mashed potatoes — eaten with chopsticks. "I still like to keep a little bit of our Japanese heritage, but I can't understand the current fascination with sushi," he says, making a face at

In his bicultural home, Shozi takes off his shoes at the door and sits down to a typical dinner of meat loaf and mashed potatoes — eaten with chopsticks.

the thought of eating raw fish. "I'm just as American as anyone else."

Well, not exactly. But that's the point.

Cluster marketing at home and abroad

The splintering society is no surprise to corporate marketers, who have been working with clusters for twenty-five years. An estimated fifteen thousand North American companies, nonprofit groups, and politicians have used clusters as part of their marketing strategies. Abroad, the need for micromarketing has fueled the creation of cluster systems in two dozen countries — with new countries being added every few months. The popularity of clustering reflects a tidal wave of demographic forces that is leaving fragmented societies in its wake. Throughout Europe, many nations are experiencing aging populations, rising divorce rates, little household growth, and declining birth rates. Less restrictive zoning laws are encouraging suburban sprawl as young families leave old city centers. Meanwhile, increasing racial and ethnic diversity is obliterating the rigid class structures of the past. One result of these changes is that fewer people define themselves by their job titles, and many no longer feel compelled to conform to traditional notions of how they should behave on and off the job.

"When I get a passport and am asked for my profession, I say, 'Geodemographic consultant,' and they respond, 'Come again?'" says Richard Webber, managing director of England-based Experian Micromarketing. "Most ordinary people don't understand the jobs their neighbors do anymore. So they can live however they like — and consume whatever products they want — to reflect their unique lifestyle."

This do-your-own-thing attitude has also spurred the growth of lifestyle segmentation systems because increasingly stringent privacy laws limit how businesses can collect and use information on individuals. In countries with fresh memories of repressive Communist governments, citizens fear that personal data can be used for surveillance. Cluster systems, however, can circumvent such concerns by relying on neighborhood-level data drawn from both public and private sources: census statistics, car registrations, electoral rolls, and independent surveys. Experian, a global leader in gathering such data, made its name as a credit-scoring agency, helping insurance companies charge rates based on neighborhood clusters. According to its fifty-two-segment British MO-

"Most ordinary people don't understand the jobs their neighbors do anymore. So they can live however they like — and consume whatever products they want — to reflect their unique lifestyle."

SAIC system, motorists from country clusters like Gentrified Villages and Rural Retirement Mix pay low fees because of few thefts and little congestion.

Throughout the world, there's remarkable similarity in the way businesses are using the cluster technology — for analyzing trading areas, profiling customers, and driving media strategies. The increasing globalization of culture is also prompting multinational companies to look to clusters as a common marketing language to reach customers across many borders. In Spain, foreign retailers like Marks & Spencer are already using cluster profiles of city consumers to decide where to open their stores. In France, Pepsi has tapped cluster profiles of shoppers at Alcampo, the hypermarket grocery chain, to determine how much to pay for a meter of shelf space to display its soft drinks. Clusters have aided Detroit carmakers analyze motorists across Europe, though sometimes the results have caused manufacturers to make a sharp turn in their thinking. When General Motors profiled buyers of its sporty Tigra sedan, company officials were shocked to find fans not among the clusters of young suburban couples, as anticipated, but in areas filled with older urban retirees, who said the car made them feel young. GM altered its marketing and media plan accordingly.

Back in the U.S.A., marketers now spend an estimated $300 million annually on clustering techniques, which have become well-accepted tools in targeting direct-mail campaigns, selecting sites for new stores, and profiling the behavior of the nation's 100 million households. With the increased precision in data collection and greater power of desktop computing, the demand for information segmented by clusters is exploding. The new marketing buzzwords are *narrowcasting, particle marketing,* and *segments of one.* Claritas now calls itself a "precision marketing" company, able to target the households on any given street. Even corporate giants are now trying to hone their messages to the diverse tastes of America's splintered consumers. Ethnic minorities control some $600 billion in annual buying power in the U.S. Today there are three TV networks and 350 newspapers catering to Latinos alone.

In the current business climate, marketing wars are being waged in microneighborhoods with surgical precision. No longer can businesses target-market a whole city or even a zip code. In 75081, the zip code of affluent Richardson, Texas, a camera store looking to sell Nikons would score big by targeting the households

The new marketing buzzwords are narrowcasting, particle marketing, and segments of one.

on Oakwood Drive, classified as Winner's Circle and filled with well-educated mobile executives and teenagers, who buy a lot of expensive photo equipment. Meanwhile, less than a mile west on Woodoak, merchants would do better selling cordless drills and circular saws to these Kids & Cul-de-Sacs households, with their large families and upscale incomes.

Such information can be translated into bottom-line results. Until fairly recently, beer was marketed as a mass-appeal product much like milk. Major brewers stuck to limited product lines, rarely launched new brands, and fought over market share during routine price wars. But today liquor stores sell dozens of microbrews, and big brewers masquerade as microbrewers — Anheuser-Busch makes Elk Mountain Amber Ale — in aggressive fights over market share. With baby boomers aging out of their wild beer-guzzling days (consumers over fifty-five drink only about half as much as twenty-something-year-old drinkers), brewers have introduced nonalcoholic beers, such as Coors Cutter, to hold on to older consumers.

And it's worked. In Urban Gold Coast, a cluster of densely populated urban neighborhoods filled with singles and young couples, residents drink imported beer at rates three times the national average but nonalcoholic beer 50 percent less often than the general population. In Gray Collars, a cluster of inner suburbs home to aging couples, consumers drink imported beer at a rate one-third below the national average and nonalcoholic beers at 50 percent above the average. To compete in this landscape of shrinking niches, Miller now targets its brews to customers one corner bar at a time.

In the past, national retail chains and catalog companies have been the most aggressive users of geodemographic marketing systems. But a new generation of small and midsized users are finding ever more creative ways to employ the cluster system and retain core customers. On college campuses, admissions officers have been particularly innovative in employing the clusters to recruit and retain students. American University in Washington, D.C., matches the clusters of its applicants with alumni recruiters to make the interview process less of a culture clash. At Concordia College, a small liberal arts school in Seward, Nebraska, marketers dispatch targeted brochures to students requesting information. The mailer sent to students from upscale suburban clusters like

Winner's Circle and Executive Suites focuses on careers previous
graduates have entered in copy titled "A Stepping Stone to Your
Future." Those from the middle-class Middle America cluster receive another, headlined "An Affordable Education" and focusing
on scholarship opportunities at the school. At Hood College in
Frederick, Maryland, officials assign roommates based on their
home clusters in an effort to reduce conflicts. "It helps link people
with similar backgrounds, so they're more comfortable in the residence hall," says Theodore Kelly, president of CERR, a cluster-
based college consulting firm in Falls Church, Virginia. "And it sure
beats making roommate assignments based on five general questions." No longer will parents hear about their child's "roommate
from another planet."

Even government agencies have turned to clusters for social
marketing projects. The Centers for Disease Control and Prevention use the clusters to ensure that their health and safety messages are understood in the communities needing assistance.
When the CDC was called on to provide workers at an Alabama
beryllium plant with safety information, a cluster analysis of the
neighborhoods surrounding the factory gave CDC field-workers
"cultural sensitivity training beyond the stereotypes to help them
better reach their audience," says Susan Kirby, a CDC marketing
communications scientist. In Kansas, adoption officials at the
state's Social Rehabilitation Services Office had difficulty finding
couples who would adopt special-needs children. Accordingly,
they cluster-coded couples who'd adopted children with physical
or learning disabilities in an attempt to find their "clones." Their
work yielded some surprises: Among the most receptive couples
were those in New Homesteaders, a midscale town cluster, and
Southside City, a downscale African American neighborhood type.
With several different target groups, Kansas officials developed a
statewide direct-mail campaign with multiple messages, featuring
a photo of a white or black youngster, depending on the cluster,
with the same caption: "A kid like this deserves a home like yours."
The response outstripped that of any previous campaign, notes
Bob Nunley, director of the Kansas Geographic Bureau. "It also
tickled the hell out of me because many of my white liberal friends
didn't believe that black couples adopt black kids. And the clusters
proved that they did."

The beauty of the cluster system is that it can reveal consumer niches in the unlikeliest of places. Executive Suites, the third-wealthiest lifestyle type, has lots of Beef Jerky fans; the blue-collar households of Rural Industria are a good market for pagers; and Golden Ponds seniors have a devilish desire to visit theme parks. Young Literati, a cluster of urban singles with a high concentration of writers and artists, displays an unusual fondness for Cheerios. When Time Inc. Ventures launched its urban culture magazine *VIBE,* its advertisers believed that the target audience was inner-city kids. But receptive readers were also found among white-collar suburbanites living in Young Influentials and Money & Brains communities — those who parrot the in-your-face street styles of the inner city. Accordingly, the magazine began selling advertising space for consumer electronics that would appeal to upscale suburban tastes.

Although market researchers have known about it for years, politicians are only now beginning to use cluster technology to sat-

Oprah Versus Book Clubs

Consumer tastes are never static. After Oprah Winfrey launched her popular monthly book club feature in 1997, she created an entirely new book-buying audience in clusters that rarely bought books. Most book club members tend to live in upscale, college-educated clusters in suburban areas out West. Oprah's book fans typically hail from downscale blue-collar clusters throughout the South and Northeast. Despite their differences, their tastes intersect when it comes to romance novels.

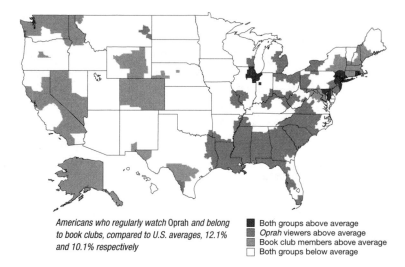

Americans who regularly watch Oprah *and belong to book clubs, compared to U.S. averages, 12.1% and 10.1% respectively*

■ Both groups above average
■ *Oprah* viewers above average
▨ Book club members above average
□ Both groups below average

Book Club Members

Top Clusters Smalltown Downtown / Urban Gold Coast / Old Yankee Rows / Upward Bound / God's Country

Top Markets Lafayette, Indiana / Bend, Oregon / New York, New York / Los Angeles, California / Colorado Springs–Pueblo, Colorado

Oprah's Book Club Fans

Top Clusters Inner Cities / Mid-City Mix / Norma Rae-ville / Hometown Retired / Latino America

Top Markets Laredo, Texas / Detroit, Michigan / Jackson, Mississippi / Columbus, Georgia / New Orleans, Louisiana

(Sources: PRIZM, Claritas Inc., Simmons Market Research Bureau)

isfy the myriad voting factions. Party-line affiliations have so disintegrated — the nation's two parties can't even muster a simple majority when electing a president — that strategists are turning to cluster affiliations to understand how allegiances shift depending on the issue at hand. During the 1996 presidential campaign, the Clinton reelection team used the clusters to identify the nation's swing voters and craft ads and speeches to help President Clinton address their concerns. Pollster Mark Penn directed a survey of ten thousand voters to probe their attitudes and lifestyles. The results yielded a profile of uncommitted voters who came from clusters like Big Sky Families and Family Scramble. As a group, they tended to be young, socially conservative voters who cared deeply about family and fiscal concerns. Acknowledging that portrait, Clinton ads began blasting Bob Dole and the Republican proposal to cut Medicare, and Clinton speeches began casting the president as the staunch defender of issues like family leave, education, and the environment. In the aftermath, election observers cited the family-friendly strategy as being key to Clinton's eventual victory with 49 percent of the vote.

The bare plurality Clinton needed to be elected president reflects an important truth: Cluster lifestyles have become a force more potent than race, geography, gender, or ideology in shaping voter attitudes. Politicians must now tap into sophisticated survey techniques that use lifestyle and demographic data to reach ever smaller divisions of the electorate. Americans are too complex to be counted on to behave as traditional voting blocs of union members, Catholics, or senior citizens; seniors, for example, don't all feel the same way. The suburban retirees who live in Pools & Patios are lapsed Republicans, wary of the party's stand on abortion and other social issues. In Mines & Mills, many aging voters still support unions and describe political issues in terms of class conflicts between management and labor; they still see government as their protector. When third-party presidential candidate Ross Perot ran for office in 1996, his supporters represented a variety of backgrounds up and down the cluster ladder: the yuppies of Young Influentials, the immigrant families of American Dreams, and the blue-collar workers of Rural Industria. All found themselves disconnected from the traditional two-party system that so often casts candidates and concerns in stark pros and cons. "On most issues, the clusters reveal a checkerboard effect," says William Krause, a survey statistician with Wirthlin Worldwide in McLean,

Cluster lifestyles have become a force more potent than race, geography, gender, or ideology in shaping voter attitudes.

Virginia. "All across America, the views of voters shift according to the issue and their perspective on the world."

Ultimately, the clusters reveal the many cultural divides that separate Americans on political and social issues. Tensions exist between the clusters of whites and minority groups on issues like affirmative action, immigration, crime, and culture. And increasingly, ideological gaps are widening as homogenizing institutions like the military draft disappear and individuals retreat to the comfort of their special interests. The 1998 debate in San Francisco over requiring school students to read literary works written by nonwhite authors can be explained in cluster terms. The top five clusters in San Francisco (Young Literati, Bohemian Mix, Urban Achievers, American Dreams, and Money & Brains) all have large numbers of Asians and foreign-born residents. They face a daily challenge of trying to balance cultural pride with the desire to be American that in the past meant celebrating a Eurocentric literary canon. The school system's compromise solution, requiring students to read at least one nonwhite author a year, is a harbinger of controversies to come in a nation of increasing diversity.

But at least such school debates are taking place. In Sun City West, Arizona, an exclusive Gray Power community west of Phoenix, elderly residents voted down tax referenda that would have funded a school district that includes a high proportion of young families classified as Boomers & Babies. At Dysart High School, the result was that the marching band had to fold, the number of librarians and school nurses was halved, and the football and basketball teams nearly disbanded because of budget constraints. Battles like this are becoming commonplace in the splintered society. Politicians call these "wedge issues," but they no longer divide the population into two adversarial camps. Instead, they now scatter a range of views into smaller factions. Today, there's little agreement on what truths Americans hold to be self-evident.

The consumer backlash

While its insights are undeniable, this clustered view of life is not universally accepted. Charges of oversimplification, stereotyping, and redlining are often leveled, and there are revolts against the "I am what I buy" mentality inherent in a consumer-based construct. There's something unnerving about being measured and pigeonholed on the basis of address or purchase patterns. Do you feel as if you belong to Money & Brains or Mobility Blues? Are you really a hunk of Brie or a country cottage by a lake? How much do you really have in common with others who watch *The X-Files* or join investment clubs?

Like many systems used to understand and predict consumer behavior, the clusters have raised privacy concerns along with the specter of an evil, all-knowing marketing monster. Many companies that operate data warehouses containing information on consumers use cluster systems, the better to divine the desired Boomtown Singles or Greenbelt Families consumers among lists of magazine readers or political contributors. And the information-gathering business is booming, projected to grow to a $10 billion industry this year. Companies like Metromail and The Polk Company gather and sort information on the lifestyles and spending habits of most of the 100 million individual households in the nation.

Of course, databases filled with personal information have existed since computers were invented, but the current explosion in data collecting — and abuses through inaccurate credit reports and zealous promotions — has understandably alarmed consumers. A 1996 survey by Louis Harris & Associates for Equifax Inc., a giant credit bureau, found that nearly nine out of ten Americans

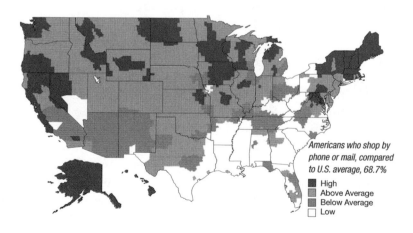

Americans who shop by phone or mail, compared to U.S. average, 68.7%

- ■ High
- ■ Above Average
- ■ Below Average
- □ Low

Home Shoppers by Phone and Mail

More than two-thirds of Americans shop by phone or mail. They typically fall into two groups: upscale metro cluster residents who haven't the time to shop in stores and middle-class exurban types who live far from malls and specialty shops. But the nation is deeply conflicted when it comes to direct marketing: Many Americans complain about junk mail and telemarketing phone calls even though the vast majority continues to respond to these pitches.

Top Clusters   Winner's Circle / Country Squires / Middleburg Managers / New Eco-topia / Executive Suites
Top Markets   Anchorage, Alaska / Burlington, Vermont–Plattsburgh, New York / Monterey-Salinas, California / Washington, D.C. / Helena, Montana

(Sources: PRIZM, Claritas Inc., Simmons Market Research Bureau)

"In the not too distant future,"
warns Democratic congressman
Bob Wise of West Virginia, "consumers face the prospect that a
computer somewhere will compile records about every place
they go and everything they
purchase."

expressed concern about threats to their privacy. In 1997, more than 8,500 privacy bills were introduced in state legislatures. And there's every fear that without strong federal oversight of the data-collection industry, breaches of privacy in the information age will increase. Today, companies rake in information from loan applications, medical histories, driver's licenses, warranty cards, and credit card receipts. "In the not too distant future," warns Democratic congressman Bob Wise of West Virginia, "consumers face the prospect that a computer somewhere will compile records about every place they go and everything they purchase."

But fears about Big Brother's power over consumers may be overstated. Cluster firms see themselves as matchmakers for parties with common interests, helping sellers understand and respond to the needs of shoppers. And no database in the U.S. — not even the census — contains complete records for every household or individual. Some industry experts estimate that as much as 30 percent of all database records on an individual or household may be inaccurate because people move, change jobs, divorce, or have children. Others note an important reason that most marketers consider privacy a low-priority issue: money. While a list of addresses in one zip code destined to receive a brochure for a new record shop may be bought for as little as thirty cents per address, it routinely costs ten times as much for information to identify particular households that bought a record in the last month. Clusters make bottom-line sense, allowing companies to simply target homes one block at a time and avoid any nasty questions about invasions of privacy. "We try to bring neighborhoods to life," declares Nancy Deck, president of Claritas. "Everything we've done to date concerns consumer behavior at the neighborhood level. And it works because cluster data gets you most of the way there while avoiding the extra cost of household data and respecting an individual's privacy."

Perhaps the most powerful defense against the abuse of cluster information is the American consumer's healthy independent streak. Marketing remains an art as much as a science, and eight out of ten new products still fail every year because consumers are too fickle to be manipulable. Contrary to the notion that America has become a totally acquisitive society, the cluster system reveals lifestyles that reject that ethic. In Single City Blues, a cluster of young, downscale urban singles, there's an almost nihilistic disdain for consumer electronics like boom boxes, video games, and cell phones that plague people in public places. Hanging over the counter at Anne Hughes's Kitchen Table Café in Southeast Portland, Oregon, is a large drawing of a flip phone with a red slash through it announcing the restaurant to be a "cell-free zone." Hughes, a bespectacled earth mother who frequently hosts neighborhood potluck dinners, refuses to buy a television set, dismissing TV as "air pollution." When a Nielsen pollster once called to ask about her viewing habits, she explained she didn't own a set (making her a member of a group that represents only 1 percent of the population). A few minutes later, the pollster's supervisor called back to make sure his associate hadn't misunderstood. Much of America looks at Single City Blues' disaffection for TV as an aberration. In Southeast Portland, that's life.

Still other critics are less concerned by the cluster systems themselves than what they reflect: an increasingly fragmented society divided by income, race, ethnicity, sexual behavior, and the percentage of fat in our diets. A recent *Newsweek* poll found that nearly 60 percent of Americans believe the national identity is threatened by the increasing diversity of the populace. Economist Paul A. Jargowsky worries about "a pronounced trend toward increasing economic segregation." In the 1990s, the United States had the least equitable income distribution among all developed nations — including England, with its aristocratic traditions. If present trends toward more fragmented lifestyles continue, this gap between Americans will only widen.

A recent Newsweek *poll found that nearly 60 percent of Americans believe the national identity is threatened by the increasing diversity of the populace.*

Concerns over a thinning social fabric can't be easily dismissed. In America's past, various institutions crossed cultural divides: public schools, the military draft, and the English language. Today, rising minority populations are threatening all these institutions and, thus, the social fabric. Sometime within the next fifty years, whites will be outnumbered by minorities in the U.S. Already, a white backlash of sorts is taking shape as evidenced by rising enrollments in private schools and an estimated eight million Americans now living in gated communities. More and more, people are turning to the private sector to insulate themselves from the rest of society; the latest retail experiment is the notion of so-called membership malls. Some critics wonder if the nation will splinter like the Soviet Union. As historian Arthur Schlesinger Jr. worried in his 1992 book *The Disuniting of America,* "Will the center hold? Or will the melting pot give way to the Tower of Babel?"

There's no clear answer. The clusters merely show that although the nation is far from being one big leafy suburb, Americans today are managing to find happiness within their patches on the national quilt. And as society continues its fragmentation in the future, cluster systems will be essential tools for understanding the changes affecting the U.S. population. One day in the future, we may be sliced and diced 275 million ways, one for every American citizen: You'll have your own personal lifestyle type known by you, your family, and any businessperson or politician with access to a database. But even in that fractured state of affairs, America will manage to endure, united in the recognition of its historic role as a great experiment in diversity. In this clustered world, you are where you live, even if your country is splintered into countless, clamorous lifestyles.

2 CHANGING AMERICAN LIFESTYLES

Reviving small-town America

It's a sweltering summer afternoon in Concord, Massachusetts, and Harold Perry is hard at work. Well, he's not actually at his desk. He's sitting next to a Japanese garden in the backyard of his $300,000 home, reading a computer magazine. Faded shorts and a gray T-shirt cover a tall and thin figure, tanned from regular rowing excursions on the nearby Concord River. Occasionally, he rises to drop another Duke Ellington disk into his CD player, thankful that as a computer consultant he can indulge his passion for classic jazz while working at home several days a week. He makes a point of breaking up his ten-hour workdays with time to enjoy the natural beauty of Concord, the historic town that's been home to Revolutionary War firebrands, Henry David Thoreau–type intellectuals, and now a new generation of urban exiles like Harold Perry.

A few years ago, Perry, forty-four, worked in the heart of Boston and lived in the close-in suburb of Melrose. Every day, he braved a tense commute, worried about his two kids' deteriorating schools, and in general expressed dissatisfaction with the stressed-out life he shared with his wife, Pam McDonough, a teacher. But when he and Pam engineered their escape, joining the migration of Americans fleeing cities and suburbs for small towns, it proved to be a salvation. "There's an embarrassment of riches here," explains Perry in an accent that hasn't completely lost its Manhattan roots. "You can't go anywhere without seeing the natural beauty of the place. I find myself reading more. I've discovered jazz out here. I keep pinching myself to make sure this is real. I'm a half hour away from a million people in Boston, but I'm out of the rat race. The quality of peace is better here."

Computer modems, faxes, e-mail,
teleconferencing — all allow pro-
fessionals to work far from the
urban centers that once formed
the core of the business world.
Between 1990 and 1998, the
number of cell phones skyrock-
eted from 5 million to nearly 60
million.

The lifestyle Perry has found is called Country Squires, a cluster that first appeared in 1990, and it represents one of the great demographic stories of the last decade. After years of losing people to cities and suburbs, rural and small-town communities are enjoying a resurgence. Nearly all of the nation's population and job growth now takes place on the periphery of larger metropolitan areas. Some two million people moved to rural America in the 1990s. (By contrast, rural areas lost 1.4 million during the 1980s.) For the first time since the 1970s, problems such as crime, crowds, and high costs are driving urbanites out of the city faster than rural folks are replacing them. Unlike the back-to-the-land trend that first drew hippies to rural communes in the 1970s, today the migration is being fueled by technological advances. Computer modems, faxes, e-mail, teleconferencing — all allow professionals to work far from the urban centers that once formed the core of the business world. Between 1990 and 1998, the number of cell phones skyrocketed from 5 million to nearly 60 million.

But the exodus to the country also reflects a shift in attitude on the part of city dwellers, and especially baby boomers, who are fed up with urban ills. Many now speak of the desire for a Norman Rockwell life of safer streets, tighter-knit communities, and cleaner air. When asked why they moved, the newcomers to Country Squires invariably invoke the notion that "less is more." Less crime. Less noise. Less traffic. Lower cost of living. Fewer school problems. "It was the schools that finally drove us away," says Perry of Melrose. "No matter what they did, it really wasn't good enough."

The migration did not take place in an economic void. The run-up in the stock market in recent years — the number of millionaires jumped from 120,000 in 1970 to an estimated two million today — contributed to the emergence of exurban clusters like Country Squires. So many wealthy Americans have moved out to bucolic settings like Charlottesville, Virginia, Doylestown, Pennsylvania, and Concord that a new portrait of "bucks in the boondocks" has emerged, home to consumers with a particular fondness for cell phones, salad bars, children's art classes, and sport-utility vehicles. While the residents of Blue Blood Estates and Country Squires have similar demographics — sky-high incomes, educations, and home values — their lifestyles are different by virtue of their settings. The suburban Blue Bloods buy classical music, imported beer, and cappuccino makers at high

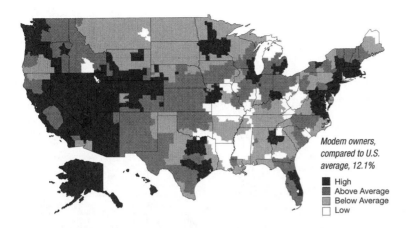

Modem owners, compared to U.S. average, 12.1%

■ High
■ Above Average
■ Below Average
□ Low

Telecommuters

The technology revolution is fueling the migration of city folks, sick of the rat race, to the countryside. All they need is a PC, fax, cell phone, and that all-important modem to service their clients far from the urban canyons. Since 1988, the number of telecommuters has jumped from fewer than 2 million to more than 12 million.

Top Clusters   Urban Gold Coast / Towns & Gowns / Country Squires / Young Literati / Upward Bound
Top Markets   Washington, D.C. / San Francisco–Oakland–San Jose, California / Boston, Massachusetts / Honolulu, Hawaii

(Sources: PRIZM, Claritas Inc., Mediamark Research Inc.)

rates; the exurban Country Squires prefer jazz, light beer, and gas grills. Blue Bloods read *Self* and *Harper's Bazaar.* Country Squires prefer *Audubon* and *Organic Gardening.*

The emergence of Country Squires reflects how the flow of affluent city dwellers can transform genteel towns like Concord. Old hardware stores and saddle shops have become chic gift shops and storefronts where one can buy latte and bagels. West Concord, which now boasts a new health food store, organic café, and granola factory, has become known as Gourmet Gulch. Local designers tell of being hired to renovate country kitchens to include computer nooks. In old stone homes, mother-in-law suites have been gutted to make way for home offices wired like the CIA for modems, scanners, and video-conferencing equipment. When a local police officer noticed someone sitting in a parked car off a busy road, he feared a potential suicide; it turned out to be a man trying to extricate himself from his car phone cord.

Inevitably, this migration of people and values causes culture clashes, often in unexpected ways. Political experts thought urban exiles would bring centrist or liberal sensibilities to these traditional conservative strongholds. In fact, many of the newcomers are right-of-center whites tired of debates over affirmative action, immigration policy, and bilingual education. Voters in Country

Squires, for instance, describe themselves as moderate Republicans and selected Bob Dole for president during the 1996 campaign. Six out of eight exurban clusters qualify as moderate to right-wing.

More common are differences in sensibility that arise when exiles from a high-rise, coffee-bar subculture parachute into a landscape of barns and feed stores. In Louisa, Virginia, a rural town that's part of the Scrub Pine Flats cluster, a torpid agrarian lifestyle was jump-started with the arrival of retirees and professionals commuting to faraway jobs in Richmond and Washington, D.C. Scrub Pine Flats residents are more likely than any other Americans to claim that they need only $50,000 to feel wealthy. In Louisa, locals complain that well-off newcomers have cluttered up Lake Anna so there's no open space to catch bluegill and rockfish. Others groan about the honking from motorists in sport-utility vehicles during the planting season, when tractors take to the country roads. "I think there should be an orientation for people who move to the country, like when you go to college," says Bradley Pleasants, forty-six, owner of the Maddox Feed Store in Louisa. "They should hear that this is the way people do things down here. Either adapt to it or don't come."

The problem is that the country is the natural place to go if you're seeking a simpler life. And that fact is also attracting businesses, hotels, and outlet stores that see the new pioneers as undermarketed consumers. Three years ago, forty-one-year-old Christopher Middaugh quit his Tagamet-a-day job managing convenience stores in Kansas City, hoping to leave behind his share of robberies, fires, and drive-by shootings. With his wife and kids, he moved to Dallas Center, Iowa, a town of 1,600 northwest of Des Moines that's classified as a River City, USA cluster. A collection of midscale hamlets found throughout the heartland, River City, USA has been particularly adept at drawing city exiles to its easy pace and old-fashioned virtues. Middaugh took over a six-lane bowling alley and pizza joint, and promptly discovered the charms of a community with six churches and no crack houses. At his bowling alley, women clip coupons between their turns on the lanes. Almost everyone in town shows up for high school football games — home and away — and kids still ride their bikes to school. For a weekend getaway, whole families will pack up tents and RVs and head for a campground that's maybe ten miles away.

"There are no pretenses here," says Middaugh, who quit his

antacid habit once he moved to Dallas Center. "People will let you use their forklift in exchange for a cheeseburger. It's more like when we were kids. We're more carefree here."

The flow of people to rural River City, USA communities has been a boon for retail chains like Target and Wal-Mart, which appreciate the critical mass of consumers now invading the countryside from Vermont to Iowa. But the opening of new Wal-Marts has also spelled disaster for small-town Main Streets, as a single megastore can wreak havoc on dozens of mom-and-pop businesses. In Dallas Center, about twenty miles from the closest Wal-Mart, several storefronts stand empty, and the former grocery store is now a law office. Le-Ann Bott-Hartman tried to realize an Alice's Restaurant fantasy by opening a country diner called the Lylah Rose in Dallas Center. She hoped to lure longtime residents and newcomers with a menu heavy with homemade soups, fresh-baked rolls, and gravy-drenched entrées. But her prices, higher than those of the usual Iowa diner, scared off locals, and her comfort food never attracted enough citified émigrés. Unable to bridge the divergent customers without a support base, she closed her restaurant and is planning to move. "The good side is that everyone knows you and it's so neighborly," she says. "The downside is it's hard to keep a business going in town." Admittedly, she'll miss the good side of the River City, USA lifestyle when she leaves. One night her beagle escaped and was still loose when Bott-Hartman turned in at eleven P.M. When she awoke in the morning, the dog was inside, having been let in by a neighbor who remains anonymous. "The life here," she concludes, "is wholesome."

The diversity divide: equal but separate

The repopulating of rural America is one of the biggest demographic trends of the decade, but it isn't the only one. Throughout metropolitan America, the most remarkable force behind changing lifestyles is the rise in immigration, the largest influx of foreigners since the first wave of Europeans came to America a century ago. Once defined in black and white, today's America is more colorful: 74 percent white, 12 percent black, 10 percent Hispanic, and 3 percent Asian. The rise in immigration means that today nearly one in ten Americans were born outside the country. And unlike the European immigrants from the last great migration, the newest immigrants are from developing countries in Asia and

Once defined in black and white, today's America is more colorful: 74 percent white, 12 percent black, 10 percent Hispanic, and 3 percent Asian. The rise in immigration means that today nearly one in ten Americans were born outside the country.

Latin America: Mexico, the Philippines, China, Cuba, India, and Vietnam. They're coming largely because of 1996 changes in the 1965 immigration law that permit the family reunification of Hispanics and Asians already in this country. That means fewer whites and more of everyone else. "The main reasons for the population's growing are more diverse immigrants and higher fertility rates among some groups," explains Claritas president Nancy Deck, a petite and energetic forty-five-year-old. "Our stew is becoming spicier."

The stew analogy is fitting. For all of America's increasing ethnic diversity, there's also evidence that these newcomers aren't blending into the proverbial melting pot. Indeed, the latest cluster system reflects a landscape of neighborhoods separated by racial and ethnic divides. Most whites continue to live in predominantly white neighborhoods. Among Hispanics, the proportion living in non-Hispanic block groups actually declined during the 1980s, from 24 to 19 percent. Language barriers are partly responsible for that development. But another factor is the desire of some immigrants not to assimilate — unlike the Italian and German immigrants of the past. In Big City Blend, a cluster filled with middle-aged, middle-class Hispanics, a large percentage of residents have gone to college and are homeowners. But many now speak English only because they feel it's necessary to help them get a decent job. At home they abide by deeply rooted traditions. With quick flights back to their homelands, cheap international phone service, and cable TV stations with ethnic fare, Hispanics needn't surrender their culture while living in America.

Maintaining their ethnic traditions in a multicultural society is the overriding concern of residents in the Latino America cluster, the 61 percent Hispanic lifestyle with the nation's most foreign-born immigrants. As the name implies, the cluster is dominated by Latin American immigrants, mostly from Mexico and El Salvador, who've settled in the nation's biggest cities, like New York, Chicago, Miami, and Los Angeles. These new residents tend to have midscale incomes — the median is $30,100 — but their large families and low education levels make for downscale lifestyles and economic hardship. Latino Americans support restricting immigration far more than the national average. In Virgil Village, California, a Latino America neighborhood in Los Angeles, many residents live in crowded apartments with three and four children to a bedroom and some sleeping in oversized closets. More than a quarter of adults never finished the eighth grade, and the unemployment rate is high.

"People here don't strive for material things. They want to make sure their bills are paid," says Geoffrey Saldivar, a community activist who founded a neighborhood watch program called Rampart Rangers. "I've known enough people with hiccups in their incomes to have their phones turned off and their cars repossessed. They live from month to month."

For Gilda Zavala, a Guatemalan-born, forty-three-year-old apartment manager in Virgil Village, the biggest concerns are less economic than cultural. She and her husband, who works as an alarm technician, have a household income of $40,000. But they worry about the impact of the area's gang and drug activity on their four children, ages twelve to twenty-one. Rather than retreat behind locked doors and barred windows, however, they've turned their apartment into a neighborhood hangout to keep their kids off the streets. In a bedroom, where a clutter of beds and bureaus are pressed against each other, her kids and their friends play Nintendo. In the living room, a handful of other teenagers sit around a computer or fuss over the family's menagerie — four dogs and six cockatiels. Several years ago, after local drug dealers offered some of their wares to her children, Zavala decided that she had to do something to protect her kids from the worst elements of the neighborhood. She began volunteering at school and working with the Rampart Rangers to help clean up the streets. "When the kids have nothing to do, they get into trouble," says Zavala, a compact woman with long black hair and a gregarious personality. "And it's difficult because sometimes the parents are so busy, they forget their kids."

Like other Latino America residents, the Zavalas live in a bicultural world. They get Spanish magazines along with *Redbook, YM,* and *Teen.* They watch Spanish *novella* soap operas along with favorites like *ER, The X-Files, General Hospital,* and *New York Undercover.* Twice a month, they head to Price Club, spending $300 at a time on tortillas, chilis, and papayas as well as milk, crackers, and SnackWell's cookies. In their living room, a bureau holds an assortment of collectibles that bespeaks a cultural polyglot: Chinese dolls, Japanese dragons, and even some Precious Moments figurines. Zavala recently took on a second job to help raise the several thousand dollars it cost to pay for her daughter's *quincinnera,* an elaborate fifteenth-birthday party marking a

Like other Latino America residents, the Zavalas live in a bicultural world. They get Spanish magazines along with Redbook, YM, *and* Teen. *They watch Spanish* novella *soap operas along with favorites like* ER, The X-Files, General Hospital, *and* New York Undercover.

The Salsa Scene

The consumption of salsa, America's best-selling condiment, generally reflects the settlement patterns of the Latino population — a segment representing about 10 percent of Americans concentrated in the Southwest. And while culinary trends typically spread from coastal cities into the hinterland, salsa's popularity has grown in a reverse pattern, starting out in rural Latino communities and then moving north and east. Today, upscale consumers in suburban, family-filled neighborhoods enjoy salsa's exotic flavor and low fat content.

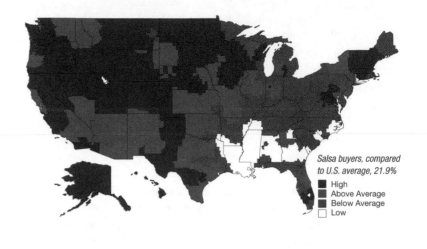

Salsa buyers, compared to U.S. average, 21.9%
■ High
■ Above Average
■ Below Average
□ Low

Top Clusters   Upward Bound / Kids & Cul-de-Sacs / Boomtown Singles / Boomers & Babies / Hispanic Mix

Top Markets   Monterey-Salinas, California / Hartford–New Haven, Connecticut / Helena, Montana / Bend, Oregon / Yuma, Arizona–El Centro, California

(Sources: PRIZM, Claritas Inc., Mediamark Research Inc.)

girl's passage into womanhood. The affair included costly gowns, a rented hall, a hired band, and enough food and drink to impress even distant relatives.

But if there's any question about the Zavalas' American identity, Gilda is the first to downplay the pull of her homeland. Several years ago the whole family returned to Guatemala to visit relatives and see the country, but after a month the kids wanted to come home. They missed America, or rather that corner of America where Spanish is the language of the streets. Sometimes she thinks about moving to a larger house in the suburbs, but there's no rush to realize that American dream. Like most of her neighbors, she knows that limited English skills are the single biggest obstacle to upward mobility. In places like Virgil Village, where residents speak sixty different languages, overcoming that obstacle doesn't seem so important. "There's a feeling among the Latinos that everybody is in this together," she explains. "I feel like I'm among my own here."

The Asian population in America grew faster than that of Hispanics during the 1980s, by 52 percent as compared to 37 percent.

But the 3 percent Asian population still constitutes a smaller proportion of U.S. residents — and they're different in other ways. Although African Americans and Hispanics tend to cluster together and dominate neighborhoods — each group accounts for five clusters — those of Asian ancestry are more likely to live in predominantly white and ethnically mixed neighborhoods. Nearly 40 percent of Asians live on mostly non-Asian blocks, mainly because their higher education and income levels result in fewer barriers to home ownership. Of the ten wealthiest lifestyle types in America — from Blue Blood Estates to Kids & Cul-de-Sacs — Asians are present in eight of them at above-average rates.

The evolution of Executive Suites, a new cluster of upper-middle-class suburbs beyond the nation's beltways, reflects the movement of Asians into upscale suburbia. With almost 11 percent of its population of Asian ancestry, Executive Suites is filled with upscale, white-collar couples raising young families in town-house condos and starter homes. Many of these neighborhoods were originally settled during the white flight to the suburbs that followed World War II. In West Springfield, Virginia, a cluster community south of Washington, D.C., Pastor Ralph Weekman of the Prince of Peace Lutheran Church remembers the founding of his congregation in 1962, when nearby subdivisions still had restricted covenants barring blacks. Weekman walked with Martin Luther King Jr. during his March on Washington and went door-to-door in West Springfield with petitions to halt the discriminatory practice. Today, the community is almost 10 percent Asian, and a sign in front of Weekman's mod-angular church announces Korean-language Sunday services. So many nonwhite families have moved into the community that today an Indian market sits between Szechuan and Italian restaurants in the local shopping center, and no one gives it a second thought.

But cultural clashes occasionally occur. At the South Run Recreation Center, middle-aged white women, many of whom are business professionals, show up for an early-morning aerobic workout and then get a quick shower before continuing on to work. The Asian women, by contrast, are more likely to be homemakers who take a leisurely soak in the pool before a dry sauna and shower. "The white women are always complaining that the Asian women move too slowly," says Karen Francona, a desk clerk at the rec center. "They're too politically correct to say, 'Oh, those

Of the ten wealthiest lifestyle types in America — from Blue Blood Estates to Kids & Cul-de-Sacs — Asians are present in eight of them at above-average rates.

Asian women.' So they just come out here and say, 'Oh, those women won't let me get to the shower,' and then sigh and roll their eyes."

For upscale African Americans, the movement of Asians into white suburbia is a stark reminder that barriers are higher for race than for ethnicity. Although blacks achieved gains in income, employment, and education during the 1980s, segregated housing and other barriers to mobility persist. Thirty years after the passage of civil rights laws, blacks remain the nation's most segregated group, with 62 percent living in predominantly black neighborhoods regardless of socioeconomic status. Typically, when middle-class African Americans move out of city neighborhoods, they settle into integrated suburbs. Too often, however, the clustering phenomenon then prompts a white flight that turns the suburb overwhelmingly black. Today, there are simply no upscale lifestyles in the PRIZM system that are predominantly black.

African Americans are present in fourteen U.S. clusters and found in high concentrations in five: Mid-City Mix (midscale singles and families), Southside City (service workers), Norma Raeville (young families in biracial mill towns), Scrub Pine Flats (older farm families), and Inner Cities (downtown solo-parent families). Wealthy African Americans live as a minority in many suburban and exurban communities — as they always have. "The patterns of residential segregation remain strong," observes Ken Hodges, chief demographer at Claritas. "You don't see a real breakdown in segregation, a block going from 90 percent white to 60 percent white. There may be greater diversity in the country today, but many neighborhoods in many areas remain heavily white or heavily black."

What has changed is the face of poverty in America. A decade ago, the big-city ghettos that comprised Public Assistance cluster ranked as the poorest neighborhoods in America. Communities like the South Bronx became symbols of decay, immortalized by the Paul Newman film *Fort Apache, the Bronx.* The streets were filled with blackened rubble from arson fires, and so many apartments had been abandoned that housing authorities painted flowers on boarded windows to give the appearance of occupancy. But ten years later, an infusion of public and private capital has swept away the burned-out skeletons. And groups like the Mid Bronx Desperadoes Community Housing Corporation have built or renovated more than 3,300 housing units, including the construction of

Thirty years after the passage of civil rights laws, blacks remain the nation's most segregated group, with 62 percent living in predominantly black neighborhoods regardless of socioeconomic status.

440 private homes. In one development, called Charlotte Gardens, middle-class families have moved into neat ranch houses surrounded by shady trees, swing sets, and attractive parks. A new $29 million shopping center has arrived, anchored by a Pathmark supermarket and stores like Old Navy and the Wiz. At one time it would have seemed like an oasis in the South Bronx. Now it's becoming commonplace to see row houses being renovated, and stores and banks moving into the area. When community activists recently discussed which new businesses they'd like to attract to the community, Ben & Jerry's ice cream, a yuppie favorite, was one of the first names to come up.

The poorest lifestyle in America today is called Southside City, a cluster of forgotten neighborhoods in the nation's satellite cities that are 70 percent African American and overwhelmingly desperate. Only 7 percent of residents have a college degree; high schools cope with exorbitantly high rates of dropouts and teenage pregnancies. Few can afford the dream of leaving. In central Petersburg, Virginia, much of the housing stock dates to the Civil War — and too much hasn't been renovated since. Dilapidated shotgun shacks with sagging roofs and crumbling walls stand near closed, rusting factories. Many of the stores on Main Street are barred; the side streets are filled with thrift shops, fast-food joints, and prowling drug dealers. When Wal-Mart announced plans for a nearby store, local business leaders only shrugged. "There's no one left to hurt," says William Patton, CEO of Virginia First Bank. For longtime residents who see prosperity on the other side of the Appomattox River in Richmond to the north, there's a feeling of both desperation and isolation. "We don't even hear what's going on elsewhere," says Marie Parham, a clerk at Crockett's Records & Tapes. "We're just surviving."

Today the wealthiest African American cluster is Mid-City Mix, a middle-class, urban-fringe cluster filled with singles and couples. In these neighborhoods, centered in the Northeast and Great Lakes regions, residents have average rates of college educations and mostly white-collar jobs. But a form of economic discrimination frequently leaves them with little more than downscale commercial choices. In Brightwood Park, a Mid-City Mix neighborhood in northwest Washington, D.C., supermarkets and department stores have fled the area to wealthier suburbs, forcing residents to make do with thrift shops, corner grocers, fast-food carryouts, and ubiquitous liquor stores. "As soon as we get a commercial vacancy, we get a liquor store or a check-cashing store wanting to move in," says Charlene Drew Jarvis, a city councilwoman who represents the neighborhood. "We don't need them. People here need hardware stores, bookstores, and clothing stores."

The isolation of black neighborhoods — no matter what their socioeconomic status — cannot be ignored. In a 1997 survey by NFO Research asking if the U.S. government should apologize for its role in slavery, 7 percent of Americans thought it was a good idea. In Mid-City Mix, more than 26 percent supported the proposal — one of the highest proportions for any lifestyle. Cluster media tastes, which favor magazines like *Jet* and *Essence* and TV shows like *Cosby, Oprah,* and *Martin* reruns, reveal the sharp color line dividing white and black America. In 1998, when *ER* and *Seinfeld* were the top-rated shows among white Americans, they ranked 18th and 54th among African American viewers, respectively. By contrast, *Between Brothers,* the most popular program among African Americans, ranked 107th among whites. Only four shows, including *Monday Night Football,* appeared on both lists of top-twenty programs, and not one was a comedy. "It's a reflection of how fragmented our society has become," observed Dean Valentine, president of the UPN network, in the *New York Times.* "Blacks generally watch black shows, and whites generally watch white shows."

The racial divide in media may be changing slowly, according to recent research showing young whites more receptive to shows like *Sister, Sister* and *The Wayans Bros.* But the jury is still out on whether today's younger generation can remain color blind as it grows older. Some clusters — especially those well established — seem incapable of reconciling the races. In Norma Rae-ville, a cluster of racially mixed mill towns concentrated in the Southeast, there's relatively little integration. Although black and white residents say that the races get along, and relations are certainly better than they were in the past, social divisions are deep. In the cluster community of Monroe, Georgia, about an hour west of Atlanta, whites and blacks have their own churches, American Legion halls, and barbecue joints. Some of the poorest citizens, predominantly black, live in shotgun shacks literally on the wrong side of the railroad tracks from more upscale parts of town. Despite the sweeping social changes of the past three decades, racial mixing is one of America's last taboos. Observes Shan Taylor,

"It's a reflection of how fragmented our society has become," observed Dean Valentine, president of the UPN network, in the New York Times. *"Blacks generally watch black shows, and whites generally watch white shows."*

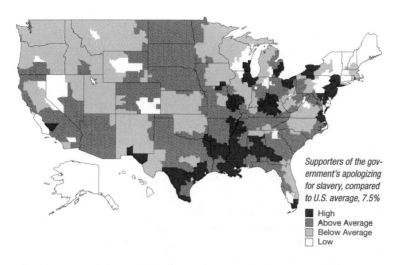

Apologizing for Slavery

In a 1997 mail survey, only a small minority of Americans — white or black — indicated that the U.S. government should apologize to African Americans for slavery. The issue resonated most among the poorest minorities, who feel the most disenfranchised from the American Dream. In Inner Cities, the downscale urban cluster, almost 40 percent of residents supported an apology; in Single City Blues, a cluster of predominantly white aging hippies, about 20 percent backed the idea.

Supporters of the government's apologizing for slavery, compared to U.S. average, 7.5%

■ High
■ Above Average
■ Below Average
□ Low

Top Clusters Inner Cities / Mid-City Mix / Southside City / Single City Blues / Hispanic Mix

Top Markets New Orleans, Louisiana / Detroit, Michigan / Greenwood-Greenville, Mississippi / Memphis, Tennessee / Miami–Ft. Lauderdale, Florida

(Sources: PRIZM, Claritas Inc., NFO Research, Inc.)

branch manager of the Monroe-Walton County Library, "I'd describe the races as still separate but amicable."

Booming boomers

No look at the changing American landscape would be complete without an update on the aging baby boomers, those 76 million Americans born between 1946 and 1964. Still the largest population segment in the nation, the so-called pig has now moved halfway through the python. More and more boomers have reached their fifties, entering their peak earning years, and have begun to grasp the reins of power. In Bill Clinton, they elected the first president of their generation. They've poured into the workforce at record numbers. And, though it took some time as they established careers and delayed childbirth, they've created a baby boomlet of their own, with more than 50 million children born since 1976 in what's been called the echo boom.

Present in twenty-eight different lifestyle types, boomer families have begun the empty-nesting process, altering the nation's dominant household types. Married couples with children, the classic family unit celebrated from the days of *Ozzie and Harriet,* now make up only one-quarter of all households. Almost half of all

American families have no children living at home; in ten years, the figure will be three in five families. Already, that trend has created a cluster called New Empty Nests, a suburban neighborhood type where the children are out of the house and upper-middle-class couples have the money to enjoy themselves. In New Empty Nests, they tend to pursue active leisure lives with a vengeance, being more likely than average Americans to go gambling, visit museums, take adult education courses, and engage in charitable volunteering. In Tucker, Georgia, residents mentor young people through the Tucker Women's Club or take financial planning courses at Rehobeth Baptist Church. Riley Deichert, a fifty-year-old wife and mother of two grown children, does some of everything, teaching exercise classes at Tucker Recreation Center, joining with her husband in neighborhood potluck dinners, visiting a lakeside resort time-share, and vacationing in the Bahamas and Disney World — without her children. "It's better without your kids," she says unabashedly. "While my friends with kids worry about drugs and drunk driving, we don't have any stresses."

The youngest boomers, by contrast, are in full child-rearing bloom and are responsible for the ongoing echo boom. While most of these echo boom kids are still toddlers, their economic impact is already being felt: Nine of the ten best-selling videos today are animated Disney features, and Club Med now draws half of its income from family resorts. This aftershock population bulge can best be seen in Boomers & Babies, the cluster with the most children, where the adults tend to be college educated, white-collar, upper-middle-class, and totally devoted to their families. These are the consumers who rent videos every week, buy Juicy Juice by the case, and subscribe to magazines like *Baby Talk* and *Child*. They fear letting their kids jump on bikes to head to parts unknown so they turn to play groups and indoor playgrounds like Discovery Zone for reassurance. Victims of their parents' search for enriching educational experiences, the kids carry a heavy load of chess clubs, music lessons, and karate classes. And they usually have a schedule of play dates; after all, their parents moved to Boomers & Babies just to be around other child-rearing families.

Of course, the boom in kid-filled neighborhoods brings flashbacks for the original boomers. The schools in Thornton, Colorado, near Denver, are so overcrowded that children are bused to distant schools. At the rec centers, long lines await anyone hoping for activities. When Janice Mueller, a thirty-five-year-old mother of

While most echo boom kids are still toddlers, their economic impact is already being felt: Nine of the ten best-selling videos today are animated Disney features, and Club Med now draws half of its income from family resorts.

two toddlers, wanted to sign up her kids for swimming lessons, she showed up three hours before registration began; a hundred parents were there ahead of her. "There are tons of little kids in the area," she says. "It's just like when we were growing up, when the schools had classes in trailers."

There is at least one important difference, however, between the parents of boomers and those of echo boomers. Nearly two-thirds of today's mothers with children under six work, and almost two-thirds of U.S. children aged three to five attend preschool. In Boomers & Babies, parents like Mueller grapple with caring for their kids. Mueller, a government accountant, first sent daughters Ashley and Stephanie to a baby-sitter and then to day care. But she worries daily if she's doing the right thing and if she's spending enough time with her daughters. "You have quality time, but you have to spend quantity time with them," she confides. "There's nights when I just don't have the patience after whatever happens through the day, and there's nights when my husband doesn't."

Like other parents in Boomers & Babies, Mueller says she'd be willing to give up income to spend more time with her family. But she and her husband, a park service ranger, can't cut their $90,000 household income in half and still pursue the lifestyle they prefer. So they send their kids to A New Generation Pre-School and Day Care Center, a bright and well-maintained facility for 150 children. Mueller believes the kids will benefit from more social interaction and activities there than at a baby-sitter's home. But she doesn't know if this choice will best prepare them for elementary school. And she occasionally wonders about the price of living in a community of sprouting subdivisions where it's rare to see anyone over fifty years old. "What's the best way to raise children today?" asks Mueller, frowning. "What's it going to be like when my daughters grow up? I have no idea."

Generation X

Trailing the baby boomers is Generation X, that group of 45 million Americans born between 1965 and 1976 who are now in their twenties and early thirties. Demographically speaking, they're of minor significance, a modest-sized population cohort initially known, somewhat derisively, by what they weren't: the baby bust generation. But the need to imbue significance in population groups with a clever label, well-understood by cluster experts, elevated their status. Journalists adopted the term Generation X

Nearly two-thirds of today's mothers with children under six work, and almost two-thirds of U.S. children aged three to five attend preschool.

Sex and Drugs,
Not Rock 'n' Roll

Baby boomers who came of age with the
Beatles and antiwar protests have main-
tained their liberal leanings on political
and social issues. Yet they're a lot more
conservative when it comes to their children. In one poll, American parents cited
drug use as the biggest threat to today's
teenagers (29.6%), followed to a lesser
degree by sexual permissiveness (10.0%).
True to their rock 'n' roll roots, these same
parents expressed relatively little concern
about violent messages in music (4.6%).

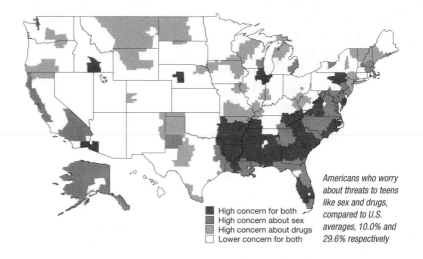

- ■ High concern for both
- ■ High concern about sex
- ■ High concern about drugs
- □ Lower concern for both

*Americans who worry
about threats to teens
like sex and drugs,
compared to U.S.
averages, 10.0% and
29.6% respectively*

Concerned About Teen Sex

Top Clusters Mid-City Mix / Young Literati / Gray Power / Big Sky Families / Greenbelt Families

Top Markets Meridian, Mississippi / Sioux City, Iowa / Fort Myers–Naples, Florida / Augusta, Georgia / Wilmington, North Carolina

Concerned About Teen Drug Use

Top Clusters Urban Gold Coast / Bohemian Mix / Scrub Pine Flats / Agri-Business / Sunset City Blues

Top Markets Great Falls, Montana / Shreveport, Louisiana / Salisbury, Maryland / Palm Springs, California / Medford–Klamath Falls, Oregon

(Sources: PRIZM, Claritas Inc., NFO Research, Inc.)

after Douglas Coupland's 1991 novel by the same name, which por-
trayed twenty-somethings as slackers, cynics, and drifters. When
it came to voting, they were allegedly politically apathetic. Their
heroes were said to be Beavis and Butt-head. Their favorite movie
reportedly was Richard Linklater's *Slacker,* filled with deadbeats
from Austin, Texas. They were said to be Net-surfing, tattooed ni-
hilists who, in Coupland's tale, imagined that in the event that an
atomic bomb were dropped, they'd probably seek sanctuary at a
shopping mall. Advertisers ran with this image and tried to make
them the next great market: cynical, hip, funky, antibrand, and
antiestablishment. Then, after making them what they were, the
media tried to kill them off. In 1993, *Newsweek* labeled them "The
Whiny Generation."

But researchers like Nicholas Zill and John Robinson found
that survey data contradicted the loafer stereotype. When Zill and
Robinson analyzed a National Endowment for the Arts survey of
public participation, they found that compared to previous generations at the same age, the Gen Xers had higher college atten-

dance rates but lower incomes, were more interested in the visual arts but less so in sports and sex, and were more scarred by divorce though more likely to live with parents. "The notion that they're slackers is contradicted by the high value they place on education and the insecurity they feel about their success in a tough job market," says Zill, director of child and family studies for Westat, a Bethesda, Maryland–based survey research firm. "There's an underlying ambition to Generation Xers."

Today, the twenty- to thirty-four-year-olds of Generation X are found in ten of the PRIZM clusters, and Boomtown Singles, a cluster of young midscale singles living in satellite cities, has one of the highest proportions. Beaverton, Oregon, is a typical cluster town, attracting young singles to jobs at Intel, Nike, and dozens of high-tech start-ups headquartered in block-long buildings. In developments like Murray Crest and Stone Creek, Boomtown Singles live in $750-a-month garden-style apartments, parking their Saturns and Suzuki Samurais beneath balconies where they sun themselves in the summer. Status in Beaverton is a creative job, like software architect or development engineer. For leisure, residents are more interested in team sports such as softball and basketball than solo exercise challenges like jogging, hiking, and walking. At Gold's Gym in Beaverton, out-of-towners being recruited by local chip makers stop in to check out the fitness scene — a critical part of their decision to head for Beaverton.

"These people are into the health scene," says Michele Briedé, manager of Gold's Gym. "They're looking for activities." Briedé, a petite twenty-nine-year-old divorcée with an effervescent personality, ticks off the kinds of activities her clients are into: biking, windsurfing, and golf — she stops herself. "But they're not doing golf for the exercise," she notes. "They're doing it for the networking opportunities." At her gym, the busiest time is between 6:45 A.M. and 8:00 A.M., before the start of a long day in front of a computer.

Unlike the many boomers who tuned in, turned on, and dropped out, Boomtown Singles are a clean-living group. Social drinking, yes; drugs, no. A typical Beaverton party features a keg of microbrew beer from Bridgeport or McMenamins brewery in Portland. "You'd never find Budweiser here," one resident notes. "You're better off to show up with nothing than with something conventional." But Boomtown Singles is still a relatively new lifestyle, and many businesses are trying to catch up. In Beaver-

*A typical Beaverton party fea-
tures a keg of microbrew beer
from Bridgeport or McMenamins
brewery in Portland. "You'd
never find Budweiser here," one
resident notes. "You're better off
to show up with nothing than
with something conventional."*

ton, only a few chains, like Red Lobster and TGI Friday's, have come to town. The streets are notably bereft of juice and sushi bars. To wind down, these workaholics surf the Net. "After their car," says Briedé, "a computer is the biggest capital expense for the guys."

On one score, politics, the slacker image fits. Less than a third of all eighteen- to twenty-four-year-olds voted in the 1996 presidential election; 42 percent of their counterparts went to the polls in 1972. Boomtown Singles tend to be moderate Republicans with few firm beliefs. They have the second-lowest proportion of registered voters of any cluster in the nation (next to the downscale seniors in Hometown Retired), and they were nearly twice as likely as average Americans to vote for Ross Perot. "It's a tolerant community," says Beaverton architect Robert Enninga. "We rarely hear about national issues like abortion. There's a willingness to accept other beliefs and welcome with open arms people of any race, color, or creed." But there's also a general distrust of government and its ability to help people. In their lifetimes they've witnessed government corruption from Watergate to Iran-Contra to Whitewater. A Third Millennium survey found that 53 percent of Gen Xers believe that the TV soap opera *General Hospital* will last longer than Medicare. "People don't talk politics when they get together," says Alice Fosse, hospitality director of the Bergfreunde Ski Club in Beaverton. "We talk about relationships."

The graying of America

The baby boomers are getting older, but they're not the fastest-growing age segment; that distinction belongs to the so-called mature generation, those Americans born between 1909 and 1945 who were shaped by the common experiences of the Depression and World War II. Between 1985 and 1997, the number of over-sixty-five-year-olds increased from 28 million to 34 million, and better medical care and an improving standard of living are the chief reasons. Since the turn of the century, the life expectancy of Americans has increased by 40 percent, to 79 years for women and 72 for men. The lion's share of today's seniors are found in fifteen clusters outside the nation's big cities, including Hometown Retired, Golden Ponds, and Mines & Mills. More and more retirement communities are appearing in rural areas as seniors push farther into the countryside in search of less stressful lifestyles. In Middleburg Managers, a collection of expanding midscale second-tier cities like Lacey, Washington, so many new subdivisions are going up near golf courses that a regular sight has become forty-foot-high net fences to protect windows from errant tee shots. "Retirement," as one local puts it, "has become our growth industry."

If the biggest retirement trend of the 1980s involved the growth of planned seniors communities classified Gray Power — with their classes in line dancing, lawn bowling, and computers — the 1990s caused the pendulum to swing back: more retirees are staying put. The emergence of Sunset City Blues, a cluster of empty-nesting suburbs around aging industrial cities in the North, indicates that not all Americans turn into snowbirds when they hit sixty-five. In Merrillville, Indiana, just south of Gary, locals have relatively low rates of travel and prefer getting together with long-time neighbors for dinner. They're big on collecting coins, plates, and dolls. They're more likely than Gray Power residents to bake from scratch and wish there were more time to entertain family and friends at home. Aging in place, the seniors of Sunset City Blues face the same concern as their Sunbelt counterparts: how to maintain their health and economic well-being over increasingly longer life spans. But they're facing these worries without the infrastructure of a Leisure World or a Sun City dedicated to homogeneous elderly residents. At the Merrillville library, guides for self-diagnosing aches and pains associated with aging are among the most popular reference books. According to librarian Lani Peterson, this is because so many retirees belong to HMOs that provide only the minimum of medical advice. "These people don't know their doctors anymore," she says. "So they get diagnosed with a disease and they come in here to find out what it means."

In Hometown Retired, a new cluster of fading industrial towns, many of the blue-collar retirees simply don't have the means to pack up and move away. In places like Cumberland, Maryland, the percentage of elderly is rising because young people have moved out in search of jobs and the seniors are staying put. "The town is dead," observes Helen Sporkey, seventy-three, a former government worker. "There are no good jobs for young people. But it's a good place for seniors because it's safe." The downscale lifestyle — the median income is $18,100 — is nothing new for residents who've struggled financially for most of their lives. Retirees here spend their days playing cards rather than golf. They hang out in the lobbies of senior-filled apartment buildings, watching TV or chatting with neighbors, many of whom have known each other for decades. At night, bingo is so popular that many apartment lobbies have standing bingo boards. "I've never understood people who work and live fifty years in one town and then pick up and retire somewhere else," says Jim Goldsworthy, business editor of the *Cumberland Times-News.* "I just don't get it."

Recent statistics show that most of America's elderly population are living in exurban areas, far from the madding crowds. And one of the fastest-growing community types is Rustic Elders, a cluster of downscale, isolated settlements where the lifestyle is pure country. Surveys show that these residents enjoy sewing and woodworking, listening to Christian faith music and country radio, fishing and camping. In Arborville, West Virginia, a hamlet of only one hundred households, residents don't bemoan the lack of organized activities; they just concentrate on the simple pleasures of their mountain home. "My favorite thing in the whole world is to sit on the front porch snapping string beans and listening to a distant dog bark," says Harold Crist, seventy-three, a retired schoolteacher. "There's no sound of traffic. You're alone more, and you feel touched more by God. When people walk, they do it for the exercise, but also to meditate. You'll see a deer, then flowers blooming, then the seasons changing."

Meditation may be nice, but Rustic Elders are somewhat isolated from mainstream messages, especially when it comes to health and fitness. In this cluster, bacon and eggs sell at high rates, and cholesterol is given little thought. "People around here say, 'My grandfather lived to ninety-two and he ate eggs every day, so why shouldn't I?'" says Crist. Smoking rates are high, and chewing tobacco is even more popular because so many workers in the cluster's logging and paper industries are forbidden to smoke around wood products. The residents' isolation also breeds parochialism: Rustic Elders have low travel rates, and in Arborville, many residents have never taken a plane or a train, never seen a museum or a zoo. In these communities, going shopping typically means driving an hour to the closest mall. In a cluster where the roads are often hilly, narrow, and made of gravel, motorists tend to own pickup trucks so they can navigate the long hauls to stores, hospitals, or fishing lakes.

Not that residents mind. Crist, for one, appreciates a community where a night on the town may mean a covered-dish supper at the local church. He has his garden, his hobby writing Civil War fiction, and his collection of Matchbox cars, antique jars, and soft-drink cans endorsed by race car drivers. But for all the collectibles, he still claims that his favorite activity is doing nothing at all. "To us, we never have a boring day," says Crist. "People's aspirations aren't very far-ranging." While the pace may sound dull compared to the nonstop activities and club meetings of Gray Power seniors living in Sun City or Leisure World, the residents of Rustic Elders are in no hurry.

When lifestyles change

In most of America, change occurs slowly. Despite America's image as a constantly churning, yearning society, mobility rates have actually declined in recent years. Today, only a third of the nation's adults say they would even consider moving to a new community someday. A 1996 survey found that the vast majority of Americans, rich or poor, say they're happy right where they are. More than two-thirds claim they can do better for themselves by *not* pulling up stakes.

But when people do move, the cluster system confirms an important principle of settlement: People may leave, but neighborhoods stay the same. The infrastructure that first attracted people to a community — housing stock, schools, and commercial base — remains relatively constant even after the original residents move away. It takes years for the steady migration of city dwellers to a small town to alter local demographics and consumer tastes. The young singles drawn to Bohemian Mix may look different from their predecessors — more tattoos, fewer spiky hairdos — but the street scenes in Manhattan's East Village and Washington's Dupont Circle still look the same as they did a decade ago. There's still an array of funky apartments, hip bars, and bleeding-edge clothing styles. There are always the drugs, the homeless people, and the periodic protest marches.

Moreover, a sense of place has a powerful influence on making newcomers conform to local customs. Sara Hope, a librarian in Lynchburg, Tennessee, grew up in California, and describes herself as "the original Valley girl" as a teenager. But she longed to settle in a rural community with her husband. When they finally moved to Lynchburg, a Shotguns & Pickups hamlet in the hill-and-holler country of middle Tennessee, she remembers feeling bothered by the lethargic pace of her new surroundings, by locals who would spend hours a day on their porches, simply rocking in chairs and

A 1996 survey found that the vast majority of Americans, rich or poor, say they're happy right where they are. More than two-thirds claim they can do better for themselves by not *pulling up stakes.*

talking to friends. "I kept thinking, these people are not doing something. Things need to get done," recalls Hope, forty-nine, a former circuit court clerk. "Then, after about six months, one day I got my husband off to work and my young kids off to school, and it was like a light being turned on. The people here enjoy their own company. They don't want excitement. This is why people sit and rock. So I went out to the porch and sat down and never felt a bit of guilt from then on. I never regretted the slow-paced life anymore."

Many clusters underwent modest shifts over the last decade as research plants opened up, neighborhoods empty-nested, and new subdivisions were built. Blue-Chip Blues, the largest cluster during the 1980s, declined in population as blue-collar jobs moved abroad and younger families left for opportunities in Sunbelt boomtowns. Old Yankee Rows, a cluster of immigrant-filled row-house neighborhoods in the Northeast, has changed in ethnic makeup — from Irish and Italian families to Asians and Hispanics. Ten years ago, the rural God's Country cluster was just beginning to attract affluent city dwellers and culture clashes erupted as newcomers complained about the smell of fertilizer and manure on area farms. Today, only 2 percent of God's Country adults work as farmers and the cluster has become a part of the exurban fringe of metro areas. New battle lines are being drawn between pro-growth and slow-growth proponents. Some God's Country families want to bring in fancy shopping malls, parks, and schools, while others want to stake out their homes on cornfields and shut down further development. In East Brandywine, Pennsylvania, a God's Country community outside of Philadelphia, the number of farms has shrunk over the last twenty-five years from eleven to one as fields have been paved over to make room for town houses and supermarkets with salad bars. Now, longtime residents fear their paradise is starting to look a lot like Detroit and are trying to slow the influx of newcomers with antigrowth measures. The township recently set up an agricultural security district to maintain some of the open space that first attracted newcomers to the area, but it may be too little too late. "Our lifestyle has become schizo-phrenic," laments resident Liz Pavlick. "On the one hand it's peaceful, on the other it's increasingly hectic."

Employment shifts are perhaps the most potent force in changing lifestyles, because people follow jobs and commercial development follows people. Ten years ago, Spring Hill, Tennessee, was a sleepy Back Country Folks community in flat farmland about an hour south of Nashville. Then General Motors built its new Saturn plant there, and the impact was like the arrival of extraterrestrials from, well, Saturn. Within a few months, real estate changed hands several times, developers arrived by the truckload, and new businesses sprang up like mushrooms. In five years, the county population jumped by 35 percent. The predominant cluster morphed into Mines & Mills, like other industrial towns where the pace of life follows the rhythm of local factory employers. In Back Country Folks, residents spend their weekends camping and hunting; in Mines & Mills, they go cruising on motorcycles and attend auto races.

Today, motorists on Spring Hill's Highway 31 pass new schools, two new firehouses, and a number of freshly painted subdivisions. White rocking chairs sit in front of the new town center, but they're one of the few vestiges of the town's agrarian past. The national chains have discovered Spring Hill, now home to a new Food Lion and Holiday Inn. Down at the Poplar House restaurant, hamburgers now cost $3.25 and a turkey plate goes for the once unheard-of price of $6.99. Onetime waitresses now own the place, and they're tickled that the new plant has increased traffic. "The old-timers who wanted to keep this a country town don't like it a

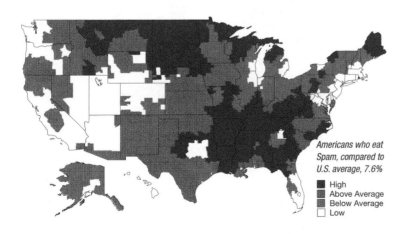

Americans who eat
Spam, compared to
U.S. average, 7.6%

■ High
■ Above Average
■ Below Average
□ Low

Spam Country

Spam's popularity among rural Americans — and heartland clusters like Blue Highways and Grain Belt — reflects the usual life cycle of consumer products in the U.S. They're first adopted by upscale metropolitan clusters before undergoing a process called "proletarian drift" that eventually sends them to the hinterland. Eventually, even Starbucks caffe latte ends up at an isolated market in Appalachia. Spam, now a century old, arrived in rural America years ago and remains a mainstay in downscale and rural pantries.

Top Clusters   Blue Highways / Back Country Folks / Hard Scrabble / Norma Rae-ville / Grain Belt
Top Markets   Hattiesburg-Laurel, Mississippi / Traverse City–Cadillac, Michigan / Jonesboro, Arkansas / Alexandria, Louisiana / Bangor, Maine

(Sources: PRIZM, Claritas Inc., Mediamark Research Inc.)

bit," one concedes. "But my feeling is that if you don't keep up with progress, you die."

To be sure, one person's progress is another's nightmare. Over the last decade, a group of urban planners has started a movement called New Urbanism that attempts to create and restore communities as alternatives to the current urban sprawl. In places like Kentlands, Maryland, Northwest Landing, Washington, and Seaside, Florida, developers have built compact communities where homes surround a village green, roads are narrow to encourage walking rather than driving, and public transit systems connect residents to shops and businesses without mind-numbing commutes. In fact, residents are encouraged to bike or walk to work. And open space is reserved for community space, not backyards, contrary to the traditional suburban model. "The problem with suburbs is that they no longer work," says Peter Katz, an urban theorist and author of *The New Urbanism*. "The suburban dream has changed. The road system is in gridlock. We can't afford the big yards. Americans initially moved to suburbs for privacy, security, and home ownership. Now, they've got isolation, congestion, rising crime, and pollution."

In response, a coalition of architects, planners, and builders have created some 150 New Urbanism developments to help foster a sense of community by recalling the charms of turn-of-the-century streetcar suburbs. The most talked-about of these communities is a new town being developed by the Walt Disney Company that resembles nothing more than a Frank Capra movie set, reflecting the deep American nostalgia for small-town life. Picket fences, Victorian-style homes, porches, and sidewalks line shady streets in Celebration, Florida, currently going up south of Walt Disney World in Orlando. In 1990, the town's zip code, 34747, was classified Big Sky Families, a cluster of upper-middle-class towns in country settings. By November 1996, when Celebration officially opened, the town had evolved into an upscale Country Squires lifestyle. Celebration was designed to encourage multigenerational households by incorporating the totems of an earlier age: gazebos, town squares, and lots of mother-in-law apartments. The only furniture store specializes in antiques and reproductions. The business district is compact, with plenty of benches and streets made of brick. There's a lake, and curvy paths to encourage walking — not to mention skating, skateboarding, and biking.

"We came because it's a real family place," says Darlene ("just like the Mouseketeer") Rapanotti, forty-nine, one of the newest residents, from her American flag–draped porch. "It's like the old-fashioned communities with people on the front porch and kids riding their bikes down the street. In other places, you rarely talk to your neighbors. Here, you do." Rapanotti heard about the project through the Disney Institute, where she used to work, and saw more information on the Disney web site. So she, her teacher husband, and their two children moved in and found themselves pleased with the atmosphere — "Like where I grew up on Long Island, years ago," Rapanotti says. True, their yard is tiny, their new house has only about half the square footage of their previous one, and the bedrooms are modest. But their high-ceilinged living room has plenty of room for Rapanotti's collection of miniature ceramic Disney creatures. And with Celebration's homes priced at $200,000 to $1 million, the community closely resembles other ritzy towns that are classified Country Squires.

Despite its trappings, Celebration hardly qualifies as a traditional small town in any authentic sense. The clerk at Downeast, a clothing store, describes its big-bang origins: "One day it was 'Boom! A town!' That's how it felt." Today, it feels rich. With the windows in Gooding's Food Market advertising "sundries and sushi," it's not likely to remind your grandparents of their corner grocery store. The picture-perfect pastel-painted homes seem more appropriate for the nearby Magic Kingdom than any traditional town. There is no trash on the streets. No bums in the alleys. No bad smells. Town officials predict that soon Celebration will be home to 20,000 people, a figure that hints at the powerful lure of theme-park fantasy as a way of life.

But the relatively small number of New Urbanism developments may suggest that not everyone appreciates such charms. One Orlando architect has described Celebration as "a subdivision on steroids." Others complain that such alternatives to suburban sprawl are often available only to those who can afford them. Because the homes typically come with big price tags, most of these alternative communities fall into the affluent family clusters of Kids & Cul-de-Sacs or Country Squires. Then there's the matter of taste, many Americans being too traditional for the progressive visions of many planners — even those trying to put a contemporary spin on the past. Suburbanites tend to want to be surrounded by people like themselves. They enjoy their homogeneous split-level homes, their big yards, their cars, and a lot of elbow room separat-

A 1998 survey found that nearly half of all motorists like driving as a time to think and enjoy some solitude.

ing them from their jobs that serves no common good except their own impulse to stretch out occasionally. A 1998 survey found that nearly half of all motorists like driving as a time to think and enjoy some solitude, leading Peter Katz to observe, "Things won't change until the pain level becomes much higher than it is today." For now, too many people still find rush-hour traffic and road rage at tolerable levels, which may be the greatest testament to America's love affair not with the hearth but with the car.

A fractured future

Every generation cluster is in pursuit of happiness, but what kind of choices will the clusters offer in the future? A lot depends on how demographic trends play out over the next decade. Already, census projections indicate that Americans will be older, smarter, more crowded, and more ethnically diverse in the twenty-first century. By the year 2050, the population is expected to grow by a striking 50 percent, to more than 380 million. The percentages of Latinos, African Americans, and Asians will zoom, leaving whites a minority. And more Americans will live to experience those changes, over longer periods of time, especially in Sunbelt communities. These shifts will be revealed in the next cluster system, which will be released a few years after the 2000 census. But with a little informed speculation, it's possible to anticipate what the next cluster map will reveal.

■ EXURBAN RISE. The largest number of new clusters likely will sprout along the fringes of what were once small-town and second-city clusters. Some of the new residents will be young families seeking affordable housing in a safe setting that could be termed Family Boom. More affluent city dwellers will continue moving to the exurbs, hauling their modems in SUVs to create a Techies & Telecommuters lifestyle. Although three out of four Americans live in metro areas, a recent Gallup poll found that more than half of them wish they could live in a small town.

■ BABY-BOOM RETIREES. The baby boomers and their children are turning the population pyramid into an hourglass. With the oldest turning fifty-five in 2001, boomers will start exiting their careers for retirement. The anticipated growth in Sunbelt states like Texas and Florida may result in early-retirement communities catering to active older boomers as part of a Southern Comfort cluster. As younger boomers enter their peak earning years, the winner-take-all impulse will likely create more millionaires and a second wealthy city lifestyle, called City Elite, to join Urban Gold Coast. America's romance with gated communities, which now total 400,000, may result in a Gated Living lifestyle, filled with boomers seeking protection from dicey urban neighborhoods. And longtime resort communities will suddenly experience pressure from boomers buying not vacation homes but retirement condos, creating a Resorts & Retirees lifestyle.

■ AGING AMERICANS. Americans are living longer and healthier lives, a trend that will no doubt continue thanks to medical advances and better health education. With more companies offering employees early retirement, retirement years are stretching out and in some cases beginning earlier than ever. Expect a new cluster of planned retirement communities called "Middlessence," a term coined by age expert Ken Dychtwald to describe fifty-five- to seventy-five-year-olds. As for the growing percentage of elderly steadfastly staying in their old neighborhoods, this group should find themselves represented in a Savvy Seniors cluster. Finally, the boom in the oldest of the old, those over eighty-five years of age, should result in more age-segregated apartments and assisted-living facilities, giving rise to an Assisted Society cluster.

■ AN EVEN SPICIER STEW. The Census Bureau predicts that from 1997 to 2050 more than half of the nation's population growth will occur among Hispanics and Asians. Hispanics are already on their way to becoming the largest minority within the population in 2010, and because Hispanics have a tendency to have more children than whites, a middle-class, family-filled Hispanic Sprawl cluster should appear shortly after the year 2000. Asians will continue to be the fastest-growing population segment, thanks to increasing immigration, and it's reasonable to anticipate a majority Asian suburban lifestyle called Asiaville. With midscale ethnic migrants pushing farther out into exurbia's formerly homogeneous communities, there's every likelihood that an Asian Pioneers cluster will join a suburban Latino Elite, reflecting the upward mobility of these two ethnic groups. Finally, look for two new clusters of African Americans: affluent Black Executives, composed of upscale families who have left downtown areas for comfortable suburbs, and upper-middle-class Upscale Managers, reflecting the new prosperity of a black management class in a handful of metros.

The baby boomers and their children are turning the population pyramid into an hourglass. With the oldest turning fifty-five in 2001, boomers will start exiting their careers for retirement.

*In the year 2000, some 35
percent of American families
are headed by singles or single
parents.*

■ SHRINKING HOUSEHOLDS. In the year 2000, some 35 percent of American families are headed by singles or single parents. Add to that widowed seniors and echo boomers entering their twenties, and American society will increasingly be dominated by single-person households. This trend will likely mean another young singles cluster in exurban areas, where industrial growth is occurring, with a name like Young Settlers. Another empty-nesting elderly cluster that might be called Senior Solos may emerge in urban areas. Because more older Americans may become dependent on their children for care, a Sandwich Generation cluster may appear with a high proportion of adult children living in the houses they grew up in with their elderly parents.

Given these demographic and socioeconomic riptides, the more important question may be how America's future clusters will get along. Some demographers see twenty-first-century America as a nation increasingly split between have and have-not, young and old, and immigrant and native born. With the predominantly white exodus to the exurban fringe, the nation could become a polarized place of coastal cities that are increasingly diverse and great swatches of the heartland that are overwhelmingly homogeneous. In this *Blade Runner* scenario, Americans will undergo constant class, racial, and ethnic strife. The social fabric will rend. Decaying cities will be surrounded by enormous gated and segregated suburbs. The gap between rich and poor will widen to a chasm.

But the clusters do contain seeds of hope that may germinate over time. There are signs that Americans are adapting to ethnic diversity: More immigrants are settling not in downtown ghettos but in suburban neighborhoods and even exurban towns. The intermarriage rate between blacks and whites is steadily rising. Latinos are marrying across ethnic lines in growing numbers. Sports heroes like Tiger Woods are bringing multicultural parentage into the mainstream, and even the Census Bureau has begun to recognize this new reality by allowing respondents to check more than one racial category when answering its questionnaires. The future may yet find Americans resembling a café au lait society in which race is no longer a significant issue. But if past cluster systems are any prologue to the future, the changes will come incrementally, the slow evolution of a mosaic society in which people get along because there's simply no other way.

3 PUTTING AMERICAN CLUSTERS TO WORK

It is only shallow people who do not judge by appearances. The mystery is the visible, not the invisible.

— Oscar Wilde

The color of clusters

Barbara J. Eichhorn, an interior designer from Kansas City, Kansas, used to conduct market research by sitting in a client's parking lot and noting what kinds of cars drove by. "I'd look to see if the cars were American or imported, if the drivers were blue-collar workers or yuppies," she recalls. Whether she was designing an office or store, whether her client was McDonald's or Charlie's Diner, she followed one truth: "You have to know your customers in order to meet their needs."

But about ten years ago, Eichhorn packed up her folding chair when she learned about clusters, realizing there was a more systematic way of understanding consumer behavior. By tapping into the PRIZM cluster system, she could profile all the lifestyles found in the community surrounding a store. She began conducting interviews with business owners and residents about their favorite shapes, colors, and values, using humanistic psychologist Abraham Maslow's famous hierarchy of needs. Were they driven by basic desires — such as food, shelter, and safety — or higher, more complex forces — like love, aesthetics, and achievement? And how could those needs be addressed in terms of interior design?

In time, Eichhorn developed a lexicon of colors, shapes, and furnishings linked to every cluster. And she used those insights to help design some fifty PRIZM-based residential and commercial projects — everything from banks to bowling alleys — as part of her business, BJ's Lifecode. Whereas marketers once used lifestyle data to decide where to open a store and how to stock it ($150 Hermès ties or $20 Dior knockoffs), Eichhorn focused on the psychology of the target customers: What color scheme would make them feel comfortable and want to return to a store again and again?

"In Money & Brains, you're talking about complex colors, like Mayflower blue, Gloucester green, and New England red," explains Eichhorn, a breezy fifty-year-old former high school art teacher. "And the fabrics they like are often hand printed, with imperfections. These upper-class consumers value old, worn, and faded things that aren't machine made. If they want wood, it's highly distressed." She pauses, flipping through a stack of sample books. "But in the Middle America cluster, they think that's junk. They want a piece of furniture to look new or shiny, like oak or mahogany. They want a Barcalounger that's padded and big. They want colors that are clean and can be described with one word: Beige. Pink. Green."

Eichhorn may sound like a slightly eccentric artist, but there's nothing kooky about the work she's done translating data on a cluster's leisure preferences into designs of brick, wood, fabric, and paint. For the midscale Middle America cluster of Ormond Beach, Florida, Eichhorn designed a fitness center with bold primary colors: blue lacquer chairs; red, white, and blue wall tiles; yellow door trim. Several years ago she designed a bowling alley in a Kansas City neighborhood filled with middle- and working-class families from Blue-Chip Blues, Middle America, and Shotguns & Pickups clusters. Couples in these clusters leave their jobs at Shell Oil and the Remington gun factory to bowl in T-shirts. So she gave the alley a bold Southwestern theme, painted in bright peach and turquoise, with wooden bar stools in the grill. Across town, in an upscale area filled with Blue Blood Estates, Winner's Circle, and Young Influentials, the bowling alley was given an art deco look in soft aqua and burgundy, a trompe l'oeil dining car out front, and elaborate bar stools in the restaurant befitting the bottoms that are brought to league nights in cushy BMWs and Acuras.

"If you're used to a two-thousand-dollar sofa at home, you're not going to like a ten-dollar bar stool in a bowling alley," says Eichhorn. "It's my belief that birds of a feather bowl together."

Because cities typically attract more than a few similar lifestyles, Eichhorn finds herself especially challenged when trying to plan a building that satisfies multiple — and sometimes competing — interests. Several years ago, she designed another bowling center in Port Charlotte, Florida, a community fairly evenly divided between Gray Power, a segment of affluent retirees, and Golden Ponds, seniors who are a bit younger, less affluent, and more rural. Many of the Gray Power folks are snowbirds who belong to country clubs back north, prompting Eichhorn to install whitewashed wood, wicker chairs, and plants for that country club look. And because their favorite colors tend toward complex shades of bright peach and Mediterranean aqua, she added flamingos and seashells. But the alley also wanted to attract the rural "youngsters" of Golden Ponds, so Eichhorn added a deep forest green color. "In the end, we had young colors and older colors in the same room," she noted, adding that the overall effect apparently worked. The new center opened to glowing reviews, with local newspaper headlines proclaiming, "Country Club Bowling Comes to Port Charlotte." Bowling receipts soared.

"You're socialized to like different colors," concludes Eichhorn. "Nobody will come inside a store in Shotguns & Pickups if the decor is pale peach. Each one of the clusters has different preferences for colors."

A product for every lifestyle

In the constant effort to understand and influence America's ever-fickle consumers, Barbara Eichhorn is hardly alone. With the first baby boomers leaving their peak earning years and household growth slowing to a 1 percent crawl, business decision makers have armed themselves with desktop computers loaded with cluster software, manipulating giant databases to discover how consumers behave in the marketplace. An increasing number of companies, ranging from General Motors and JC Penney to neighborhood banks and mom-and-pop shops, now use cluster systems as a sophisticated attempt to predict the kinds of products people want or the kind of pitch they'll respond to. A 1991 study by information consultants Deloitte & Touche found that 50 percent of Fortune 500 companies were using high-tech marketing databanks to identify customers and pinpoint prospects for campaigns. Just two years earlier, it was barely 30 percent.

But it's not just the commercial sector that's turning to lifestyle segmentation systems. Many state and local agencies have adopted business management approaches for social marketing projects, viewing their constituents as "customers" to be mapped and profiled like any consumer niche. Government officials now tap lifestyle clusters to tailor and promote their services, whether

"You're socialized to like different colors," concludes Eichhorn. "Nobody will come inside a store in Shotguns & Pickups if the decor is pale peach. Each one of the clusters has different preferences for colors."

the goal is to encourage adoptions, increase seat belt use, or heighten health awareness. In Georgia, state health officials have linked diseases to lifestyle types in order to earmark funds to areas that need them most. Antismoking campaigns, for instance, are now dispatched to communities filled with clusters like Scrub Pine Flats, a lower-middle-class cluster with a high concentration of retirees, where lung cancer traditionally has been a problem. To advance seat belt use, the U.S. Department of Transportation conducted a cluster analysis of the 56,000 Americans killed in highway accidents each year. Afterward, DOT launched a seat belt promotion campaign targeted to the clusters where motorists failed to buckle up — places like Norma Rae-ville and Grain Belt — instead of sending out costly nationwide messages.

The popularity of cluster-based marketing reflects a growing acknowledgment by business leaders as well as social scientists that American society is increasingly fragmented. Many applauded PRIZM's growth from forty to sixty-two clusters because of the increased power to discriminate among different kinds of consumers. When cable television giant Cox Communications wanted to increase subscribers in Phoenix, Arizona, it was happy to find that the sole Hispanic cluster of the 1980s had grown to five distinct clusters in the '90s. "We could now find Hispanics who were middle income rather than just going after the downscale Hispanic Mix," says Charlotte Siegel, a Cox market research analyst. Indeed, one of its top target groups consisted of just two predominantly Latino midscale clusters: Mobility Blues (young blue-collar families) and Big City Blend (ethnically mixed urban families). To encourage these residents to sign up for cable, Cox opened local payment centers, allowing customers to pay their monthly bills with cash. Because recent immigrants are reluctant to open checking accounts, fearing reprisals by the Immigration and Naturalization Service, the cash payment option was critical to capturing them as subscribers. The cluster system told Cox exactly where to locate its payment centers, mostly in neighborhood grocery stores near its best prospects.

The rise of new lifestyle types within the metropolitan sprawl requires new cluster segments to explain consuming patterns in finer detail. Throughout the 1980s, much of Fairfax County, Virginia — the wealthiest suburb in the Washington, D.C., area — was classified Furs & Station Wagons, the third most affluent neighborhood type. But following the 1990 census, the cluster system revealed twenty-nine different lifestyle types, from small-townish Middle America to millionaire pockets of mansions overlooking the Potomac River that are classified as Blue Blood Estates. Most county residents fell into two lifestyle types: the young, child-filled families of Kids & Cul-de-Sacs, and the older, empty-nesting couples of Executive Suites. And they behave differently. When the Fairfax County Park Authority wanted to build eight recreation centers, it programmed the Wakefield RECenter, near Kids & Cul-de-Sacs subdivisions, with lots of pee-wee swimming classes for the preschool set. At South Run RECenter, surrounded by Executive Suites, it featured water aerobic classes, a cardiovascular center equipped with Nautilus devices, and a gourmet coffee vending machine to cater to that cluster's craving for caffe latte. Over a three-year period, season pass revenues jumped by 63 percent. Says marketing research manager Nick Duray, "The sixty-two clusters moved us, in microscope terms, from a ten-power lens to a fifty-power lens."

The strength of the larger cluster system lies in its ability to uncover customers in unlikely places. When Claritas looked at the buyers of cigarette rolling papers, staffers expected to find high numbers in urban singles clusters like Urban Gold Coast and Bohemian Mix, where pot parties are still common. They even anticipated a target group among downscale rural clusters like Grain Belt and Hard Scrabble, where tradition and economics might result in do-it-yourselfers hand rolling their own tobacco smokes. But what they didn't expect was a strong market among upscale suburban clusters like Kids & Cul-de-Sacs and Boomers & Babies, where aging boomers have settled with families into comfortable split-level lives. Apparently, many otherwise staid and respectable former potheads have trouble denying their counterculture roots and keep stashes hidden away in Ethan Allen hutches. "You could see this aging group of boomers still partaking in an occasional joint," says Claritas analyst Michael Mancini. "It's their little weekend escape."

In this fragmented marketplace, the clusters aid companies in extending their brands to reach more market niches. So a nameplate like Lincoln can offer a sport-utility vehicle like the Navigator to prevent its upscale consumers from shifting to the Chevrolet Suburban, and Mercedes-Benz can brand its logo on an M-Class SUV to spread the status symbol farther across the suburbanite landscape. When Chrysler created its popular new minivan mod-

Low-Tech Americans: Call-Waiting Fans

Income is a powerful predictor of consumer patterns. But low-tech products like call-waiting attract an unusual, two-tiered audience: upscale suburban families with teenagers who don't want to miss calls from friends, and working-class urban minorities who rely on the telephone as a lifeline to friends and family. On average, African Americans talk on the phone for 100 minutes per day — triple the norm.

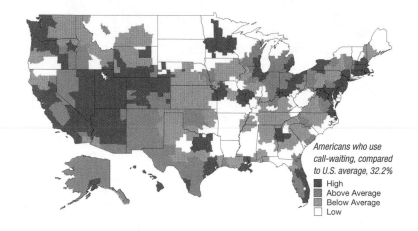

Americans who use call-waiting, compared to U.S. average, 32.2%

■ High
■ Above Average
■ Below Average
□ Low

Top Clusters   Boomers & Babies / Single City Blues / Gray Collars / Kids & Cul-de-Sacs / Mid-City Mix
Top Markets   Las Vegas, Nevada / Baltimore, Maryland / Detroit, Michigan / Philadelphia, Pennsylvania / Providence, Rhode Island–New Bedford, Massachusetts

(Sources: PRIZM, Claritas Inc., Mediamark Research Inc.)

els, it unveiled corporate triplets, the Chrysler Town & Country, the Dodge Caravan, and the Plymouth Voyager — identical vehicles but geared to very different segments of the motoring public. To capture upscale executive men, Chrysler featured rich wood trim and leather on the Town & Country, and its ads featured tony images to reassure the buyer that this land cruiser was very much like a luxury car. To capture educated upper-middle-class couples who like to comparison shop, Dodge's ad campaign used spokesman Edward Herrmann to tick off fact-filled features on a stark set. For middle-class moms, Plymouth ads offered frolicking family scenes set to jazz music, portraying essentially the same vehicle as a wonderful way to haul the kids.

The result: Town & Country's audience consists of more upscale men from clusters like Winner's Circle and Country Squires. Plymouth Voyagers are disproportionately purchased by midscale women from Greenbelt Families and Boomers & Babies. And Dodge is driven by exurban couples from God's Country and Big Fish, Small Pond. Men may be from Mars and women from Venus, to paraphrase author John Gray, but when it comes to minivan selection, men are from Winner's Circle and women are from Green-belt Families.

Even long-held sociological beliefs can be shattered by cluster profiles of American activities and consumption patterns. It's commonly believed that the nation's liberal neighborhoods are concentrated in the largest cities, where young singles are inclined to be more tolerant of alternative ideas — whether the subject is New Age medicine or gay sex. Indeed, some of the nation's most well-known gay neighborhoods, such as Greenwich Village in New York and Dupont Circle in Washington, are classified Bohemian Mix and typically found in large coastal cities. But a cluster profile of the 40,000 subscribers of a gay newspaper, *The Advocate,* found a disproportionate number of readers in upscale suburban clusters like Executive Suites and Young Influentials — even a satellite-city cluster like Middleburg Managers. The paper's marketing executives brought these findings to advertisers of upscale products to encourage displaying their wares in the paper. At the same time, an analysis of the 3,000 members of the International Society for the Study of Subtle Energy and Energy Medicine (ISSSEEM), a New Age medical group in Boulder, Colorado, found high concentrations in exurban America. New Age types were found to be living in rustic clusters like Country Squires, God's Country, and New Homesteaders, where surveys show that high numbers of residents believe in extraterrestrial life. Increasingly, alternative lifestyles are spreading to the hinterland, following the exodus of aging boomers away from the nation's big cities.

"Conventional wisdom holds that rural Americans would find New Age things to be frivolous," says geographer Bob Nunley, who consulted with ISSSEEM. "But it turns out that people willing to put up with longer drives and more inconvenience in the country are also interested in alternative lifestyles. They believe in massage therapy as part of their health maintenance program."

Perhaps the most difficult job facing businesses is marketing a new product for which there's no obvious audience. Each year, some 14,000 new products are introduced in the U.S. marketplace — and 80 percent will be gone within a year. A&E Television Networks faced that perilous challenge in 1994, when it decided to launch its new History Channel. At the time, only PBS and a handful of cable networks aired history shows with any regularity, and A&E had no way to gauge the audience. How many history buffs

New Age types were found to be living in rustic clusters like Country Squires, God's Country, and New Homesteaders, where surveys show that high numbers of residents believe in extraterrestrial life. Increasingly, alternative lifestyles are spreading to the hinterland, following the exodus of aging boomers away from the nation's big cities.

Each year, some 14,000 new products are introduced in the U.S. marketplace — and 80 percent will be gone within a year.

lived in the United States, and were there enough of them to support twenty-four-hour history programming? A&E wondered. What periods of history piqued their interest? And which local cable operators had the most of these viewers in their subscriber areas?

Moira Clinton, a thirty-two-year-old researcher for A&E, set out to find the size of the nation's history audience. She began by developing a database from the subscription lists of ten magazines — titles such as *American History, Great Battles, Wild West, Military History, Vietnam,* and *World War II* — and the buyers of three kinds of A&E home videos — biographies, documentaries, and programs featuring military and historical subjects. Soon, Clinton's History Channel database consisted of 1.4 million names. Analyzing the names by address and interest from her thirteen information sources, she identified clusters that had a strong preference in only a few topics, dubbing them Niche Buffs, and those with a moderate interest in a number of categories, whom she named Broadbased Buffs. For instance, the upscale city dwellers of Urban Gold Coast, who are fans of *Masterpiece Theatre* and American Movie Classics, were classified Niche Buffs because they bought documentary and historical videos and enjoyed *Great Battles* magazine — but not much else. Similarly, the career soldiers who lived in Military Quarters also had niche tastes, being big fans of *Military History* and *Great Battles* magazines but indifferent to life in early America and the Western frontier. By contrast, the educated suburbanites of Blue Blood Estates and Winner's Circle had wide-ranging interests in military history, biographies, documentaries, and early American culture. "They seemed to enjoy history for history's sake," says Clinton. "They just had a thirst for knowledge."

While the History Channel analysis showed that many Americans harbor a general interest in history, some specialized pockets exist. The baby boomers of American Dreams and Kids & Cul-de-Sacs, with above-average concentrations of Asian-born residents, share an interest in the Vietnam period. The Wild West plays well in remote clusters like Hard Scrabble and Agri-Business, perhaps because their lifestyle — filled with hunting, farming, and horseback riding — isn't so different from that of pioneers a century ago. Early Americana finds its fans in New Eco-topia, where city dwellers have fled the metros for a more rustic lifestyle. And the Civil War attracts interest in many clusters — from the yuppies of Young Influentials to the suburban families of Greenbelt Families — though Southern residents still refer to it as the War Between the States. "It's just one of those interesting periods in our past when everybody was affected," observes Clinton. "And it wasn't that long ago." In all, the analysis found armchair historians in forty-seven of the sixty-two clusters.

Ultimately, Clinton and her colleagues lumped the hot clusters into target groups and mapped where they could be found in markets across the country. Then cable operators in the hot markets began signing up for the History Channel — in droves. Clinton's research panned out, and within two and a half years, the History Channel could be seen in 39 million households, making it one of the fastest-growing cable networks in history. Says Clinton: "We became known as 'the little network that could.' We just hit an untapped reservoir of interest in history."

Marching to different beats

In a nation awash with advertising — each American sees an estimated three thousand messages daily — many companies have turned to cluster-based marketing to cut through the information fog. This is especially true for direct-mail pitches, which must speak the language of a cluster resident to avoid getting tossed as junk mail. When WGMS, a classical radio station in Washington, D.C., wanted to increase its listenership during its spring 1995 ratings period, Colorado-based Eagle Marketing suggested a cluster-targeted sweepstakes offer. Generally, classical music lovers are concentrated in affluent suburban clusters like Blue Blood Estates and Executive Suites. But an analysis of station listeners showed a surprising number of younger, less affluent fans in Young Influentials areas. Eagle's creative artists wanted a mailer to speak to these newly discovered, active and hip classical devotees. "Too often, creative marketing people try to reach classical music lovers with stuffy, corporate-looking themes," says Linda Brown, Eagle's research director. "But we noticed that these are fun-loving, luxury-minded people. They're living well, shopping at fancy stores, and flying to Europe on holiday."

With a nod to the rock classic "Born to Be Wild," the WGMS mailer featured a colorful caricature of Johann Sebastian Bach cooking hotdogs on a backyard grill, his apron scrawled with the words "Born to B Major." In the accompanying copy, the station offered prizes for a "Bachyard Barbecue," including a gas grill and barbecue fixings for the summer. But the grand prize was the big hook to lure them in: a new BMW, the ultimate status symbol for Young Influentials residents. Although Young Influentials generally respond poorly to sweepstakes, the classical music mailer struck a chord with them. Compared to an overall response rate of 12 percent, an impressive 26 percent of Young Influentials replied, besting even traditional classical music havens like Blue Blood Estates and Gray Power. "To Young Influentials, it's not 'your father's classical music' anymore," says Eagle's Brown, paying homage to another advertiser's slogan, "Not your father's Oldsmobile," which sought a younger audience for a product long associated with granddads. "Young Influentials wouldn't mind having a new BMW, especially if it's free. To them, that's cool."

Such promotional messages tailored to audience niches can be surprisingly powerful. When Eagle Marketing analyzed the listening audience of radio station WRDU in Raleigh, North Carolina, it discovered that a disproportionate number of residents were classified Back Country Folks, a cluster of rural blue-collar families who like to crank up "dinosaur" rock 'n' roll by the Rolling Stones and Lynryrd Skynyrd. To encourage those clusters to tune in, the station mailed out contest brochures boldly stating, "Work Sucks If You Can't Rock 'n' Roll," and offered a free "Work Sucks" T-shirt for the first 500 people who returned a business-reply card. Again, the company struck a chord — or perhaps a nerve. Nearly 17 percent of the contest respondents hailed from Back Country Folks — double the marketwide rate. The morning after the mailing hit the streets, fifty people stood outside the radio station to personally turn in their reply cards and secure T-shirts.

Americans' taste in music can be fairly predictable. Surveys show that the music they fall in love with as teenagers often remains their favorite genre the rest of their lives. This explains the continued aging of audiences for big band music, Broadway musicals, and even oldies radio, whose typical listener is now over fifty years old. Classic rock, which found its early fans among college kids in the dorms and beat-up VW Bugs of the nation's Towns & Gowns communities, now plays to upscale Kids & Cul-de-Sacs, where residents live in split-levels and drive Lexus sedans. But this forever-young approach to music appreciation can change with the arrival of crossover artists who expand traditional boundaries of taste. When country artists like Garth Brooks and the Judds added stepped-up rock tempos to create the Young Country

Traditional country music is enjoying a fresh audience among the Hispanic immigrants of clusters like Latino America and Hispanic Mix.

Speaking Cluster Languages

To cut through the clutter of junk mail, Eagle Marketing of Fort Collins, Colorado, developed cluster-tailored brochures to increase the audiences of different radio stations — be they classical, alternative, or country rock. When Pittsburgh station WDVE solicited ideas on how to improve the station with the humorous come-on "Free Sex," some recipients thought it tasteless. Those from Military Quarters loved it.

(Sources: Eagle Marketing, PRIZM, Claritas Inc.)

sound, their CDs no longer appealed simply to hayseeds in pick-ups. Their biggest fans today live in midscale town clusters like New Homesteaders and Red, White & Blues. Meanwhile, more traditional country music is enjoying a fresh audience among the Hispanic immigrants of clusters like Latino America and Hispanic Mix, where listeners appreciate romantic themes reminiscent of their small-town roots in Central American countries.

Through numerous direct-mail campaigns, Eagle Marketing has learned much about the kinds of messages that move America's radio listeners. But its failures have also taught it plenty. Eagle once headlined a rock station mailer "FREE SEX," and included caricatures of the deejays inside, naked but for some strategically placed greenery. Inside, the station solicited ideas on how to better serve its listeners, noting that the "free sex" suggestion from one fan was appreciated though hardly practical. But the eye-popping come-on — not to mention the illustration of a couple of hairy, out-of-shape deejays — proved a mixed message at best. The mailer failed to move recipients at either end of the cluster ladder, their sensibilities understandably offended. By contrast, in blue-collar, middle-class clusters such as Military Quarters, Middle America, and Red, White & Blues, an impressive number of recipients found the ribald message amusing enough to respond to the mailer. "It's testosterone humor," observes Brown, a thirty-year-old former medical illustrator. "It works for a young male audience. They don't think it's disgusting. They think it's funny."

Politically correct clusters

Although the clusters have had only limited use in the political arena, they did play a small role during the 1996 presidential campaign. In June of 1995, with Bill Clinton's reelection campaign adrift and threatened by inroads from leading Republican contender Bob Dole, Democratic pollster Mark Penn suggested a ten-thousand-person nationwide survey to identify the swing voters and the messages that would push them into the Clinton camp. Traditionally, swing voters are tough to pinpoint because of secret balloting; they can be inferred by laboriously examining previous election rolls to see if they voted for a Republican one year and a Democrat the next. But Harvard-educated Penn, a partner in the consulting firm of Penn & Schoen, had another idea. He'd worked with clusters for corporate clients to help identify customers most likely to switch brands. For Clinton's reelection effort, he suggested a "neuropersonality poll" designed to sift out uncommitted voters and determine their lifestyle clusters. With this sampling, he could then identify which five or six clusters held the nation's swing voters, map out where they lived, and try to reach them before election day. *Time* magazine reported that Clinton was at first doubtful but later became intrigued by the concept and gave the project the go-ahead.

From company sites in Denver and Manhattan, Penn's pollsters began phoning people and asking a battery of seemingly unrelated questions ("What movies do you like? What is your attitude toward religion? Are you happy with your current situation?"). The answers, the surveyors discovered, were surprising. Although Dole and Clinton seemed locked in a dead heat among all voters if you looked at preferences by age and sex, Penn's survey showed that the critical factor to voters was family life. Those voters in child-filled clusters like Upward Bound and Big Sky Families preferred Dole to Clinton by as much as 15 percentage points. And their greatest concern wasn't the economy, which had been the key issue in the 1992 election, but family values: school discipline, TV violence, caring for aging parents, lengthening maternity leave, and banning tobacco ads aimed at children. Clinton had a lock on the traditional liberal wing of the Democratic Party, the clusters

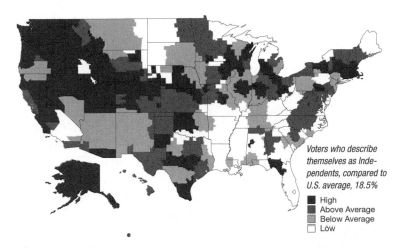

Voters who describe themselves as Independents, compared to U.S. average, 18.5%

■ High
■ Above Average
■ Below Average
□ Low

Swing Voters

Nearly one in five U.S. voters is a self-described Independent, unaffiliated with Democrats or Republicans and part of a sizable voting bloc that shifts according to the candidate and the issue. These swing voters represent a checkerboard of cluster lifestyles, from the college students of Towns & Gowns to the retirees of Sunset City Blues.

Top Clusters   Towns & Gowns / Greenbelt Families / Family Scramble / Sunset City Blues / Executive Suites
Top Markets   Gainesville, Florida / Austin, Texas / Lansing, Michigan / Santa Barbara–Santa Maria–San Luis Obispo, California / Eugene, Oregon

(Sources: PRIZM, Claritas Inc., NFO Research, Inc.)

filled with young singles and minorities such as Southside City and Towns & Gowns, which backed affirmative action, abortion rights, and gun control.

Beyond the cluster angle on political issues, the interviews yielded a treasure trove of information about the psychological and lifestyle profiles of the candidates' supporters. For instance, Clinton voters often made decisions based on emotions. They liked to watch *Friends,* tune in to MTV, and listen to classical, rap, and Top 40 music. By contrast, Dole's backers were more concerned with facts when making decisions. They watched *Home Improvement,* enjoyed *Larry King,* and listened to '70s music. As for swing voters, Penn's poll discovered, the news was not encouraging for the Clinton campaign. Faced with choices, they tended to be thinkers, not feelers. They liked technology, enjoyed sports like baseball, and were big fans of camping out — hardly the sort who looked with favor on Clinton's forays to Martha's Vineyard and gadabouts with the Jackie O. jet set.

After digesting the survey results, the Democrats began experimenting with the president's image. For Clinton's summer 1995 vacation, then-consultant Dick Morris suggested a mountain holiday. And Clinton did just that, hiking in the national parks and camping in a tent in Wyoming — though he managed to get in a few rounds of golf as well (ignoring the sport's popularity among

Dole supporters). But subsequent polls found that Clinton's numbers were flat, and the president called Morris on the carpet for taking the cluster concept too far. According to his book *Behind the Oval Office,* Morris stood by his theory, suggesting that presidential decisions continue to be linked to survey results. He blamed Clinton's stagnant numbers on the golf.

In the broader political arena, however, Penn's cluster survey carried more weight. For stump appearances that fall, Penn suggested Clinton make a thoughtful, fact-filled case for his reelection to capture swing voters. He needed to win over young, socially conservative families not with appeals to religious values but with secular concerns like protecting their children and caring for their parents. Toward that end, Penn developed two target groups. Swing I voters (29 percent of voters) consisted of Democratic-leaning Independents in clusters like Starter Families and Smalltown Downtown. Swing II (25 percent) were the Republican-leaning Independents in clusters such as Big Sky Families and Family Scramble. Both shared similar concerns except on fiscal issues like taxes and welfare, where the two groups fell back on their party's traditional thinking. Penn's advice to Clinton: Combine toughness with compassion. Grab the Swing IIs with tough talk on crime but soothe the Swing Is with touchy-feely words on flextime and family leave.

In August, the Democrats launched an ad campaign attacking the Republican proposal to cut Medicare and portraying Clinton as the trusty defender of the elderly and families. In September, Clinton honed his message to balance the budget in a way that protected family values and defended Medicare, Medicaid, education, and the environment. In fact, the reelection team used this formula so often that they eventually took to calling it the M2E2 strategy. During the State of the Union address in January of 1996, Penn rated every position according to how it fared with four voter groups: Clinton stalwarts, Dole backers, Swing I, and Swing II.

Although it's hard to quantify the impact of clustering on the final election results, political analysts cited Clinton's positive, family-values message as critical to his victory. In December 1994, polls showed Clinton had only 33 percent of the vote in a two-way contest with Dole. By February 1996, Clinton had locked up 53 percent against Dole in a two-way race and 50 percent in a three-way race with third-party candidate Ross Perot. Ultimately, Clin-

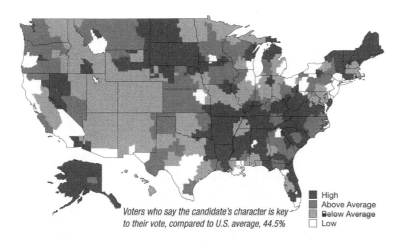

Where Character Counts in Politics

"It's the economy, stupid" was the rallying cry of Bill Clinton campaign workers during the 1992 presidential election, reflecting the issue uppermost in the minds of Americans. Today, after two terms of robust economic growth and an impeached president, the character of political candidates is a top concern of voters. It's especially significant to young baby-boomer families who've prospered in the Clinton years.

Voters who say the candidate's character is key to their vote, compared to U.S. average, 44.5%

High
Above Average
Below Average
Low

Top Clusters Boomers & Babies / New Homesteaders / Second City Elite / New Beginnings / New Eco-topia
Top Markets Glendive, Montana / Palm Springs, California / Anniston, Alabama / Florence–Myrtle Beach, South Carolina / Bangor, Maine

(Sources: PRIZM, Claritas Inc., NFO Research, Inc.)

ton won the election with 49 percent of the vote — about where the polls had him pegged following his State of the Union speech.

Clustering against type

Traditionally, cluster systems allow marketers to identify their best customers in order to find more of the same among prospects. But in recent years, cluster-based marketing has been used to find opposites — or at least dissimilar types — and determine ways to retain them as well. College and university admissions counselors who once concentrated on finding standout high school students now use the clusters to achieve more diversity on campus and to keep those students who do attend happy. For several years, CERR, a Virginia-based enrollment consulting firm, has been helping colleges fine-tune their recruiting drives. Based on his experience with more than a hundred colleges, CERR president Theodore Kelly believes that a student's mobility is one of the key factors in college choice. According to his theory, college students can be lumped into three groups: those who live at home so their mothers will do their wash, those who live close enough so they can bring their wash home, and those who go far enough away so they do their own wash. In other words, school choice is related to the discomfort level associated with living away from home. High school students from clusters with high mobility rates (Middleburg Managers, Country Squires) are more willing to go to far-off colleges and presumably do their own laundry than students from lifestyles where they have remained in the same home for years (Middle America, Blue-Chip Blues).

Kelly's theory proved to be on target when predominantly white, middle-class Miami University of Ohio set out to increase the diversity of its student body of 15,600. Logic told recruiters to concentrate on major cities throughout the Southern Black Belt, but their efforts to recruit African American students from Atlanta's inner city proved disappointing. An analysis of the city's most common high school family clusters — Middle America, God's Country, and Shotguns & Pickups — revealed the flaw in the university's plan: low mobility rates among residents. These students just didn't feel comfortable leaving home to go to college. "Distance from home had a lot to do with their school choice," admits Jim McCoy, Miami's director of admissions.

In the aftermath of that analysis, McCoy and his colleagues targeted minority students living closer to Miami University's campus in southwestern Ohio. Recruiters visited high schools in Mid-City Mix, an African American cluster found in Ohio's three-C cities — Cincinnati, Columbus, and Cleveland — as well as the downscale rural cluster of Scrub Pine Flats, present in Appalachia. "We went into schools we hadn't been to before," says McCoy, "where a lot of the families were poor and their kids were the first generation to go to college." Miami's recruiting letters talked about scholarships, high retention rate of students, and postgraduation jobs. It was the kind of message that resonates in downscale but upwardly striving clusters. Over five years, the percentage of minority students at Miami rose from 2 percent to 10 percent. Today, computer-based letters help the university's recruiters reach out to students from different geographic regions, socioeconomic levels, and ethnic groups to achieve a desired mix of students. "We're trying to do what's best for the institution, the students applying, and the students already here," says McCoy.

Cluster marketing has been useful for more than attracting students to college; it's also helped keep students from dropping out. At Pratt Institute, a fine arts college in Brooklyn, New York, more than 20 percent of the freshman class in 1992 did not return for sophomore year. Some were leaving for academic reasons, unable to keep up with the demands of college-level art. But when Judith Aaron, a newly hired vice president of enrollment, investigated the problem, she found that culture shock was the main cause. A disproportionate number of dropouts came from upscale, exurban clusters like Second City Elite and Upward Bound, where residents live in comfortable homes in leafy subdivisions. Follow-up interviews revealed that they were simply uncomfortable with Pratt's urban setting. "They came from areas with cleaner streets, nicer supermarkets, no graffiti, and no insect problems," says Aaron. "It was a shock for anyone from the suburbs who'd never had any experience with city living."

Pratt's solution took several approaches. First, campus recruiters began concentrating on high school students from closer-in suburbs like Winner's Circle and Pools & Patios, as well as midscale urban clusters such as Old Yankee Rows, Latino America, and Urban Achievers. Second, counselors developed telemarketing messages and recruiting letters with different themes. For the parents of students from the upscale suburbs, the letter focused on the difficulty of sending your child to an urban school and how Pratt was dealing with safety issues. "We'd say that there are mentors and somebody is watching over the kids," explains Aaron. The parents of students in the midscale urban clusters learned about financial aid and the successful jobs that Pratt graduates land. "We wanted to preserve the diversity we have here," explains Aaron, "but we also wanted students to stay here and do well." Third, and perhaps most important, the school budgeted more money to improve classrooms and dorms to make all its students — and potential students — happier with campus life.   •

The results were undeniable. Between 1992 and 1994, the attrition rate dropped 20 percent. By 1996, the number of applications had ballooned from 1,000 to 2,800. And even though Pratt had curtailed recruiting in exurban, second-city clusters, the freshman class nearly doubled, from 273 to 500. "We felt that if they really wanted to come enough, they'd be fine," says Aaron. "But we concentrated our efforts on those likely to stay here. And that's worked." If "location, location, location" has long been the mantra of real estate agents, the new breed of marketers would amend that line to "cluster location, cluster location, cluster location."

Defensive cluster maneuvers

Cluster-based marketing campaigns aren't always intended to increase sales. Some are defensive in nature, designed simply to
maintain market share against overwhelming competition. Imagine, for instance, being the owner of a retail shop when a competitor many times your size moves in down the street. That's what
happened in 1992 to the Burnsville Center, a modest-sized mall located outside Minneapolis, when the Mall of America, as large as
thirty-four shopping centers, opened its doors only a ten-minute
drive away. The fallout was palpable at shopping centers for
twenty-five miles around, but Burnsville was hardest hit. One survey found that 42 percent of Burnsville Center's customers soon
were shopping at the Mall of America, in large part because of the
greater store variety and the megamall's indoor amusement park.
In an age when shopping is entertainment, the Mall of America aspires to be the Disneyland of retailing.

For traditional shopping malls like Burnsville Center, cluster
segmentation systems are nothing new. They've long been used to
identify the best sites for new centers based on the clusters in the
trading area, and, increasingly, they've been consulted to determine the best advertising medium and message for promoting the
center. After the Burnsville Center conducted a cluster analysis of
those most likely to shop there, it found its prime market in Greenbelt Families and Suburban Sprawl — upscale, suburban, nuclear
families who spend a large chunk of their disposable income on
their school-age kids. Taking a cue from their stressed lifestyle,
the center adopted a direct mail campaign in 1994 focusing on the
family-friendly message that "we're more convenient, more local,
more neighborly." Then it added a lighthearted, little-guy billboard
campaign, proclaiming itself: "The Mall (That Takes Up Very Little) of America." To remind busy parents that the center's core
business is shopping, not entertainment, another billboard declared: "Hey, you'll be incredibly disappointed with our roller
coaster."

In succeeding months, the center continued to draw young
families with local promotions, such as "Cash for Class," which
awarded money to schools based on Burnsville Center receipts
collected by students. Area teens were tapped as models for center fashion shows, and raffles were held, the management carefully

selecting prizes that appealed to the target clusters: a $4,200 fishing boat, motor, and trailer, for instance. Today, the Mall of America is no longer eating away at Burnsville Center sales. And Burnsville has lured even more shoppers with favorite Greenbelt Families and Suburban Sprawl stores, such as Ethan Allen, Brookstone, and Mervyn's. Consumers from these upper-middle-class clusters are early adopters when it comes to fashion and household gizmos, but they're always looking for bargains.

Targeting mass media

Like other cluster companies, Claritas offers all its clients detailed profiles of media preferences in their customers' clusters, the better to understand whether a target audience is more inclined to read fashion or fitness magazines, watch network news or a Nick at Nite sitcom. Isuzu, for instance, found that placing ads in lifestyle magazines worked better than advertising in newsweeklies. The buyers of designer jeans tend to watch cable channels like BET, Cinemax, and the Cartoon Network. Among the first users of cluster marketing were advertisers in the 1970s who bought ad space in "zoned" editions of general interest magazines like *Time* and *McCall's* — essentially subsets of their subscriber lists targeted to upscale readers in Blue Blood Estates and Money & Brains clusters.

But the ongoing debate among advertisers between using mass media like newspapers and niche media such as cable channels or specialty magazines has shifted. Today, newspapers are trying to recast themselves as no longer a mass-market medium but a targeted vehicle for editorial and advertising content, able to compete just as effectively as television and direct-mail marketers. As the newspaper-reading population ages and younger Americans turn to TV for news, chains like Gannett have tapped cluster profiles to find effective messages to increase subscribers. In Fort Collins, Colorado, a community heavy with Towns & Gowns and Boomtown Singles, the *Coloradoan* used premium gifts such as skis, mountain bikes, and CD equipment to help build circulation. In Blue Blood Estates–rich Palm Springs, California, the *Desert Sun* appealed to the altruistic values of residents who, let's face it, have whatever money can buy. If a household subscribed, the newspaper would make a forty-dollar donation to its favorite charity. The paper recorded a 31 percent response rate for that direct-

The buyers of designer jeans tend to watch cable channels like BET, Cinemax, and the Cartoon Network.

mail promotion. When the *Des Moines Register* wanted to increase the twenty-five- to forty-four-year-old subscribers in its primary clusters — like God's Country and Greenbelt Families — the paper conducted focus groups to discover what they wanted from the daily. After redesigning its lifestyle section and promoting its news-you-can-use features on health, entertainment, and relationships, the *Register* landed 1,900 new subscribers.

At the *Houston Chronicle,* database marketing coordinator Tony Phillips believed the city's hodgepodge of communities made it a natural candidate for a cluster-based targeting campaign. "In Houston, you'll see an upscale suburban cluster next to a middle-class city neighborhood next to a rural downscale one," he observes. "In one mile, you can go from Money & Brains to Agri-Business. It's nuts." But Phillips, a former Claritas analyst, believed that clusters are particularly adept at divining lifestyles in diverse neighborhoods, and he had a candidate in mind who could use the help. Every Christmas season, Toys "R" Us would blanket the Houston area with advertising circulars inserted into 300,000 newspapers and mailed to 150,000 homes. For years, it worked well and the costs were modest. But as printing and mailing expenses began to climb, the toy retailer needed to find a way to get more bang for its advertising buck.

Phillips set out to determine the best distribution formula for Houston's patchwork landscape. The first step involved a cluster analysis of the *Chronicle*'s 445,400 subscribers by carrier route (200 to 300 households) and 213,800 Toys "R" Us customers from its sales database. Then he compared the two profiles and ranked the clusters according to the most promising matches, from Blue Blood Estates, where 86 percent of all residents buy Toys "R" Us toys and read the *Chronicle,* to Towns & Gowns, where only 5 percent do both. Finally, he classified a handful of similar, top-ranked clusters into target groups and pinpointed the carrier routes that fit those profiles. For instance, Phillips named the top-performing group Upscale Suburban (which included Kids & Cul-de-Sacs, Boomers & Babies, and Suburban Sprawl) and noted that these parents would promise their kids a trip to Toys "R" Us as a reward for good behavior. The analysis also teased out another target group, Regular Gift-Givers, which surprisingly, contained households with no children. Instead, these older singles and couples from clusters like Gray Power and Middleburg Managers fre-

"In Houston, you'll see an upscale suburban cluster next to a middle-class city neighborhood next to a rural downscale one. In one mile, you can go from Money & Brains to Agri-Business. It's nuts."

quently bought toys for their friends' children or their grandchildren. After all, you can't show up empty-handed when visiting a kid-filled family, or so the thinking went.

The resulting map of targeted carrier routes carved the Houston cityscape into odd chunks. But from that portrait, Toys "R" Us was able to decrease the distribution of costly direct-mail pieces from 105,000 to 75,000 and increase the number of its cheaper newspaper inserts from 300,000 to 350,000 — for a bottom-line savings of $10,000 per holiday distribution. As for the impact, when many toy stores experienced a sales decline during the Christmas 1996 season, Houston's Toys "R" Us sales remained strong. "The client was able to reduce the quantity of mail and increase store sales," says Phillips. And everyone was happy — everyone, that is, except the U.S. Postal Service, which lost the fees from 30,000 pieces of bulk mail. Today, the postal service uses the clusters as well to market its services.

Better living through clusters

The successes that corporate marketers have found with lifestyle clusters have not been lost on the nonprofit community. Since the earliest days of geodemographics, public service agencies have sought ways to link lifestyle type with social marketing initiatives. Throughout the '90s, the American Cancer Society used the PRIZM system in fund-raising campaigns geared to the differing attitudes cluster residents have toward charity. After analyzing their database of 10 million donors, the society's Atlanta-based home office learned which clusters are naturally sympathetic to the cause (the senior-filled Golden Ponds and Gray Power), which are reluctant givers (the small-town families of Big Fish, Small Pond and Greenbelt Families), and which would donate at social events. When the society hosted a Cattle Barons' Ball in Denver, area Blue Blood Estates residents flocked to the fund-raising event, as much to be seen as to support a worthy cause. In San Francisco, organizers had to turn away thousands of Bohemian Mixers at a blues club for a lineup of live retro '70s bands. Shotguns & Pickups isn't known as a particularly charitable cluster, but the cancer society found a way to tap the altruistic spirit of these rural, blue-collar families. In 1997, it sponsored a "Relay for Life" marathon in Hall County, Georgia, where most residents are classified Shotguns & Pickups. With a cluster profile of area residents in hand, organizers showed the marketplace preferences of consumers to local businesses when asking them to sponsor prizes and entertainment.

"We said, 'Hey, these people we're going after are the same ones who use your product,'" recalls Michael Schneider, director of market analysis for the American Cancer Society. "We showed them a site analysis like any good business." And the race went off like any slick corporate promotion, becoming a major social event and attracting donations for the fight against cancer from 5,000 of the 6,000 households in the county. Mind you, this occurred in the heart of a cluster where surveys show high consumption of tobacco products and fatty foods that have been linked to high cancer rates.

There's irony in both health advocates' and alcohol and tobacco companies' using the same cluster-based marketing techniques in the hopes of achieving opposite effects. While businesses know that where you live is a strong predictor of dietary habits and recreation patterns, epidemiologists have begun to realize that cluster lifestyles also contribute to chronic illnesses such as cancer, diabetes, and heart disease. And understanding that link can be useful in reducing and treating those ailments. "We recognize that marketing data is often used to push products like alcohol and tobacco that create poor health outcomes," says Teresa Lofton, chief of the Health Assessment Section for the Georgia Division of Public Health. "But if you learn who's drinking and smoking excessively, you can turn that around with messages that promote better health. The data can be used for good."

Few states have done more in the area of social marketing than Georgia, where the Division of Public Health has cluster-profiled the state's entire population to assist in opening health clinics, targeting prevention programs, designing promotional messages, and determining local health needs. In one project, officials sent mobile mammography screening vans to neighborhoods classified Norma Rae-ville and Mines & Mills, downscale mill town clusters where women have low rates of breast cancer testing. In another, health investigators targeted older homes in Hometown Retired and Gray Collar, aging factory areas, for safety messages to reduce accidents, fires, and lead paint hazards. To decrease underage smoking, they worked with the University of Georgia to pinpoint communities with high levels of tobacco use and then dispatched underage college students to go undercover and buy cig-

While businesses know that where you live is a strong predictor of dietary habits and recreation patterns, epidemiologists have begun to realize that cluster lifestyles also contribute to chronic illnesses such as cancer, diabetes, and heart disease.

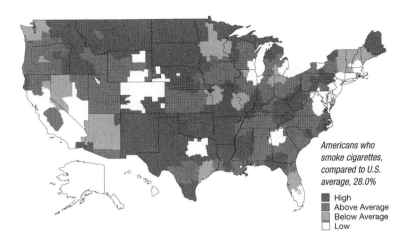

Americans who smoke cigarettes, compared to U.S. average, 28.0%

- ■ High
- ■ Above Average
- ▨ Below Average
- □ Low

Targeting Smokers for Health

Most marketing campaigns help retailers increase sales of their products and services. But a new breed of social marketers uses cluster-based maps to reduce chronic illnesses such as lung cancer and heart disease that are linked to lifestyle. In Georgia, epidemiologists have used statewide smoking maps to launch new health clinics and prevention programs where they're needed the most — especially in communities like Scrub Pine Flats and Norma Rae-ville.

Top Clusters   Military Quarters / Hard Scrabble / Family Scramble / Norma Rae-ville / Scrub Pine Flats
Top Markets   Bluefield–Beckley–Oak Hill, West Virginia / Laredo, Texas / Alexandria, Louisiana / Alpena, Michigan / Albany, Georgia

(Sources: PRIZM, Claritas Inc., Mediamark Research Inc.)

arettes and chewing tobacco from convenience and package stores. If cashiers complied, store owners were to be busted and fined.

Profiling communities by lifestyle cluster has not only helped Georgia's health officials target programs to its neediest citizens, it's also altered the way they look at disease. For instance, one analysis showed that the highest death rates from circulatory disease in Fulton County, Georgia, occurred in the poor, urban neighborhoods of Atlanta. But an analysis of four million hospital records found that although several clusters — including upscale Money & Brains and Gray Power — exhibited a high rate of circulatory disease, those segments with the highest rates of death due to circulatory disease were Southside City, Inner Cities, and Smalltown Downtown, clusters with some of the oldest and poorest residents. Public health planners, who had often lumped together all members of a racial group in terms of their mortality risk, now recognize that a cluster's socioeconomic rank is a more important factor. Compared to average Americans, residents from this group of downscale clusters are less likely to exercise aerobically and more likely to smoke tobacco. Georgia health officials have targeted preventive health information to 55 of the 146 census tracts in the county that share the same downscale lifestyle types — even though many have not exhibited high mortality figures. The hope is that the state can prevent a "disease cluster" from developing in fifteen years.

"What the clusters show is that the condition of a community drives the health status of an area, not an individual's behavior," says Lofton, former director of the Georgia Center for Health Statistics. "A teenager in some areas may run a high risk for getting AIDS, but not because she is promiscuous. She could be living in an area with high levels of HIV infection and get infected the first time she has sex."

Health officials are working toward crafting heart disease prevention messages based on the dietary and recreation patterns of the targeted clusters. Consumer surveys show that Southside City residents are more likely than average consumers to smoke cigarettes, eat pork, drink alcohol, and frequent fast-food restaurants. So Georgia officials want to respond with an education campaign encouraging Southside City residents to increase their consumption of low-fat milk and lean meats and decrease their consumption of alcohol and cigarettes. Meanwhile, Money & Brains consumers tend to spend more on fish and greens, but also on high-fat ice cream, alcohol, and snacks. Accordingly, Money & Brains residents were urged to reduce their consumption of alcohol, snacks, and buttery foods at restaurants. "We've seen a cultural propensity to buy food as a group, so we want to break the patterns of associations between food," explains Lofton. "If someone with a cholesterol count of two hundred fifty liked bacon and eggs, we'd try not to torment them to ban everything. We'd say have your egg but not bacon one day and substitute foods the next."

Granted, not all diseases are cluster sensitive. Airborne illnesses like pneumonia and influenza are equal-opportunity diseases found among rich and poor. But chronic ailments like cancer, diabetes, circulatory diseases, and pulmonary diseases can be linked to lifestyle. And to Lofton, the clusters provide a "postindustrial age disease model," linking affluence, psychology, and lifestyle to both health problems and their marketing-driven treatment. When Georgia transplant Jane Fonda once criticized conditions in the rural part of the state as resembling "some developing countries," she was promptly skewered by Governor Zell Miller. But the health division's cluster analysis of area residents, with its disproportionate concentration of Hard Scrabble, the poorest of rural lifestyles, proves that she was right on target.

Selling to the haves

While it's tempting to believe that traditional demographic measures — age, sex, and income — predict most consumption patterns, the lifestyle clusters show that's hardly the case. Take America's rich, who aren't just different from you and me but different from each other: Just compare the twenty-five-year-old Wall Street wunderkind spending every penny of his $200,000 annual income and the fifty-something couple headed to retirement with a $1 million nest egg. The affluent market is growing: About 12 million households earn more than $100,000 a year, and, as the baby-boom generation ages, that figure is increasing by 5 percent annually. But their needs are different, depending on their age, life stage, and values. More and more companies, from brokerages to casinos, are using extensive lifestyle databases to forge a personal relationship with these elusive, hot prospects. And they're tapping segmentation models to better understand the specific preferences of clusters within the affluent market.

Consider three different affluent American lifestyle clusters. The lower end is Young Literati, filled with urban dwellers between twenty-five and fifty-four years old who fit the fiscal stereotype of the yuppie. They earn between $50,000 and $150,000 but have relatively few assets. They may have yet to acquire homes or sock away significant savings, so they're prime targets for gold credit cards, adventure travel, and designer jewelry; indeed, their susceptibility to such offers may be the reason they don't have many real assets. While financial planners strike out with this group, travel agents make out like bandits.

Then there are the couples in their thirties and forties with children living in Kids & Cul-de-Sacs. Savvy marketers tailor their appeals to the people in this group who really control the family's pocketbook — the kids. Resorts in the Southwest have even started kids' clubs, tempting them to come with frequent-guest programs. Parents in this cluster came of financial age in the past two decades and remember double-digit mortgage rates, stock market turmoil, and, more recently, white-collar unemployment. In a 1994 survey of households that make $100,000 a year and have a half million in assets, not including their homes, 60 percent of respondents agreed with the statement "I am very concerned that I will outlive my retirement savings." Their most important financial goals are to ensure a comfortable retirement and to maintain their current standard of living.

In contrast to the yuppies and suburban parents, empty-nesting couples in the affluent Pools & Patios cluster are in their fifties and sixties, and they relate less to retail products and more to people. They tend to be civic-minded and give to charities because they feel it's the right thing to do. They are culturally inclined, reading epicurean and leisure publications as well as attending the theater, ballet, opera, and symphony concert performances. In their wallets, they have money to spend but not quite enough to burn. They're much more likely to spoil their grandchildren than themselves with toys.

This last cluster is the segment that Chrysler went after when it introduced its $35,000 New Yorker in 1993. Company marketers knew that consumers of highbrow culture tend to be skewed toward the affluent and educated types of Pools & Patios due to theater tickets' costing upwards of $100. So Chrysler sponsored a series of symphony galas in five key markets, spending $250,000 to target an audience of 15,000 people. For one Boston Symphony Orchestra performance, Chrysler put eight gleaming New Yorkers on display in the symphony hall lobby, plastered logos on every imaginable surface, and distributed hundreds of concert programs explaining why Chrysler was sponsoring that night's performance. Normally, 60 percent of all programs are left behind; that night only 2 percent were forgotten. During intermission, nearly 500 people gathered around the cars, asking questions, climbing in, and playing with the compact disc players. Chrysler also mailed several hundred thousand promotional videos to orchestra subscribers, which included a disproportionate number of Pools & Patios residents. As a result of the campaign, Chrysler recorded sales of several hundred cars — and profits of more than 30 percent per car. Within a year, the cluster was buying New Yorkers at one of the nation's highest rates, 27 percent above the U.S. average.

The wealthy may be easily found at highbrow affairs, but the clusters can suggest some counterintuitive sources of upscale consumers as well. When Buick wanted to increase sales of its luxury Park Avenue model to minority buyers, it noticed that African Americans frequently have lower rates of home ownership but more disposable cash than whites at similar income levels. Affluent African Americans, the company discovered, were being ignored as potential Park Avenue purchasers simply because their status as renters didn't fit the traditional buyer profile. As a result, although the company normally targeted its vehicles to households with at least a $60,000 median income, it searched for census tracts in clusters like Mid-City Mix and Bohemian Mix, where at least 40 percent of households were minority and the median income was only $40,000. The number of prospects increased from 50,000 to 650,000 households. After lifestyle surveys showed that current owners enjoyed gourmet magazines, Buick created the "Taste of Park Avenue" promotion, with a direct-mail piece offering potential customers in twenty-five markets a free dinner if they came into the showroom for a test drive. Some 3,000 people took advantage of the offer, and the company judged the promotion a wild success.

"A lot of companies pay lip service to targeting minority groups," says Patrick Harrison, marketing line manager at Buick. "But we wanted our Buick dealers to develop a personal relationship with African Americans. And this is how we found a way of bringing minorities into our dealerships."

The privacy dilemma

As the technology grows increasingly sophisticated, more and more companies will use clusters to forge personal relationships with elusive and hard-to-please customers. Already in the advertising industry, cable companies have begun distributing specific ads to specific homes. Grocery store scanners allow manufacturers to print on-the-spot coupons based on a shopping cart's worth of household purchases. Even in cyberspace, consumer interests can be tracked with on-line surveys and so-called cookies, those hidden programs that download to a Net surfer's computer and examine what sites the user has visited.

But this information-collecting binge has had unwanted side effects. Many Americans dislike the avalanche of junk mail and those annoying telemarketer phone calls that interrupt dinner. A 1997 Louis Harris survey found that eight of ten computer users felt that consumers had "lost all control over how personal information about them is circulated and used by companies." A consumer backlash has resulted in a boom in unlisted phone numbers, the increasing popularity of encryption software among Net surfers, and the sharp decline in the number of people who respond to surveys. Many Americans who do respond make them-

A 1997 Louis Harris survey found that eight of ten computer users felt that consumers had "lost all control over how personal information about them is circulated and used by companies."

selves out to be richer or poorer on surveys, depending on how they think the interviewer wants them to appear.

For businesses, however, modeling consumers by clusters allows them to infer sensitive information that individuals no longer feel comfortable providing. The goal is to re-create the personal touch of a small-town store, where the owner knows each customer's likes and dislikes without intruding on the customer's privacy. Because the respondents of nationwide surveys are coded by cluster, the results can be projected into each U.S. neighborhood by virtue of its composition of lifestyle types; chocolate's fans, for instance, tend to live in neighborhoods filled with Winner's Circle households anywhere in the country. As a result, marketers are increasingly relying on those cluster insights overlaid with other marketing data to help provide personalized service without the neighborhood busybody's looking in.

In the magazine industry, the Meredith Corporation has taken the technology a step further into on-line analysis to permit one-on-one marketing. In the past, when readers of home-improvement magazines circled the names of advertisers on the reader response cards, they waited six weeks for a company to respond. But that didn't help the advertisers because, surveys showed, readers typically started their home renovation projects within ninety days of reading a specialty magazine like *Kitchen and Bath Ideas* or *Window and Wall.* In 1996, the Meredith Corporation, which publishes forty *Better Homes and Gardens* specialty publications each year, began an Internet project designed to respond to information requests in three days. The company had its fulfillment house immediately record the names of respondents and fill their requests when they arrived. Then, with every batch of 1,000 requests, the names, addresses, and cluster classifications of the respondents would be posted to a private web site that advertisers could access. "The result was an instant snapshot of the advertiser's customers," says publisher Stephen Levinson, noting that the company processed more than one million customer requests in its first year of operation.

For the advertisers, the on-line clustering provided multiple benefits: Window and shade manufacturers traditionally sell to wholesalers and not directly to customers, but the cluster profiles offered them an opportunity to learn more about their end consumers. In addition, their understanding of the top-earning clusters like Winner's Circle and Country Squires helped concentrate their marketing dollars. "If it costs a company twenty dollars to fulfill a product request, it can decide whether to spend fifteen dollars for a lead from Winner's Circle and only five dollars on a lead from somewhere else," says Levinson. Just as important, the program provides companies with access to the names and lifestyles of interested customers twenty-four hours a day. "If you get someone to raise their hand," says Levinson, "you better satisfy their interest as quickly as possible."

In the auto industry, marketing consultant Leonard Wanetik has used clusters to help carmakers respond to consumer requests for information about their models. Traditionally, manufacturers treated all customers the same way, dispatching brochures by third-class mail. But Wanetik devised a system to differentiate the responses according to a prospect's cluster. After assigning a customer to a cluster, based on zip code information taken during a toll-free call, he'd peg the response according to a matrix of options linked to the customer's likelihood of buying a particular model anytime soon. A prospect from Red, White & Blues might receive an extra $500 cash-rebate offer because such blue-collar motorists tend to respond well to cash-back programs and use the money for down payments. A caller from Winner's Circle might get an attractive leasing promotion because such white-collar professionals are fans of leasing packages. The best prospects would receive a fat promotion package in overnight mail. The worst, a plain brochure sent third-class mail. And the matrix changes depending on the car model. "For a given van, a woman caller from a range of family clusters would be considered a home run," says Wanetik. "With a particular truck, you'd hope for a man from one of the midscale exurban clusters."

Such insights into managing customer responses may seem like minor marketing tricks, but they can mean big savings for an automaker that receives thirty thousand calls a month and offers billions of dollars in incentives. And with the specter of more invasive data-gathering in the future — huge data warehouses have begun sprouting around the country — the new value of clusters may be in helping protect consumers from intrusive marketers while helping businesses fulfill their long-sought goal of reaching the right consumers one at a time. "Nowadays people are so unreliable in reporting their income and other information that you can

"For a given van, a woman caller from a range of family clusters would be considered a home run. With a particular truck, you'd hope for a man from one of the midscale exurban clusters."

actually infer better information from a cluster profile," says Wanetik. "It's the strangest situation." Or maybe not so strange, after all. In the information fog surrounding Americans today, the clusters reveal that the truth is not in what we say but rather in how we live.

4 CANADA: A KINDER, GENTLER, DIVIDED NATION

*When they said Canada, I thought
it would be up in the mountains
somewhere.*

— Marilyn Monroe

Fewer people, more lifestyles

The sprawling community of Malvern, located east of Toronto, Ontario, is like many American metropolitan suburbs. Connecting the courts and crescents, wide, curvy streets meander past compact split-levels and town houses. On a clear summer morning, kids head for the local recreation center, with its indoor hockey rinks and outdoor soccer fields, or meet at Malvern Town Centre, where they join other mall rats hanging out at the McDonald's. By noon, sidewalks teem with joggers, walkers, and youngsters flipping soccer balls to each other as they move.

But Malvern should not be confused with a white-bread Kids & Cul-de-Sacs suburb of Chicago or Kansas City. Like many Canadian suburban communities, Malvern defies the American stereotype as a haven for white middle-class families. In multiethnic Malvern, for instance, the library houses books in seventeen languages — from Tagalog and Tamil to Polish and Hindi — and each week overflow crowds flock to instructional classes in English. Many residents have college degrees but only modest jobs at nearby factories, and some residents cannot afford a car. Outside the giant, appropriately named No Frills supermarket, the cabs queue up like a conga line, awaiting shoppers who emerge pushing carts heavily laden with discount staples and produce. Like the drivers, many wearing Indian Sikh turbans, the customers have only recently arrived from countries in Asia and the Caribbean. And while they may lack the wherewithal to possess wheels, they do have enough money to fill their homes with consumer toys like CD players and large-screen TVs. As one resident observes, "In Third World countries, it takes months to own a TV. Here you can get one for a week's wages."

In the vernacular of Canada's largest geodemographic company, Compusearch Micromarketing Data & Systems, Malvern is a Kindergarten Boom community, a cluster of young, ethnically diverse midscale families located in outer-ring suburbs. Many families, living in compact town houses and ramblers, have three or more children. And unlike the bedroom suburbs that spread across America's urban fringes following white flight, Kindergarten Boom is typically an entry point for immigrants. They come for the inexpensive apartments, abundant blue-collar jobs, ethnic shops, and from the desire to be near relatives and friends who have emigrated there before them. They just don't stay for too long. Kindergarten Boomers tend to view places like Malvern as stepping stones to more upscale neighborhoods with larger homes and bigger yards. "It's hard to have a strong community group because of the transient population," says Krish Prashad, a Guyana-born émigré who directs the Malvern Community Residents Association. "We're always going through a reorganization because people keep leaving."

Kindergarten Boom is typically an entry point for immigrants. They come for the inexpensive apartments, abundant blue-collar jobs, ethnic shops, and from the desire to be near relatives and friends who have emigrated there before them.

Compared to America — and most discussions about Canadian culture inevitably end up in just such comparisons — Canada is no geodemographic clone. According to Compusearch, the Toronto-based marketing firm founded in 1974, the nation today consists of sixty lifestyle types as defined by its PSYTE cluster system. Like PRIZM, the PSYTE clusters reflect demographic and socioeconomic characteristics of small areas of Canadian geography — called enumeration areas, which average 250 households — as well as consumer preferences for 1,500 different products, brands, and categories. Unlike PRIZM in the U.S., PSYTE divides Canadian lifestyles by dominant language; 22 percent of Canada's 30 million residents are French speaking.

Why sixty clusters for a country whose population is one-tenth that of America with its sixty-two lifestyle types? "We're just as diverse as America but have ten times fewer people," explains Steve Rayner, a senior research analyst at Compusearch. "We have prairie farmers, executives, suburbs, and fishing villages. But we also need boutique-y clusters in order to cover the French in Quebec."

Based on current census data, the sixty PSYTE clusters show Canada to be a country of stark contrasts not unlike America in the 1940s, prior to suburban sprawl, white flight, and the decline of the urban core. The cities are denser, the hinterland more vast.

Canadian Lifestyles

Compusearch's PSYTE cluster system has identified 60 dominant Canadian lifestyles, grouped below by level of urbanization and socioeconomic rank (1 equals most affluent; 6 equals least).

Urban 1
Canadian Establishment
The Affluentials
Urban Gentry

Urban 2
Europa
Asian Mosaic
High Rise Melting Pot

Urban 3
Conservative
    Homebodies
High Rise Sunsets

Urban 4
Young Urban
    Professionals
Young Urban Mix
Young Urban Intelligentsia
University Enclaves
Young City Singles
Urban Bohemia

Urban 5
Euro Quebec
Old Quebec Walkups
Quebec Town Elders
Aging Quebec Urbanites
Quebec's New Urban
    Mosaic

Urban 6
Struggling Downtowns
Aged Pensioners
Big City Stress
Old Grey Towers

Suburban 1
Suburban Executives
Mortgaged in Suburbia
Technocrats &
    Bureaucrats
Asian Heights

Suburban 2
Boomers & Teens
Stable Suburban
    Families
Small City Elite
Old Bungalow Burbs

Suburban 3
Suburban Nesters
Brie & Chablis
Aging Erudites

Suburban 4
Satellite Suburbs
Kindergarten Boom

Suburban 5
Participaction Quebec
New Quebec Rows
Quebec Melange
Traditional French Canadian
    Families

Town 1
Blue Collar Winners
Town Boomers
Old Towns' New Fringe

Town 2
Old Leafy Suburbs
Town Renters
Nesters & Young
    Homesteaders
Young Grey Collar
Quiet Towns

Rural 1
Northern Lights
The New Frontier
Rustic Prosperity
Pick-ups & Dirt Bikes
Quebec's Heartland
The Grain Belt

Rural 2
Agrarian Blues
Rod & Rifle
Down, Down East
Big Country Families
Quebec Rural Blues
Old Canadian Rustics

(Sources: PSYTE, Compusearch)

PSYTE features twenty-three urban clusters compared to PRIZM's thirteen. And Canada has fewer income extremes than the U.S., fewer wealthy pockets and poor urban areas. Because downtown areas are not centers of crime — the murder rate in Canada is one-quarter what it is in the U.S. — more middle-class families still live in city neighborhoods. Another reason is that the choice to move out to the 'burbs is often not available. Strict zoning laws and a federal government that rarely subsidizes highway construction have kept the number of suburban subdivisions down. Canada boasts one-quarter as many freeways and half as many cars per capita as the U.S. The result is limited exurban sprawl, little of the "wired cottage" phenomenon of telecommuting consultants, and few isolated retirement communities like Sun City, Arizona. Canadian retirees with money simply spend the winter in the American Sunbelt; Florida is sometimes referred to as Canada's thirteenth province.

Because there are fewer tax breaks for homeowners in Canada, Canadians tend to rent rather than own, and living in an apartment carries no social stigma. Whereas renting in the U.S. is often a life-cycle phenomenon reserved mainly for young singles before marriage, children, and the inexorable pull of suburbia, Canadian students, singles, and families of all ages will rent together in the same neighborhood. In fact, most Canadian colleges are located in big cities. Without the university land grants that created America's Towns & Gowns communities like Bloomington, Indiana, or Gainesville, Florida, Canada lacks distinct college towns whose main industry is teaching psychology to twenty-year-olds. There's no northern equivalent of Boulder, Colorado, with its campus buildings surrounded by funky group houses, pizza joints, and health food stores.

Although small towns look about the same in both countries, cities in Canada are more crowded: about 10,000 people per square mile versus 8,000 in the U.S.

Although small towns look about the same in both countries, cities in Canada are more crowded: about 10,000 people per square mile versus 8,000 in the U.S. Canada's cities are home to about three-quarters of the populace — more than in the U.S. and much like highly urbanized countries in Western Europe. Over the last decade, Canada's central cities actually gained population, and not just in young single clusters like Young Urban Professionals and Urban Bohemia. Four of the five most affluent urban lifestyle types are filled with families. One study found that nearly 60 percent of Canada's central city neighborhoods are still seen as suitable for family life, with sound school systems and low crime rates. Unlike America's wealthiest neighborhoods, which are concentrated in suburbia, Canada's highest-income neighborhoods, filled with million-dollar manses on modest-sized lots, are close to downtown cores — and classified Urban Gentry (affluent and cultured singles and couples) and Canadian Establishment (extremely wealthy established families).

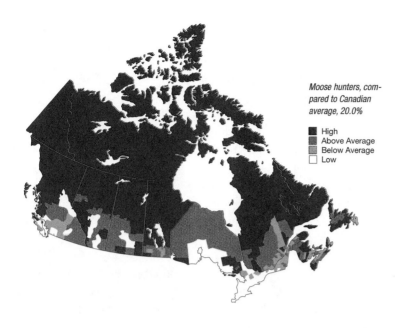

Moose hunters, compared to Canadian average, 20.0%

■ High
▨ Above Average
▥ Below Average
□ Low

Endangered Moose Hunters

One in five Canadians like to go moose hunting, but those numbers are dropping. As more and more Canadians leave their rural northern towns for better jobs in metro areas along the southern border, they've adopted more citified pursuits and find less time to travel back to moose country. Knowing which clusters prefer which leisure activities allowed the Ontario Ministry of Natural Resources to develop lifestyle-based land-use plans for the province's wilderness holdings, with areas designated specifically for camping, logging, or moose hunting.

Top PSYTE Clusters The New Frontier / Northern Lights / Down, Down East / Pick-ups & Dirt Bikes / Quebec Rural Blues
Top Canadian Markets Labrador City, Newfoundland / Thompson, Manitoba / Kitimat, British Columbia / Fort McMurray, Alberta / Whitehorse, British Columbia

(Sources: PSYTE, Compusearch, Ontario Ministry of Natural Resources)

Take Forest Hill, one of the nation's wealthiest neighborhoods, just miles north of Toronto's business district. Classified Canadian Establishment, this enclave of million-dollar Georgian and Victorian houses on quarter-acre lots is home to corporate executives, lawyers, and doctors who appreciate its close proximity to theaters, art galleries, and restaurants. The lifestyle is much like that of any affluent community in the world. Every morning, residents drive off to executive jobs in their Mercedes sedans or Suburban sport-utility vehicles. As in Blue Blood Estates in America, on weekends residents host pool parties, head to lakeside cottages, and attend black-tie balls for this symphony or that hospital. Local stores cater to what used to be called the "carriage trade," that is, the wealthy who don't mind paying premium prices for gourmet foods — or have servants to do the shopping. When the local bus service proposed a cutback on route 33, nicknamed the "nanny bus" for its usual cargo of Forest Hill child-care workers, no one protested. Instead, residents simply provided cab money for the hired help. "When you think of Forest Hill, think of Beverly Hills," says one Forest Hill real estate agent. "People here live the same way and think the same things."

Yet Canada's affluent may show subtle, less ostentatious forms of status compared to Americans. Surveys of the residents of the Canadian Establishment cluster show they spend more time reading, going to the theater, and doing charity work than do their American counterparts. They have more collections of books and paintings, fewer private planes and yachts. Howard Muchnick, a Bronx-born businessman who lives in Forest Hill and owns a chain of bagel shops, confirms the polls showing that Canadians travel less than America's elite. "They're less worldly, less likely to have visited New York, which I find astonishing," he says. Yet many Canadian status symbols still follow the path of trendsetters to the south. "You will see big cars, big cigars, big steaks," he says. "It used to be Rolex, but now everyone has Breitling watches costing four thousand dollars. Suntans are back. Hair transplants are in. Spas are booming." But stiff tax laws and relatively high unemployment keep Canada's affluent from wild spending and high living. "Everyone is always worried about the bubble bursting," says Muchnick.

One issue that has not crossed the forty-ninth parallel to any large extent is crime, the fear of which greatly influences many American lifestyle choices. There are far fewer criminals in Canada, so few that the police carry bullets in their pockets, not in their guns. Canadian newspapers rarely feature police-blotter roundups, and it's only recently that a Vancouver version of the TV-vérité show *Cops* made it to the airwaves. With Toronto's low crime rate — only sixty-five murders in all of 1996, about one-half the number in Miami — you won't find a security gate, perimeter fence, or private police force in Forest Hill. Lately, younger residents have called for fences to keep their children from drifting into the street, but there's no desire to wall off the community. "Gated communities are many, many years away," says resident Stanley Taube, a semiretired lawyer. "There's just less fear of criminals here." Indeed, when Canadian activists uncovered an ex-Nazi living nearby, the local Jewish community — which includes many Forest Hill residents — demanded neither his jailing nor his expulsion. "To us, he's an old man," explains Taube, sixty-one. "Now, if he were found in Brooklyn, the community would be up in arms. But we're a more peacefully restrained, laid-back community."

Entrepreneur Howard Muchnick confirms the polls showing that Canadians travel less than America's elite. "They're less worldly, less likely to have visited New York, which I find astonishing," he says.

The Canadian mosaic

Though historically linked to Great Britain and France, Canada today is a closer lifestyle cousin to the United States than the Continent. Demographically, both countries have identical age distributions and average ages. Both populations share a common language and even some cultural institutions, including major league baseball. With the world's longest unguarded border between two countries along the forty-ninth parallel, trends in media and popular culture flow freely up from the south. About three-quarters of all Canadians live within a hundred miles of the U.S. border, explaining why the country is sometimes thought of as America's fifty-first state (to the ire of Canadian nationalists). The top television shows in Vancouver look much like those in Seattle. Toronto residents can get their caffe latte grande at a corner Starbucks or listen to Elvis Presley at the Hard Rock Cafe. Several years ago, surveys showed a high recognition factor among Canadians for Clorox products, though none could be bought in Canada.

By contrast, polls consistently reveal Americans to be woefully ignorant of their northern neighbors. The number of Canadians who've made an impact on American culture is legion and includes Peter Jennings, Jim Carrey, Alanis Morisette, Michael J. Fox, k.d. lang, and Dan Aykroyd, to name a few. Encouraged by the 1994 North American Free Trade Agreement, Canada now trades some $365 billion worth of goods annually with the U.S. — more than any other country. But a 1995 poll found that only 1 percent of Americans knew that the Canadian prime minister was Jean Chrétien — a statistic that didn't surprise Canadians. American ignorance taps a deep vein of resentment among Canadians, who believe they've produced a superior society. And it goes beyond being offended when a magazine like the *New Republic* nominates "Worthwhile Canadian Initiative" as the most boring headline ever written. "Canadians fear losing their identity," observes Compusearch senior vice president Tony Lea. "No one talks about the percentage of Americans who live within a hundred miles of the Canadian border. It's always 'America, America, America.'"

Confronted with a vast land, a harsh climate, and three founding national identities (aboriginal, French, and multicultural English speaking), Canada's founders knew that sharing was the key

Encouraged by the 1994 North American Free Trade Agreement, Canada now trades some $365 billion worth of goods annually with the U.S. — more than any other country.

Downtown Computer Owners

Most Canadian computer owners live in the country's wealthiest neighborhoods, which, unlike the suburbs in the U.S., are located close to the centers of major cities. About three-quarters of all Canadians live within 100 miles of the U.S. border, indicating the concentration of city dwellers, upscale clusters, and computer owners along the 49th parallel.

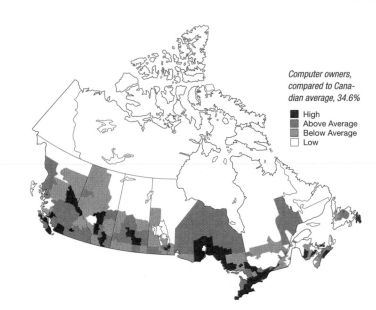

Computer owners, compared to Canadian average, 34.6%

■ High
■ Above Average
■ Below Average
□ Low

Top PSYTE Clusters   Asian Heights / Canadian Establishment / Suburban Executives / Mortgaged in Suburbia / The Affluentials
Top Canadian Markets   Toronto, Ontario / Oshawa, Ontario / Vancouver, British Columbia / Calgary, Alberta / Ottawa-Hull, Ontario

(Sources: PSYTE, Compusearch, Print Measurement Bureau)

to survival. Canada's modern social legacy was built on the notion that social security, and especially health care, is the right of all citizens. Its policies designed to eliminate class and ethnic differences have made Canada one of the most popular destinations among the world's immigrants, and the country welcomes more than 200,000 newcomers each year. Seventeen of the PSYTE lifestyle types are filled with residents who speak languages other than English; five million Canadians — one in six — have neither French nor English as their mother tongue. Compared to the U.S., Canada is more British (21 percent to 10 percent) and more French (23 percent to 3 percent), but less German (3 percent to 18 percent). And thanks to open immigration policies, Canada admits three times as many immigrants as America each year. While the U.S. is primarily white, African American, and Hispanic, Canada is more Asian (6 percent to 3 percent) and less black (1 percent to 12 percent); Latinos are practically nonexistent in Canada.

With newcomers encouraged to maintain their ethnic ties rather than assimilate as in America, Canada is more a mosaic than a melting pot. Asian Heights, a cluster of upscale suburban family neighborhoods, is largely the result of Chinese immigration since 1987. Concentrated in Vancouver and to a lesser degree in Toronto, it's home to immigrants from Hong Kong, Taiwan, and mainland China who fled their homeland for economic and political reasons. During the last decade, Canada opened its doors to immigrants with professional skills and money to invest in opening businesses. Unlike America, with its stricter immigration policies, Canada requires only $300,000 and the willingness to start a business. Today, many Asian Heights residents are under fifty, university educated, and members of the business class. Surveys show they enjoy going out to restaurants, traveling to the Caribbean, watching tennis on TV, and drinking white wine; only Canadian Establishment residents own more cellular phones.

Like other assimilated ethnic groups in Canada, Asian Heights residents tend to read and write, if not speak, proficient English. But they also try to maintain their cultural roots. At the Chartwell Shopping Centre in an Asian Heights section of suburban Scarborough, every store in the mall is Chinese owned, from the supermarket (Wan Fai) and camera shop (Guide Light Photo) to all the storefronts in the food court (Happy Wok, Seventh Heaven, Yogi's Noodles). At the herb store, there are a dozen different kinds of ginseng, and rows of jars filled with eggs, fungae, and odd-shaped mushrooms. Both shopkeepers and shoppers, mostly families with young children, speak Chinese. And in the early morning hours, before most stores are open, a group of about twenty retirees performs tai chi exercises along the corridors. Then it's off for mah-jongg or morning dim sum.

Though the mall is bustling on a typical weekend afternoon, not all the shops do a booming business. Nor do they expect to. It's well known that some immigrants invest their money in tiny gift shops, do the minimum in hiring employees just to get their citizenship papers, and then, after several years, allow their operations to fold. "After three years, they'll lose sixty thousand dollars, but at least they'll have permanent residence," says Tom Chang, a forty-five-year-old engineer who emigrated from Hong Kong in 1975. "A lot of people are setting up shops just for the status of becoming Canadian."

At the Chartwell Shopping Centre, this immigration loophole creates a revolving door of small Chinese businesses. But the difficulty of running a successful business has done little to reduce

Some immigrants invest their money in tiny gift shops, do the minimum in hiring employees just to get their citizenship papers, and then, after several years, allow their operations to fold.

Canada's popularity among Asian immigrants, with real estate markedly cheaper than anything in pricey, politically uncertain Hong Kong. A thousand-square-foot condo in Hong Kong could cost $1 million; in Scarborough, it runs less than $200,000, leading many Chinese apartment dwellers to move into comfortable homes in neighborhoods like Brimley Forest. Locals can usually pick out the new immigrant homeowners by their ragged yards. Most didn't have any land in Hong Kong and don't know how to care for grass or shrubs. In Hong Kong, you have to be a multimillionaire to own a home with a yard.

Like many in Asian Heights, Tom Chang leads a bicultural lifestyle, trying to retain his roots, which emphasize family, education, communal activities, success, and respect for social conventions. He'll tell you that he's happy that his mother-in-law lives in his spacious split-level and is a bit irked that his own parents choose to live in their own home. He reads books on Chinese culture and enjoys watching Chinese soap operas on television. He and his wife speak Chinese to their sixteen-year-old daughter and thirteen-year-old son, and every Saturday the kids are sent to a math enrichment class as well as to a Chinese language school. "I want them to take the opportunity to learn about the culture because one day they may need it," says Chang as ginseng soup simmers on the stove, pinkish roots visible through a glass pot. But Chang resembles a lot of longtime Canadian residents who do their own landscaping, take their kids camping, and have discovered the mixed blessing of being a baseball parent-chauffeur. In fact, he's no longer surprised to bump into a long-lost relative or friend at his son's baseball games — someone he may last have seen in Hong Kong twenty-one years ago.

"The melting pot has its advantages," Chang says. "In the U.S., everyone says, 'I'm an American,' and that's good. But since Canada can't be a world power, it's good to have your own identity. We all have something in common as Canadians, but we have our own spice. We just have to learn how to live together."

This peaceful image of Canada helps explain the success of its immigrant invasion. Opinion polls show Canadians to be well-mannered, law-abiding citizens. Polls confirm that they rarely hang up on telemarketers, answering machines, or computer-generated phone pitches. They have a higher response rate for direct-mail pitches than Americans (but because Canadians receive a third less junk mail, this finding is somewhat skewed). Canadians are a

"Canadians are hopelessly polite," says Compusearch chief R. Bruce Carroll. "They're loyal to brand names. They buy retail. They think discounting is seditious."

less litigious people, supporting 118 lawyers per 100,000 people — 64 percent fewer than in the U.S. After a U.S. Marine Corps color guard mistakenly flew the Canadian flag upside down at a 1992 World Series game, irate Toronto Blue Jays fans purchased thousands of upside-down American flags but refrained from waving them inside the Sky Dome because they thought it unmannerly. R. Bruce Carroll, the Canadian-born senior vice president of The Polk Company, which owns Compusearch, reports that Canadians are the kind of pedestrians who wait on the corner at all red lights, even at a deserted intersection at two in the morning. Some 95 percent voluntarily answer government surveys, and 22 percent answer those product-use surveys conducted by marketing companies — far above American figures. Because there is little product competition in many areas, Canadians agreeably pay higher prices for goods and services.

"Canadians are hopelessly polite," says Carroll, a fifty-two-year-old geodemographics veteran who's lived around the world while designing segmentation systems like PSYTE, PRIZM (U.S.), Persona (U.K.), and PSYTE USA. "They're loyal to brand names. They buy retail. They think discounting is seditious."

For businesses and nonprofit organizations, the challenge is trying to satisfy the needs of Canada's many lifestyles. Already, multinational companies like Volkswagen, Campbell's soups, Sony, and Clairol feature multilingual product packaging and Chinese-language marketing campaigns. At Toronto's Harbourfront Centre, a cultural hub that sponsors 4,000 dance, theater, music, and art

Survey Issues	Canada	U.S.
Prefers "neighbors of my own race"	14%	22%
Wishes to reduce number of immigrants	55%	67%
Has contacted a politician over an issue	37%	43%
Believes "all great religions equally true and good"	67%	55%
Says religion is important part of life	58%	79%
Prays weekly	47%	71%
Cites jobs as top concern facing country	46%	9%
Cites defense/international issues as top concern facing country	4%	24%
Cites crime/violence as top concern facing country	4%	20%

(Source: Angus Reid Group Poll, 9/96–10/96, funded by The Pew Charitable Trusts)

The Border Gap

How different are Americans from Canadians? Let's count the ways. A 1996 two-nation survey entitled "God and Society in North America" found profound distinctions in social, religious, and political attitudes. Canadians tend to be more tolerant on social issues, more concerned about economic ones. Americans are more religious and more international in political outlook, but less tolerant of diversity at home.

events annually, marketers analyzed its 100,000-name database to better target attractions to specific audiences. The yuppies of the Young Urban Professionals cluster are big fans of traditional drama, and the students in University Enclaves flock to the cutting-edge dance programs. Marketing manager Bruce Hutchinson makes sure that brochures of classical music productions end up in Toronto's Canadian Establishment and The Affluentials neighborhoods, and that flyers on children's programs go to those in the Mortgaged in Suburbia and Technocrats & Bureaucrats clusters.

But when Harbourfront found itself sponsoring a little-known, avant-garde English production of *The Three Lives of Lucie Cabrol* in the fall of 1996, it adopted a crossover cluster approach to sell tickets. Directors of the art and dance divisions created an 8,000-piece direct-mail campaign for their subscribers who'd shown receptivity to innovative arts events. Then brochures about the production were distributed to libraries, bars, and restaurants located near likely theatergoers: The Annex neighborhood, which is filled with University Enclaves and Young Urban Professionals, and The Beach area, home to the Young Urban Professionals and more downscale Urban Bohemia residents. Finally, the center advertised in the *Toronto Globe and Mail,* which cluster surveys showed was popular among theatergoers.

As a result, five of six performances in the 445-seat theater were complete sellouts, with 65 percent of the sales made through direct mail. "We hit the right buttons on the right people," says Hutchinson, forty-four. "No one knew what the production was about, so there was a degree of trust that we were offering them a program they would want. But it worked."

For Canadian marketers, luring people across ethnic lines to attend Harbourfront events like the Asian Heritage and Caribana festivals remains a challenge. "Most groups will come to their own cultural events and then not come back," Hutchinson concedes. At the Canadian Broadcasting Corporation, whose mandate is to serve the nation's disparate populations, this is no small concern. The CBC's TV programming changes almost hourly — a Chinese-language cooking program may be followed by a European news roundup — which prompted marketers to look beyond the ages and genders of viewers to their clusters. "We treat our schedule like forty separate magazines," Mark Leslie, CBC's television marketing services manager, says of the network's major weekly programming blocks. "So imagine the waste of advertisers spending millions to reach adults aged eighteen to forty-nine. Clustering allows us to match consumers of a particular product with their favorite program." When surveys showed that Canadian Establishment residents were 15 percent more likely than the general population to watch the nightly *National News* telecast, CBC increased the cost of a thirty-second spot, about $10,000, by 15 percent to reflect that cluster's desirable status. Advertisers like Fidelity Investments, the giant mutual fund company, were happy to pay the premium to reach well-off viewers.

Analyzing the cluster audiences for CBC's varied lineup also revealed some surprises that helped advertisers pick out previously hidden audiences. The link between upscale and educated residents and nightly newscasts is almost universal in terms of media consumption. But CBC programmers were startled to learn that its premier sports program, *Hockey Night in Canada,* had an upscale audience from clusters like Brie & Chablis and Town Boomers. Meanwhile, its investigative journalism show, *The Fifth Estate,* had a decidedly downscale profile, as shown in town clusters Young Grey Collar and Nesters & Young Homesteaders, where viewers appreciated a program that dug up corporate dirt. Some lifestyles have relatively low rates for watching TV, including the time-poor Kindergarten Boom and those with language barriers in Asian Heights. Urban Bohemia, filled with young singles who spend a lot of their time on bicycles, in bars, and at cafés, consider TV a symbol of crass materialism and are notorious for below-average audience levels. Yet this cluster registers high for watching *This Hour Has 22 Minutes,* a political satire show whose name even spoofs the fact that the show's length is reduced by commercials — a joke that Urban Bohemians appreciate.

For Urban Bohemia residents like Ben Smith Lea, a thirty-eight-year-old computer consultant who lives in Toronto's Niagara neighborhood, an off-the-wall perspective helps. He calls his neighborhood "slipper country" because of its mix of mental health patients and Vietnamese immigrants. "There are hookers on the corner and poor people and crazy people here," he says, adjusting steel gray wire rims beneath a blond buzz cut. A self-described bicycle activist, he's strung parking tickets through his row house living room as a commentary on what he views as Canada's auto-obsessed society, and he's decorated one wall with product advertisements to ridicule commercialism. When Starbucks wanted to open one of its coffee bars in the area, protestors

CBC programmers were startled to learn that its premier sports program, Hockey Night in Canada, *had an upscale audience from clusters like Brie & Chablis and Town Boomers.*

staged a demonstration. "The people didn't want one more American chain to come in," says Smith Lea. "They make fun of America." But he also admits that bashing anything American is an easy out. "It gets us off the hook," he adds. "We don't have to work as hard to complain compared to coming up with an original idea."

Niagara is known for its Chinese and Portuguese groceries and restaurants, and that's typical of Urban Bohemia neighborhoods. In many of Canada's largest cities, ethnic minorities dominate the landscape. English is a minority language in Vancouver, where the Chinese population, now 18 percent, is expected to grow to nearly a third of all residents by the year 2010. Fully 40 percent of Toronto's population was born outside the country, and the city has more Italian speakers than any other city in the world except Rome. Despite this diversity, social segregation remains. In Toronto's high school cafeterias, white, black, and Asian students tend to congregate in separate groups during lunch. While Canadians invariably disparage the gated communities where as many as eight million Americans live, in Canada invisible gates seem to separate Chinese, Greek, French, and Italian neighborhoods. In Europa, a cluster of communities filled with older first- and second-generation Italian families, these invisible gates have succeeded in keeping time at bay as well.

At nine o'clock on a summer Friday morning, the sidewalks start coming alive off College Street in the Little Italy section of Toronto — a classic Europa community. Older men walk their dogs, young women push prams, and the kids home for summer vacation ride their bikes on shady walkways lined with dark brown row houses and cluttered porches. But most of the activity is taking place down the street inside the Church of St. Francis of Assisi, an imposing stone edifice, where a rich chorus of voices, some two hundred strong, offers an ethereal sound track to the action on the streets. While some churches would thrill to have as many worshipers on a Sunday morning, in Europa residents flock to their churches daily. Many are first-generation Italians, now retired from years of work in the construction and craft trades, and the church remains a central part of their lives every day of the week. Older couples go to mass in the morning, visit with friends and neighbors, and then stroll to a nearby baker or butcher for the day's food shopping. Their homes are filled with crosses and other religious items sprinkled among the heavy mahogany furniture

Fully 40 percent of Toronto's population was born outside the country, and the city has more Italian speakers than any other city in the world except Rome.

and TV sets that locals claim get only two channels — the RAI station from Italy and Toronto's Italian channel. Most afternoons, elderly men gather at the Joseph Piccininni Recreation Center to play boccie and cards, ignoring the man who occasionally breaks into an operatic aria for no particular reason. On a Saturday night, couples gather for dinner with relatives; surveys show they'd rather eat at home than go out to dinner. "What do they talk about all the time? Families, of course," says Father Gregory Botte, the husky Boston-born Franciscan leader of the church. "Who married, who died, who's going to have a baby. That's the way it's always been."

Although Italians in America assimilated relatively quickly, those in Canada's Europa neighborhoods refused to admit they had left the Old Country. "Italy has changed and moved on," Botte explains, "but life here is like Italy in the 1950s. People speak Italian on the street and in their homes. For the summer, one-third of our parish goes to Italy. The travel agencies have just one route, from Toronto to Rome."

Research reflects these ties: Europa residents are three times as likely as the general population to drive Alfa Romeos, twice as likely to drink Italian wine, and nearly twice as likely to shop at Italian clothing and food stores. On St. Clair Avenue West, a major commercial strip called Corso Italia, the sidewalks are cluttered with racks of shoes, blouses, carpet remnants, jewelry, and all manner of fruits and vegetables. A steady stream of shoppers promenades by, fifty-year-old women carrying heavy purses and plastic bags filled with outfits for their grandchildren, and twenty-something women in platform shoes, skintight stretch pants, and oversized white blouses, their faces heavily made up with bright lipstick and black eyeliner. Some of the shops display mod European fashion, with names like La Scala, Viola Designs, Versace, and Valentino. Signs in green, white, and red — the colors of the Italian flag — advertise Sicilian ice cream. Italian pop tunes blare out of bars; inside clothing stores the radios are turned to Italian news and variety shows.

"There's no better place for retirees," says Gino Cucchi (pronounced "cookie"), a community leader and owner of a local clothing store. "They don't need a car to buy food, clothing, or shoes. They know everybody. They feel safe. They come in and talk and move to the cafés. They don't stay home and watch TV and feel

[Canada's] Europa residents are three times as likely as the general population to drive Alfa Romeos, twice as likely to drink Italian wine, and nearly twice as likely to shop at Italian clothing and food stores.

sorry for themselves. They meet and embrace and kiss each other." Cucchi, who hosts a monthly broadcast on CHIN radio featuring Italian music and guests, is something of a local celebrity and has plastered one wall of his shop with photos of himself and area dignitaries. "When the mayor of Toronto walks down the street with me, people say, 'Who's that with Gino?'" he quips.

But Cucchi, a dapper fifty-eight-year-old with dark hair and elegant gestures, turns serious when he talks about changes coming to his aging Europa neighborhood. Parents still watch over the neighborhood kids from porches, but the lure of the streets is undeniable. Nowadays the grandchildren of immigrants are exposed to drugs, and the fear of being stripped of *bella figura,* literally "good image," is no longer enough to keep them out of trouble. Losing their ethnic identity is a constant concern among the older generation. Cucchi remembers the day in 1982 when the Italian soccer team won the World Cup championship, sparking a spontaneous celebration that lasted three days in his Toronto neighborhood. "There was a sea of flags and happy people from little ones to those eighty-five years old," recalls Cucchi. "Older people who didn't know about soccer still felt that pride. From then on Italian culture exploded. The kids who couldn't speak it began speaking it." Today, he and other Little Italy merchants are raising money to build a statue dedicated to Canada's Italian immigrants. "As soon as an Italian puts his foot in America, he becomes American," says Cucchi of the continuing allure of Europa. "I came here thirty-seven years ago, and I'm still Italian. But I worry about the next generation."

Divided they stand

Nowhere is the concern over the disappearance of cultural identity expressed more often — or with more fervor — than in Quebec, home to most of the seven million French-speaking Canadians, about a quarter of the populace. When it comes to Quebec, the peaceful image of Canada is shattered. To Americans, observes McGill University professor William Watson, Canada's periodic votes on giving Quebec independence make it appear as "a society on the verge of a nervous breakdown, the political equivalent of the mild-mannered citizen who one day inexplicably goes out on a ledge with a gun and a hostage."

In a way, the Quebecois illustrate what happens when the

clustering principle is taken to extremes: An indigenous population threatens to separate and form its own nation. This separatist
movement has deep roots: For generations, the French-speaking
residents were Quebec's oppressed minority, forced into the worst
jobs and poorest schools. In 1961, Francophone Montrealers
earned a third less than Anglophones. That changed between 1960
and 1975 in what's been called the Quiet Revolution, a period of
unprecedented economic and social reform that also resulted in
the rise of a new generation of artists, politicians, and business
leaders. In 1976, the separatist Bloc Quebecois came to power in
the provincial government and started turning pride into law:
French became the official language of Quebec. At first, all product labels had to be bilingual, then no label could be printed in English. Schwartz's Montreal Hebrew Delicatessen became Chez
Schwartz, Charcuterie Hebraic de Montreal. Soon, all immigrants
and their children were forced to attend French schools. In the
words of Quebec culture and communications minister Louise
Beaudoin: "We have to be vigilant. There is no free choice for
newcomers because we want them to integrate to the French
majority."

Yet such zealous vigilance on the part of Quebec's Office de la
Langue Français has created a backlash. Many English-speaking
residents have fled — some 325,000 Montrealers have left since
1971 — fed up with the language police's enforcement of signs,
software, and menus. In 1996, Jewish Quebecers were especially
infuriated over an affair that became known as Matzogate when an
ardent language inspector sparked the seizure of all boxes of
matzo arriving in Montreal during the Jewish holiday of Passover
because the packaging was written in Hebrew and English, not
French. Outrage over the incident prompted the government to
allow kosher matzos in English packaging to enter the province for
sixty-five days a year around the time of the holiday. But that
wasn't enough to earn forgiveness from critics, including novelist
Mordecai Richler. "If I were crossing the border into the United
States, I would be very careful not to have any marijuana or cocaine or heroin on me," he told one CBS-TV interviewer. "But coming in here, you better not have any kosher matzos." Today, some
English speakers and immigrants living in Quebec charge that the
Francophones are discriminating against them in the province's
civil service.

Top-Rated Television Shows

The Quiet Revolution in Quebec did more than produce economic reforms and create a nationalist movement. It resulted in the rise of a new generation of artists and the development of Quebec-produced television shows that now top the ratings throughout the province. By contrast, nine out of ten of Vancouver's top-rated TV shows are American produced and look very much like those in Seattle.

Quebec City	Vancouver
Urgence (hospital drama)	*X-Files*
Cher Olivier (comedy)	*NewsHour with Jim Lehrer*
La Petite Vie (wacky comedy)	*Seinfeld*
Edition Quebec (news)	*Friends*
Les Machos (teledrama)	*3rd Rock from the Sun*
Piment Fort (comic quiz show)	*ER*
Juste pour Rire (comedy festival)	*Single Guy*
J.E. (consumer fraud cases)	*Canucks [hockey] on BCTV*
Le Masque (hockey star miniseries)	(British Columbia Television)
4 et Demi (singles apartment sitcom)	*Drew Carey*
Bouscotte (drama)	*Frasier*
	Melrose Place

(Sources: BBM, Spring 1997; Compusearch)

Not surprisingly, the marketplace behaviors of Francophones and Anglophones are strikingly different. Francophones are more likely to gamble, use coupons, shop at warehouse clubs, and drive European and Asian imports like Toyota and Hyundai, for instance, compared to the Jeeps and Suburbans popular among Anglophones. They're less likely to attend a sporting event than to play in one. They respond to businesses that communicate in French — and not just poor translations from the English. Eight of their top ten TV shows are made in Quebec, shows with names like *La Petite Vie,* and *4 et Demi* (the Quebec version of *Friends*). They consume more alcohol than average Canadians but prefer local microbrews over national beer brands like Molson. And they have a collective sweet tooth that far exceeds that of other Canadians. While Coca-Cola is popular in most other provinces, so many Quebecers drink sweeter Pepsi that they're sometimes nicknamed Pepsis. Quebecers, according to surveys, don't just buy more continental fashion, they care deeply about the latest French and Italian styles. "Women in Montreal will not eat to have perfume," one businessman observes. "You must look put together when you go outside."

Hardly a monolithic ethnic group, French Canadians dominate no less than a dozen different PSYTE clusters — from the upper-middle-class families of Participaction Quebec to the poor singles who live in Quebec's New Urban Mosaic. Each cluster has distinct consumption patterns and voting behaviors, even when it comes to the issue of Quebec's sovereignty. When voters in Quebec rejected a 1995 referendum granting provincial independence by a slim 50.56 percent majority, Compusearch analyzed the results to determine how the clusters voted. Their findings showed no particular geographic pattern: The opposition came from cities, towns, and satellite suburbs. But Quebec's 125 electoral districts were polarized along lifestyle lines: Those Quebecers who most wanted to hold the nation together included the richest and poorest citizens — clusters 1 through 8 and 58 through 60 on the socioeconomic scale. In addition, they included some upscale suburban clusters like Technocrats & Bureaucrats, as well as many non-French-speaking immigrant clusters like Europa, Asian Mosaic, and Euro Quebec.

To the cluster analysts, the biggest surprise came from the fact that the vote for Quebec's sovereignty did not break along French-speaking versus English-speaking lines. The more telling indicator came from clusters that were unique to Quebec versus those that were found throughout Canada. For instance, many young, educated French-speaking city dwellers who were against the separatist movement lived in clusters that were not distinctly French Canadian: Young Urban Professionals, University Enclaves, and Satellite Suburbs clusters — lifestyles typical of cities like Toronto and Vancouver. By contrast, those who wanted to break away often came from rural French-speaking Quebec, including traditional blue-collar union strongholds like Quebec Town Elders and the more rustic Quebec Rural Blues. And they included some of the newer activist immigrants from French-speaking countries in the downscale urban cluster called Quebec's New Urban Mosaic. Meanwhile, voters were split in Quebec Melange, a French-speaking cluster of middle-class, middle-aged suburbanites who tend to be traditional, conservative, and brand loyal. On the issue of a separate Quebec, however, they did what one cluster observer describes as the "ultimate in brand switching — changing nationalities."

The ambivalence toward Quebec sovereignty is perhaps best expressed in Old Quebec Walkups, a diverse cluster of lower-middle-class urban singles and couples concentrated in multilevel apartment buildings in Montreal and Quebec City. The typical Old Quebec Walkup household is a working-class family living in a $700-a-month triplex on a street lined with shops, cafés, and overhanging balconies. The Plateau section of Montreal, an area of

100,000 people, is a microcosm of Canadian schizophrenia characteristic of Old Quebec Walkups. The population is a mix of students, new immigrants, younger blue-collar families, and even some affluent couples drawn to gentrifying commercial strips. Residents live like Parisians, stopping for breakfast at corner cafés and shopping at the local butcher and grocer. For leisure, they take walks in the park and ride their bicycles to theaters, art galleries, and other cultural activities. But they worry about too much traffic, not enough parking spaces, crime, education, and the arrival of gentrification-minded developers who will convert the older shops to fashionable boutiques and sushi bars.

"The culture is different between the French and English, but the families are the same," says Ginette Richard, a fifty-year-old French-speaking day care provider who lives in The Plateau. "We live more like European people. We eat a lot and drink a lot and speak French to maintain the language. Bad taste is speaking English."

But residents in Old Quebec Walkups can't decide which way

An Independent Quebec: *Oui* or *Non*?

In 1995, when Quebec voters rejected the provincial referendum to gain independence by a slim 51-to-49-percent majority, cluster analysts discovered that the vote didn't break along French-speaking and English-speaking lines. The real determining factors were those lifestyle types unique to Quebec and those found throughout the nation. Those who most wanted to hold the nation together included the richest and poorest Canadians.

	PSYTE Clusters	Pro-Independence Index
Favoring Independence	Northern Lights	155
	Town Boomers	133
	Young Grey Collar	127
	Quebec Rural Blues	123
	Quebec Town Elders	121
Ambivalent About Independence	Town Renters	104
	New Quebec Rows	103
	Blue Collar Winners	100
	Agrarian Blues	99
	Old Quebec Walkups	95
Opposing Independence	Canadian Establishment	23
	The Affluentials	30
	Young Urban Mix	39
	Satellite Suburbs	41
	University Enclaves	64

An index of 100 equals the Quebec average for independence; 121 means 21 percent above average; 64 means 36 percent below average.

(Sources: PSYTE, Compusearch)

to go. The issue of separating Quebec from Canada frightens many of the traditional working families, and, as Liberal Party national director Terry Mercer notes, "People won't vote for change if they don't understand the consequences." In contrast, students and new immigrants in The Plateau are more separatist; they speak French to maintain their culture and they vote for the Bloc Quebecois to push for the province's independence. Every July 24, these Canadians party to celebrate the day in 1967 when Charles de Gaulle declared on a visit to Canada, *"Vive le Quebec libre."* And some locals predict that in the next referendum, Quebec will become free. "For sure," claims Pierre Klépock, a thirty-three-year-old steelworker turned student who remembers marching to allow French to be spoken in the workplace. Asked about the most important object in his home, he responds, "My books: Karl Marx, Lenin, and a lot of Quebecois revolutionary books."

Today, Quebec is very much a nation within a nation, and the separatist movement remains the great drama of Canada. When a statue of de Gaulle was unveiled in 1997, three decades after the French president visited Quebec, fights broke out across Canada between pro- and anti-separatist citizens. And the 1997 national election ushered in a Parliament more regionally fractured than at any time in the country's 130-year history, with the Liberal Party maintaining control of Ontario and the majority of provinces, the Bloc Quebecois taking Quebec, and the Reform Party sweeping the west. Constitutional recognition of "the distinct society" in Quebec remains as divisive an issue as ever.

The Canadian sell

For Canada's national political parties, trying to build a consensus and keep the country from imploding has become a major concern. In 1993, the majority Liberal Party began using the PSYTE clusters to provide information to its candidates about voters and to target party communications to their concerns. At first, Liberal officials developed mailings targeted to forty different constituencies destined for hundreds of thousands of voters. Issues-based letters to Young City Singles and University Enclaves focused on the rising cost of education and the growing unemployment that had occurred under Brian Mulroney's Conservative Party administration. Mailings that went to suburban professionals and their families in Mortgaged in Suburbia and Technocrats & Bureaucrats emphasized improving the government's finances by bringing in solid management people who could create jobs and control the deficit. "These voters understood debt," says Liberal Party leader Mercer. "They had relatively high mortgages, and either one or both in the family had been unemployed and worried about it. These people were ready for a change."

The Liberal Party letters were supplemented with a media-buying campaign that included an effort to target homemakers in clusters like Nesters & Young Homesteaders. Mercer purchased ads on their favorite television programs, soap operas like *Another World* and *General Hospital,* leading to confusion among party regulars. "Some people in the party complained that they never saw our advertising," he recalls. "But that's because they weren't our target audience. They were women. And the soap operas were important to us." Although the outcome of a political campaign can rarely be attributed to one marketing effort, Mercer believes that the targeted letters were critical to the Liberal Party's sweeping victory that brought Jean Chrétien to power. Of the forty riding districts sent letters — each riding holds between 80,000 and 120,000 voters — thirty-five ended up in the Liberal Party column, electing party candidates across the country.

Ironically, many French Canadians feel a closer kinship with Americans than with their English Canadian countrymen. They envy America's history and seek inspiration from the American Revolution that overthrew British rule. Young Quebecois talk admiringly of Benjamin Franklin's visit to the province in 1775. Football fans in Montreal often claim allegiance to the New England Patriots of America's National Football League, adopting their logos as symbols of Quebec's own campaign for independence. That support is one reason that America's Super Bowl garners a larger audience in Canada than the Canadian Football League's Grey Cup championship game.

The passage of the North American Free Trade Agreement brought both countries closer together economically and raised expectations of a single continent-wide market. Multinational corporations hoped that they could reduce marketing and advertising costs by employing a single promotion campaign for American and Canadian consumers. However, even as technology has improved and trade barriers have fallen, few cross-border geodemographic marketing efforts have been attempted. To spur interest, in 1992 Claritas and Compusearch teamed up to create a joint PRIZM Canada cluster system, but lack of cluster conformity resulted in

Ironically, many French Canadians feel a closer kinship with Americans than with their English Canadian countrymen.

only modest success. There are no American lifestyles, for instance, that correspond to the dozen French-speaking neighborhood types of Quebec. And Canada lacks predominantly African American lifestyles like Norma Rae-ville and Inner Cities; the nation didn't even conduct a racial census until 1998. By blending several lifestyle types and downplaying racial and language factors, PRIZM Canada ended up with twenty-four clusters that had some limited applications. Several automotive manufacturers used the system to compare consumer profiles for similar cars across the border. Other carmakers have used the clusters for their preferred list orders, helping to determine how many cars and models each dealer should be allotted given the cluster profile of customers in their trading area.

But the broad brush strokes of PRIZM Canada diluted differences among communities to the point where the system was not very powerful. Eventually, Compusearch and Claritas each returned to promoting their own more finely tuned cluster systems and dropped the project. The failure of PRIZM Canada showed that the acceptance of a product — whether across national boundaries or subdivision boundaries — still depends on local culture, climate, settlement patterns, economic conditions, and retail arenas. Together, those forces create very different consumer societies from one country to the next.

Canadians, for instance, spend 35 percent less money on transportation than Americans. They own fewer cars, drive less, have fewer highway miles per capita, and use public transportation more to go to work and to shop. Malls are generally bigger in Canada, in part because when people do go out, they want a huge variety of stores at their destination. And motorcycles are generally more popular in Canada, but not because the nation has more leather-clad biker clubs. In Canada, a significant number of motorcycle buyers are affluent city dwellers with much higher socioeconomic levels than the working-class bikers who tend to purchase Harley hogs in the States. It's not uncommon for a lawyer or an insurance salesman to drive a GoldWing motorcycle to work in Toronto.

PRIZM Canada showed that the same product requires different positioning when it crosses borders. The Nissan Sentra, a second car for suburban families in the U.S., is the first car for French Canadian city dwellers in Quebec. The Lincoln Town Car, a luxury car in U.S. suburbs, plays better in Canada's older small towns.

Canadians, for instance, spend 35 percent less money on transportation than Americans. They own fewer cars, drive less, have fewer highway miles per capita, and use public transportation more to go to work and to shop.

Similar forces are also at work with the Ford Crown Victoria, which, in America, is a car of choice for upscale professionals from midsized cities — the Middleburg Managers of the PRIZM cluster system. In Canada, the Crown Victoria finds its fans among heartland farmers like those in Rustic Prosperity, the kind of folks who want a sturdy vehicle for driving on rutted and gravel roads. "You can put the family up front and two goats in the back," quips Compusearch's Tony Lea, fifty-one, who holds a Ph.D. in geography from the University of Toronto.

More than a few behavioral differences are attributable to natural causes, like weather. Canada's northern latitudes mean longer winters, more snow, and a higher percentage of residents who ski. In the U.S., skiing, with its hundred-dollar-a-day passes in New England mountains, is an upscale suburban phenomenon, but Canada's working-class residents from small-town clusters like Rod & Rifle can ski all day on a forty-dollar pass. By contrast, a downscale American activity like fishing translates into more of an upscale one in Canada, thanks to the large number of fully stocked lakes in sparsely settled northern stretches. Status among the wealthy Canadian Establishment families in Ontario and British Columbia is owning a cottage near an isolated lake where they can take clients ice fishing.

With many Canadian residents renting rather than owning

Gone Fishin'

Fishing is a much more upscale, urban activity in Canada than in the U.S., according to PRIZM Canada, a segmentation system that classifies Canadian lifestyles using PRIZM's U.S. clusters. The affluent in Canada often own rustic cottages on lakes — the more isolated, the higher the status — and cultivate clients on fishing trips just as Americans do on country club golf courses. At noon on Friday, traffic jams begin appearing out of Toronto as businesspeople head for their remote weekend cottages three hours away.

Top Ten PRIZM Canada Clusters for Fishing

Canada	U.S.
Bohemian Mix	Hard Scrabble
Mid-City Mix	Blue Highways
Young Literati	Grain Belt
Money & Brains	Shotguns & Pickups
Blue Blood Estates	Military Quarters
Inner Cities	Back Country Folks
American Dreams	Big Sky Families
Urban Gold Coast	River City, USA
Winner's Circle	Mines & Mills
Upward Bound	Sunset City Blues

(Sources: PRIZM Canada, Claritas, Compusearch)

their homes, economists might expect Canadians to enjoy a fair amount of disposable income. On the contrary, higher taxes — wealthy Canadians pay 54 percent compared to 40 percent in the U.S. — result in less discretionary spending. Canada's government makes up for it with a costly social welfare system that provides citizens with health care, education, and cultural arts. But the lack of disposable income encourages Canadian consumers to be fiscally conservative. As a result, Canadians buy fewer stocks and more life insurance than Americans. The joke among personnel officers is that job candidates ask first about pensions and benefits, and only then get around to salaries.

The quickest way to start a debate among Canadian sociologists is to ask about the cultural lag from the time American products and ideas appear to when they make their way north of the border. Recent surveys have found that only a third of Canadians want to improve their health, a much lower figure than Americans would admit to. Eating beef, which has largely gone out of fashion among America's educated, cholesterol-conscious metro residents, remains popular in all kinds of Canadian clusters. Knowledge of the hazards of smoking still hasn't reached critical mass in many Canadian communities. Nearly a third of all Canadians smoke, thanks partly to French Canadians who take their cue from European smokers. When the city council of predominantly English-speaking Toronto passed a smoking ban in bars and restaurants, editorials in predominantly French-speaking Montreal condemned the move as "so Toronto."

But it would be an error to conclude that Canadians are always behind Americans in accepting new and innovative ideas. They're more likely to do their banking over the Internet, and they buy computers, watch movies, and read books at similar rates. Canadians have a much higher purchase rate for imported products, in part because their multi-ethnic communities have strong ties to foreign countries. The French sensibility that's so pervasive in Quebec makes cheese as much a staple there as in France. While imported cheese in the States is consumed primarily by upscale urban- and suburbanites who can afford steep prices, in Canada imported cheese is priced competitively and has made its way into more rural, downscale communities — the type of heartland communities that comprise "Buy American" country in the States.

"The pride in being Canadian is to feel no guilt about buying

Nearly a third of all Canadians smoke, thanks partly to French Canadians who take their cue from European smokers.

Smoking Their Way Across Canada

The health revolution has been slower to overtake educated consumers in Canada than in America. Canadians are less concerned about smoking cigarettes, drinking alcohol, and eating high-cholesterol foods. Smokers in Canada include young singles and families whose stateside counterparts cut back their consumption long ago.

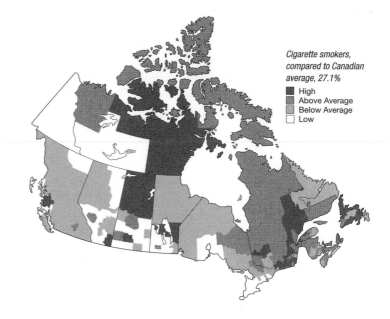

Cigarette smokers, compared to Canadian average, 27.1%
- ■ High
- ■ Above Average
- ■ Below Average
- □ Low

Top PSYTE Clusters   Brie & Chablis / Quebec's New Urban Mosaic / Young Urban Intelligentsia / Euro Quebec / Young Grey Collar
Top Canadian Markets   Saint-Hyacinthe, Quebec / Saint-Jérôme, Quebec / Hawkesbury, Ontario / Joliette, Quebec / Moose Jaw, Saskatchewan

(Sources: PSYTE, Compusearch, Print Measurement Bureau)

Dutch cheese," says cluster analyst Steve Rayner. "The pride in being American is buying a Wisconsin-made Gouda so you don't put some fellow American out of business."

Advertising affects the popularity of products, but Canadians have a different sensibility about messages spilling into their country from the U.S. Ads with overtly American themes, such as the cowboy riding through Central Park pitching Stetson cologne, rarely prove effective. Nor do hard sell approaches work, as Manulife, one of Canada's largest insurance companies, discovered several years ago. In a campaign to market financial planning services for women, the company found that its prime market was middle-management professional women living in clusters like Urban Gentry, Young Urban Professionals, and Young Urban Mix. These consumers would rather do their financial planning with a company representative over an 800 number than face-to-face with an agent. In focus groups evaluating marketing materials, these women rejected the spokeswoman with the blond hair and bright lipstick in favor of sandy brown hair and no lipstick at all. "It has to be a low-key approach," says Rene Montgomery, the company's marketing database and segmentation consultant. "You have to tell the consumer, 'It's easy, it's convenient, and it's your way.'"

Such differences between Canadians and Americans are well appreciated by Casino Niagara, Canada's largest casino, located on the Ontario side of the border at Niagara Falls. The casino attracts some 10 million players each year and, through surveys and computerized "membership" cards that indicate how often they play and how much they bet, has gathered information on hundreds of thousands of customers: their demographics, interests, and gaming patterns. Employing both PSYTE and PRIZM clusters to analyze players, Casino Niagara has uncovered sharply dissimilar gambling styles on either side of the border. The Americans, who tend to live in midscale PRIZM clusters like Blue-Chip Blues, Single City Blues, and New Empty Nests, play the slot machines three times more often than any other casino game. The Canadians, from more upscale PSYTE clusters such as Europa, Mortgaged in Suburbia, and Asian Heights, are more likely to play table games such as roulette and blackjack. Through its understanding of how players from each cluster like to bet, the casino has developed loyalty promotions using coupon offers for complimentary meals and coins.

More recently, Casino Niagara has made imaginative use of the clusters in designing advertising campaigns to attract more of the kinds of people who've already discovered it. Andrew White, manager of database marketing for the casino, recalls the delicate balance of crafting a refined image that nonetheless appealed to blue-collar gamblers from the U.S. One mailer for the American clusters, entitled "Bingo Schmingo," spoofed Canada's popular charity bingo games and positioned Casino Niagara as a flashy, Vegas-style resort with glitzy photos of slot machines surrounded by bright gold-and-red lettering. A TV commercial reinforced the vibrant image by showing the casino's falls observation tower shooting purple lightning across the landscape, causing coins to gush out of slot machines like water from a spigot. "We didn't want to be too sophisticated, but we struggled with not looking too cheesy," says White. "The message was, 'You just have to come here to experience it.'"

For the casino's more sophisticated Canadian audience, another popular mailer looked like a personalized invitation to a charity ball. Printed in forest green, silver, and black, the "exclusive to you" invitation to the casino highlighted the facility's five-star Mediterranean restaurant and valet parking. A TV spot was similarly understated, with soft jazz accompanying a James Bond–like figure in white tuxedo as he enters the casino to gamble between romantic embraces with an attractive woman. "We needed a softer sell for an executive audience," notes White. "That's the Canadian way."

Twin cities

Despite the marketplace differences, analysts see a number of lifestyle parallels between Canada and the U.S., especially along north-south axes. Canadians who live in the Maritime Provinces tend to have lifestyles more similar to those of New Englanders than those of Canadians in British Columbia. In many respects, the farmers of Manitoba and Saskatchewan are more akin to those from Minnesota and the Dakotas than they are to the residents of industrial Ontario and the French-influenced Quebec. Fans of rodeos would be at home in Alberta or Texas. Shopping malls in suburban Calgary and Denver are similar in location, market orientation, and layout.

In fact, the U.S. and Canada share a handful of "twin cities" with strikingly similar demographics and lifestyles. A 1995 Compusearch analysis to match neighborhood types across the border revealed these "separated at birth" metropolitan areas:

■ WASHINGTON, D.C., AND OTTAWA-HULL, ONTARIO: It probably comes as no surprise that the capitals of both countries have white-collar, bureaucratic workforces. Both have high concentrations of well-educated and affluent professionals who live with their families in large suburban homes. And both report large numbers of young, mobile high-tech workers; Ottawa-Hull is known as the Silicon Valley of the north. In Washington, the three most prevalent clusters are all upscale and white-collar: the families of Upward Bound (9 percent) and the couples in Executive Suites (9 percent) and Winner's Circle (7 percent). In Ottawa-Hull, the market includes more midscale families in satellite towns: Technocrats & Bureaucrats (13 percent), Suburban Executives (6 percent), and Participaction Quebec (5 percent), one of the principal clusters representing the 43 percent of French speakers in the market. As for consumer patterns, both communities rank high for computers, books, museums, frequent flying, and low-cal frozen entrées, but low for canned beans, bowling, and religious radio.

Canadians who live in the Maritime Provinces tend to have lifestyles more similar to those of New Englanders than those of Canadians in British Columbia.

■ DENVER, COLORADO, AND CALGARY, ALBERTA: These two western boomtowns share a young, upscale workforce, a number of wealthy residents, and relatively few ethnic or poor neighborhoods. Bustling Calgary holds the second-largest number of corporate head offices in Canada and is the center of the Canadian oil industry and an area rich in ranchland. Its top clusters include the young families of Kindergarten Boom (15 percent), the downtown renters of Young City Singles (10 percent), and the midscale families of Technocrats & Bureaucrats (9 percent). In more diverse Denver are found singles and families from a range of income levels between upscale and lower-middle-class: Kids & Cul-de-Sacs (7 percent), New Beginnings (4 percent), and Smalltown Downtown (4 percent). Together, they share a decidedly yuppie lifestyle, surprisingly cosmopolitan for their respective heartland settings. Consumer surveys show a strong preference for skiing, exercise, rock music, and Mexican food; *The Simpsons* plays well in both cities.

■ DETROIT, MICHIGAN, AND HAMILTON, ONTARIO: You'd think that Detroit would be a likely match with the city right over the river, Windsor, Ontario. Actually, Detroit's closer twin is Hamilton, across the water from Buffalo and known by its big-city neighbors as Steeltown. With their former industrial bases shifting from manufacturing to service jobs, these two cities have similar, diverse populations: struggling young and often single-parent families combined with more successful blue- and white-collar families. Hamilton's top clusters include the older couples of Conservative Homebodies (15 percent), the upper-middle-class families of Satellite Suburbs, and the upscale town cluster known as Blue Collar Winners (8 percent). Detroit has more socioeconomic extremes: the poor residents of Inner Cities (11 percent), the upper-middle-class Blue-Chip Blues families (7 percent), and the upscale, child-filled subdivisions of Kids & Cul-de-Sacs. Residents in both cities are big on cars, fishing, lotteries, and golf.

■ TUCSON, ARIZONA, AND SASKATOON, SASKATCHEWAN: When the temperature hits ninety degrees in Tucson, the ground may still be covered with snow in Saskatoon, but don't let the weather fool you. Beneath the surface, these cities have a lot in common. Both are home to young, midscale renters as well as upscale retirees and pockets of strongly ethnic neighborhoods. Saskatoon, or "Toon Town" to locals, is a prairie market with a college, many younger white-collar families, and, considering that it's heartland, an uncommonly high percentage of Eastern European ethnic groups. Its highest-ranked clusters are Kindergarten Boom (13 percent), Struggling Downtowns (11 percent), and Technocrats & Bureaucrats (10 percent). Dry and dusty Tucson, with its mix of college students and retirees, also has a number of younger families working at blue-collar jobs in clusters like Family Scramble and Smalltown Downtown as well as recent college graduates living a Towns & Gowns lifestyle. These diverse communities create yuppified consumer markets with high rates of interest in books, the arts, health food, and exercise.

Beyond these cluster twins, Canada is close on the heels of other American trends, primarily one demographers have dubbed the Great Population Turnaround. For the first time in a century, Canadian census figures are indicating the start of a reverse migration, from southern cities and suburbs to the formerly spurned countryside. Already, the spread of city dwellers into exurban towns has created a kind of rural renaissance, bringing new life and wealth to recently declining communities. In 1993, an Old Canadian Rustics hamlet named Rossburn, Manitoba (population 660), gained fame when it took out a Toronto newspaper ad in an effort to lure disenchanted city slickers with the promise of wide-open spaces and cheap housing. Officials were swamped with 560 replies. Many who responded were members of an increasingly overstressed and economically insecure middle class who wanted to get off the treadmill for the slower pace of small-town living. Canadian psychotherapists have even given a name to this fast-lane urban ailment: the TINS syndrome, for Two Incomes, No Sex.

But, as in America, picking up roots and moving across cluster chasms can create tensions. Old Canadian Rustics is a neighborhood type of poorly educated and rural retirees — a real lifestyle leap for metro sophisticates, even those fed up with the urban rat race. After the initial flush of publicity, only eight families that came to Rossburn decided to stay, leaving a net population gain of seventeen. Some newcomers fled complaining of not enough activities for their children. Others failed to find an audience for their businesses, such as a citified café and a New Age reflexology practice. "There's a very fossilized pattern of habits in Rossburn," observes Dorothy Pot, who later moved to the more upscale Old Leafy Towns community of Swan River, Manitoba (population 4,500). "You can't make a living there."

Still, many Canadians and Americans tell researchers they are

For the first time in a century, Canadian census figures are indicating the start of a reverse migration, from southern cities and suburbs to the formerly spurned countryside.

willing to sacrifice income levels for a better quality of life. There's an undercurrent of concern among Canadians that their cities are becoming more like America's, more violent, more commercially absorbed, and more brash. Residents were shaken when riots broke out in Toronto after the Rodney King verdict in Los Angeles. Recent polls show that residents fear that too many of the immigrants who arrive are not adopting Canada's "live and let live" values. Demonstrations against immigrants have sprung up ("Honk if you hate Gypsies," read one sign at a Toronto rally). And a boom in suburban development is causing Canadians to worry about what impact more asphalt, more snow plowing, and more commuting will have on their environment. In the quest for a manageable life, Canadians are discovering that America's problems can't be contained by a line drawn on a map.

Canada's sixty diverse lifestyle types bespeak a nation that is nurturing numerous cultures in the face of pressures within and outside its borders. Its success recently earned it recognition from the United Nations as the most livable country on the planet. But the peaceful mosaic is threatened by the Quebec separatist movement, and no one can guarantee how an independent Quebec would affect Canada's future. In many ways, secession is the ultimate act of clustering. But for most geodemographers, who devote their careers to studying that principle, the breakup of a nation would hardly be cause for celebration.

When people buy a house, they're not just getting a roof and four walls. They're also buying into the image of a neighborhood that tells a lot about who that person is. And it's the same all over the world.
— Richard Webber

The clustering of the world

From the sidewalk in front of his terraced town house in London's Highgate neighborhood, Richard Webber surveys a row of Edwardian homes with their angular roofs, bay windows, and tiny porches. "A theatrical agent lives there, a lighting designer there, a fashion buyer there, and a public relations person over there," he says, pointing out neighbors in a soft English accent. "You see, they all have jobs in the creative arts."

Webber, a lanky, thoughtful man with a dry wit, chuckles at the shared distinction. According to the MOSAIC segmentation system he helped create, Highgate is a Chattering Classes community, a collection of dense urban-fringe neighborhoods filled with well-educated professionals in the arts, politics, education, and the media. With comfortable salaries, they've settled in quaint, desirable corners of cities like London, Cambridge, and Bristol. But their progressive ideas — Chattering Classes residents are the biggest consumers of newspapers and magazines — reflect a quirky, antiestablishment perspective. "These are reasonably educated people who aren't very materialistic," Webber explains. "They're upwardly mobile but haven't forgotten their proletarian roots." In other words, his neighbors are happy to live in half-million-dollar homes, drive clunky-but-safe Volvos, enjoy tawdry soap operas, and watch proletarian soccer matches — all integrated into a lifestyle that's found throughout Britain.

With the push by Prime Minister Tony Blair's Labour Party to turn stuffy old Britain into "Cool Britannia," the envy of a dynamic European community, there is no lifestyle more influential than the Chattering Classes. Surveys show that these residents tend to be international in their orientation, favoring ethnic foods, imported wine, and traveling abroad — Spain, Cuba, and Romania were hot destinations in the summer of 1997. But whereas they may be the first to try a new Vietnamese restaurant, they're the last to pick up on a new piece of technology: Cell phones and answering machines are considered intrusive and overly commercial. In the high-ceilinged homes of Clifton, a community in Bristol, the decor typically features primitive art from other cultures, a study with no degrees on the wall, a rack of classical CDs, and an older-generation computer. As the MOSAIC literature notes, the Chattering Classes are "articulate but skeptical influencers and opinion formers who direct the cultural and political agenda of the nation. . . . They're often uninterested in technology for its own sake, more comfortable with ideas and opinions than with the operational details of day-to-day management."

All of which would be a pretty fair description of Richard Webber — except the part about being a technological Luddite. Quite to the contrary, Webber is more involved in the technology of geodemographics than nearly anyone else in the world. As the fifty-year-old chief of Experian Micromarketing, based in Nottingham, England, he oversees a sprawling empire of MOSAIC cluster systems that analyze consumers in nineteen countries, from Australia and Belgium to South Africa and the United States. In linking all the countries into a single segmentation system called Global MOSAIC, Experian qualifies as the top marketer of the global village. Webber's computers have boiled down 631 different MOSAIC types in the various countries to come up with 14 common lifestyles, classifying 800 million people who produce roughly 80 percent of the world's gross domestic product. Beyond industrialized nations, Webber has set his cluster computers on underdeveloped countries. Next stop: South America.

Although the formation of the fifteen-nation European Union implies a social convergence, cluster systems illustrate the uniqueness of each country as a result of differing geographies, cultures, and histories — and especially as it relates to freedom of expression. Norway, which has about two million households, is divided into thirty clusters, including Maritimers, Older Craftsmen, and Mountain Farmers. Belgium, with twice the number of households, has only twenty-seven segments, such as Couples Starting Out, Mining Villages, and Active Retired People. Apartheid may have ended in South Africa, but almost half of all black citizens still live in poor, dense neighborhoods that challenge analysts to distinguish the different degrees of poverty: Urban Decay, Crammed Chaos, and Shack Settlements are among the thirty-eight clusters designated for five million households. The largest lifestyle in South Africa, representing 11 percent of the population, is called Matchbox Houses.

Some of the cluster differences between countries reflect settlement patterns that have evolved over time. In Latin America and Southern European countries like Spain and Italy, the elite tend to live in city centers and the poor on the urban fringe, the exact opposite of the U.S. and England. No one looks down on apartment renters in Classic Bourgeoisie Neighbourhoods, Spain's wealthiest neighborhood type, where the most prestigious buildings typically were built before World War I and the ownership of units is passed down through inheritance. The concentration of wealth in the central core of European cities dates to the Middle Ages, when the barons of estates lived inside castle walls and the serfs lived outside, without protection from marauding armies. In most European countries, the high-end specialty clothing and jewelry stores are still concentrated in city centers. And the farther away from the downtown area, the poorer the housing becomes. France's most impoverished lifestyle is a rural cluster called Agrarian Decline; Belgium's is Farmers & Agricultural Areas.

As with the U.S., not all countries appreciate this clustered view of life, with its implicit message that people can be sorted into several dozen lifestyle types. The Japanese, on the other hand, dislike clustering not because it pigeonholes but because it has *too many* pigeonholes for its homogeneous populace of 126 million. The Japanese ethic of working in groups and sacrificing for the good of the country helped the nation rise from the ruins of World War II and become an economic powerhouse. Even so, Experian analysts studying Japan found thirty-nine lifestyle types, with names like High Status City Household, Small Town Mix, and Long Distance Commuters. There's such a disparity between the clusters in the countryside, where residents tend to be poor, traditional homeowners, and the metropolitan areas, where they are relatively upscale, modern apartment-dwellers with the world's longest working hours, that Japan appears to be two distinct countries.

In the cities of Japan, time-starved residents have created the vending capital of the world, where customers can buy hundred-dollar ties, whiskey, boxer shorts, and life insurance from sidewalk

In Latin America and Southern European countries like Spain and Italy, the elite tend to live in city centers and the poor on the urban fringe, the exact opposite of the U.S. and England.

machines. Gadget-crazy city dwellers snatch up wristwatches that double as TV remote controls, and the fashion conscious look to American pop culture for the latest consumer trends, whether it's donning sunglasses at night, striking poses like the models from the Gap, or melding English expressions into Japanese. Tokyo office workers now sit at their computers to *"daburu-kurikku"* (double-click) the *"mausa"* (mouse) on an *"ai-kon"* (icon).

Despite anticluster sentiments, businesses in nearly every industrialized nation have recognized the death of traditional mass markets and the need for micromarketing to reach fragmented customer niches. Consumers who once made marketplace choices based on functionality are now selecting products based on brand, emotion, and the image of themselves they wish to project. In Spain, political freedom following the death of Francisco Franco in 1975 unleashed decades of pent-up consumerism that is only now being satisfied with new malls, and suburban housing. At the same time, companies are increasing their product choices to cater to

Around the World in 18 Clusters

In many countries, the widest socioeconomic gap between clusters is the one that separates prosperous inner-city neighborhoods from those characterized by rural poverty. The largest cluster, however, tends to be unique to each country, based on history, geography, and tradition. Here are highlights of cluster systems from seven countries, representing 256 lifestyle types.

	France	Germany	Great Britain	Japan	South Africa	Spain
Population	58 million	84 million	57 million	126 million	42 million	39 million
# clusters	52	38	52	39	38	37
Largest cluster	Rural Industry	Village Inhabitants	Pebble Dash Subtopia	Lower Status City Workers	Matchbox Houses	Daytours & Detours
% households	7.7%	4.5%	4.2%	5.1%	11.1%	8.2%
Richest cluster	Inner Metro Elites	Attractive City-Center Buildings	Clever Capitalists	High Status City Households	Upper Crust	Classic Bourgeoisie Neighbourhoods
% households	0.8%	2.1%	1.4%	2.0%	0.9%	1.2%
Poorest cluster	Agrarian Decline	Younger Rural Population	Upland and Small Farms	Old People's Home	Forgotten People	Small, Scattered Stagnant & Secluded Rurals
% households	3.7%	3.1%	1.4%	0.3%	0.6%	1.0%

(Sources: MOSAIC International Network, Experian Micromarketing)

new marketing niches. In English supermarkets, yogurt choices have grown from fewer than five to more than fifty over the last twenty years. The breakup of the Soviet Union and the decline of Communist dictatorships have forever altered a once-stagnant consumer landscape, as Procter & Gamble and Burger King march into Iron Curtain countries offering Woolite and Whoppers and a taste of what these countries have been missing for decades.

Across Europe, businesses are now using clusters much as their North American counterparts do: to analyze customers, select business locations, target direct mail, and crunch sales data. In England, insurance companies use the clusters to determine premiums for home or car insurance and to predict the payoff in case of an accident. In Ireland, newspaper ad salespeople use clustered circulation maps to show advertisers which products are most likely to be bought in different subscriber locations. Every year, more than two hundred companies use the Dutch MOSAIC system to reach forty-one lifestyle types; the country's equivalent of the Red Cross targets donors with cluster-tailored social marketing campaigns.

Increasingly, multinational companies are discovering the value of multicountry cluster systems in understanding the idiosyncracies of shoppers across national boundaries. Last year, Denmark-based Bang & Olufsen turned to the international MOSAIC network when it wanted to develop a marketing strategy for its global chain of high-end audiovisual stores. Beginning in England, the company used British MOSAIC clusters to analyze its existing customer base, confirming its biggest fans among upscale suburban clusters like High Income Families and Rising Materialists. That enabled Bang & Olufsen to identify promising sites for new stores in areas with a high concentration of those clusters, as well as target direct-mail pieces to neighborhoods near existing stores that contained the targeted clusters.

But when Bang & Olufsen tried to imitate this model in countries on the Continent, it discovered different lifestyle and shopping patterns. To be sure, the company's best customers were still affluent audiophiles. But in countries like France and Spain, they tended to live in city neighborhoods, in French MOSAIC clusters like Directors & Executives and Bourgeois Antiquity, and in Spanish MOSAIC clusters such as Urban Elites and Classic Bourgeoisie Neighbourhoods. Although these customers could afford to shop anywhere, they tended to stay near home when buying audio

Every year, more than two hundred companies use the Dutch MOSAIC system to reach forty-one lifestyle types; the country's equivalent of the Red Cross targets donors with cluster-tailored social marketing campaigns.

equipment. The company's British stores attracted consumers from great distances, but its outlets in France and Spain reported most of their traffic within a single kilometer. For Bang & Olufsen, these findings were critical in developing a marketing plan that identified how many stores any market could support — whatever the country, however urbanized the setting.

With the forces of globalization gaining ground daily, it's inevitable that similar lifestyles will crop up in different countries. Every day in England, Holland, and Spain, tens of thousands of young people put on their Levi's, watch a *Star Wars* video, and chow down at Pizza Hut. Movies, TV shows, and popular fiction cross borders freely. In April 1997, at least three of the top five best-sellers in Britain, Germany, and Australia were written by American authors. In Germany, only two books on that country's fiction best-seller lists were by Germans, and four legal thrillers by John Grisham were among the top fifteen hardback and paperback titles.

Every day in England, Holland, and Spain, tens of thousands of young people put on their Levi's, watch a Star Wars *video, and chow down at Pizza Hut.*

But one country's particular cup of tea isn't always the object of universal desire. Bingo, a downscale game in the U.S. and U.K., is chichi in Spain, where residents don their finest to play. When Marks & Spencer, one of Britain's most successful retailers, went looking to expand on the Continent, it found that upscale shoppers among Barcelona's Urban Elite were less interested in the clothing and home furnishings so popular among the store's British clientele. In Britain, the store's target audience is concentrated in the upper-middle-class Stylish Singles suburbs around London's M25 beltway — known to marketers as the Gin and Jag Belt (for the drink and the car). Instead, Barcelona's affluent snapped up the prepared foods, wine, and toiletries. In France, the popularity of Marks & Spencer's sandwiches has even changed the country's leisurely two-hour lunch. Now, so many Parisian office workers eat shrink-wrapped sandwiches at their desks that the nation's culture guardians have criticized Marks & Spencer as an assault on French corporate culture as menacing as American slang is to their language.

The Marks & Spencer experience underscores the need to check cultural expectations at the border. Mercedes may be a trendy nameplate for affluent motorists in England, but it's considered the declassé sedan of farmers in Sweden, where homegrown cars like Volvos are hot among the well-to-do. Budweiser, the largest beer brewer and a mainstream label in the U.S., is considered an upmarket product in Britain. Neighborhood pubs charge four dollars a bottle for what one British marketer describes as "the essence of cool America." When Citibank moved to Spain, it opened bright branches with glass walls. Spaniards hated them. "They want their privacy," says David Monsó, an account executive with Experian MOSAIC Iberia, in Madrid. "They like dark places and lots of walls to do their banking."

Political groups in Europe have also taken to cluster systems. During the 1994 Swedish referendum campaign on joining the European Union, Experian identified areas of "floater voters" for a pro-EU group that unleashed a small army of telemarketers to help convince them to vote yes. Using psychographic studies that explore attitudes, Experian determined that the EU's biggest backers among Sweden's 6.5 million registered voters were those city-dwelling Conspicuous Consumers who, in terms of attitude, were into "self-exploration." Those most opposed were blue-collar workers from small industrial towns who were both reluctant to change and collectivist in their attitude. Psychographically, they were belongers who backed the trade unions and the welfare state in Sweden, and feared the changes that would come from joining the EU.

Using a selective campaign, the proponents targeted only 680,000 swing voters characterized as collectivists who were nevertheless open to change, mostly in the southwestern part of the country. After identifying what messages would appeal to different clusters, they launched an extensive direct-marketing campaign called "Yes to Europe," using telemarketing scripts and direct-mail pitches tailored specifically to the undecided residents in clusters like Average Areas and Dynamic Families. "These folks are not big readers, but they'll pick up information in front of them that provides facts," says Experian senior analyst Andrea McDonald. "So the brochure was designed to explain the effects of voting yes or no." Before the campaign was over, organizers had made 500,000 phone calls and sent out follow-up brochures stressing the message that if Sweden didn't join the union, it would result in more change than if it did. Although polls predicted the referendum would be defeated, 53 percent of Sweden said yes to the European Union. And in follow-up interviews, a healthy majority of those who received phone calls from "Yes to Europe" said they'd supported the move.

While political and demographic trends have conspired to bring the world closer together — 300 million Europeans now share a single currency in the euro — cultural distinctions nevertheless remain. Every country has a unique lifestyle mix evocative of its psyche. For better or worse, some national tastes and trends defy globalization, as shown in the following thumbnail portraits of several clustered countries.

■ FRANCE. In a country where American products are seen as a form of imperialism, some critics attribute France's cultural snootiness to an underlying xenophobia. It's true that the French travel less than other Europeans and sign up for fewer packaged holidays abroad. But they don't have to. The growing number of urbanites — France is one of the few industrial countries where people from the country are moving to the city — simply vacation at country homes in Brittany or Provence. And France's small percentage of immigrants also contributes to low rates for travel abroad. Where the French do excel is in sporting activities, enjoying cycling, soccer, and rugby at high rates. And they purchase a disproportionate quantity of certain foods: bread, steak, cheese, oysters, and snails. France's highest concentration of residents lives in small towns that attract both tourist and industrial activity. The largest cluster, Rural Industry, is home to nearly 13 percent of the population and is characterized by young blue-collar families who live in pre-World War I housing and own multiple cars.

■ ITALY. Psychographic surveys show Italians to be more open, stylish, and interested in new fashion and ideas than citizens of other European nations. Compared to those of the British, their furnishings and clothes are more colorful, their cars more snazzy looking than speedy driving. And Italians have more of a global view, ranking among the biggest supporters of the European Union, American movies and music, and imported products. Yet Italians still value traditional commercial practices; they have yet to embrace outlet malls and hypermarkets, preferring to do business at corner shops and family-run stores. Their largest lifestyle type, In the Factory, representing about 6 percent of the populace, is a collection of small towns filled with modestly educated blue-collar workers. Italy also has some of the most fanciful cluster names, including Once Upon A Time (aging pensioners living in working-class areas of big towns), Thanks Mom (a high percentage of grown-up children still at home in industrial areas), and

Fireplace Angels (older rental communities in southern Italy with a disproportionate number of housewives).

■ GERMANY. German consumers are health fanatics, concerned about their bodies as well as their environment. They're big buyers (and producers) of pharmaceutical drugs, beauty care products, and alternative medical treatments like reflexology. They worry about ecological issues, especially waste management and pollution. Although they travel around the world at high rates — the highest proportion of their leisure budgets is spent on vacations — they're relatively slow to adopt new technology and consumer goods at home. Only 18 percent of Germans own computers, about half that of Americans. Nationwide tastes in food and cars reflect a parochial passion for things German; it was no surprise to cultural historians that President Helmut Kohl's recent cookbook featured traditional German sausage in many recipes. Among the nation's thirty-eight clusters, the largest, with 4.5 percent of the population, is a classic rural one, Village Inhabitants, with high concentrations of large families living in older homes in the countryside. Since the unification of Germany in 1990, social and income inequalities between the former East and West Germany have steadily grown, widening the gap between the clusters of rich and poor citizens.

■ SOUTH AFRICA. Blacks constitute the largest underclass in South Africa, but by no means are they uniformly poor. In fact, a bigger factor influencing poverty is living in the countryside rather than the city. There are relatively prosperous black families living in clusters like Self Starters, located in historically black townships, and All Sorts, a mix of races, languages, and ethnic groups. The largest cluster, Matchbox Houses, is predominantly black. It contains more than 11 percent of the population, and its name is especially apt. Most residents here live in tiny apartheid-era four-room houses, built on tiny plots arranged in endless rows, with modest comforts; less than 1 percent of South Africans own a computer. But the end of apartheid brought a rapidly expanding consumer society, and a huge market for basic goods like cars, washers, refrigerators, and food. Credit card balances have skyrocketed. Gambling and nightclubbing are popular, as if the end of a divided society unleashed a hedonistic spirit. And sports, especially soccer, are bringing the races together. Today, the world's fastest-growing cities are in South Africa.

In South Africa's largest cluster, most residents live in tiny apartheid-era four-room houses, built on tiny plots arranged in endless rows, with modest comforts; less than 1 percent of South Africans own a computer.

New Britannia

To more fully appreciate the evolution of lifestyles around the world, consider the development of two cluster systems: MOSAIC, one of the oldest geodemographic systems in Europe, which classifies lifestyles for the industrialized society of Great Britain; and MOSAIC Iberia, one of the newest cluster systems, which covers the emerging economy in Spain.

Of all the cluster systems in Europe, the most widely used is Experian's MOSAIC system for Great Britain. Despite Britain's reputation as a rigid society of upper crust and lower classes, those distinctions are blurring. The fifty-two neighborhood types divined by MOSAIC — including Affluent Blue Collars, Gentrified Villagers, and Ageing Professionals — reflect a nation where the family you were born into has less impact on your career than your education and ambition. The largest lifestyle in England, Pebble Dash Subtopia, represents 4.4 percent of the population and defies any simple notion of class. Most of the residents are low-level white-collar couples living in small-town neighborhoods in places like Surrey. The communities first appeared in the 1930s, during the boom in semidetached houses with half-timbered gables and gravel-and-stucco exteriors (hence "Pebble Dash"). With their garages, gardens, and frosted-glass doors — letting in light but not prying eyes — these homes met the aspirations of young families fleeing the grime and congestion of the city.

Despite Britain's reputation as a rigid society of upper crust and lower classes, those distinctions are blurring.

Today, however, younger managers move to closer-in cosmopolitan areas, and the suburban row houses of Pebble Dash Subtopia are considered passé, their residents aging and out of touch. As consumers, they're among the last to pick up on new fashions. As voters, they're the silent majority who feel marginalized by the media. When Princess Diana died in a car accident in 1997, the media elite from the Chattering Classes cluster thought the widespread public display of affection at her funeral was vulgar and embarrassing. Not so the residents of Pebble Dash Subtopia, who surrounded Buckingham Palace with tons of flowers and mourned her passing with spontaneous, heartfelt grief. "These were people who weren't rooted in any social matrix," explains Experian's Richard Webber, "and could relate to Diana's loneliness in a vicarious way." Eventually, the royal family took note of their sympathies for "the People's Princess" and promised to be more in touch with the modern concerns of its subjects. For a royal family whose every public appearance was so formal and proscribed, this declaration was a rare triumph for the commoners of Pebble Dash Subtopia.

As the country takes on the mantle of the modern leader of Europe, the biggest changes are occurring in Britain's largest city, London. Here, the predominant lifestyle among the city's seven million residents is classified Victorian Low Status, a collection of communities where residents tend to live in cramped nineteenth-century row houses surrounded by betting shops, ethnic cafés, and greengrocers. Seventeen percent of the city's population fits that description, and for them, status is owning a hundred-dollar pair of athletic shoes and playing Nintendo games — both of which they enjoy at rates more than twice the national average. The second-largest cluster group, Stylish Singles, represents about 16 percent of London's populace and is more likely to live in expensive garden-style flats. But these suburban folks are well educated and involved in their work, having put off homes, families, and gardens until later in their lives. They're into fashion, foreign travel, the arts, entertainment, and eating out. Surveys show that their favorite car is a Mercedes, their favorite newspaper the conservative *Evening Standard*. And their outlook on life is, naturally, much different than that of Victorian Low Status. People in Stylish Singles favor putting health warnings on cigarettes and avoiding too much salt and sugar in their foods. In Victorian Low Status, residents are heavy smokers and big fast-food eaters.

Just as British and American lifestyles share a common heritage, the histories of the MOSAIC and PRIZM cluster systems are similar. In fact, Webber's interest in geodemography goes back to 1974, when he built a cluster system to help target deprived areas of Liverpool for government funding — much like PRIZM creator Jonathan Robbin's early work for the U.S. Department of Housing and Urban Development, helping to target housing grants to cities with a history of rioting. In 1980, after the British census became linked to addresses and commercially available for statistical modeling, Webber helped build his country's first geodemographic system, called ACORN (A Classification of Residential Neighbourhoods). Six years later, he left ACORN to join a credit reference agency, CCN (which later bought TRW Information Systems & Services and changed its name to Experian), and developed

British Lifestyles

MOSAIC defines 52 clusters and 12 lifestyle groups for Great Britain.

High Income Families	*Council Flats*	*Mortgaged Families*	*Town Houses & Flats*	*Country Dwellers*
Clever Capitalists	Families in the Sky	Brand New Areas	Bijou Homemakers	Gentrified Villages
Rising Materialists	Graffitied Ghettos	Prenuptial Owners	Market Town Mixture	Rural Retirement Mix
Corporate Careerists	Small Town Industry	Nestmaking Families	Bedsits & Shop Flats	Lowland Agribusiness
Ageing Professionals	Mid Rise Overspill	Maturing Mortgages	*Stylish Singles*	Rural Disadvantage
Small Time Business	Flats for the Aged	*Institutional Areas*	Studio Singles	Tied / Tenant Farmers
Suburban Semis	Inner City Towers	Military Bases	Town Centre Singles	Upland & Small Farms
Green Belt Expansion	*Low-Rise Council*	Non Private Housing	College and Communal	
Suburban Mock Tudor	Co-op Club & Colliery	*Victorian Low Status*	Chattering Classes	
Pebble Dash Subtopia	Better Off Council	Bohemian Melting Pot	*Independent Elders*	
Blue-Collar Owners	Low Rise Pensioners	Victorian Tenements	Solo Pensioners	
Affluent Blue Collar	Low Rise Subsistence	Rootless Renters	High Spending Greys	
30s Industrial Spec	Problem Families	Sweatshop Sharers	Aged Owner Occupiers	
Lo-Rise Right to Buy		Depopulated Terraces	Elderly in Own Flats	
Smokestack Shiftwork		Rejuvenated Terraces		

(Sources: MOSAIC, Experian Micromarketing)

MOSAIC using more current marketing and behavioral data. Over the next decade, he pushed MOSAIC into other countries, overcoming spotty census surveys and strict privacy laws to build his segmentation systems with local partners. Today, each of the MOSAIC systems depends on a differing blend of private information sources to develop the clusters, including car ownership information, electoral registers, and independent surveys.

As in America, all the cluster systems abroad are based on the sociological notion that people live where — and how — they do because of their age, household, and socioeconomic status. And all follow the guiding principle that lifestyle types influence consumer behavior more acutely than demographic characteristics alone. Take Studio Singles and Military Bases, two MOSAIC clusters with high concentrations of young middle-class singles in modestly priced flats, yet whose lifestyles are as different as night and day. Military Bases residents, disproportionately male, lead highly mobile lives with little home ownership; much of their discretionary

In Britain,
Same Demographics,
Different Lifestyles

Not all young middle-class British singles are the same, as is shown here in selected consumer habits of Studio Singles and Military Bases.

Product / Activity	Studio Singles Index	Military Bases Index
Secondhand cars	98	108
Satellite / cable TV	97	115
Red wine	202	60
Canned lager	110	115
Instant potatoes	97	257
Eat-in restaurants	205	180
Bingo	75	105
The Guardian	348	70

An index of 100 equals British national average; 115 equals 15 percent above average, 70 equals 30 percent below average.

(Sources: MOSAIC, Experian Micromarketing)

income is spent on sporting goods, home entertainment, and music. By contrast, Studio Singles is home to emerging professional or white-collar childless workers in their first homes. Developing professional skills is more important to them than fashion or the acquisition of lifestyle products, and they have high rates of owning computers and taking out college loans.

"A consumer's behavior is as much determined by the type of neighborhood he or she lives in as by personal demographics," Webber observes. "And no one scale of geography explains all consumer behavior." In other words, the street where you live affects what kind of car or dishwasher you own. What kind of neighborhood you live in affects leisure patterns such as hunting or aerobics. And what cluster you live in influences the sum total of your consuming patterns, voting behavior, and social concerns — and vice versa.

For all the lifestyle similarities between the U.S. and the U.K., there still are many differences; for instance, it would be an overstatement to say that British class structure has completely disappeared. The continued use of aristocratic titles, the presence of enormous country estates, and the political powers granted descendants of past members of the House of Lords indicate a class system that has not been completely drained of its blue blood. When Tony Blair launched a 1997 effort to reform the House of Lords, it touched off a constitutional crisis that led to political resignations, threatened the nation's entire legislative agenda, and resulted in bitter recriminations between those supporting an elected chamber and others hoping to preserve this vestige of aristocracy. Until recently, fewer than 10 percent of all British students went to college, and only 2 percent attended the country's topflight universities, like Oxford and Cambridge. The English government has tried to promote egalitarianism through higher education, and loans initiated by the Thatcher government have helped double the number of university students over the last decade to 1.2 million. But success among working-class students has been elusive. A 1991 cluster analysis of applicants to higher education institutions found that students who came from upscale MOSAIC types like Chattering Classes and Clever Capitalists were two and three times more likely to be accepted than those who hailed from downscale Suburban Semis and Blue Collar Owners. And those children of upper-level white-collar parents were nearly twice as likely to attend academic universities than technical colleges. For the children of blue-collar laborers, the findings were exactly opposite, with more attending technical schools.

"A distinct pecking order still exists between universities and polytechnics," observes Mark Farr, the business development manager at Experian who investigated the issue. "While the polytechnics draw from a much wider audience, the combined system is still elitist." A major factor in choosing a university over a technical college was a student's prior exposure to travel. Because there are fewer universities than technical colleges, students have to travel farther to the elite schools. "People from a more wealthy background seemed more comfortable traveling away from home to school because they've been accustomed to traveling abroad on holidays," says Farr. "If your father is rich, he'll travel more than if your dad's a dustman."

Although mobility in England is relatively low — about 12 percent of the populace moves each year — the upward progression of Thatcher's "children" arising from her government's initiatives is changing lifestyles at the top. In Britain's wealthiest cluster, Clever Capitalists, life hardly resembles the aristocratic world of the past. Accounting for 1.5 percent of the population, this lifestyle is mostly pursued by new-money residents who came to prominence during the Thatcher years of the 1980s. Typically found in the outer-ring commuter belts of big cities like London and Manchester, these areas boast a large number of company executives and affluent foreign-born residents with high rates of owning stocks and bonds. Like America's wealthiest clusters, Clever Capitalists contains single-wage-earner families with children who attend the

Class Counts in British Colleges

Nowhere is Britain more class conscious than in its higher education system. Below are 1991 acceptance indices by MOSAIC lifestyle groups for universities and polytechnic schools in the U.K., showing a direct correlation between socioeconomic origins and the likelihood of earning a college degree.

MOSAIC Group	University Index	Polytechnic School Index
Older Couples / Leafy Suburbs	265	196
Country Dwellers	154	135
Young Mortgaged Families	152	141
Families / Inter War Semis	136	144
Singles & Flat Dwellers	76	85
Older Communities	61	83
Go-Getting Council Tenants	57	67
Older Council Tenants	39	40
Worse-Off Council Tenants	29	43

Index of 100 equals British national average.

(Sources: University Central Council on Admissions, Experian Micromarketing, Lancaster University. Group names are from an earlier MOSAIC system and differ slightly from current designations.)

same elite universities their parents attended. These high achievers appreciate the material symbols of success: BMWs and Jaguars in the driveway, membership at the country club, a time-share in Spain. When they go out for a drink, they'll order an imported Belgian lager like Stella Artois, whose catch phrase is "Reassuringly Expensive," at $3.50 a bottle. Clever Capitalists are happy to pay the price of status.

The Clever Capitalist sheen can be found in most corners of Berkhamsted, a picturesque town of 16,000 west of London. On hilly streets stand stately, century-old brick homes that cost more than $500,000, with new Jaguars casually parked around their circular driveways. Many of the homeowners are newcomers, highly paid professionals who moved here for the prestigious schools and the relatively short commute to London (about forty-five minutes by train). But they've stayed for the small-town pace, the extensive green space — a golf course and a heath-filled park border the town — and a commercial district that caters to the nouveau riche. It's hard to keep track of all the grand openings of wine bars, clothing boutiques, and chic restaurants offering Thai, Italian, and French cuisine. Not long ago, a four-hundred-year-old pub closed down to make way for Café Rouge, a trendy chain restaurant with a French bistro theme. Only a few residents expressed dismay.

Julian and Caroline Omerod are typical Clever Capitalists. Recently married and both in their early thirties, they chose Berkhamsted as the logical place to buy their first home, an Edwardian town house, and plan a family. They commute each day to London, where they work long hours for high pay: he as a marketing executive, she as an events planner for a bank. Dinner often doesn't take place until nine P.M., and it is eaten in front of a TV newscast. Weekends are reserved for exercise, renovating their house, and trying new foods, either at the area's restaurants or in their kitchen filled with gourmet seasonings, pasta, pâté, sausage, and fresh vegetables. Like other Clever Capitalists, the Omerods are future-oriented consumers who put extra money into their pension plans and eagerly embrace new products and services. "I think it's important to try new things, different sports, ethnic restaurants, and holidays," says Julian, a tall and muscular former championship rower. "We like being adventurous."

But the Omerods' drive and ambition aren't shared by some of their neighbors, who are quite content to indulge in daily luxuries provided by Clever Capitalist–sized incomes. "There are a lot of people who have made money quickly, and they're a little rough around the edges," says Caroline, whose trim figure bespeaks an earlier life as a phys ed teacher. "There are women here who have their morning coffee, play tennis, go to an exercise class, take their kids to school, and then go shopping. They seem to kill time very easily here."

Britain's stringent zoning controls have kept distinct suburban towns like Berkhamsted, Wimbledon, and Epsom from meshing into that indistinguishable suburban sprawl that characterizes many U.S. metro areas. The concept of surrounding communities with officially designated "green belts" arose after World War II, and today huge ribbons of undeveloped land, totaling 3.8 million acres — about 12 percent of the countryside — remain throughout Britain. Many communities have barely expanded beyond their 1975 borders, putting pressure on cities and towns with expanding populations and no place to go with them. Government officials estimate the need for 4.4 million new homes by 2016 and have begun giving county leaders new housing quotas for the first time. When Parliament passed a measure in the winter of 1997 outlawing fox-hunting, commentators regarded the move as the death knell for life in the countryside.

For now, families in search of cheap housing are cramming into booming satellite towns in exurban settings. In Yate, an ex–mining town outside of Bristol in the Nestmaking Families cluster, all the trappings of a burgeoning family community are present.

The concept of surrounding communities with officially designated "green belts" arose after World War II, and today huge ribbons of undeveloped land, totaling 3.8 million acres — about 12 percent of the countryside — remain throughout Britain.

Most of the 25,000 residents are young, middle-class, and live in new town-house developments dotted with churches and soccer fields. There's little in the way of adult entertainment: no movie theater, only one nightclub, and few pubs. Kids fare somewhat better. Every neighborhood has mom-and-tot groups, but the schools are overcrowded. "You have to put your children on a waiting list as soon as they're born," complains one mother. The central mall, Yate Town Centre, is jammed every Saturday with kids crowded around a clown show and merry-go-round in the open-air plaza. Bargain-hunting parents make their way to the House of Pine furniture shop, the Lidl Discount Supermarket, and stores featuring inexpensive toys, car parts, and sporting goods. "It's a new town, functional but with no character," says Paul Hitchings, a stocky thirty-one-year-old engineer for the Ministry of Defense.

"It's pretty tacky," continues Paul's wife, Maxine, a twenty-eight-year-old part-time secretary with wire rims and a blond shag. "You see a lot of tracksuits and white stilettos, girls from Essex whose boyfriends drive a Ford Escort. We call them 'Wayne and Sharons.'"

In the Hitchingses' home, a $90,000 town house on a cul-de-sac, the Nestmaking Families lifestyle resembles that of many child-rearing subdivisions in exurban America. On a weekend afternoon, three-year-old son Alex is watching a video of *The Little Mermaid* while Maxine heats up a can of Heinz Barbie noodles in the microwave. A toy-strewn hallway leads to a small bedroom with a queen-size bed, nylon carpeting, computer, and small TV set. Like most Nestmaking Families, the Hitchingses are in the borrowing phase of their lives and spend little on entertainment. "If you want to go out drinking, you're looking at a baby-sitter for three dollars an hour and hiring a cab both ways," says Maxine. Most of their leisure time is spent with Alex, going to playgrounds during the day and watching videos or sports on television at night. When they go out to dinner parties, the conversation usually turns to dreams of making a larger salary and moving to a bigger house. Indeed, gambling is big in the area, and the Hitchingses alternate between different lotteries each week. "People live here, but they aspire to a bigger house with a nicer lifestyle," says Maxine. "If wages go up, people will move."

Where will they go? Farther into the countryside, Paul and Maxine agree. "People check out your status by what kind of house you live in, not by what you earn," says Paul. "And you can get more house farther out. As people advance, you see their migration from towns to the country."

In Nestmaking Families communities like Yate, the demand for day care is stiff among mothers who want to work part-time and be at home for their kids after school and during holidays. But that's typical in a country with arguably the worst day care system in Europe — a fact that didn't escape the notice of the Minneapolis-based day care company KinderCare. Eager to expand into this underserved market, KinderCare conducted an analysis of communities with high concentrations of progressive, upper-middle-class families with children ages five to nine. Among the hot clusters filled with this target group: Rising Materialists, Corporate Careerists, and Suburban Mock Tudor — all lifestyles of high-income families in quiet suburbs. In 1994, after ranking hundreds of communities according to population density — the company wanted 40,000 people within a two-mile radius — the presence of owner-occupied homes, and households with at least two cars, KinderCare opened its first center in Warrington, a town near Manchester filled with $200,000 Tudor-style split-levels. A waiting list immediately formed after the seventy-five available slots were filled, and the company quickly began working with other property surveyors to find similar sites across England.

The migration of families to country towns has left big cities like London and Manchester younger and more ethnically diverse

The McDonaldization of Britain

Like many multinational companies, McDonald's began its European expansion in upscale urban neighborhoods, where affluent, well-traveled consumers are the first to accept foreign products and services. Now, with more than 700 restaurants in the United Kingdom, McDonald's has saturated the biggest cities, especially around Greater London, and is moving into smaller fast-growing town markets — and clusters like Brand New Areas and Prenuptial Owners.

Top MOSAIC Clusters   Military Bases / Victorian Tenements / College and Communal / Brand New Areas / Prenuptial Owners
Top British Markets   Tooting, Greater London / Stratford, Greater London / Hammersmith, Greater London / Battersea, Greater London / Merton, Devon

(Sources: MOSAIC, Experian Micromarketing, BMRB Ltd.)

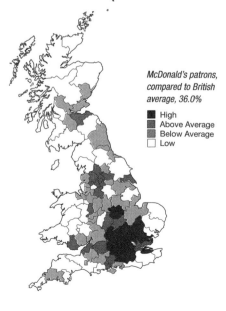

McDonald's patrons, compared to British average, 36.0%

■ High
▨ Above Average
▧ Below Average
□ Low

Britain lacks neighborhoods

where a single ethnic group is concentrated, like the Little Italys and Chinatowns of American cities. Instead, émigrés of many different nationalities live in the same community in a cluster like MOSAIC's Bohemian Melting Pot.

than the general population, as singles and immigrants settle in urban neighborhoods. But in terms of ethnicity, English and American cities are quite different. Ethnic groups in Britain represent only about 8 percent of the population, compared to 25 percent in the U.S., and their presence is more dispersed. Britain lacks neighborhoods where a single ethnic group is concentrated, like the Little Italys and Chinatowns of American cities. Instead, émigrés of many different nationalities live in the same community in a cluster like MOSAIC's Bohemian Melting Pot.

In Willesden Green, a Bohemian Melting Pot section of northwest London, many residents are recent immigrants from Asia, Ireland, and the Caribbean, single men working in trade jobs and living in Victorian-era flats inside two-story row houses. Pictures of their homelands decorate the walls along with framed degrees, and copies of the *Mirror,* a working-class tabloid, sit on side tables. The streets are lined with Indian grocers, Irish pubs, and Turkish kabob shops, in part because these residents lack both spouses and kitchens. Betting parlors are popular, and pubs feature Guinness or an Indian beer whose label appeals to the cultural longings of Indian expatriates. The Willesden Bar even posts the soccer scores for Pakistani teams. But the area also attracts people who thrive on diversity and feel uncomfortable around nuclear family values. There's a high proportion of gays, students, divorcés, and single parents. Men drift through the area in ponytails and dreadlocks, wearing sweat suits picturing American cultural icons like Michael Jordan and Shaquille O'Neal. Women drive secondhand vans and aging subcompacts with bumper stickers proclaiming "NO NUKES."

"The only community feeling I've experienced is the fear of being burgled," Rachel Hyland, a twenty-two-year-old Bohemian Melting Pot resident, told one reporter. "This is just an area where all sorts have ended up."

CableTel, one of the largest cable companies in the United Kingdom, understood this lifestyle well when it began offering Bohemian Melting Pot cable TV service in 1991. Because cable TV access is sold in concert with telephone service, CableTel knew its best customers were downscale people who had lost their phone service from British Telecommunications, the giant phone company, when they couldn't pay their bills. But wiring a home costs CableTel as much as $500, so the company had to find customers among the poorer clusters who would be able to pay their bills over the long term. "We soon realized that the easy sale to a down-scale customer isn't always the best one," says Mike Rankin, president of Cable Precision Marketing. After conducting a cluster analysis, Rankin targeted the immigrants in Bohemian Melting Pot for CableTel's promotional effort. These consumers not only pay their phone bills to keep in touch with family back home, but they also enjoy watching the international soccer matches on cable.

To businesspeople like Rankin, the future of target marketing involves merging geodemographic and psychographic surveys to understand why people buy products and services at the rates they do. The 1996 launch of Beamish Red, a premium Irish ale that costs about three dollars a bottle, aptly demonstrates this interplay of demographics and consumer personality. Knowing that Chattering Classes residents are early adopters as well as opinion makers, the brewer targeted the ale to these upmarket, individualistic drinkers with the nonconformist message "Be Red. Be Proud." The plan worked, as the Chattering Classes not only drank the stuff but talked it up to other customers. While the introduction of Beamish Red drew a market share of about 2 percent (compared to 11 percent for a national brand like Guinness), it had a 4 percent share of Chattering Classes households. At the same time, Beamish Red barely registered a blip of interest among Nest-making Families, who, weighed down by house and car debt, tend to order cheaper bitters. Likewise, the unemployed young males of Problem Families, who routinely go out for long drinking sessions featuring inexpensive lagers, showed no interest in being Red. On the other hand, a cluster profile of customers at 1,500 drinking establishments revealed Beamish Red drinkers among the students of Bohemian Melting Pot, who, despite being stretched for cash, don't mind splurging on a premium brew.

The style in Spain

Lifestyle cluster systems first appeared in countries with well-developed economies and high population densities that made it possible to target consumer segments efficiently. But in recent years, several companies have begun building classification systems in emerging markets like Mexico, India, and Spain, where younger populations have relatively low incomes. As in the developed nations, these cluster systems are effective in revealing settlement patterns and consumer tastes — as well as consumer niches in the unlikeliest of places.

In Spain, a consumer society is just now emerging after decades of being stalled by the dictatorship of Franco, which ended with his death in 1975. When Experian MOSAIC Iberia conducted its first analysis of 40 million Spaniards in 1992, almost half of the thirty-seven lifestyle types were classified as rural, with names like Tractors & Tradition, Land Labourers & Peasants, and Landless Labourers. To marketers, this portrait was still an improvement over the commonly held belief that Spain consisted of only two kinds of consumers: rich city dwellers and poor country folk. For the first time, demographers detected the presence of suburban areas (albeit accounting for less than 10 percent of the population) and detailed the behavioral differences between residents of minor cities, provincial towns, and touristy villages. The flood of tourists to coastal villages in southern Spain created the Sun, Sea & Seasonal Services cluster, where local residents work in the hospitality industry. And pockets of wealth, long concentrated in older city centers, were detected in small-town clusters like Regional Service Hubs, where residents spend their leisure time going to museums and traveling abroad, trading in their Mercedes sedans every twenty-four months.

Historic events have done much to craft Spain's unusual social structure. One lifestyle, called Struggling Smallholders, is centered in Galicia and Asturias, where the rustic landscape looks much like the rugged highlands of Scotland — and for good reason. Celtic tribes began arriving in Spain around 900 B.C., and during the late sixteenth century, Spain tried to conquer England as part of its expanding empire. When that effort failed, troops returned to northern Spain carrying some of the British farming traditions they had observed. Similarly, it's not uncommon to see camels in Caliph and Granada, across the Mediterranean from Morocco. Muslims lived in Spain until 1608 and left their mark in the Moroccan-flavored architecture. In this region today, a center for a cluster called Telly Addict Subsistence, residents with little formal education work as laborers in the construction, hotel, and retail industries. With high unemployment and little income, they excel in one leisure pursuit: watching television. In their meager flats, they often have two or more sets and tune in at rates far above the national average.

The impact of Franco's dictatorship continues to reverberate through Spanish society. After his death, waves of rural residents moved into cities like Madrid and Barcelona, creating lifestyle

Spanish Lifestyles

MOSAIC Iberia defines 37 clusters and 12 lifestyle groups for Spain. A quarter-century after the end of the Franco regime, Spain's economy is making up for lost time. More than two-thirds of the clusters are home to blue-collar workers.

Elite	*Blue Collar Metropolitans*	*Smokestack Classics*	*Living off the Land*
Classic Bourgeoisie Neighbourhoods	Aged Working Classes	Recession Victims	Tractors & Tradition
Urban Elites	Better Off Immigrants	Blue Collar Traditionals	Land Labourers & Peasants
New Residential Elites	Modest Manual Workers	Aged & Affluent Blue Collar	Aged & Abandoned
	Junior Clerks in the Service		Landless Labourers
Well To Do	Sector	*Breaking Away*	
Families from the 1980s Boom	Metropolitan Manual Workers	Regional Service Hubs	*Remote Rurals in Rejected*
Families from the 1970s Boom		Small Urban Business	*Regions*
City Professionals	*Tourist Class*	Struggling Smallholders	Deprived in Distant & Deserted
Settled Professionals	Sun, Sea & Seasonal Services		Districts
	Daytours & Detours	*Mixed Sector in Transition*	Small, Scattered, Stagnant &
Conspicuous Consumers		Telly Addict Subsistence	Secluded Rurals
Professionals from the Outskirts	*New Industrial Areas*	Rural Types Close to Industry	
White Collar Consumerists	Young Families & Light Industry	Rural but Diverse	*Unclassified*
Urban Periphery Senior Clerks	Families in New Industrial		Institutional
White Collar Provincials	Towns		Social Fringe

(Sources: MOSAIC, Experian MOSAIC Iberia)

types dubbed Families from the 1970s Boom (upper-middle-class older couples) and Families from the 1980s Boom (upper-middle-class young families). Both groups today hold white-collar jobs and have enough disposable income to own luxury cars, travel abroad, and attend the theater. In Spain's Basque region, where one million Spaniards live in the rocky hills and industrial towns hugging the Pyrenees, a separatist culture has survived some four thousand years with its own language and customs. Franco forbade anyone to speak Basque in public or study it in school, a prohibition that fueled the separatist movement in the late 1950s. Today the Basque region is home to working-class clusters like Blue Collar Traditionals and Recession Victims, households that were hit hard by the industrial downturn of the 1980s. These areas feature a high percentage of recent immigrants, a low rate of college degrees, and large numbers of unemployed.

The combination of downscale living and long-repressed culture has created a Basque separatist movement unlike that of the relatively peaceful Quebecois in Canada. Basque separatists are known for the violence of the terrorist group ETA (Euskadi Ta Askatasuna). Over the past three decades, the ETA has been responsible for the deaths of nearly eight hundred people, mostly politicians, judges, and policemen. In response, the Spanish government has infused $1 billion into a redevelopment campaign designed to nourish nationalism while undercutting the separatist movement. In Bilbao, the effort is bringing in high-tech firms, a new library, a cultural center, and a branch of the Guggenheim Museum. Says Bilbao deputy mayor Ibon Areso, "We think culture will help combat the violence."

Over the years, public policies have influenced Spain's social structure, helping define what lifestyles are or are not present in the nation. Like many countries, Spain underwent a baby boom in the 1960s, abetted by state subsidies for families with children. But ever since that policy ended, Spain has had one of the lowest birthrates in Europe, 0.6 children per couple, resulting in fewer child-rearing lifestyles. A stagnant economy — its 12 percent unemployment rate in 1997 was one of the worst in Europe — has reduced the number of upscale lifestyles. The repressive regime of Franco prohibited the type of counterculture movement that produced Woodstock in the U.S. and the Summer of '68 in France. Nor does the MOSAIC Iberia system include clusters of aging leftists comparable to Single City Blues in the U.S. or Bohemian Melting Pot in the U.K.

In many ways, Spain is a traditional society, with half of all women homemakers, and children typically living at home until they're married. Less than 20 percent of all households have computers, and only a small fraction have Internet access. Consumers still shop daily at the local butcher or baker. Indeed, not until 1985 did Spain have its first shopping malls. In blue-collar neighborhoods in Madrid, stores still specialize in selling only milk, honey, or chicken. Frozen food is considered a progressive purchase; low-cholesterol products are a foreign concept.

But these attitudes are slowly beginning to change. Over the past two decades, Spain has democratized its political system and opened up its economy. Consumers now buy a third of their groceries at hypermarkets, and the most popular shopping time is from five P.M. to ten P.M., when half-off sales are featured. Cable TV finally arrived in the fall of 1997, though the vast majority of residents still make do with six woeful channels and precious few programming choices. On a typical night, the offerings may include

Spain has had one of the lowest birthrates in Europe, 0.6 children per couple, resulting in fewer child-rearing lifestyles.

one soccer game, two talk shows, a poorly dubbed Gary Cooper movie, and a documentary on retired soccer players reminiscing about their glory days. (Soccer shows accounted for all of Spain's top twenty programs in 1994.) The nightly lineup often features an odd assortment of American shows dubbed in Spanish: *Beverly Hills 90210, Melrose Place, Home Improvement,* and *Hangin' with Mr. Cooper.* Still a mass-market medium, Spanish TV airs commercials during a single program that shift jarringly from laundry detergent to cellular phones to sports cars. When cable television first became available in Spain, experts predicted 35,000 customers a month would sign up for the new service. In fact, 135,000 households requested cable in the first month alone.

Among Spain's wealthiest citizens, prestige means living in the centers of big cities where the sports stadiums and chic shops are located; Madrid actually has a higher proportion of upscale neighborhoods than London. The nation's richest residents tend to live in historic districts classified Classic Bourgeoisie Neighbourhoods. They own big flats and vacation homes, drive luxury cars, and use financial services at high rates. When the public treasury in Spain wanted to sell stocks and bonds, it tailored its messages to the types of callers who'd responded to a free phone number for information. For a rural type, skeptical farmers worried about the weather and their crops, the theme was reassuring: "Be confident in the public treasury. It's as secure as a bank." In contrast, the elite in Classic Bourgeoisie Neighbourhoods were told, "Be happy; you've made a good choice."

Raquel Roch, who lives in the Retiro Park section of Madrid, inherited from her grandfather the apartment building where her family resides. "Most of the people who live here have inherited property from their families," she explains through an interpreter. The thirty-nine-year-old property manager estimates that her flat, with its high ceilings, chandeliers, and columned dining room, is worth $700,000. Roch has filled her apartment with nineteenth-century bureaus and hutches in dark mahogany and oak, and she spends her free time refurbishing antique furniture and attending auctions. Her apartment building's greatest asset is its location, she says, so close to shops, offices, and the park where she takes her kids to romp. But lately, historic buildings like hers have been converted into offices, and she's noticed fewer people on the streets at night.

For the intelligentsia in Spain's Classic Bourgeoisie Neighbourhoods, life is different from that of other elite Europeans. Technological innovations play a lesser role: Roch has no computer in her home, and she watches little television, preferring to read novels. She's working on a master's degree in environmental education, but while other educated women may be nutritionally conscious, she boasts, "I don't buy food that is low in anything. We eat a lot of milk, cheese, and yogurt, as well as meat — normal food." Cigarette smoking, barely tolerated among the educated Americans, is openly enjoyed in the Roch home. Hearing that U.S. laws ban smoking in public buildings, bars, and restaurants, she shakes her head dismissively. "How horrible," she exclaims. "How do people stand it?"

In big cities like Madrid, many blue-collar residents were born in farming villages but, over the last two decades, moved to the city for work.

In big cities like Madrid, many blue-collar residents were born in farming villages but, over the last two decades, moved to the city for work. Still, they long for their rural past. In bars in Carabanchel, a working-class section of Madrid classified Modest Manual Workers, pictures of the owner's hometown are hung next to the de rigueur bullfighting posters. In the three-bedroom flat of Angela Manteca and Juan Azcona, their prized possessions are family heirlooms from their childhood — a milking pail and a clay jug — as well as a framed rural landscape that on closer inspection turns out to be a jigsaw puzzle. "I put it together," says Azcona, a stocky forty-five-year-old, "because it reminds me of home."

In areas filled with Modest Manual Workers, residents face an uncertain economic future. Manteca is a hospital housekeeper, Azcona recently lost his job as a salesman for a food supply company, and their neighbors work as policemen and taxi drivers. "Most of the people in the neighborhood work; they just don't have careers," says Azcona. They do have enough money to own a VCR, fax, and TV, and Manteca watches game shows during the days that she's not working. "They teach us a little bit about everything," she says, explaining why the family set is on four or five hours a day. She and her husband complain about high unemployment and poor job prospects for their twenty-three-year-old son, who is living at home while attending technical school. "There's a saying around here that money doesn't buy happiness," says Azcona, "but if that's the case then I don't want to be happy."

Those Spaniards who remained in their country villages are witnessing a transformation. In Moralzarzal, a small town classified Tractors & Tradition an hour outside of Madrid, the landscape is dotted with poor dairy and cattle farms. But in the center of town, stucco town houses are going up — the new weekend getaways for upscale city dwellers. In the last five years, the population has doubled to 4,000 residents. A formerly vacant corner of town holds sixty new houses, many valued at $85,000 — far more than the typical brick row house where residents still heat their homes and cook their food with wood stoves. "We need the money that the people bring," concedes Justo Garcia, the twenty-four-year-old owner of Bar El Ladrillo. "But it bothers me that they're destroying the prairie and the nature nearby."

To longtime resident Miguel Angel Alonso, a forty-one-year-old construction worker, the old ways are disappearing. A grizzled, burly man who enjoys a beer and sausage for breakfast at the local bar, he describes Moralzarzal as a quiet town that used to have no worries. The kids grew up and went to technical schools or worked nearby. Most of the local farmers had second jobs to make ends meet, or stayed at home and watched TV all night. For vacations, they'd have someone watch their cows and head to the Spanish coast. But the migration of city dwellers to the countryside has changed the sleepy community. Now residents are fighting over land and accusing each other of selling out to developers. "We're no longer a village," says Alonso. "We're almost a city."

Across Europe, suburban developments are luring people from the city centers into formerly green space. Low-density areas are filling up for the same reason as in the U.S.: Cheaper housing is attracting retirees and young families who seek a slower pace and better schools, new roads have made rural areas accessible to commuters, and inner-city crime is a far-off problem. At the same time, many chain stores are leaving the cities and following this suburban population boom.

For companies doing business in Spain's emerging markets, the shift in lifestyles has meant having to throw out old business plans. In Madrid, a fast-food chain called A Hueva ("To Egg") was launched more than a decade ago using McDonald's as its business model. It quickly opened a dozen 150-seat outlets in high-rent districts in the city center, catering to office workers who'd eat in or take out three-course meals during their traditional two-hour lunch breaks. A home-style meal of soup, chicken, dessert, and a soft drink cost about eight dollars. The concept was an immediate hit, and revenues grew by 15 percent a year.

But in 1992, sales slowed and then dropped 20 percent annually for the next four years. With shorter lunch breaks starting to

Hot Videos in Spain

With the lack of television choices in
Spain — until 1997, the country had
no cable TV and only six broadcast
channels — videos are a big business.
Fifty-five percent of all Spaniards own
VCRs, and video stores like Blockbuster
are found throughout metro areas. Contrary to the expectations of research
analysts that videos would be most popular in affluent in-town neighborhoods,
Blockbuster found its biggest audience
among economically diverse families on
the urban fringe.

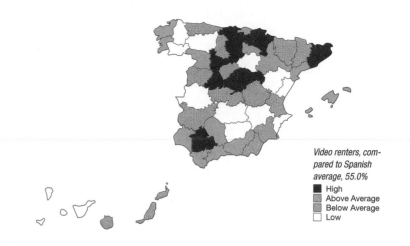

Video renters, com-
pared to Spanish
average, 55.0%
■ High
■ Above Average
▨ Below Average
□ Low

Top Spanish MOSAIC Clusters   Families in New Industrial Towns / Rural Types Close to Industry / Urban Elites / Families from the 1980s Boom /
Urban Periphery Senior Clerks
Top Spanish Markets   Alava / Madrid / Guipúzcoa / Navarra / Cantabria

(Sources: Spanish MOSAIC, Experian MOSAIC Iberia)

take hold as companies modeled their schedules after British and
American workdays, A Hueva's business plan became outdated.
Company officials tried to halt the slide by opening outlets in supermarkets, encouraging shoppers to get their takeout as they
picked up groceries. But people had trouble balancing trays atop
their shopping carts, and the idea was dropped. At the chain's
fourteen restaurants, sales dove 70 percent in 1996.

To stem the flow of red ink, Campofrio, the food distribution
conglomerate that owns the chain, hired Gustavo Durán, a polished thirty-four-year-old marketing whiz with prior experience at
Kentucky Fried Chicken. After transforming the chain into a
phone-in, take-out business, the new company director set his
sights on his chief competitor, Telepizza, a home-delivery success
with 220 outlets. Durán was convinced that A Huevo could best
that company by offering "ten families" of products — such as
hamburgers, tortillas, chicken, sandwiches, Tex-Mex dishes, *and*
pizza. For the next four months, he conducted tests at four stores,
mailing 10,000 brochures weekly to each outlet's trading area,
then analyzing the orders of 7,000 customers. The results revealed
some basic rules of operation: The company needed at least

50,000 households in a store's trading area to succeed, and the marketing plan required 10,000 menus mailed out each week. At that pace, Durán figured a new store would need eleven months to break even.

But when two new A Huevos opened in distinctly different neighborhoods on the same day, Durán quickly realized where the chain's greatest potential was to be found. In an upscale section of Madrid called Santa Gria, filled with Classic Bourgeoisie Neighbourhoods and Urban Elites, one outlet reported a customer base of 700 regulars. In a far less affluent suburb called Alcoverda, with its Metropolitan Manual Workers and Families in New Industrial Towns lifestyles, the store boasted 2,000 regular customers. "In these homes, both parents worked," Durán explains in impeccable English. "They didn't have a domestic to cook their meals and go shopping. So they didn't have a refrigerator full of food. They arrived late from work to their bedroom suburbs, and they didn't want to cook." Whereas receipts dropped off during soccer matches at the in-town stores, they jumped 44 percent in the new suburban shops.

Based on the cluster information, A Hueva reinvented itself yet again, changing its name to Chef Line in 1997 and rapidly expanding by opening a new store a week in Spain's growing suburban areas. All the new locations mimicked the winning formula of the Alcoverda shop, responding to the new economic realities in Spain: shorter lunch breaks for office workers and working couples living in far-out suburbs. "It's difficult to compete with someone's wife," Durán notes, "so we push à la carte fun food." Today, the Santa Gria store has closed, but Durán is bullish on the future of Chef Line in Spain and has even started expanding to Portugal and South America. With the suburbs' lower lease rates, the new stores are reaching their break-even point in five, not eleven, months. And like other emerging consumer societies, Spain exhibits a drive to catch up with its developed European neighbors that will certainly result in more suburban lifestyles craving more take-out meals.

"The future," as Durán puts it, "is in enjoying the home." It's a refrain being echoed throughout a resurgent Spain, and one that increasingly unites Spanish consumers with those of other European nations. In a world without borders, working couples from the suburbs cope with long hours and draining commutes the same way: They dial up a pizza.

6 **LIVING** IN THE **GLOBAL VILLAGE**

*It's a small world, after all. It's a
small, small world.*
— Richard M. Sherman
and Robert B. Sherman

When culture crosses borders

On a crowded stage shimmering with spotlights and vibrating with
the buzz of electric guitars, a nine-piece band tears into a song
called "Thunder." The music recalls 1970s rock, a meld of soaring
guitars, thumping bass, and feel-good vocals, all wrapped in a slick
corporate production. Band members shake their long hair to the
beat and dance across the stage wearing an assortment of colorful,
hippieish costumes: puffy tunics, granny dresses, and embroi-
dered vests in paisley patterns. Seated in the front row of the audience, a knot of preteen girls screams nonstop, the same tearful
ecstasy the Beatles might have induced in their mothers three
decades earlier.

The band on stage is the Kelly Family, and if you haven't heard
of them, you're not alone. According to some music critics, the
Kellys may be the world's most popular rock band still unknown in
North America. Based in Cologne, Germany, the family of nine
children of an Irish American musician began singing for tips on
European street corners in 1976, and gradually they worked their
way up to larger, indoor venues. Today, the multilingual Kellys,
ranging in age from sixteen to thirty-four, perform two hundred
concerts a year, routinely in 100,000-seat stadiums. In the last
decade, they've sold 12 million records on their way to earning
$100 million and a 100,000-member fan club complete with
groupies who camp out in parking lots wherever the family is playing. Their sugary brand of rock — "Imagine the Grateful Dead
meets Disney," one music executive puts it — has made them teen
idols in Asia and Europe, now the world's largest market for
recorded music.

But it's their marketing savvy, pushing their sixteen albums, eleven videos, and wardrobe of T-shirts through mail-order catalogs, that has kept them on top of the world. When the Kelly Family finally decided to invade America, however, they recognized that success would require more than standard marketing tactics. In 1996, they hired Robert Wilson, vice president of the Nashville marketing company Wilson & Associates, to help introduce them to U.S. audiences. "Theirs was not a story easily told," Wilson explains. "They didn't want to come to America and start playing in small venues to work their way up. And they didn't want to release a record on an American label, because we knew the snobs at the record label would turn up their noses at them for being uncool." Wilson settled on a novel approach: Air a cable television infomercial in selected markets to drum up interest in an eventual concert tour.

But which cable markets would be most receptive to a Kelly Family concert? What kind of Americans would latch on to an unknown, retro rock group with an Irish name, and a German home? "Their Dad said, 'Go to Boston, where the Irish are,'" recalls Wilson, a shaggy-haired forty-year-old with a languid Southern drawl. "But we weren't sure. We just knew that we didn't want to start in New York or Los Angeles because we knew that we'd get killed there."

Wilson knew about U.S. lifestyle clusters from his fifteen-year stint with a billboard advertising company. This time, he turned to the Global MOSAIC system for help in correlating the Kellys' German fans with their likely U.S. counterparts. A cluster analysis using the German MOSAIC system showed that the highest concentration of Kelly fan club members lived in diverse neighborhood types like Classic Rural Families, Young and Prosperous Urban Families, and Older Villagers in Older Houses — "honest workers" is how father Dan Kelly likes to describe his kids' audiences. When those lifestyles were translated into the Global MOSAIC clusters, the five types with the greatest number of Kelly Family fans turned out to be two urban clusters (Old Wealth and Career Focused Materialists), two rural ones (Farming Town Communities and Agrarian Heartland), and a cluster of retirement villages called Greys, Blue Sea & Mountain. Wilson then ranked all the media markets in America according to their concentration of those five Global MOSAIC clusters and sorted out only those metro areas with at least 200,000 people to ensure a sizable base. The

The five Global MOSAIC types with the greatest number of Kelly Family fans turned out to be two urban clusters, two rural ones, and a cluster of retirement villages.

Global Fans of an Irish Rock Band

A global cluster system allows businesses to identify residents of the same lifestyle type anywhere in the world. When a German-based Irish rock band called the Kelly Family wanted to tour the U.S., organizers first classified members of the band's German fan club by Global MOSAIC cluster and found they tended to live in regionally important midsized cities. Then marketers ranked U.S. markets with high concentrations of the same clusters and targeted their promotion campaign there.

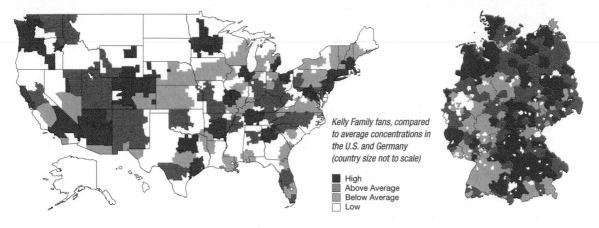

Kelly Family fans, compared to average concentrations in the U.S. and Germany (country size not to scale)

- High
- Above Average
- Below Average
- Low

Top Global MOSAIC Clusters Agrarian Heartlands / Career Focused Materialists / Farming Town Communities /
Greys, Blue Sea & Mountain / Old Wealth
Top U.S. Media Markets Minneapolis, Minnesota / Seattle, Washington / Dallas, Texas / Nashville, Tennessee / Boston, Massachusetts
Top German County Markets Unteraligäu / Bernkastel-Wittlich / Hildburghausen / Cloppenburg / Donau-Ries

(Sources: Global MOSAIC, Experian Micromarketing, Microm Micromarketing-Systeme und Consult GmbH)

analysis identified markets such as Minneapolis, Nashville, Seattle, and — much to the family's relief — Boston. Wilson now knew where to buy time for his thirty-minute infomercial.

In mid-1997, the Kelly invasion began. A slickly produced montage of concert footage, documentary clips, and profiles of the Kelly Family began airing in the targeted markets. It wasn't long before American residents of Old Wealth and Agrarian Heartland clusters were listening to Kelly recordings, ordering Kelly T-shirts, and inquiring about concert dates. Wilson and the Kellys were pleased with the promotion. They had spent about $400,000 to produce and roll out the infomercial, and by the end of the year they'd recouped about half that in tape and CD sales. Just as important, the campaign had netted some 80,000 names and addresses of Americans who'd either made a purchase or requested a low-cost promotional video of the band. From past experience, Dan Kelly has estimated that every database name is worth forty dollars in future sales of tapes and T-shirts. And the increased awareness would bode well for the Kellys when they finally did tour America or their albums began appearing on the shelves of national chains like Wal-Mart or Kmart. After all, it never hurts to have a display declaring "As Seen on TV."

The Global MOSAIC system shows that the honest workers who love the Kelly Family in Germany can also be located in the United States with astonishing accuracy. In fact, the Kelly Family can find potential fans just about anywhere in the world where geodemographic systems have been developed, including Spain, Peru, and South Africa. "It's a small world and getting smaller," Wilson observes. "People are basically the same when it comes to music or cars or other products. The only difference is language."

Parallel universes

A generation ago, Marshall McLuhan coined the term "global village" to describe a world where nations have become increasingly interdependent. What McLuhan could not have foreseen is how rising consumerism and falling trade barriers have so erased cultural differences that our global village now looks more like a cookie-cutter megamall straddling borders. As individual cluster systems have shown, each country has its own parochial and idiosyncratic lifestyles that evolved from its unique mix of geography, history, and demographics: Provincial Shiftworkers, a Belgian cluster of downscale textile workers in semidetached housing, would never be mistaken for any lifestyle in Sweden, where rural retired mineworkers belong to a one-of-a-kind cluster called Mail Order & Mining. That said, nearly every country is home to neighborhoods of old-money flats and new family suburbs, working-class rural villages and waterfront retirement areas. And the consuming patterns of each lifestyle tend to be the same throughout the world: Whether residents of the same cluster live in Italy or Australia, they tend to drive the same kinds of cars, enjoy the same kinds of entertainment, and worry about the same kinds of political issues.

College kids with Eurail passes may have always known as much, but these observations weren't measurable until 1996, when Experian went beyond its network of single-country cluster systems and launched Global MOSAIC, which now includes fourteen common lifestyle types found in nineteen countries in North America, Europe, Africa, Asia, and South America. Developed in

Whether residents of the same cluster live in Italy or Australia, they tend to drive the same kinds of cars, enjoy the same kinds of entertainment, and worry about the same kinds of political issues.

Nottingham, England, Global MOSAIC is based on two central ideas. First, the clustering principle is universal — that is, people with similar demographics and lifestyles tend to live together regardless of what country they live in. Second, cities throughout the world tend to share common residential patterns, whether the setting is Boston, Barcelona, or Bonn.

Drawing on the age, family status, urbanization, and income of residents, Global MOSAIC shows that every country has its exclusive enclaves of Career Focused Materialists, its immigrant-filled ghettos described as Inner City Melting Pot, and its bedroom suburbs filled with Midscale Metro Office Workers. The richest cluster, Old Wealth, consists of well-established urban neighborhoods where corporate managers and small-business owners have a culture of restrained luxury. The bottom of the lifestyle ladder, Shack & Shanty, is found in the impoverished villages of Third World economies, where low-income consumers struggle to achieve a subsistence lifestyle in poorly built housing. Each Global MOSAIC cluster has its own demographic characteristics, consumer preferences, and psychological motivations — just like the national cluster systems.

Behind this clustered-world view is a nexus of several social, technological, and business megatrends. Advances in communications technologies have created instant global demand for products. CNN can be watched in two hundred countries. Web sites and virtual malls on the Internet allow small companies into the marketplace without "brick and mortar" stores or large capital outlays. The increasing globalization of multinational brands is helping to create common tastes in food, products, and media. In 1996, more than fifty different U.S. retailers had a major European presence: the Gap with 71 stores, Levi Strauss with 278 locations, and Blockbuster Video with a whopping 764 outlets. McDonald's earns half of its total receipts from overseas sales — $15.4 billion in 1997 alone, including a two-dollar Maharajah Mac made of lamb sold in Delhi.

The net effect of these globalizing forces is the creation of similar desires and cookie-cutter stores everywhere on the planet. These days, a shopping mall in upscale Bal Harbour, Florida, has more in common with one in Madrid's Retiro Park than its suburban Miami counterpart a few miles away in Sunny Isles: the same Gucci and Chanel stores, identical polished marble and glass fittings, the same diamond-studded clientele. The poor miners in

Lifestyles of the Global Village

The Global MOSAIC system classifies neighborhoods in 19 countries into 14 common lifestyles. Below are the names and descriptions of those clusters, along with the countries that are part of the Global MOSAIC network.

Old Wealth — Affluent metro sophisticates who prefer premium products and conservative ideas.

Career Focused Materialists — Upscale suburban families who are heavy users of credit, early adopters of technology, and prime followers of leisure pursuits.

Educated Cosmopolitans — Young urban professionals who enjoy nightlife, diverse cultures, and alternative lifestyles.

Midscale Metro Office Workers — Middle-class suburban commuters who live in mortgaged houses, are future-oriented in their purchases, and seek value for their money.

Farming Town Communities — Remote towns of midscale families whose ideas and lifestyles are influenced by local networks of friends, shopkeepers, and social groups.

Greys, Blue Sea & Mountain — Scenic areas with a service economy catering to vacationing tourists and well-off retirees.

Inner City Melting Pot — A downscale mix of urban neighborhoods with a high concentration of immigrants and foreign-born singles and families.

Agrarian Heartlands — Remote agricultural areas where families tend to be traditional, self-reliant, and dependent on the land.

Blue Collar Self Sufficiency — Working-class families in booming areas who have parlayed manual skills into middle-class, materialistic lifestyles.

Lower Income Elderly — Downscale retirees living in low-density, sometimes government-owned housing, with few children, low mobility rates, and relatively little consumer spending.

Hardened Dependency — Inner-city areas with a high rate of unemployed residents, welfare recipients, elderly poor, and single-parent families struggling at basic levels of survival.

De-Industrial Legacy — Very poor industrial areas where craft workers retain old-fashioned tastes in food, clothing, and furnishings.

Shack & Shanty — Impoverished villages concentrated in Third World countries that are home to indigenous people in poorly built housing who retain rural, traditional lifestyles.

Non-Family Residences — Institutional residences like college dormitories, military barracks, or prisons where most food, housing, and furniture is purchased by the institution.

Countries linked by the Global MOSAIC network: United States, Canada, Belgium, Great Britain, Northern Ireland, Ireland, France, Spain, Denmark, Norway, Sweden, Finland, Germany, Netherlands, South Africa, Australia, New Zealand, Greece, and Peru.

(Sources: Global MOSAIC, Experian Micromarketing)

West Virginia would feel at home in the industrial neighborhoods of Bilbao, Spain, and Nokpink, Sweden. And though there may be some housing differences — the miners in West Virginia live in country shacks and those in South Wales live in terraced houses — their consumer patterns and attitudes are similar. Show up at a local bar at breakfast and you'll see the same rugged men downing glasses of beer with whiskey chasers and complaining about big government as one factory shift ends and another begins.

"There are neighborhoods in Manhattan that are more similar to ones in Milan than in Brooklyn," observes Emily Eelkema, director of Experian's Global Micromarketing Division. "The yuppie on the Upper East Side of New York has more in common with a yuppie in Stockholm than with a downscale person in Brooklyn. The neighborhoods in Fargo, North Dakota, are very similar to Freisland in the Netherlands as well as Calabria in southern Italy. From a day-to-day perspective, their lifestyles, attitudes, motivations, and products are all very similar. They're more provincial and concerned with family and friends."

Exploring Global MOSAIC can shatter some long-held claims to nationalistic fame. Australians and New Zealanders often fight over which is the more progressive country, but the cluster system shows that New Zealand has more than twice as many residents classified in the two most upscale lifestyles, Career Focused Materialists and Educated Cosmopolitans — 20 percent compared to Australia's 9 percent. The French may pride themselves on their cultural sophistication, but nearly 30 percent of them still live in the remote, parochial clusters of Agrarian Heartlands and Farming Town Communities, with little link to the latest Parisian trends in fashion, arts, or philosophy. In the United States, by contrast, less than 9 percent of the population resides in those rural clusters.

The international clusters also serve as a practical guide to living in today's global village. For instance, Americans looking to retire abroad would do well to look up communities of Greys, Blue Sea & Mountain, a cluster of country villages and scenic resorts that cater to tourists and retirees. Whereas older people in Europe used to retire to urban areas by the sea — much like their American counterparts in Miami or Atlantic City — more are now settling down in pleasant countryside homes throughout Spain and France. They're doing so because pensions are providing them greater income, advances in medicine are allowing them to live independently well into their eighties, and the picturesque villages

Searching for Common Lifestyles

Every country has a unique lifestyle profile, as shown in the concentrations of five Global MOSAIC clusters in selected countries below. A company can find desirable areas for retirees by mapping the Greys, Blue Sea & Mountain cluster — and learn that Spain is a haven for well-off senior citizens. A beer manufacturer would do well to introduce a new lager in Great Britain before rolling it out across Europe.

Global MOSAIC Clusters	France	Germany	Great Britain	South Africa	Spain	U.S.
Agrarian Heartland	4%	14%	5%	5%	23%	2%
Greys, Blue Sea & Mountain	7%	6%	8%	0%	19%	3%
Midscale Metro Office Workers	6%	7%	15%	4%	7%	15%
Old Wealth	12%	16%	10%	2%	1%	9%
Shack & Shanty	0%	0%	0%	50%	0%	0%
Consumer Patterns						
Household savings rate	13%	12%	9%	NA	11%	4%
Credit card use	19%	17%	58%	8%	20%	59%
Own a computer	19%	18%	30%	1%	25%	35%
Attend movies	55%	31%	54%	16%	47%	53%
Smoke cigarettes	31%	33%	28%	28%	24%	27%
Drink beer	NA	32%	45%	33%	NA	30%
Belong to health club	3%	3%	3%	4%	7%	7%

(Sources: Global MOSAIC, Experian Micromarketing; EGM Survey; Simmons Market Research Bureau; Embassy of France. "NA" designation indicates no available data.)

of Greys, Blue Sea & Mountain typically come with affordable cottages. And their numbers are growing, especially in rustic Spain and northern France, where the opening of the Channel Tunnel has turned coastal villages into London's exurbia. For $100,000, one-third the cost of a vacation home in Britain, British retirees can snap up a French country house in a sleepy hamlet where the food and wine are cheap and plentiful.

As geodemographers admit, wealthy clusters are more similar from one country to the next than poor clusters. Mobility plays an important role in blurring country distinctions among the rich, and it stands to reason: Affluent people tend to travel the most — whether for business or pleasure — and they rub shoulders with their ilk at the same restaurants and beach resorts the world over. Similar views and consumption patterns are bound to emerge in these groups.

By contrast, residents of the world's poorer clusters are far more sedentary and tend to cling to their provincial ways. So while coal miners in Britain and Spain may share the same De-Industrial Legacy demographics, the sports they enjoy are different, as are the foods they buy — whether it's a tortilla in Bilbao or tripe in Lancashire. In Spain's industrial towns, blue-collar workers may stop at a bar for cheap brandy and coffee, while Britain's drinkers order up a pint of bitter. "These people are very different in their dress, eating habits, and behavior," says Experian director Richard Webber. "They're the least international. They're the last to pick up anything new and the least interested in going abroad." But don't be fooled by regional differences. Deep down, these cluster residents share the same values. They're politically conservative, resistant to change, and believe in a firm division of gender roles: the men in the pubs and the women in the home. These cluster cousins are simply unaware that they're living in parallel universes.

Whither the yuppie?

Consider the yuppies, those young, upwardly mobile professionals deified during the go-go 1980s for their trendsetting tastes and avid acquisition of grown-up toys. More than a subculture of the baby boomers, yuppies became a target group for pushing all manner of costly goods and services: Rolex watches, sushi-to-go restaurants, BMWs (called Beemers everywhere), and imported beers.

"The ad community blew up the concept of yuppie, so it became a self-fulfilling prophecy," says Jonathan Robbin, who left Claritas to found Bethesda, Maryland–based Ricercar Inc. "Because people consume by perception, if a person perceives himself to be a yuppie, he can act out the image. There's a great power in consensus."

Nowadays, the yuppie concept has reached the end of its life cycle in the U.S., and media attention has moved on to Generation X and the teenagers of the echo boom, sometimes called Generation Y. But yuppies are thriving abroad. Like other icons of American culture — Madonna, Rollerblades, and Sylvester Stallone movies among them — yuppiedom has become a booming worldwide import. In Europe, yuppies are seen as the educated elite from the top schools in Oxford and Heidelberg. They're the white-collar professionals who work for international companies. And they're the earliest adopters of imported products and ideas. In Italy, yuppies have taken up jogging in neon-colored Gore-Tex

Like other icons of American culture — Madonna, Rollerblades, and Sylvester Stallone movies among them — yuppiedom has become a booming worldwide import.

outfits that make them look like outer-space insects. In Argentina, they're the hip fans of Robert Johnson who line up at Buenos Aires' trendy blues clubs. In Japan, used Adidas and tattered jeans have become a sign of yuppie status. Denim jeans fished out of Goodwill depositories in the U.S. now fetch $100 a pair in Tokyo boutiques.

Late Night with David Letterman, one of the most popular yuppie television shows, has spawned talk-show imitators from Australia to Slovakia, complete with Dave clones who use deadpan humor and skits that employ crew members. In Russia, the set of the talk show *Good Evening* features a nighttime vista of Moscow copped from Letterman's New York skyline. In Argentina, the host of *Duro de Acostar* cracks up a bandleader while presenting a Letterman-esque "Top 5" list on a current event. Guests on an Australian Letterman rip-off used to be prepped by producers with the advice, "Just pretend you're on the Letterman show." And while Letterman may be getting thrashed in the ratings game at home by Jay Leno and Ted Koppel, the overseas wanna-bes are the hottest shows since *Baywatch* went into international syndication. In terms of values and lifestyles, their yuppie audiences appreciate the same wry expressions and slicing hand gestures no matter the thievery, no matter where their TV set is located. They simply relate to a universal Letterman body language.

That language tends to be spoken in Educated Cosmopolitans, the Global MOSAIC cluster with the highest concentration of yuppies. Found in large cities and university towns, these well-informed individuals are dispersed in varying concentrations throughout the world: 8 percent of Norwegians and 4 percent of Australians are classified as Educated Cosmopolitans. And their proportion affects the receptivity to foreign goods and ideas in their respective countries. With jobs in the media, arts, and politics, Educated Cosmopolitans are avid readers of newspapers and magazines, frequenters of restaurants and urban entertainment, and champions of new ideas and experiences — not unlike MOSAIC's Chattering Classes in Britain and Urban Brahmins in America. Drawn to the diversity and vitality of the city, Educated Cosmopolitans are more likely than any other cluster to pursue alternative lifestyles (read: gays, unmarried couples, and group households). And they tend to pursue leisure activities like golf and tennis that are costly, exclusive, and desirable when enjoyed in a financially frivolous setting. Ask British yuppies where they

The Yuppie Index

Yuppies can be found the world over, but they're not present in equal proportions in all countries. Educated Cosmopolitans, the Global MOSAIC cluster with the highest concentration of young, upwardly mobile, urban professionals, plays a special role in every country: Its residents are the first consumers to accept new products and ideas, spreading the globalization of lifestyles.

Percent of Households

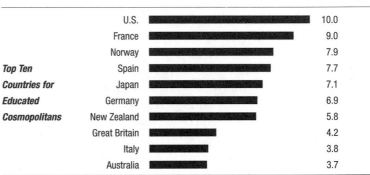

		Percent of Households
	U.S.	10.0
	France	9.0
	Norway	7.9
Top Ten	Spain	7.7
Countries for	Japan	7.1
Educated	Germany	6.9
Cosmopolitans	New Zealand	5.8
	Great Britain	4.2
	Italy	3.8
	Australia	3.7

(Sources: Global MOSAIC, Experian Micromarketing)

like to vacation and the response is "Skiing in Aspen." Ask a Spanish yuppie (pronounced "joopie") the same question and the response needs no translation: "Skiing in Aspen."

Wherever they're found — in neighborhoods like the Clifton section of Bristol, England, or the Georgetown enclave of Washington, D.C. — Educated Cosmopolitans share the same cares and concerns. In both Clifton and Georgetown, the complaints are the same: not enough parking, too many uncurbed dogs, an overload of noisy beer drinkers from the nearby colleges, and a shortage of decent grocery stores. The housing stock is similar — three-story stone and brick town houses with elaborate grillwork, monitored by architectural boards that prohibit garish paint jobs and plastic flamingos. The streets and private driveways are lined with the same models of Jaguars, BMWs, and sport-utility vehicles. The commercial base is founded on chic boutiques, wine shops, and pricey restaurants rather than franchises. At the Clifton library, the hottest books are popular fiction by Stephen King, Dean Koontz, and Danielle Steele — just like at the Georgetown library. And both communities have charitable streaks, supporting such philanthropic concerns as the Junior League in Georgetown and

Oxfam in Clifton. Clifton librarian Lone Howell sports a "Friends of Greenpeace" bumper sticker on her car. "Politically," she says, "liberals have everyone's sympathies."

A visitor need go no farther than Clifton's Brown's Bar to find the universal yuppie type in full regalia. Contrary to the stereotypical image of British pubs, Brown's is no dark, draft-filled haven for dart throwers and working-class heroes downing pints of Guinness drawn by local lasses. At Brown's, male bartenders sporting bleached hair and earrings serve mostly bottled beer from Mexico, Germany, and the U.S., of all places. Costing four dollars a bottle, Budweiser and Rolling Rock are considered premium brews. The first drink listed on the cocktails blackboard is a Long Island Iced Tea. And the decor is basic California fern bar, with high ceilings, palm fronds, and globe light fixtures — "A continental bar with pretensions of English colonialism," observes pianist Mauro Montuschi, who plays a Bobby Short–style repertoire of American jazz standards like "Ain't Misbehavin'" and "Jeepers Creepers."

More than the decor, it's the crowd that sets Brown's Bar apart from the typical British pub. With the stiff cost of a bottle beer, the patrons are an upscale group of twenty- and thirty-year-olds in natty suits and pressed chinos who've come to be seen. Most dispense with glasses just so they can march around showing off the labels on their beer bottles. The talk is of trips to Spain, divorcing friends, where to find white designer jeans, the sorry state of the theater. Occasionally, students from the University of Bristol show up in flannel shirts and faded jeans, propping cell phones alongside their Jack Daniel's and Cokes.

Except for the accents, the same scene is repeated almost nightly in bars like Clyde's or Nathan's or Champions in the heart of Georgetown.

Naturally, every country has its own spin on the universal yuppie model. In Japan, many young single men escape the high rents by living in drab company-subsidized dormitories during the week and commuting to their parents' homes on weekends (one reason nearly 40 percent of Japanese women twenty-five to twenty-nine years of age are still single). In Spain, where young single men and women often live with their parents until marriage, many yuppies still sleep in the bedrooms where they spent their toddler years. Their consuming patterns are sometimes skewed in surveys because middle-aged mothers buy their food or their clothes. José González, a twenty-eight-year-old highway contractor and M.B.A.

In Japan, many young single men escape the high rents by living in drab company-subsidized dormitories during the week and commuting to their parents' homes on weekends (one reason nearly 40 percent of Japanese women twenty-five to twenty-nine years of age are still single).

graduate, still lives with his grandmother and two sisters in the central Madrid apartment he lived in when he attended college. Like his cluster cousins abroad, he drives a snappy subcompact, plays tennis, and meets his friends for barhopping on Saturday nights. But a relatively low salary keeps him living with his family, sleeping amid the heavy antique furniture and coming home to meals prepared by his grandmother's cook. If he and a date want a romantic night together, they do what most yuppies do in Madrid. "We go to a hotel," he explains. "Living with my grandmother may seem strange to foreigners, but I'm more or less like all my friends."

Because of their role as cultural bridges, the yuppie clusters are critical to the globalization of culture and lifestyles. As big consumers of media who are open to new experiences and ideas, yuppies are more aware of trends in their own countries and abroad. Their relatively high rate of computer and Internet activity provides them access to ideas from all over the world. Their tendency to travel puts them in close contact with others who share similar trendsetting urges. And they have the money to pay for a bottle of Absolut vodka or a pager featuring a running stock ticker. But why yuppies abroad glom on to certain products (cell phones, Starbucks frappacino, Beemers) and not others (pickup trucks, Velveeta cheese, video games) is still something of a mystery that multinational companies are trying to solve.

Dr. Richard Fenker, a mathematician who directs a Fort Worth, Texas–based marketing company called Tangram, believes that global yuppies develop shared interests in a way analogous to infants' learning common language structures at certain points in their development. "I see a kind of synchronicity taking place among yuppies all around the world," he explains. "There's an unconscious knowledge base that's creating more common products and more common tastes. We're moving more toward a group mind." Fenker, who teaches psychology at Texas Christian University, believes that the Internet is encouraging this convergence, spreading ideas around the global market to receptive consumers. "There was an American consensus of what a yuppie was twenty years ago. Now there's an international sense of yuppieism that's more common across the world."

A generation ago, countries in the throes of political upheaval blamed American imperialism for their troubles. But as dictatorships and Communist regimes have fallen in Europe and South

America, the cries of "Yankee, go home" have faded. Rising incomes and greater access to goods and information are breeding consumerism and a passion for everything stamped "U.S.A." And it's not just Russians lining up for Whoppers or Londoners wearing Michael Jordan T-shirts. The U.S. produces over 40 percent of the TV programming in seventeen foreign markets. And American-style malls are popping up like mushrooms around the world; in Mexico, the man who created Minneapolis's Mall of America has built three million-square-foot shopping centers, anchored by U.S.-based JCPenney and Dillard's department stores. Major players like Kmart, Domino's Pizza, Arby's, and Sam's Club rack up impressive sales overseas. In 1997 alone, Wal-Mart made over $10 billion in foreign sales.

Why are foreign consumers suddenly finding things American cool? Jonathan Robbin's explanation is consumer envy. "Americans are world-class consumers. It's our favorite indoor sport," he says from a cluttered home office. "We're not slaves to the marketer. We don't act like lemmings marching to stores. And people from other countries respect our experience." The result is the continued expansion of American products abroad.

Of course, the downside of all this creeping Americanization is graceful boulevards in Madrid and Bonn punctuated by advertisements for Dunkin' Donuts and Burger King, and mediocre American sitcoms airing in Rome and Caracas. "Yuppies are a disease the world over," declares one shopkeeper in that yuppie haven of Bristol, England. In Vancouver, British Columbia, an anticonsumption group called the Media Foundation rails against an ailment it calls "affluenza," a spiritual and environmental disease brought on by American-style overconsumption. The organization has declared the day after Thanksgiving, traditionally the busiest shopping day for Americans, Buy Nothing Day. Its monthly magazine and web site fight the spreading consumer society and multinational commerce by celebrating home-grown businesses and consumers who pursue a simple life. Its organizers believe that American-style consumption results in social and environmental ills.

This anticonsumerist sentiment isn't limited to Vancouver. In every society, there are population segments that resist mass-marketed products: the poor who can't afford them; the rich who, preferring one-of-a-kind boutiques, ignore them; the isolated consumers who have no access to them; and the individualistic types who detest them. Many of the counterculture types inhabit

"Americans are world-class consumers. It's our favorite indoor sport," Jonathan Robbin says from a cluttered home office. "We're not slaves to the marketer. We don't act like lemmings marching to stores. And people from other countries respect our experience."

Global MOSAIC's Inner City Melting Pot cluster, with its diverse neighborhoods of immigrants and downscale singles, ramshackle row houses and health food eateries. In places like Toronto's funky Kensington Market, filled with hippie clothing shops, corner markets, and music clubs, locals have scrawled graffiti on walls with antiracist and antitobacco messages; cigarette company billboards, for example, have been repainted so the manufacturers look like murderers. "You won't find chains or cutesy shops here," says Bob Wilson, a thirty-five-year-old neighborhood activist and president of the Kensington Business Association. "There's an element of chaos here to keep out yuppie intruders." Wilson, who owns a laundromat that doubles as a rehearsal site for several punk rock bands, describes his neighbors as a mix of "artists, anarchists, and squatters" who resent any sign of encroaching gentrification. "Anyone who has an urge to rebel gravitates to this area," he explains. "They're attracted to the anticorporation feel."

Yet such views remain a minority in a world where Polish consumers are crying out for washing machines and credit card balances are at an all-time high in South Africa. Wilson's anticonsumerism calls in Toronto are drowned out by the din of cash registers. Despite its many drawbacks, consumerism — whether it's of Big Macs or Rollerblades — creates common experiences and connects people around the world. Given humanity's propensity for killing each other over small cultural differences, the opportunity to come together in the global marketplace is more appealing than battling each other with tanks. Today's generation of political leaders might adopt as its slogan "All we are saying is give consumerism a chance."

The final marketing frontier

One day, most products and services will be marketed around the world like Germany's Kelly Family. As more and more companies seek customers beyond their home borders, they'll turn to global clusters to differentiate consumers, select business locations, and target advertising — and not just to acquisitive Educated Cosmopolitans. When the Country Music Association recently went looking to expand its audience for country music TV into foreign markets, it found that the highest concentration of U.S. fans lived in the Global MOSAIC clusters of Farming Town Communities and Blue Collar Self Sufficiency. After charting these clusters in other countries, the group found the best markets for Garth Brooks and

Reba McEntire to be in Ireland, Spain, and Portugal. Experian calls this process "glocalization: global branding with local implementation."

The power of Global MOSAIC lies in its ability to identify cross-cultural similarities and each nation's cluster concentrations using a common currency of lifestyles. Knowing the prime consumers for premium red wine in one country, a company can attempt to replicate its popularity in another — provided there's a large enough cluster base. Career Focused Materialists, the global cluster with the highest marks for red wine drinkers, represents 15 percent of Belgian households but just 5 percent of Spanish households. Blue Collar Self Sufficiency households are more prevalent in Japan, at 17 percent, than in Germany, where only 2 percent of households belong to this cluster. The college dorm–size refrigerators that are found in the cramped homes of Japanese factory workers wouldn't cut it in Germany, with its larger kitchens, smaller blue-collar workforce, and higher expenditures on food and drink.

But international clusters have their limitations as marketing tools. Not all global brands are perceived the same way — nor do they permit identical advertising — across national boundaries. Indeed, the Global MOSAIC system sometimes provides insights into how dissimilarly the same product is viewed among consumers in different countries. For instance, Beemers are popular as an upscale suburban family car in Britain but are preferred more by affluent city couples and singles in Sweden. There, upscale suburbanites tend to drive big Volvos and regard BMWs as little cars for speed-driven guys; they have a low brand appeal. "The Global MOSAIC clusters let you see if your brand has a similar profile in each country," explains Experian's Richard Webber. "Maybe your product needs to be advertised differently because it appeals to quite different sorts of people."

But to date, relatively few organizations have used the Global MOSAIC system, and critics claim that with only fourteen clusters, Global MOSAIC's discriminatory power isn't strong enough to effectively distinguish a country's consumer niches. Even Webber concedes that Global MOSAIC doesn't help direct-mailers seeking population niches within neighborhoods. Every country has quirks of history and demographics that create a Fireplace Angels in Italy and a Mountain Farmers in Norway.

Despite these criticisms, competition in the global market-

Knowing the prime consumers for premium red wine in one country, a company can attempt to replicate its popularity in another — provided there's a large enough cluster base.

Garth Brooks on Irish Television?

When the Country Music Association wanted to globally market Country
Music Television, Experian Micromarketing used Global MOSAIC to show the
best markets abroad. In the U.S., where 13.0 percent of Americans watched
Country Music Television, the residents of three clusters — Agrarian Heartlands, Farming Town Communities and De-Industrial Legacy — were nearly
twice as likely to tune in. Abroad, Ireland had the highest percentage of those
clusters and the best chance of cheering country music TV.

Potential Audience Size

	U.S.	25.3%
	Ireland	19.8%
	Spain	18.0%
Top 10	Belgium	17.4%
Nations for	Sweden	17.3%
Country	Italy	17.0%
Music TV	Finland	17.0%
	Japan	16.8%
	Australia	16.6%
	France	16.4%

(Sources: Global MOSAIC, Experian Micromarketing)

place will compel businesses to accept the death of traditional
mass markets and embrace cluster-based international marketing.
The North American Free Trade Agreement, which eliminated tar-
iffs and border restrictions between the U.S., Mexico, and Canada,
has created a giant consumer market with more than 350 million
people and $6 trillion in economic activity. Meanwhile, the Euro-
pean Union has opened up fifteen European nations to a free-trade
zone and a common currency that will be implemented by 2002.
Despite nationalistic disagreements large and small, the forces of
trade and technology are driving countries toward greater integration. Consumer markets are thriving throughout the world, and
geodemographic companies have responded with expanded cluster systems. While Experian launches new cluster systems in Asia
and South America, Claritas is pushing ahead with its own models
across Europe, and Compusearch's parent company, The Polk
Company, has introduced its own American cluster system to compete with the other players on the Continent. As the calendar
moves into the twenty-first century, cluster systems are emerging

in Chile, China, Mexico, and India, reaching new consumers and revealing new insights on the international scene.

A century ago, Polish philologist Ludwig Zamenhof invented an artificial language called Esperanto that he hoped would become the world's lingua franca. It never happened. Though the Universal Esperanto Association meets biannually and its last convention drew more than a thousand enthusiasts from fifty-five countries, Esperanto remains an academic curiosity. But in fact, a universal language exists, and cluster systems like Global MOSAIC provide the vocabulary. With words like *rap, Coke,* and *Reebok* spoken around the world, with Russians eating pizza and Britons singing along to karaoke music, the universal clusters have become a common language throughout the world. And in the next century, cluster systems will continue to define how people live, dismantling territorial frontiers as they show our commonalities of behavior. As national boundaries continue to disappear, the global village will once and for all become a clustered world.

*We expect to eat and stay thin, to
be constantly on the move and ever
more neighborly . . . to revere God
and to be God.*
— Daniel J. Boorstin

Forget sex. Forget race, national origin, age, household composition, and wealth. The characteristic that defines and separates Americans more than any other is the cluster. From sea to shining sea, the clusters reflect the diverse patterns of how Americans live, what they buy, and where they share the same lifestyle with others around the country. Every household has been assigned to one of these clusters, and their tastes and attitudes have been predicted by census data, market research surveys, public opinion polls, and point-of-purchase receipts. According to cluster theory, people with similar demographics naturally gravitate to one another and share similar tastes in products, services, media, and homes — whether they live down the block or in another cluster community across the continent.

What follows are profiles of the sixty-two PRIZM clusters developed by Claritas for America's 275 million residents. The sources for the portraits are varied and authoritative: The demographic data is based on the latest statistics from the U.S. Census Bureau. The preferences for product and lifestyle information as well as radio and TV programs (current and syndicated) come from the giant market research companies, Mediamark Research Inc. and Simmons Market Research Bureau. Car and truck figures were compiled from motor vehicle registrations by The Polk Company. And the political and social issues information was derived from surveys conducted by NFO Research, Inc. Finally, to better understand the meaning behind the statistics, every profile comes with a map showing the concentration of cluster residents and a descriptive account of life in one of the cluster's neighborhoods — an archetypical community selected by computer from among U.S. census tracts (areas averaging 1,200 households). Individually, each of these sixty-two quintessential American lifestyles represents millions of people.

One warning: As sophisticated as the technology is at measuring neighborhood activities, there are many characteristics missed in this portrait-by-numbers. The clusters reveal little about the friendliness of an area, whether trees provide shade when someone walks a dog, if the children are happy. And the portraits may not exactly match every household in a neighborhood because the cluster system operates on the law of averages, providing tendencies and correlations for a group of households. What the cluster profiles do reveal is how people behave in the public realm: what they buy in stores, where they play after work, how they vote at the ballot box, and — more importantly — how they compare to others from different lifestyles.

Here, then, are snapshots from the front, America in all its diversity: from the top to the bottom of the socioeconomic ladder,* Blue Blood Estates to Southside City, SER (socioeconomic rank) 1 to SER 62. Better buckle up. You're in for a strange and wondrous ride.

*The socioeconomic ranking of clusters is not based strictly on median income but a composite score of affluence based on income, home value, and educational achievement.

SER 1

blue blood estates

0.8% of U.S. households

Primary age group: **35–54**

Median household income: **$113,000**

Median home value: **$452,000**

Thumbnail Demographics

elite suburban super-rich families

single-family housing

predominantly white and Asian households

college graduates

white-collar professionals

Politics

Predominant ideology: moderate Republican

1996 presidential vote: Bob Dole

Key issues: more military spending, eliminating
    affirmative action, pro abortion rights

Sample Neighborhoods

Potomac, Maryland 20854

Saddle River, New Jersey 07458

Winnetka, Illinois 60093

Old Westbury, New York 11568

Rolling Hills, California 90274

It's a world of million-dollar homes and manicured lawns, high-end cars and exclusive private schools. Blue Blood Estates, the nation's wealthiest lifestyle type, stands at the top of America's class ladder, a cluster of such desired addresses as Scarsdale, New York; Winnetka, Illinois; and Potomac, Maryland. Concentrated in the well-manicured suburbs of major cities, Blue Blood Estates is home to doctors, lawyers, and business executives as well as trust fund–supported families. With a median income of $113,000 — one in ten residents is a multimillionaire — these are not the frugal and inconspicuously wealthy entrepreneurs celebrated in the book *The Millionaire Next Door* by Thomas J. Stanley and William D. Danko. The residents of Blue Blood Estates are the well-heeled Americans who enjoy the embellishments of money — lavish homes, expensive clothes, luxury cars, and private club memberships — in a gilded suburban setting with others who share the same values.

A family-filled cluster, Blue Blood Estates prepares its children for a life of privilege. Youngsters attend private schools supplemented by pricey lessons in ballet, horseback riding, and ice skating. By the time they're sixteen, many possess credit cards, cellular phones, and sports cars. But growing up amid such affluence poses challenges, like peer pressure to keep up. "You'll go to the mall and a girlfriend will buy five pairs of shoes at a time," says a Potomac sixteen-year-old whose everyday life might resemble a scene from the

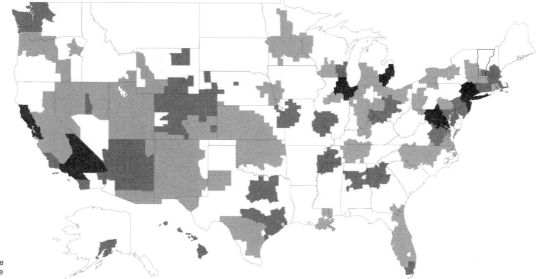

■ High
■ Above Average
■ Below Average
□ Low

country clubs   pita bread   *Wall Street Journal*   classical radio   Ferraris   first-class foreign travel

movie *Clueless.* As one longtime resident observes, "This is a nice place to visit — as long as you realize it's not the real world."

But Blue Blood Estates is the real world for more than 2.25 million Americans, who come for the expansive homes and stay for the exclusive setting. Half of all homes cost more than $452,000, not including all the interior decorator extras that are de rigueur. "People here want narcissistic bathrooms with fifty linear feet of closets and everything in marble and glass," says one real estate agent from Potomac. Privacy fanatics, many of these residents live behind security gates and tall shrubbery, discreetly exercising with personal trainers or working out in basement gyms and backyard swimming pools. "We live in a community of McMansions," says Michael Abelson, a forty-seven-year-old attorney, describing his imposing Potomac home, which his wife, Lyndsey, decorated with silk chairs and Lalique bowls. One neighbor observes, "You're envied if you have a live-in housekeeper who won't steal from you."

Though they may kick around in ratty jeans and sweats, Blue Bloods pull out the glitz for political fund-raisers, philanthropic dinners, and charity balls; a recent trend is taking courses in how to give away your money. Status can also be seen in their cars of choice: They are more than fourteen times as likely as average Americans to own Jaguars, Infinitis, and Ferraris. Shopping centers feature gourmet carryouts, Parisian boutiques, and book shops with window displays featuring titles like *Eating Well Is the Best Revenge.* For leisure, many Blue Blood Estates residents choose tennis because it offers a quick and competitive workout. "It's a cutthroat game," observes Potomac tennis pro Jeff Wilke. "Winning is the most important thing in this community."

Although Blue Blood Estates is America's most affluent lifestyle type, it is by no means one without challenges. Most residents must still work for a living, and work hard to afford their $7,000 monthly mortgage payments. "The phrase 'no money, no honey' applies to this community," says Potomac restaurateur Fritz Siegfried. And preserving their exclusive lifestyle is the chief concern of most residents. Politically, many are fiscal conservatives and social liberals who voted for Bob Dole in 1996. They tend to support tax reform, abortion rights, and gun control. Many have become increasingly tough on criminals and the homeless, given their preoccupation with security in their neighborhoods. Indeed, with so many homes connected to alarm systems, when one goes off, many neighbors assume it's an accident and pay little attention.

PREFERENCES

(index of 100 = U.S. average)

Lifestyle / Products

what's hot

country clubs 471

first-class foreign travel 323

tennis 317

investments > $50,000 316

Price Club 280

housekeepers 244

cellular phones 240

theatergoing 215

premium credit cards 191

charitable volunteering 145

what's not

Burger King 80

power tools 71

Medicare / Medicaid 68

satellite dishes 61

Kmart 58

chiropractors 56

freshwater fishing 47

weekly groceries < $50 44

veterans' clubs 38

baby food 38

Food / Drink

pita bread 261

imported wine 260

veal 178

imported cheese 159

Caffeine-Free Diet Coke 154

Post Grape-Nuts 152

Domino's pizza 147

egg substitute 141

fresh fish 140

soy sauce 131

Magazines / Newspapers

Wall Street Journal 607

Longevity 481

Architectural Digest 425

Fortune 424

Gourmet 322

Town & Country 285

Martha Stewart Living 267

Inc. 219

Time 218

National Geographic Travel 177

Television / Radio

classical radio 509

Masterpiece Theatre 258

Wall Street Week 240

pay-per-view concerts 225

Charles Grodin 214

Mystery 188

Face the Nation 176

Homicide 160

Nightline 150

Nova 127

Cars / Trucks

Ferraris 2146

Land Rovers 1816

Jaguars 1582

Infinitis 1455

Mercedes-Benzes 1359

Lexuses 1124

Saabs 1076

Dodge Vipers 1025

Volvos 987

Acura Legends 945

Backyard necessity:
private tennis court

SER 2
winner's circle

1.9% of U.S. households

Primary age group: **35–64**

Median household income: **$80,600**

Median home value: **$247,900**

Thumbnail Demographics

executive suburban families

single-family housing

predominantly white and Asian households

college graduates

white-collar professionals

Politics

Predominant ideology: moderate Republican

1996 presidential vote: Bob Dole

Key issues: improving the economy, reducing size
of government, pro environmental programs

Sample Neighborhoods

East Cherry Hill, New Jersey 08003

Birmingham, Michigan 48009

Lexington, Massachusetts 02173

Mercer Island, Washington 98040

Woodland Hills, California 91367

"A lot of people around here have careers you never heard of fifteen years ago," says Susan Bass Levin, mayor of Cherry Hill, New Jersey. It's an observation fitting Winner's Circle communities throughout the nation. The second most affluent cluster is home to a disproportionate number of executives in emerging fields of technology, consumer services, and pharmaceuticals — as well as more traditional doctors, lawyers, and stockbrokers. It's typically found in the new-money suburbs of major cities, dotted with parks, golf courses, and upscale malls. With a median income of $80,000, Winner's Circle residents are big spenders who like to travel, whether it's heading abroad at three times the national average or going out to eat, taking in a show or catching a pro basketball game at high rates. Their most popular consumer electronic device is the car phone.

In Winner's Circle, four out of five adults have gone to college, and they pursue leisure activities reflecting an educated populace: surfing the Internet, going to museums, and frequenting libraries. At the Cherry Hill Free Public Library, patrons check out not just books but works of art — prints by painters such as Matisse, Chagall, and Monet. A reference desk is cluttered with financial periodicals for local investors who are skilled in conducting their own research. There are three computers in the children's section — and nine in the adults' section — with Internet access on many of them. "People wear out the library here," says librarian Miranda Van Horn, who

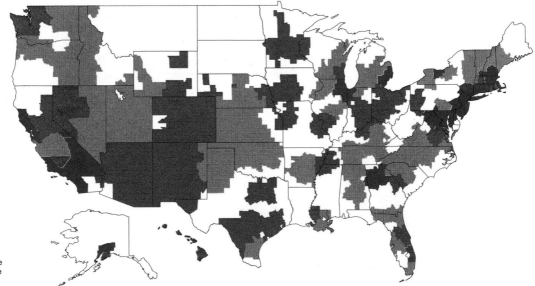

High
Above Average
Below Average
Low

car phones   gourmet coffee beans   *Kiplinger's Personal Finance*   news radio   Land Rovers

notes that the facility recently approved a plan to open an on-site cappuccino bar.

Throughout Winner's Circle, businesses cater to time-pressed, well-off consumers. There are plenty of takeout restaurants and video stores but few do-it-yourself shops. "Most of my neighbors couldn't change a lightbulb," notes Cherry Hill lawyer Steven Polansky. "They'll tell you they just don't have the time." In East Cherry Hill, the row of strip malls along Route 70 West is filled with jewelers, clothing boutiques, and high-end specialty shops. Bob Danzeisen, owner of Danzeisen & Quigley Sporting Goods, notes that his customers aren't overly concerned about finding the cheapest equipment for skiing, golf, or biking. "They want the K2 skis or the Callaway golf clubs," says Danzeisen. "They want the names with all the bells and whistles." This passion for top-of-the-line brands extends to cars as well: Porsches and Mercedes-Benzes are bought at six times the national average in Winner's Circle communities.

But the cost of living is high, despite the six-figure incomes. In East Cherry Hill, it's not uncommon for the cost of a bar or bat mitzvah, the celebration of when a Jewish child turns thirteen, to top $50,000. "There's a lot of new money here, and a lot of people living right up to their means," says David Butler, a commercial designer and president of the local Jewish Community Center. Spoiling their children is common, and the communities are known for supporting soccer leagues and drama clubs. Most kitchens boast calendars cluttered with appointments for grown-ups as well as children. "No kid stays home for the summer," observes David's wife, Maxine, a psychotherapist. "Sometimes it's a little too easy to be a kid here."

Politically, Winner's Circle is a middle-of-the-road community type. "We don't like extremists," says one voter flatly. Progressive on social issues, Winner's Circle residents support gay rights, abortion rights, and gun control — "No one can understand how you can be against that," one declares. However, they're more conservative on fiscal issues, backing low taxes and balanced budgets. "Voters here want government to be run like a business," says Cherry Hill's Susan Bass Levin. "They think it shouldn't interfere with your life and it shouldn't waste money." And most of all, they think it should keep the schools well funded, knowing that education is the ticket to prepare their children for jobs that don't yet exist.

PREFERENCES

(Index of 100 = U.S. Average)

Lifestyle / Products

what's hot

car phones 242
travel agents 234
car-rental credit cards 227
personal computers 197
pianos 170
mystery novels 153
gambling casinos 150
trivia games 149
swimming 149
gardens 143

what's not

new-car loans 90
Wendy's 86
in-home purchases 80
Montgomery Ward 79
roller-skating 77
oven cleaners 76
condoms 73
rap music 73
smoking 72
shocks changed by self 72

Food / Drink

gourmet coffee beans 240
domestic wine 206
veal 173
bagels 169
Kellogg's Special K 167
avocados 145
brown rice 145
boxed chocolates 138
pretzels 137
fresh fish 125

Magazines / Newspapers

Kiplinger's Personal Finance 233
Money 221
PC Magazine 194
Smithsonian 174
Self 173
House Beautiful 158
USA Today 141
Newsweek 135
Consumers Digest 134
People 132

Television / Radio

news radio 310
Wall Street Week 248
TV tennis 174
Meet the Press 169
Caroline in the City 151
Frugal Gourmet 139
Larry King Live 132
Saturday Night Live 123
Murphy Brown 114
Law & Order 105

Cars / Trucks

Land Rovers 662
Porsche 911s 655
Audis 649
Mercedes-Benzes 627
Toyota Previas 616
Saabs 576
Volvos 554
Infinitis 527
Toyota Land Cruisers 506
Honda Accords 228

Most dog-eared library book:
Fodor's Europe

el agents   domestic wine   *Money*   *Wall Street Week*   Porsche 911s   gambling casinos   TV tennis

SER 3
urban gold coast

0.5% of U.S. households
Primary age group: **mixed**
Median household income: **$59,300**
Median home value: **$363,500**

Thumbnail Demographics

elite urban singles and couples
renters, multi-unit housing
predominantly white and Asian households
college graduates
white-collar professionals

Politics

Predominant ideology: liberal Democrat
1996 presidential vote: Bill Clinton
Key issues: pro abortion rights, human rights abroad,
reducing job stress

Sample Neighborhoods

Upper East Side, New York, New York 10021
Woodley Park, Washington, D.C. 20008
Lincoln Park, Chicago, Illinois 60614
Marina Del Rey, California 90292
Radio City, New York, New York 10019

It's hard to mistake the Urban Gold Coast, America's densest lifestyle type. No place has more singles, more residents per square mile, or a higher per-capita income — and none has fewer children, cars, or pets. Urban Gold Coast boasts these characteristics because of an architectural oddity: The neighborhoods are dominated by high-rise apartment buildings found in only a handful of big U.S. cities. Residents pay dearly to live in this crowded, vertical world; a one-bedroom apartment on Manhattan's Upper East Side can rent for $3,000 a month. But the in-town location also provides a vibrant social scene, with more bars, restaurants, coffee shops, and boutiques located on just one block than in many small towns. And most are dedicated to operating on the cutting edge of trends.

It takes money to live in the Urban Gold Coast, the third-wealthiest cluster, and more than 90 percent of all residents are white-collar professionals and executives. These type-A jobs require long hours, which in turn encourages an active nightlife and a thriving service economy of waitpeople, dog walkers, and housekeepers. "My most important relationship is with my dry cleaner," says Debra Lusman, twenty-four, a New York brokerage house analyst. "He makes sure that I'll have something to wear to work each day." On the Upper East Side in New York, lines form outside the trendy restaurants at ten P.M., health clubs stay open until eleven, and many delis deliver twenty-four hours a day. Typically young and unattached,

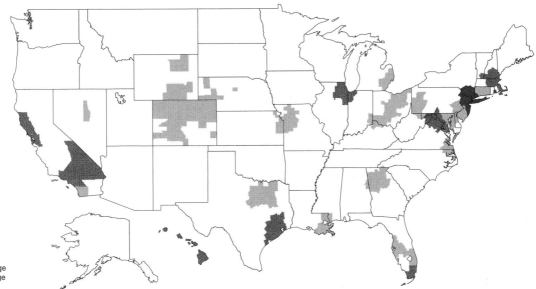

■ High
▨ Above Average
▧ Below Average
□ Low

Saks Fifth Avenue avocados *New York Times* *Late Night with Conan O'Brien* Ferraris foreign vide

Urban Gold Coast residents tend to play hard and work hard, jogging, Rollerblading, and working out at health clubs at high rates. At the New York Sports Club on East Eighty-sixth Street, seven thousand members have signed up, not as much for the meat market as the sweat shop. "People come here to lose themselves in exercise," says general manager Paul Slater. "No worries — it's a great outlet to get rid of your tensions."

Living in the high-rent heart of the city, Urban Gold Coasters are early adopters, the first to try palm pilots, visit the hottest Internet site, sip the oddest-color cocktail. "Everyone thinks of themselves as cutting edge," says Earl Geer, owner of the Hi-Life Restaurant and Lounge on the Upper East Side, which serves new and emerging microbeers. "They're either quite successful and wealthy or trying to become the next big shot." Businesses respond accordingly, striving to produce the best products in ever-smaller niches. One-of-a-kind stores may sell only roses, decorative hangers, or Hungarian books. Because of the postage stamp–sized kitchens in most apartments, relatively few residents do their own cooking — hence the low purchase rates for grocery items — but local restaurants thrive, providing sustenance as well as society. "The staples around here are coffee, bagels, and sushi," observes securities lawyer John Singer, twenty-nine. "Everyone has their favorite places."

Still, there's a hard edge to life in the Urban Gold Coast. Residents talk less about how hip they are than how they cope with the cramped quarters, crowded subways, harrowing cab rides, and hostile sidewalks. To protect their personal space, many residents put up psychic and physical barriers: wearing Walkmans while out on the streets, rarely communicating with next-door neighbors. Though once known for its political activism — the term "limousine liberals" referred to affluent Manhattanites — the cluster's politicism has ebbed as freshly minted college grads with bipartisan apathy have moved in. One aide to New York mayor Rudolph Giuliani has observed that many Upper East Siders can't name their U.S. congressperson; political protests are unheard of. The only issue to generate any local fervor recently was a threat to rent control, which for years has allowed tenants to take advantage of below-market rates. When state leaders suggested that the toniest residents were abusing the subsidies, Democratic assemblyman John Ravitz put the neighborhood reaction in perspective: "If you are making a hundred thousand dollars as a family living on the East Side of Manhattan, you are living paycheck to paycheck."

PREFERENCES

(Index of 100 = U.S. Average)

Lifestyle / Products

what's hot

Saks Fifth Avenue 620
foreign videos 335
dance performances 319
banking by PC 303
dry-cleaning 285
passports 280
museums 252
computer software 239
jogging 219
espresso makers 206

what's not

large-screen TVs 80
starch 73
financial planners 70
lottery tickets 48
power tools 41
JCPenney 40
grocery lists 39
hot tubs / whirlpools 34
dogs 32
family videos 30

Food / Drink

avocados 255
imported beer 227
Brie cheese 204
Cornish hens 166
pita bread 164
canned hash 156
beef 151
yogurt 139
Domino's pizza 132
pretzels 109

Magazines / Newspapers

New York Times 2325
Vanity Fair 516
Vogue 279
Essence 269
Gourmet 253
GQ 242
Fortune 239
Metropolitan Home 239
Rolling Stone 233
Playboy 146

Television / Radio

Late Night with Conan O'Brien 806
news radio 440
urban-contemporary radio 296
Nightline 173
American Movie Classics 167
Masterpiece Theatre 152
Nick at Nite 151
Saturday Night Live 144
MTV Video Awards 138
Simpsons 127

Cars / Trucks

Ferraris 897
Alfa Romeos 695
Porsche 911s 505
Infiniti Q45s 373
Audi 90s 366
BMW 325s 359
Jaguars 344
Volkswagen Corrados 327
Saabs 316
Mercedes-Benzes 296

Kitchen staples:
sushi, balsamic vinegar, cilantro

country squires

1.0% of U.S. households

Primary age group: **35–54**

Median household income: **$75,600**

Median home value: **$230,300**

Thumbnail Demographics

elite exurban families

single-family housing

predominantly white households

college graduates

white-collar professionals

Politics

Predominant ideology: moderate Republican

1996 presidential vote: Bob Dole

Key issues: eliminating affirmative action, pro abortion
rights, tax reform

Sample Neighborhoods

Concord, Massachusetts 01742

Chagrin Falls, Ohio 44022

Bethel, Connecticut 06801

Doylestown, Pennsylvania 18901

Woodbury, Minnesota 55125

"People come here," a Country Squires resident muses, "to join a reading group and learn to speak Italian." Quaint pursuits, surely, but one should not underestimate their allure. For more than a decade, affluent city dwellers have been moving to Country Squires, the wealthiest small-town community type, to indulge such passions. In places like Leesburg, Virginia, and Concord, Massachusetts, baby-boom families have settled into $400,000 restored homes with artsy flags on the front doors. They've buzz-cut their shrubbery and renovated their interiors to become user friendly for working couples, computer-literate kids, and freelance consulting businesses. "People want baby-sitter suites that will one day become home offices," says Concord architect Holly Cratsley. "You're less likely to have a TV in the kitchen than a computer nook."

Country Squires communities are often tucked away behind wooded tracts in coastal states, and residents like the rustic solitude. In Concord, with its population of 17,000 west of Boston, there are no movie theaters, malls, or McDonald's; local zoning discourages fast-food joints by requiring silverware and ceramic plates. "Anyone who wants nightlife has to leave town," one resident notes. Specialty shops sell duck decoys, homemade tea cakes, and organic food. "People don't want to go to a mall and wonder if anyone will give them service," says Mary Johnson, manager of the Mary Curtis

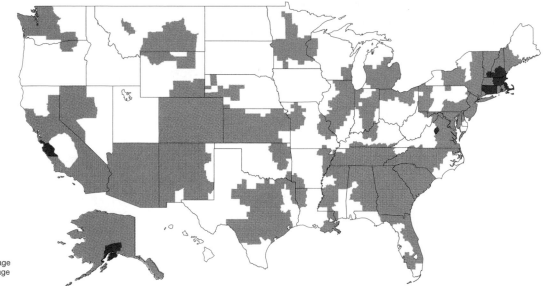

■ High
▨ Above Average
▨ Below Average
□ Low

sailing   scotch   _Martha Stewart Living_   classical radio   Saab 9000s   business trips by air

Gift Shop, which will special-order bridal gifts from anywhere in the world. "They want the good names."

With their deep pockets — theirs is the fourth-most-affluent U.S. lifestyle — Country Squires enjoy club sports like tennis, swimming, and golf. And with their cultivated tastes for opera and the symphony, they attend such performances at high rates. These are the folks who tell pollsters they wish they could spend more time reading books. Three out of four adults have gone to college, far above the national average, and most kids can operate computers before they can read. School bonds pass easily in Country Squires communities. And residents have the ecological sensitivity to want green products that promote health and the environment. There are enough safety freaks to make Volvos more popular than Mercedes — albeit, all equipped with cell phones.

Politicians recognize the independent streak of Country Squires — these are middle-of-the-roaders whose votes are often up for grabs — and typically press the flesh at the town dump on a Saturday morning. Volunteering is deeply ingrained, and in Concord, parents compete to be soccer coaches. So many volunteer at the local schools that newcomers face a waiting list to help out in classrooms. Civic pride gives towns a sense of security, and residents may even keep their house and car doors unlocked. When the administrator of a prison in Concord met with townspeople to discuss contingency plans in the event of a prison break, he noted that the facility would sound a warning siren so they could retrieve their car keys before a convict drove away with a pricey import.

But Country Squires isn't utopia. Local zoning fights break out between developers and pro-environment parents who want to preserve the land for their children's recreation. And gentrification is following the migration of yuppies to this small-town world. In Concord, the old lumber yard today is a trendy restaurant, the harness shop a drugstore. Still, the city dwellers arrive with the belief that they can find heaven in a slower, simpler lifestyle. "The American Dream is being on top of the management of your time," says Harold Perry, a Concord resident who punctuates his home computer-consulting business with river-rowing trips and jazz concerts. In Country Squires, he feels, people have the space and pace to craft a Renaissance lifestyle.

PREFERENCES

(Index of 100 = U.S. Average)

Lifestyle / Products

what's hot

sailing 283

business trips by air 247

pianos 193

personal computers 189

mail-order shopping 187

downhill skiing 185

tennis 184

premium credit cards 180

theatergoing 178

time-share residences 171

what's not

country music 83

fast-food Mexican 82

bus travel 79

baby equipment 72

pagers / beepers 70

Mary Kay cosmetics 69

pipe tobacco 61

life insurance < $20,000 55

Medicare / Medicaid 50

home-improvement loans 29

Food / Drink

Scotch 239

gourmet coffee 179

veal 165

brown rice 158

low-fat cottage cheese 148

turkey bacon 141

baking chips 135

Diet Coke 131

pasta 117

barbecue sauce 112

Magazines / Newspapers

Martha Stewart Living 228

Popular Photography 212

Forbes 194

Cooking Light 179

Skiing 175

Newsweek 172

Prevention 146

Vogue 144

Parade 139

Popular Science 128

Television / Radio

classical radio 222

Frasier 164

TV golf 160

Late Show with David Letterman 156

Nova 153

progressive-rock radio 151

Washington Week in Review 142

This Old House 135

Travel Channel 130

Kentucky Derby 130

Cars / Trucks

Saab 9000s 970

Audi 90s 775

Dodge Grand Caravans 769

Land Rovers 692

Jaguars 571

Porsches 543

Toyota Supras 515

Volvo 960s 491

Subaru SVXs 463

Mazda Millenias 407

Favorite home feature:
computer nook in the kitchen

money & brains

1.1% of U.S. households

Primary age group: **45–64**

Median household income: **$59,000**

Median home value: **$222,000**

Thumbnail Demographics

sophisticated urban-fringe couples

single-family housing

predominantly white and Asian households

college graduates

white-collar professionals

Politics

Predominant ideology: liberal Democrat

1996 presidential vote: Bill Clinton

Key issues: environmental causes, gun control, gay
rights

Sample Neighborhoods

Glen Rock, New Jersey 07452

Skokie, Illinois 60076

Floral Park, New York 11001

Wedgwood, Seattle, Washington 98115

Samp Mortar, Fairfield, Connecticut 06432

When entrepreneurs wanted to open a Dunkin' Donuts in the heart of Glen Rock, New Jersey, local residents reacted as if it were a proposed toxic waste dump. The fare would be greasy, they complained. The setting would turn into an unsightly hangout. It just wouldn't fit in on a block where merchants sold gourmet fish and rare coins. So it never opened. But that's not surprising in Money & Brains, where residents tend to be sophisticated consumers who like to be surrounded by good taste. Many of these affluent residents are married couples with few children and dual incomes, allowing them to afford their fashionable homes on small manicured yards in urban neighborhoods. With high rates of college attendance and foreign travel, there's a cultured atmosphere to these communities. Whereas some households display American flags above their front stoops, Money & Brains homeowners hang artsy banners of colorful flowers. A typical bumper sticker reads, "Friends Don't Let Friends Eat Meat," reflecting not just the politically correct concerns of those against drunk drivers but the cluster's preoccupation with health food. At Gary & Margee's, a children's shoe store in Glen Rock, the kids who've been fitted with oxfords leave not with a sugary lollipop but a fresh pretzel rod.

Concentrated on the urban fringe of several dozen major metros, Money & Brains neighborhoods are known for their desirable Tudors and colonials, top-rated schools, and quick commutes to

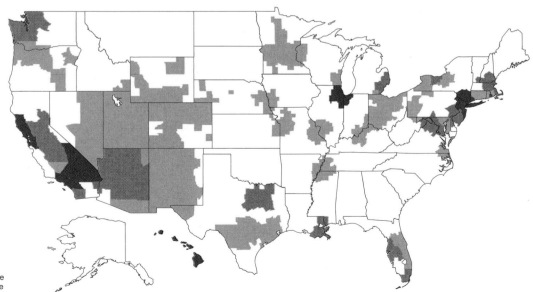

High
Above Average
Below Average
Low

espresso makers   imported wine   *Wall Street Journal*   news radio   Alfa Romeos   stock-rating service

downtown jobs. In these established communities, residents pride themselves on low-key taste rather than ostentatious display. They may hire a designer to put together a *Metropolitan Home*–quality living room with a custom glass coffee table and Romanesque chair, but they certainly don't brag about it. Women occasionally frequent designer-label boutiques, but they're really turned on by steals at discount designer stores. And when it comes to cars, area motorists are just as likely to choose a safety-conscious Volvo as a rugged Land Rover. Many teenagers receive a car for their sixteenth birthday, though it's not a flashy BMW but a modest Neon or Saturn.

In Money & Brains, residents place more stock in intellectual than financial achievements. Status is whether your child attends a prestigious college, if you're conversant in the latest *New York Times* best-seller. "Our basement is overflowing with books," says Sherry Satine, forty-eight, who estimates she buys fifty books a year. "My favorite gift to people is fiction." Her cluster neighbors tend to listen to news radio and subscribe to business, news, and travel magazines. Their TV tastes may range from A&E biographies to *Mad About You,* but they'll also tell you that "we should be watching more public television." When they go out, it's routinely to the theater.

Politically, Money & Brains is a schizophrenic cluster. Voters describe themselves as everything from liberal to conservative, but Democrats have the edge. They're fiscally moderate, but on social issues, voters swing to the left, supporting abortion rights, environmental causes, and gun control. Those liberal views come to an abrupt halt, however, when it comes to problems like crime and congestion threatening the community. "People have worked hard to get here, and they're very protective of keeping what they have," explains Glen Rock administrator Robert Freudenrich.

Even with its urban setting, Money & Brains often resembles an affluent suburban enclave. Every morning, these neighborhoods empty of their dual-income couples, to fill back up at night. Their local stores usually include gourmet markets, specialty wine stores, jewelers, travel agencies, and art galleries. Residents care about exercise — joggers and walkers abound — but not about home-cooked meals. Dinners are often microwaved affairs of Lean Cuisine or takeout. On Saturdays, locals meet at recycling centers, which were operating long before recycling came into vogue around the country. In Money & Brains, people support political correctness and multiculturalism simply because, intellectually and morally, they believe it's the right thing to do.

PREFERENCES
(Index of 100 = U.S. Average)

Lifestyle / Products
what's hot
espresso makers 254
stock-rating services 237
American Express cards 202
security alarms 185
frequent-flier miles 185
Gap 174
contributing to public broadcasting 170
theatergoing 161
science fiction 157
supporting environmental causes 142
what's not
needlepoint 79
smoking 78
power boats 75
romance novels 73
roller-skating 65
baby food 64
home-improvement loans 62
campers 51
banking by PC 41
Wal-Mart 34

Food / Drink
imported wine 189
Brie cheese 169
Kellogg's All-Bran 169
Entenmann's snacks 165
olive oil 152
Diet Pepsi 142
low-fat cottage cheese 125
bagels 123
fresh fish 117
yogurt 114

Magazines / Newspapers
Wall Street Journal 257
New Yorker 220
Skiing 179
Smithsonian 177
Vanity Fair 174
Fortune 170
Travel & Leisure 167
Elle 146
Time 134
Runner's World 131

Television / Radio
news radio 376
classical radio 339
TV tennis 199
Masterpiece Theatre 178
Washington Week in Review 175
Meet the Press 155
American Movie Classics 142
Melrose Place 141
Mad About You 123
Frugal Gourmet 121

Cars / Trucks
Alfa Romeos 455
Volvo 240s 418
Mercedes-Benzes 404
Jaguars 396
Infinitis 390
Land Rovers 331
BMWs 328
Saab 900s 315
Audis 273
Toyota Previas 295

Common sighting:
winter tans from Caribbean holidays

SER 6

young literati

1.0% of U.S. households

Primary age group: **25–44**

Median household income: **$52,100**

Median home value: **$245,200**

Thumbnail Demographics

upscale urban couples and singles

single-unit owners and multi-unit renters

predominantly white and Asian households

college graduates

white-collar professionals

Politics

Predominant ideology: liberal Democrat

1996 presidential vote: Bill Clinton

Key issues: gay rights, pro abortion rights, defusing racial tensions

Sample Neighborhoods

Walnut Creek, California 94598

Montclair, New Jersey 07042

West Los Angeles, California 90025

Cambridge, Massachusetts 02140

Studio City, North Hollywood, California 91604

Visit Walnut Creek, California, on a Saturday morning, and the busiest area in town is the Countrywood Shopping Center around Noah's Bagels and Starbucks Coffee. There, the young singles and couples show up in sweat suits and bike togs, taking a break from their exercise for some of the staples of the Young Literati lifestyle. By noon, there's a line of cars at the recycling bins in the parking lot and a small crowd at Larry's Book Nook, where a whole section is titled "Simplicity" and devoted to New Age self-help books for those who want to stop and smell the caffe latte. "I serve as the local bartender in the community," says Larry Sydes, the store's avuncular proprietor. "People come in and tell me their problems, and I recommend books to help solve them."

The books, the exercise, and an ecological mind-set are all signs of life in Young Literati, a collection of upscale urban-fringe neighborhoods, often near universities. Filled with tasteful apartments and condo developments, the cluster is a haven for Generation Xers who support a commercial base of fitness clubs, clothing boutiques, and all types of bars — from juice to coffee to microbrew. Most residents have parlayed college educations into information-intensive jobs, and the latest technology goes over here like Yanni music at a self-actualization retreat. These are the folks who log on-line daily and do their power walks with cell phones tucked into their Gore-

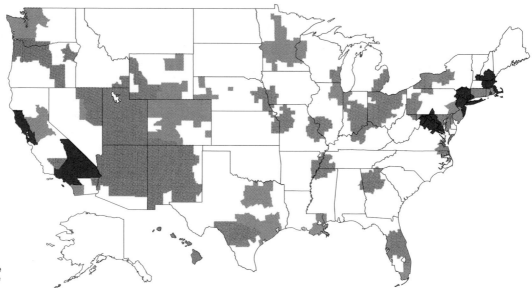

■ High
▨ Above Average
▨ Below Average
□ Low

downhill skiing gourmet coffee beans *Scientific American Face the Nation* Audi 90s Price Club

Tex windbreakers. In Walnut Creek, population 72,000, the phone company recently added a second area code simply because of the number of cell phones and modems hooked up to home computers.

Culturally, Young Literati are not your usual couch potatoes. Surveys show that they'd rather read, attend a concert, or see a movie than veg in front of the TV. "Television is just pathetic," one Walnut Creek local observes. Without the responsibilities of having children, residents have the time to travel, take adult education classes, or go to the theater. In the cultural oasis of Montclair, New Jersey, a community of 40,000 people supports four theatrical companies. The Walnut Creek Arts Center puts on 650 shows a year featuring all manner of performing arts. "People enjoy seeing something that might be Broadway bound," notes director Scott Denison. "It makes them feel sophisticated."

Young Literati is often about young people with deepening pockets learning about the good life. It's a place where a thirty-something woman thinks nothing of hiring two financial planners and a personal shopper at Nordstrom. At the gourmet Oakville Grocery in Walnut Creek, experts are on hand to help shoppers choose from among a hundred kinds of cheese and learn the difference between California premium and extra virgin Tuscan olive oil. "People come to us for education," says manager Julie Scott. "A cheese for twenty-two dollars a pound is not something you buy unless you understand it." In the nearby condo of Pamela Wisecarver, thirty-one, the magazine rack teeters precariously from the weight of *Metropolitan Home, Martha Stewart Living, Vanity Fair,* and *Bon Appétit* — typical journals in the cluster. "When I'm invited to a dinner party, people will call up and say, 'Make one of those Martha Stewart things,'" she says from her kitchen outfitted with a Cuisinart, espresso machine, and juicer. "Foodies are big around here."

Liberal in sensibility, these residents wear their leftist values on their sleeves — often of a rough cotton fiber. In Young Literati, a visit by conservative Republican Newt Gingrich draws protests. During election years, cluster voters lobby for slower growth, protecting endangered animals, and expanding the jogging trails. In Walnut Creek, the arts center warns patrons if any actors will be smoking cigarettes onstage as part of the performance; it's received too many complaints from audience members about secondhand smoke. And why not? Area residents are empowered with the education and the sophisticated sensibility to know what they want.

PREFERENCES

(Index of 100 = U.S. Average)

Lifestyle / Products

what's hot

downhill skiing 287
Price Club 247
passports 256
American Express cards 218
foreign videos 203
tennis 200
Gap 183
pro baseball games 153
attending the theater 144
cooking 131

what's not

camcorders 76
bowling 72
stationary bicycles 71
Burger King 70
coupons 68
Kmart 63
new-car loans 61
bargain shopping 59
watching TV 29

Food / Drink

gourmet coffee beans 203
tequila 160
liquid breakfasts 156
olive oil 142
Nabisco Shredded Wheat 133
reduced-fat yogurt 120
bagels 119
frozen boneless chicken 117
low-cal frozen dinners 114
Coca-Cola Classic 112

Magazines / Newspapers

Scientific American 425
Bon Appétit 390
Esquire 334
Rolling Stone 283
Star 211
Business Week 206
Time 197
Self 177
Smithsonian 177
Inside Sports 154

Television / Radio

Face the Nation 202
Melrose Place 199
progressive-rock radio 195
Comic Strip Live 192
pay-per-view sports 176
Simpsons 170
A&E Investigative Reports 168
Late Show with David Letterman 161
Frasier 150
Friends 138

Cars / Trucks

Audi 90s 447
Volkswagen Corrados 377
BMWs 333
Volkswagen Golfs 306
Nissan 300ZXs 284
Acuras 278
Toyota Land Cruisers 255
Mitsubishi Monteros 247
Toyota Supras 234
Lexus LS400s 227

Indispensable kitchen appliance:
espresso machine

SER 7

second city elite

1.7% of U.S. households

Primary age group: **35–64**

Median household income: **$58,800**

Median home value: **$147,500**

Thumbnail Demographics

upscale executive couples and families in second-tier cities

single-family housing

predominantly white households

college graduates

white-collar professionals

Politics

Predominant ideology: moderate Republican

1996 presidential vote: Bob Dole

Key issues: reducing size of government, tax reform, toxic waste disposal

Sample Neighborhoods

Northport, New York 11768

Huntsville, Alabama 35810

West Chester, Pennsylvania 19380

Cheshire, Connecticut 06410

Denville, New Jersey 07834

The malls and giant warehouse clubs are a short drive away, but the thriving Main Street of Northport, New York, reflects a central truth about Second City Elite communities: There's money here and the will to spend it to support local businesses. The residents of these satellite cities tend to be prosperous executives who adorn their stately homes with antiques, computers, and the latest golfing equipment. In Northport, a community of 7,500 an hour east of Manhattan, status is which country club you belong to and what kind of $40,000 car you drive. As one resident observes: "Typically, your work car is a Mercedes and your family car is a Suburban." Many households are composed of working couples seeking relief from the hassles of urban life. "There's resistance to going back into the city," says Northport attorney Douglas McNally, forty-five. "It's as much a factor of exhaustion as fear." Indeed, the break between metropolis and satellite city is so complete that in Northport, the local high school offers an entire course on nearby New York City simply to teach kids about urban living.

With above-average numbers of children, life in Second City Elite revolves around families. "There are a lot of Soccer Moms and Soccer Dads here," says one resident. Video stores and health food stores are hot, nightclubs and billiard halls are not. Generally, neighborhood associations are active, PTA meetings are packed, and parents pride themselves on getting involved in the schools. In

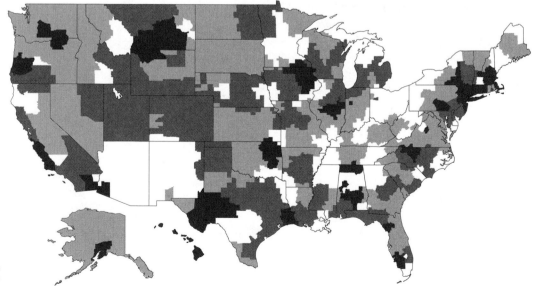

High
Above Average
Below Average
Low

country clubs   Scotch   *Wall Street Journal*   TV golf   Mercedes-Benzes   car phones   low-fat sour

Northport, where the 1996 hit movie *In & Out* was filmed, parents compete ferociously for the chance to chaperone their kids on class trips to Washington, D.C. "It's partly out of a feeling of guilt because they don't spend enough time with their kids," concedes one parent of his dual-income neighbors.

In this lifestyle, residents are well educated — more than two-thirds have gone to college — and they take their media seriously. The Second City Elite subscribe to highbrow magazines like *Smithsonian, Audubon,* and *Eating Well,* and live by public broadcasting. "People will listen to NPR as much as watch *Everybody Loves Raymond,*" says librarian Stephanie Heineman. In Northport, the center of community life is the library, where opera and ballet programs are featured on Sundays. Of 36,000 people in the library's service area, 34,000 have book check-out cards.

While Second City Elite residents have the deep pockets to be active consumers, they're somewhat uncomfortable in that role. "One of the biggest stresses is the conspicuous consumption we're all sucked into," a Northport resident observes. One remedy is to shop through catalogs — Lands' End and Talbots are popular — and some people have taken to cutting the designer labels from clothes to avoid any obvious status statements. Uninterested in gambling and lotteries, they're big on building nest eggs for college and retirement through stocks and mutual funds. "People want to live long enough to make a lot of money — and to spend it," says one cluster investor.

Far more conservative than their suburban peers, the elite of these satellite cities tend to be Republicans who support tax reform and oppose low-income housing that may reduce property values. The exurban settings of Second City Elite also makes for an environmental consciousness: As boaters and gardeners, they worry about toxic waste and water pollution; they sport bumper stickers that read, "Think Globally, Act Locally." Fighting the forces of metropolitan sprawl, the Second City Elite try to preserve a villagelike way of life. "How can we beat the malls?" asks clothier Dorothy Walsh. "We provide friendly, personal service, and our customers appreciate that." At Northport's Barefoot Image casual-wear store, proprietor Fred Richtberg keeps the swimsuit racks stocked year-round for shoppers heading off to a Caribbean getaway or a last-minute business trip to Italy. "Customers come in and say, 'Dress me for a trip to Europe. Here's my suitcase. I'm leaving tomorrow,'" notes Richtberg. And no one in the store will blink.

PREFERENCES

(Index of 100 = U.S. Average)

Lifestyle / Products

what's hot

country clubs 199
car phones 177
power boats 175
camcorders 161
on-line services 160
attending the theater 159
mail-order shopping 148
walking for exercise 135
gardens 134
charitable volunteering 132

what's not

veterans' clubs 80
baby food 78
volleyball 78
condoms 77
work boots 71
hunting 69
Motel 6 66
watching TV 58
campers 57
rolling papers 35

Food / Drink

Scotch 201
low-fat sour cream 164
low-cal frozen dinners 159
skim milk 158
low-calorie bread 141
pretzels 134
olives 132
pickles 132
Wendy's 129
pork chops 117

Magazines / Newspapers

Wall Street Journal 223
Golf Magazine 217
Outside 204
Eating Well 182
Boating 167
Money 163
Byte 151
Audubon 151
National Geographic 148
home / garden section 137

Television / Radio

Wall Street Week 256
Rush Limbaugh 194
news radio 156
TV golf 149
Nightline 144
golden-oldies radio 143
Nature 130
Tony Awards 127
Live with Regis & Kathie Lee 126
Tonight Show with Jay Leno 124

Cars / Trucks

Mercedes-Benzes 352
Mazda Millenias 324
Saabs 306
Cadillac Sevilles 306
Lincoln Continentals 285
Oldsmobile Auroras 272
Mitsubishi Monteros 260
Volkswagen Cabriolets 241
Buick Park Avenues 240
Mazda Miatas 237

Status:
luxury sport-utility vehicle

SER 8
executive suites

1.2% of U.S. households

Primary age group: **25–44**

Median household income: **$58,000**

Median home value: **$166,400**

Thumbnail Demographics

upscale white-collar couples

single-family housing

predominantly white and Asian households

college graduates

white-collar professionals

Politics

Predominant ideology: moderate Independent

1996 presidential vote: Bill Clinton

Key issues: saving endangered animals, public education
funding, balancing the budget

Sample Neighborhoods

West Springfield, Virginia 22152

Glastonbury, Connecticut 06033

Huntington Beach, California 92649

Lake Grove, Oregon 97035

Piermont, New York 10968

Ask residents of Executive Suites about the center of community life, and they scratch their heads. "Is it the mall?" ponders one in the cluster community of West Springfield, Virginia. "Maybe the corner gas station," another muses. "There is no center of community life," declares Kenneth Whetzel, pastor of Messiah United Methodist Church. "We live in a classic suburban sprawl."

That's as succinct a description as any for Executive Suites, a collection of upper-middle-class subdivisions just beyond the nation's big-city beltways. Settled during the postwar baby boom, today Executive Suites is a haven for white-collar professionals drawn to comfortable split-levels and town houses within a manageable commute to downtown jobs, restaurants, and entertainment. Residents take pride in their quiet streets, decent schools, and green parks free of big-city crime. But they recognize that their lifeblood is tied to their car, and transportation is the Achilles heel of the Executive Suites lifestyle. "Every politician runs on a platform of reducing traffic congestion," observes Addison Smith, president of the West Springfield Civic Association. "So far no one's accomplished it." Indeed, locals sometimes leave cluster communities because a fifteen-mile trip to work or a ten-mile shuttle to soccer practice can take an hour — on a good day.

In this, the eighth-richest neighborhood type, residents tend to be comfortable but not affluent; the median household income is

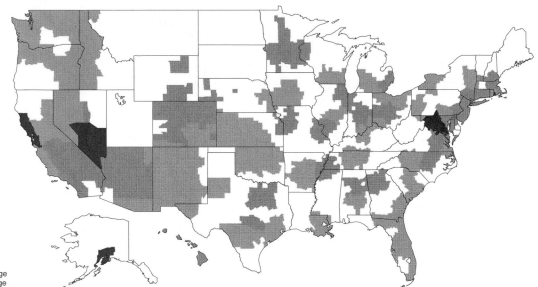

■ High
▨ Above Average
▨ Below Average
□ Low

banking by PC   gourmet coffee   *Inc.*   classical radio   Lexuses   electric juicers   DoveBars   *Skiing*

$58,000. Their two-car garages are more likely to hold Acuras and Toyotas than BMWs and Mercedes. Out of their conservative business suits, they shop the local strip malls in sweats, Dockers, and dungarees. When they travel abroad, which is often, they're less interested in chic resorts than in towns that have art galleries and historic churches. In Executive Suites homes, end tables typically bulge with business and gourmet-cooking magazines. Health-conscious consumers, they buy more fresh foods than processed products, often owning bread machines and pasta makers. At one recreation center, where swimming and aerobics are the popular activities, vending machines serve up hot cups of cappuccino. "Around here, people are into boneless chicken breasts big time," says Rick Makeley, a grocery store manager, noting residents' desire for convenience. Yet they also find it difficult to splurge on themselves. "If they see a five-dollar slab of imported cheese, they'll ask you to cut it in half before they buy it," says David Neuman, regional vice president for a health food supermarket chain.

Executive Suites is conservative in other ways. Because so much of residents' incomes are tied up in mortgages — the median home value is $170,000 — their homes are relatively bare of expensive art, fancy consumer electronics, and backyard tennis courts. "You don't see a lot of social climbing here," says Elaine McConnell, a county supervisor representing West Springfield. "People want to protect their secure way of life." In this politically moderate community, they worry about preserving their jobs, local schools, and financial investments. "I wouldn't want to win the lottery," confesses Robert Leonard, a forty-four-year-old Housing and Urban Development official who owns a pristine town house with his statistician wife and two children. "It would be too disruptive of our lifestyle."

And yet, change is occurring, at least in the ethnic makeup of Executive Suites. When the cluster's communities sprang up after World War II, most residents were white GIs buying their first homes in sometimes restricted neighborhoods. Today, Asians make up an important minority in the area, with ethnic restaurants, markets, and church ministries now commonplace. High mobility rates and stressful jobs have begun fraying family bonds, and local churches feature support groups dealing with divorce, AIDS, and corporate downsizing. Religion offers an island of respite from the hectic pace, and rituals reflect local mores. Each Easter, several churches in West Springfield host sunrise services on a local golf course.

PREFERENCES

(Index of 100 = U.S. Average)

Lifestyle / Products

what's hot

banking by PC 376
espresso makers 238
exercise at clubs 220
mutual funds > $10,000 207
dry-cleaning 196
racquetball 175
travel agents 158
photography 149
electric juicers 148
novels 144

what's not

six-month CDs 86
stamp collecting 82
cigarettes 82
woodworking 78
life insurance < $20,000 68
freshwater fishing 67
satellite dishes 62
lottery tickets 58
needlepoint 44
auto races 38

Food / Drink

gourmet coffee 200
DoveBars 182
Brie cheese 175
Kellogg's Fruitful Bran 172
low-alcohol beer 159
Diet Pepsi 148
brown rice 146
Cornish hens 135
salsa 122
yogurt 119

Magazines / Newspapers

Inc. 343
Skiing 295
Wall Street Journal 257
Sunset 254
Metropolitan Home 251
airline magazines 219
Cooking Light 209
Smithsonian 202
Self 193
Newsweek 148

Television / Radio

classical radio 344
Caroline in the City 176
NewsHour with Jim Lehrer 166
Wimbledon 160
VH1 139
CNN Prime News 138
Rush Limbaugh 132
Saturday Night Live 130
Mad About You 129
Chicago Hope 125

Cars / Trucks

Lexuses 382
Toyota Supras 373
Alfa Romeos 368
Acura Integras 340
Nissan 300s 329
Toyota MR2s 322
BMWs 321
Volvo 800s 301
Volkswagens 205
Mazdas 173

Daily routine:
his-and-her carpools

SER 9

pools & patios

1.9% of U.S. households

Primary age groups: **45–64, 65 +**

Median household income: **$58,000**

Median home value: **$167,000**

Thumbnail Demographics

established empty-nesters

single-family housing

predominantly white and Asian households

college graduates

white-collar professionals

Politics

Predominant ideology: moderate Republican

1996 presidential vote: Bob Dole

Key issues: environmental causes, improving the economy, gun control

Sample Neighborhoods

North Waltham, Massachusetts 02154

Secaucus, New Jersey 07094

Stratford, New York 06497

Olive, Orange, California 92665

Elmhurst, Illinois 60126

Founded by the children of the Depression, Pools & Patios has evolved from a neighborhood type of new bedroom suburbs to one of mature empty-nesting communities. When the first families moved in during the postwar years, the big attractions were the spacious split-levels and Cape Cods. Backyards soon filled with swing sets and — as the cluster nickname suggests — pools and patios. But as time passed, this upscale cluster quietly aged, the children grew up and left, and their parents eased into retirement. In North Waltham, Massachusetts, a Pools & Patios suburban community west of Boston, residents no longer get together with neighbors for cocktail parties after work. "We're getting too old for that," says Nancy Perry, president of the Piety Corner Club, a venerated neighborhood association. "We all go to bed early now." At the Waltham Athletic Club, the slowing pace is apparent as the most popular classes have shifted from high-impact aerobics to yoga. When residents gather at Waltham Common for summer concerts, the musicians often perform the sounds of an earlier era: big band music.

But Pools & Patios residents aren't ready for retirement communities yet. Many still work and are at the top of their careers, earning median incomes of $58,000. Having reached their postchild years, they can indulge their leisure pursuits. Lifestyle surveys show that they go to the theater, museums, and dance performances at high rates. Residents also travel to Europe and visit gambling casi-

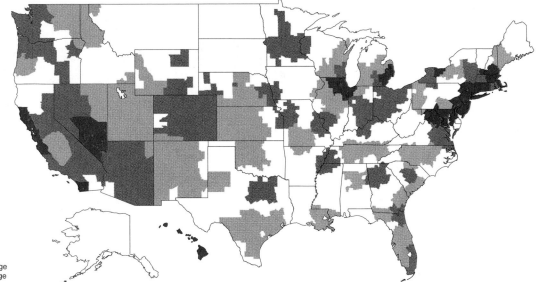

High
Above Average
Below Average
Low

pasta machines   skim milk   *Sunset*   soft-contemporary radio   Saabs   exercise at clubs   Scotch

nos more often than the general population. These Americans have amassed nest eggs to actively play the stock and mutual-fund markets; *Money* and *Forbes* are two of their favorite magazines. And they've reached a stage in their lives where they appreciate the camaraderie of gardening clubs, fraternal orders, and social organizations. The Piety Corner Club in Waltham meets monthly for no other purpose than to fly kites, play bingo, or tour a new library. In Pools & Patios, residents are more likely than average Americans to read books and see movies; book clubs are as common as tennis foursomes.

As they approach retirement, cluster residents have begun making concessions to age. At the grocery store, they purchase low-fat foods and diet soft drinks at disproportionate rates. Residents like to take walks after dinner; weekends are reserved for gardening and cookouts. In public-opinion polls, Pools & Patios residents concede they wish they could spend more time exercising, and they should. The owner of one health club says the average blood pressure of his clientele is borderline hypertense. Unlike other seniors who retire to warmer climates and active-retirement complexes, most Pools & Patios retirees prefer to stay in their area. "They've gotten older in place, and they're happy here," says Ed Tarallo, councilman from North Waltham. "But it does mean that you end up going to more wakes than farewell parties around here."

Politically moderate, Pools & Patios residents are the kind of voters who swing between economic conservatism and liberal social causes. They voted for Bob Dole in the 1996 election, but at the same time they told pollsters that they support gun control, abortion rights, and defusing racial tensions — all Clintonesque positions. And they have the time and inclination to be effective volunteers for whichever candidate addresses their particular pet peeves. To fight a development, they'll write letters, call their council representatives, and pack a council meeting, even paying for legal help for their grassroots campaigns with yard sales. In Waltham, residents of the Goldencrest-Hobbsbrook Neighborhood Association recently stopped one commercial developer whose project threatened a nearby wetlands area. But no one would mistake these protestors for radical Earth First! members. "It's not that they worry about the environment so much as their property values," says Harrison Sheppard, staff writer of the *Waltham News Leader*. "They want to maintain an area that's very residential, very suburban." The American Dream, as one resident notes, is to have enough money to retire without a loss in lifestyle. And without moving an inch.

PREFERENCES

(Index of 100 = U.S. Average)

Lifestyle / Products

what's hot

pasta machines 227
exercise at clubs 204
tennis 170
gambling casinos 167
passports 165
housekeepers 157
auto clubs 153
7-Eleven 152
gasoline credit cards 152
adult education courses 134

what's not

three-way calling 86
religious clubs 86
banking by PC 85
Kmart 83
foreign videos 79
baby furniture 77
Pizza Hut 75
college basketball games 69
chiropractors 62
cigars 61

Food / Drink

skim milk 162
Scotch 154
DoveBars 148
liverwurst 146
low-cal frozen dinners 144
Post Grape-Nuts 140
egg substitute 137
canned ham 134
fresh cold cuts 129
liquid breakfasts 119

Magazines / Newspapers

Sunset 171
Money 162
Eating Well 150
bridal magazines 145
travel magazines 142
American Health 141
Smithsonian 134
Inside Sports 122
USA Weekend 120
U.S. News & World Report 117

Television / Radio

soft-contemporary radio 219
Siskel & Ebert 178
news / talk radio 175
NewsHour with Jim Lehrer 168
TV tennis 159
Wall Street Week 150
Masterpiece Theatre 147
TV baseball 141
Law and Order 136
Murphy Brown 128

Cars / Trucks

Saabs 294
Toyota Previas 285
Lexus SC300s 285
Volvos 282
Acura Legends 274
Infinitis 265
Mercedes-Benzes 255
Mercury Sables 235
Jeep Grand Cherokees 206
Cadillacs 195

Cluster dress code:
$300 suits to work, old sweats
to exercise, no Spandex

SER 10

kids & cul-de-sacs

3.0% of U.S. households

Primary age group: **35–54**

Median household income: **$61,600**

Median home value: **$142,900**

Thumbnail Demographics

upscale suburban families

single-family housing

predominantly white and Asian households

college graduates

white-collar professionals

Politics

Predominant ideology: conservative Republican

1996 presidential vote: Bob Dole

Key issues: family values, tax reform, public school funding

Sample Neighborhoods

Wheaton, Illinois 60187

Eden Prairie, Minnesota 55346

Wilmington, Massachusetts 01887

Westminster, Colorado 80030

Allen, Texas 75002

On the main drag of Wheaton, Illinois, population 51,464, the movie theater advertises two-dollar tickets for *Flipper* and *Homeward Bound II*. Nearby, a magic shop vies for pint-sized customers with an ice cream parlor, a popcorn stand, a Stride Rite shoe store, and Igor's Comic Book Emporium. No, we're not in Urban Gold Coast anymore, Toto. Kids & Cul-de-Sacs is the premier lifestyle for both married couples with kids and families numbering more than four people. In these kid-filled neighborhoods, strollers compete with pedestrians for sidewalk space, often creating off-road traffic jams. On summer evenings, the cars line up a block deep at the Dairy Queen. Local travel agents will tell you that the favorite vacation destination is Disney World. And throughout the curvy streets lined with split-level homes, you see knots of children skateboarding, Rollerblading, and shooting hoops. It's hard to find a house on some blocks that doesn't have a basketball backboard in the driveway or a Weber grill out back. "We have thirty kids on our block alone," says Wheaton resident Jeanne Mehlberg, a forty-one-year-old mother of three, "probably twenty under the age of eight."

Characterized by upscale suburban subdivisions, Kids & Cul-de-Sacs is a refuge for college-educated, white-collar parents with well-paying professional jobs and a median income of $61,600. Their nexus of education and affluence translates into active lives for their

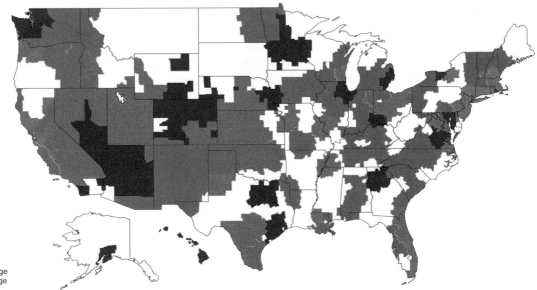

High
Above Average
Below Average
Low

Price Club   Kraft Macaroni and Cheese   *Golf Digest*   soft-rock radio   Toyota Previas   computer

children. It's not uncommon for parents to put in fifty miles a day carpooling their kids to after-school karate classes, piano lessons, and soccer practices. Residents are twice as likely as average Americans to own minivans and sport-utility vehicles, and to them the imported models are the smart choices. Surveys show cluster residents visit zoos, museums, and theme parks at high rates. The big concern of many parents is whether their kids are overprogrammed with activities and need more downtime for free, unstructured play.

Not surprisingly, marketplace behavior in Kids & Cul-de-Sacs reflects the influence of young consumers. Households here are more likely than those of average Americans to buy low-fat yogurt, pizza, and candy bars. Shoppers tend to spend more than $150 a week on groceries, buying milk and juice by the gallon as well as pasta and peanut butter in industrial-sized containers; Price Club is a favorite haunt. Kids & Cul-de-Sacs is a casual area where, as Wheaton clothier Harold Gaedes observes, "People show up in church just shy of wearing jeans and ripped-up shirts." Still, they like brand-new consumer electronics and are early adopters of computers, large-screen TVs, and camcorders for capturing scenes of their kids' busy days. For leisure, these Americans are more likely than the general population to throw barbecues, watch videos, and play board games. A typical Saturday night involves pizza and videos with the kids. "We're usually one extra or one light on the kids," says Bob Mehlberg. "Somebody's always sleeping over at somebody else's house."

Protecting their child-centered world is preeminent in the minds of conservative Kids & Cul-de-Sacs households. They express concern about education, crime, the state of the economy, and especially issues that they believe undermine family values, such as drugs and gay rights. With 76 percent of all residents married, there are a lot of stay-at-home moms. "We worry about the erosion of the family," one mother explains. "We don't want our children to get some funny California ideas." These are the nation's prime supporters of the V-chip and big opponents of legalizing marijuana. On the Fourth of July, Bob Dole marched in the Wheaton parade — unconcerned about protestors — and handily won votes that fall. Around town, you'll still see faded bumper stickers reading, "Don't Blame Me, I Voted for Bush." "If you're a Democrat around here," says travel agent Jeanne Frank, "you don't say it."

PREFERENCES

(Index of 100 = U.S. Average)

Lifestyle / Products

what's hot

Price Club 212
computer CD-ROMs 185
cellular phones 174
zoos 158
two or more VCRs 155
health clubs 154
book clubs 154
kite flying 146
theme parks 145
in-home pregnancy tests 133

what's not

campers 91
freshwater fishing 88
rap music 84
Saks Fifth Avenue 83
life insurance < $20,000 82
Domino's pizza 82
smoking 77
hunting 75
Woolworth 59
Medicare / Medicaid 53

Food / Drink

low-fat sour cream 158
Entenmann's snacks 148
candy bars 137
imported beer 135
Caffeine-Free Diet Coke 134
yogurt 126
fast-food Mexican 124
seasoned rice 122
children's frozen dinners 121
Kraft Macaroni and Cheese 107

Magazines / Newspapers

Golf Digest 230
Bicycling 215
Travel & Leisure 210
PC World 193
Money 177
National Geographic Traveler 165
Working Mother 147
USA Today 141
Consumers Digest 136
Glamour 130

Television / Radio

soft-rock radio 160
Wall Street Week 152
news / talk radio 152
Mad About You 133
Law & Order 136
TV tennis 132
This Old House 124
NYPD Blue 115
Simpsons 108
Disney Channel 107

Cars / Trucks

Toyota Previas 323
Nissan Quests 300
Mercury Villagers 290
Mazda MPVs 282
GMC Safaris 234
Mitsubishi Diamantes 248
Acura Integras 234
Infiniti J30s 234
Dodge Grand Caravans 231
Ford Windstars 227

Bumper sticker:
"My Child Is an Honors Student"

SER 11

God's country

2.7% of U.S. households

Primary age group: **35–54**

Median household income: **$57,500**

Median home value: **$135,900**

Thumbnail Demographics

executive exurban families

single-family housing

predominantly white households

college graduates

white-collar professionals

Politics

Predominant ideology: moderate Republican

1996 presidential vote: Bob Dole

Key issues: tax reform, terrorism, saving
    endangered animals

Sample Neighborhoods

East Brandywine, Pennsylvania 19335

Mystic, Connecticut 06355

Prudhoe Bay, Alaska 99734

Richfield, Ohio 44286

Pembroke, Massachusetts 02359

When city dwellers and suburbanites began moving to the countryside in the 1970s, God's Country emerged as the most affluent of the nation's exurban lifestyles. Today, wealthier enclaves may exist in the hinterlands, but God's Country is the most widespread of upscale clusters in the boonies, representing eight million Americans. In these areas once known for their solitude and scenery, sleepy farms have been plowed under to make way for town houses and split-levels. And the pace has quickened. Jeeps and Volvos now zip along the back roads, carrying residents to distant jobs and nearby malls. Inevitably, this land rush has created a clash between pro- and antigrowth residents. "The old-timers like their privacy and quiet to keep things as they are," says Scott Piersol, administrator of East Brandywine, Pennsylvania, a pastoral township of 6,000 about an hour west of Philadelphia. "Most of the newcomers are working couples and have a frenetic lifestyle. They want recreational areas built for their children. It's a tough balancing act."

Part of the allure of God's Country is escaping big-city stresses, and, to some degree, residents are successful. Hiking, biking, and gardening are all pursued at high rates. "It's considered bad taste if you don't mulch your flower beds," one East Brandywine resident observes. Yet life in God's Country isn't entirely as the cluster name implies. Most residents are dependent on their cars to find civiliza-

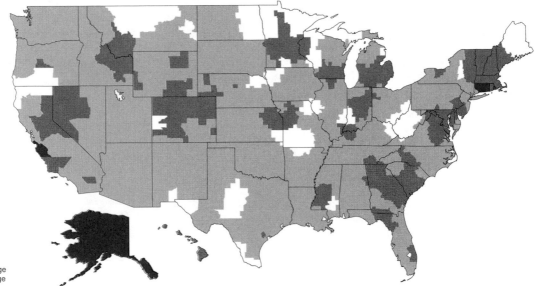

High
Above Average
Below Average
Low

cross-country skiing   Light 'n' Lively Kid Yogurt   *Golf Magazine*   soft-rock radio   GMC Safaris   hot

tion — typically a twenty-minute drive away — and those with kids seem always to be on the road to extracurricular activities. Developers apply constant pressure to build more homes and malls as metro sprawl moves farther out. Although newcomers profess that a laid-back lifestyle drew them to God's Country, many now admit they can't wait for shopping centers and amenities to follow. "I want stores and bakeries and a deli that makes a decent cannoli," says Carlene Stover, forty, an urban exile from Camden and Cherry Hill, New Jersey. "Bring them all in. I don't care about the traffic. I want convenience. I want *stuff* here."

With an increasingly professional and white-collar populace, God's Country boasts consumer patterns similar to the upscale tastes of metropolitan sophisticates. These households own camcorders, hot tubs, and gas grills at rates above the national average. They're big on clothes from the Gap and Liz Claiborne. Their refrigerators hold disproportionate amounts of fat-free ice cream, salsa, white wine, and Caffeine-Free Diet Coke, but there are not a lot of staples in the pantry for home-cooked meals. Cropper's Market in East Brandywine recently opened a giant seafood and salad bar to reflect shoppers' need for convenience foods. "With all the kids' activities, it's impossible to cook every night," says Liz Pavlick, a forty-seven-year-old teacher and mother of three. "With two people working, we're on the run all the time."

God's Country's mix of upscale families in a rural setting contributes to a moderate political streak. Residents care about issues like family values, welfare reform, and low taxes, but they also have a strong environmental stake in trying to preserve the natural beauty of their communities. The lack of minorities causes some residents to be concerned about prejudice directed at anyone "who is not white and upper-middle-class," as one resident put it. Though the newcomers are more liberal than the older residents, God's Country remains a hotbed of Republicanism. "I know people who'd vote for an old dog so long as it's a Republican," says Jack Williams, a sixty-five-year-old barber from a shop cluttered with bumper stickers like "God, Guns and Guts Made America Free." But the influx of urban exiles has called into question the insular streak of longtime residents who continue to resist the call — and cost — of new schools, sewer lines, and malls. "These people want country living with city features," one old-timer says derisively. The newcomers would unapologetically agree.

PREFERENCES

(Index of 100 = U.S. Average)

Lifestyle / Products

what's hot

cross-country skiing 202

hot tubs / whirlpools 188

Victoria's Secret 175

computers > $1,000 161

gas grills 159

financial planners 157

Builder's Square 164

frequent-flier miles 146

camcorders 140

what's not

condoms 84

Kentucky Fried Chicken 82

home-improvement loans 79

weekly groceries < $60 70

pro basketball games 66

bus trips 65

chewing tobacco 57

keeping up with fashion 48

boxing matches 7

Food / Drink

Light 'n' Lively Kid Yogurt 205

Caffeine-Free Diet Coke 147

dry mix salad dressing 145

frozen boneless chicken 139

Nutri bars / snacks 133

domestic wine 132

seasoned rice 125

Stove Top Stuffing 122

salsa 120

Magazines / Newspapers

Golf Magazine 167

Elle 152

Car and Driver 143

Sassy 137

PC Magazine 134

Organic Gardening 133

USA Weekend 132

Business Week 131

National Geographic 127

Better Homes and Gardens 126

Television / Radio

soft-rock radio 152

progressive-rock radio 142

NewsHour with Jim Lehrer 133

ER 131

Home Improvement 127

Wall Street Week 122

TV golf 122

Frontline 121

Entertainment This Week 120

Barbara Walters Show 114

Cars / Trucks

GMC Safaris 334

Saab 9000s 319

Plymouth Grand Voyagers 316

Subaru Legacys 265

Ford Econoline Club Wagons 243

Ford Windstars 240

Pontiac Bonnevilles 236

Volvos 226

Saturns 222

Volkswagen Passats 222

Indispensable tool: garden tiller

SER 12
young influentials

1.1% of U.S. households

Primary age groups: **under 24, 25–44**

Median household income: **$44,100**

Median home value: **$136,700**

Thumbnail Demographics

upwardly mobile suburban couples and singles

single-family housing

predominantly white and Asian households

college graduates

white-collar professionals

Politics

Predominant ideology: moderate Democrat

1996 presidential vote: Ross Perot

Key issues: eliminating affirmative action, legalizing
marijuana, tax reform

Sample Neighborhoods

Redmond, Washington 98052

Canterbury Square, Portland, Oregon 97223

Dunwoody, Atlanta, Georgia 30338

Sherman Oaks, Van Nuys, California 91403

Plantation, Fort Lauderdale, Florida 33324

Once upon a time, in the 1980s, Young Influentials was home to the nation's yuppies, a cluster of acquisitive young couples who bought inordinate amounts of imported wine and designer clothes, and drove only Beemers. Times change. Over the last decade, yuppiedom has faded and half of all Young Influentials residents have married and moved away, typically to suburban subdivisions in Kids & Cul-de-Sacs. Today, the cluster still retains some of the avaricious ethic, but most of the young singles and couples living here are more preoccupied with balancing work and leisure pursuits. In their upscale suburbs, biking and Rollerblading paths snake through the condominium and apartment developments. Shopping centers feature health clubs, athletic-gear stores, and little else. Those looking to shop for basic necessities and apparel must travel elsewhere. "These people don't care about malls. They want open space," observes real estate broker Mary Wilhelm in Redmond, Washington, the corporate home of Microsoft and Nintendo. When developers recently built the mixed-use Redmond Town Center, they left more than a third of the 120-acre project undeveloped for trees, bike trails, and even a salmon-spawning pond.

As in the past, Young Influentials have college degrees, white-collar jobs, upper-middle-class incomes — the median is $44,100 — and type-A temperaments. They travel abroad, buy computers, and

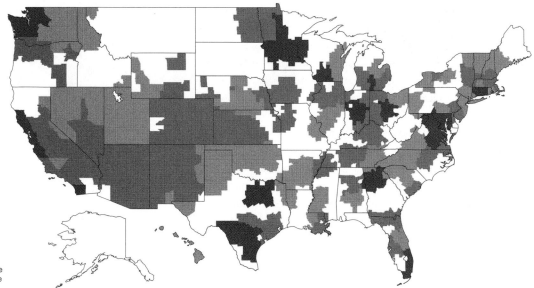

High
Above Average
Below Average
Low

jazz CDs / tapes   Brie cheese   *Us*   progressive-rock radio   Nissan 300ZXs   on-line services   Kellogg

wear designer-label clothes, whether it's Armani or Gore-Tex, at high rates. But the status cars have shifted from sleek sedans to Jeeps and sport-utility vehicles with roof racks for skiing, mountain climbing, and biking gear. REI, a recreational equipment outlet in Redmond, notes the rising popularity of OXT (outdoor cross training), which may involve biking, jogging, and mountain climbing throughout the course of a week. Not surprisingly, Young Influentials' favorite sports are often reflected in their interior decorating. No one blinks at the sight of a kayak sitting in someone's dining room. Status is owning a Bayliner ski boat or a mountain cabin — preferably accessible only by backpacking through virgin forest.

Befitting its role as a singles address — 57 percent of residents are unattached — the Young Influentials lifestyle is heavy on dating and mating activities. Although going to bars is popular, today's residents are more likely to gather in groups at coffee bars, folk music clubs, and microbreweries. Being health conscious comes with the territory, so food surveys show a preference for low-cholesterol fish- and chicken-based meals. The popularity of culinary magazines reflects a fondness for gourmet and trendy cooking. In Redmond, residents will ignore the chains to go to local purveyors for a gourmet pizza topped with the latest "in" combinations, like feta cheese, fresh cranberries, and artichoke hearts. One recent piece of graffiti read, "Meat Eaters Suck."

The voters of Young Influentials tend to be political independents with few party loyalties. In 1996, residents were more than twice as likely as average Americans to vote for Ross Perot and almost as likely to identify themselves with neither party. The cluster, which is 88 percent white and 8 percent Asian, supports the elimination of affirmative action. And most residents express concern about money issues, supporting tax reform and a balanced-budget amendment. "Economics is something we all look at and care about," explains Manda Schossberger, a twenty-eight-year-old Harvard-educated product manager at Microsoft. "A lot of people are straight out of college and are highly motivated about trying to build a company." Her twelve-hour days seem typical of Young Influentials, who in polls express a strong desire for more time to pursue activities like exercising, cooking, and entertaining friends. But the number one desire is to have more time to devote to financial investing. In Young Influentials, some things never change.

PREFERENCES

(Index of 100 = U.S. Average)

Lifestyle / Products

what's hot

jazz CDs/tapes 247
on-line services 242
stock transactions 216
frequent-flier miles 211
downhill skiing 188
backpacking / hiking 162
banking by phone 158
bars / nightclubs 156
housekeepers 150
photography 147

what's not

gardens 82
book clubs 81
dogs 81
Red Roof Inn 80
Montgomery Ward 77
freshwater fishing 74
bus travel 73
gas lawn mowers 73
Christian / faith music CDs / tapes 60
in-home purchases 50

Food / Drink

Brie cheese 237
Kellogg's Fruitful Bran 201
tequila 170
Taco Bell 159
low-fat sour cream 158
liquid breakfasts 153
light beer 136
butter substitute 124
fresh fish 112
low-cal frozen dinners 107

Magazines / Newspapers

Elle 438
Vanity Fair 283
Harper's Bazaar 251
Scientific American 249
Us 238
Bon Appétit 237
Kiplinger's Personal Finance 222
Rolling Stone 211
GQ 205
computer magazines 180

Television / Radio

progressive-rock radio 192
Melrose Place 177
Nature 170
Late Show with David Letterman 143
pay-per-view movies 142
Frasier 141
Mad About You 136
MTV Video Awards 136
Inside Edition 127
X-Files 120

Cars / Trucks

Nissan 300ZXs 285
Volkswagen Corrados 280
Hummer trucks 271
BMW 318s 263
Mazda MX-5 Miatas 252
Honda Preludes 248
Lexus SC300s 245
Jeep Grand Wagoneers 240
Mitsubishi 3000GTs 211
Toyota Land Cruisers 197

Cluster necessity:
health club membership

SER 13
upward bound
2.0% of U.S. households

Primary age group: **25–44**

Median household income: **$54,500**

Median home value: **$137,600**

Thumbnail Demographics
young upscale white-collar families in second cities

single-family housing

predominantly white and Asian households

college graduates

white-collar professionals

Politics
Predominant ideology: conservative Republican

1996 presidential vote: Bob Dole

Key issues: more military spending, reducing size of government, supporting capital punishment

Sample Neighborhoods
Federal Way, Washington 98023

Marietta, Georgia 30060

Nashua, New Hampshire 03062

Columbia, Maryland 21045

Manassas, Virginia 22111

When political pundits proclaimed the 1996 presidential election the Year of the Soccer Mom, they gave mythic status to all stressed-out, minivan-driving suburban mothers. But if anyone doubts their existence, he or she need look no farther than Upward Bound, home to a disproportionate number of Soccer Moms — and Dads, for that matter. In this cluster of suburban satellite cities, young upper-middle-class families live comfortably amid a landscape of parks, malls, and new-home subdivisions. "We call it 'cul-de-sac city,'" one resident says. Parents tend to be college educated and dual income, the kids are preschool and elementary school aged, and most families take upward mobility for granted. More than 25 percent moved in the last year, and many consider their homes temporary rest stops on the child-rearing road. Once the kids outgrow their toy-cluttered rooms in $140,000 homes, these families will move on to larger houses with bigger yards. "No one thinks they'll stay in the same house all their lives," says one cluster homeowner. "They want to buy up."

Kid obsessed is the way to describe the Upward Bound lifestyle, and for good reason. In Federal Way, Washington, just south of Seattle, nearly a third of the 76,000 residents attend local schools. Talk shows devote lengthy segments to discussing suitable places for skateboarding. Homes are dressed in elaborate decorations on Halloween and Christmas, and birthday parties routinely become com-

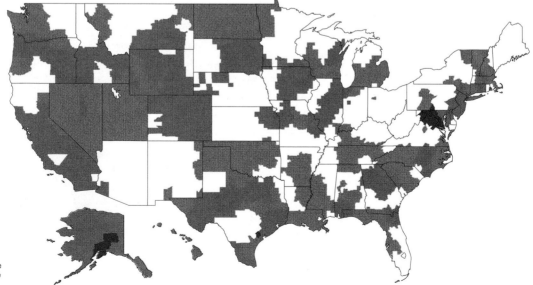

High
Above Average
Below Average
Low

Price Club   veal   *Tennis*   golden-oldies radio   GMC C2500 Suburbans   computer books   children's

petitive events to see who can provide the best entertainment: bowling or miniature golf, Barney or the Red Power Ranger. Homes typically have three-car garages because, as one resident observes, "We live in our cars around here." When they're not in school, children have cluttered calendars of music lessons and organized sports, faithfully chauffeured by parents who believe in the primal power of "structured enrichment." "Parents may not glamorize how busy they are, but they will glamorize how busy their kids are," comments the Reverend Gary Hundrup, pastor of the Steel Lake Presbyterian Church. And because everyone owns a van for hauling kids around, status is driving a flashy sport-utility vehicle — just to be a bit different. "The Isuzu Trooper dealer kicks butt around here," says Lynn Castle, manager of Sea-Tac Mall. "Every family has at least one sedan and a sport-utility vehicle."

With the preponderance of young families, Upward Bound residents lead stretched lives, pulled by work, home, school, and church. One of the essential acquisitions of Upward Bound residents is a car phone. Surveys show that adults have relatively little time for individual sports; they're more inclined to go to swimming pools or the beach with the whole family. They read magazines like *Tennis, Outside,* and *Bon Appétit* for vicarious thrills; most adults could write passionate sonnets to their microwave ovens for no-fuss meals. When they go food shopping, it's often to wholesale clubs for jumbo containers of peanut butter, cereal, pretzels, and noodles. "We'll get twelve pounds of pasta to last four months," says Pamela Elliott, a thirty-six-year-old mother of three who likes to bake cookies from scratch and describes herself as "a stereotypical fifties mom caught in a time warp." She continues, "We're more into bargains than brands."

Like other child-filled neighborhoods, Upward Bound is politically conservative. Voters backed Bob Dole and are big supporters of capital punishment, tax reform, and balancing the budget. Part of this right-wing streak is a reaction to the first sightings of gangs, drugs, and homeless persons in their family-filled neighborhoods. But child-rearing Americans usually worry less about world affairs than domestic concerns — especially what's affecting their own families. In Upward Bound, you'll see far fewer political bumper stickers than ones proclaiming, "My Child Is an Honor Roll Student." "I'm not too concerned about national issues affecting the country," admits Elliott, a PTA president. "Right now, we have to focus on what's going on in our immediate world."

PREFERENCES
(Index of 100 = U.S. Average)

Lifestyle / Products

what's hot

Price Club	202
computer books	188
car phones	179
stationary bicycles	153
gasoline credit cards	150
two or more VCRs	145
beachgoing	133
theme parks	133
electric juicers	133
dogs	125

what's not

lottery tickets	84
fast-food fish	82
volleyball	82
Saks Fifth Avenue	76
rap music	69
pro football games	64
rolling papers	63
Woolworth	61
weekly groceries < $60	60
diet pills	46

Food / Drink

veal	158
children's vitamins	145
Caffeine-Free Diet Coke	144
salsa	140
decorative icing	132
fast food	124
seasoned rice	119
pretzels	113
bananas	112
packaged pasta salad	109

Magazines / Newspapers

Tennis	229
Fortune	199
Bon Appétit	176
computer magazines	163
GQ	163
Omni	162
Shape	146
Popular Mechanics	145
People	136
Prevention	135

Television / Radio

golden-oldies radio	162
Disney Channel	142
progressive-rock radio	137
Frontline	129
TV golf	127
Entertainment This Week	126
Nick at Nite	125
VH1	124
Nova	117
Star Trek: Deep Space Nine	116

Cars / Trucks

GMC C2500 Suburbans	267
Nissan Quests	250
Toyota Previas	249
Acura Vigors	238
Mazda Millenias	230
Mercury Villagers	228
Mazda RX-7s	226
Toyota MR2s	225
Volkswagen Vanagons	225
Mitsubishi Monteros	213

Hot local issue: building a new skateboard park

SER 14
American dreams

1.4% of U.S. households

Primary age group: **35–54**

Median household income: **$51,700**

Median home value: **$180,900**

Thumbnail Demographics

established urban immigrant families

single-family housing

ethnically mixed households

college graduates

white-collar professionals

Politics

Predominant ideology: liberal Democrat

1996 presidential vote: Ross Perot

Key issues: gun control, pro-life movement, eliminating affirmative action

Sample Neighborhoods

Buena Park, California 90620

Jamaica, New York 11428

Dunning, Chicago, Illinois 60634

Garden Grove, California 92640

Cerritos, California 90703

American Dreams is a hint of what the nation will look like in the mid-twenty-first century: an ethnically diverse cluster whose population is 21 percent Asian, 18 percent Hispanic, and 17 percent African American. In these multiracial and multilingual neighborhoods, older immigrants and their children live in the relative harmony afforded by upper-middle-class status. They typically own $200,000 homes, drive newly imported sedans, and fill their driveways with boats and recreational vehicles. In Buena Park, California, a community of 75,000 just east of Los Angeles, many of the neat ranch houses have carefully landscaped lawns, ornamental iron fences, and neatly painted signs proudly welcoming visitors to The Bohannons or The Perezes. In the schools their children attend, there may be fifteen native languages spoken in one class.

Despite this ethnic mélange, no one seems to have told American Dreamers about the melting-pot concept. While ethnic groups live side by side, there's not a lot of socializing beyond backyard-fence chatter. "We have all kinds of nationalities, but most people like to hang together with their own kind," says Nick Van Kampen, the Dutch American owner of a nursery in Buena Park. Ethnic groups frequent their own stores, churches, and restaurants; Buena Park even has an all-Dutch soccer club. "We talk in English at home," says Van Kampen, "but when we have parties, we sing in Dutch."

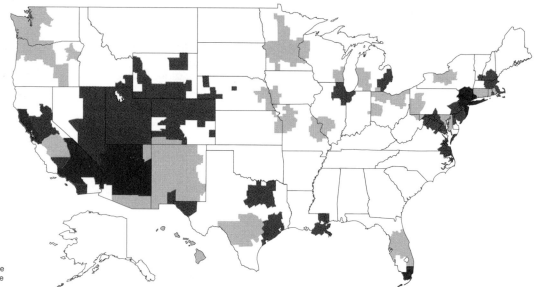

High
Above Average
Below Average
Low

foreign travel   avocados   *New York*   news radio   Toyota N93 pickups   gambling casinos   condoms

In this lifestyle, being American means carrying a beeper, owning more than three television sets, and installing a hot tub in the bathroom. Residents like to read ethnic newspapers and watch foreign-language TV shows, but they also enjoy *Sunset* and *New Yorker* magazines, as well as *Melrose Place* and *The Late Show with David Letterman* at high rates. American Dreams consumers are the kind of shoppers who buy designer-label children's clothes at Sears and JCPenney so they know they will fit in. But the adults still haven't reached that higher-planed comfort zone where they belong to country clubs or fraternal orders. For leisure, they tend to stick to their families and ethnic clubs. For vacation, American Dreamers enjoy visiting theme parks, going to gambling casinos, and traveling abroad — often to their native countries.

Although they think of themselves as liberal Democrats, American Dreamers are not traditional leftists by any means. Having pulled themselves up by their bootstraps, these voters support welfare reform, oppose affirmative action, and express ambivalence about immigration. "The country can absorb the immigrants," as one puts it, "but a lot of them come in here and just have their hands out." Unlike those of other immigrant clusters, American Dreams residents vote, and in the Buena Vista area in 1996, they elected a Hispanic woman to Congress for the first time. Loretta Sanchez rode into office partly as a reaction to Proposition 187, which cut back benefits for legal immigrants. With its urban setting, the cluster isn't so isolated that residents can remain complacent about crime and the threat of ethnic gangs; these areas frequently have neighborhood watch programs and debates about the merits of gated communities. But authorities believe that time and succeeding generations will help assimilate the diverse groups and ease any ethnic tensions. Time, and intermarriage, may ultimately turn American Dreams into a real melting pot.

Just how do people define the American Dream in their namesake cluster? The same way most native-born Americans do: as the freedom to pursue happiness and to create a better life for their children. "They want to be able to eat pizza and participate in the Little Leagues and not have to worry about prejudice," says Dave Roque, editor of the *Buena Park / Anaheim Independent*. "They just want to be treated like any other Americans."

PREFERENCES

(Index of 100 = U.S. Average)

Lifestyle / Products

what's hot

foreign travel	208
gambling casinos	190
Amway products	189
Victoria's Secret	174
ice hockey games	149
condoms	163
credit card balance > $451 / month	156
jogging	149
adult education classes	143

what's not

Builder's Square	72
cats	71
country music CDs / tapes	71
gas grills	70
Mary Kay cosmetics	63
homeowners insurance < $50K	57
college football games	54
boating	53
country clubs	52

Food / Drink

avocados	233
cognac / brandy	178
Domino's pizza	156
Entenmann's snacks	152
Diet-Rite cola	149
bottled water	146
canned hash	141
Cornish hens	132
yogurt	117
Kentucky Fried Chicken	107

Magazines / Newspapers

New York	314
Essence	198
Sunset	191
New Yorker	172
Vogue	172
Modern Bride	163
Business Week	162
Motor Trend	137
Discover	137
Parents Magazine	128

Television / Radio

news radio	315
Spanish radio	302
Showtime	184
BET	178
American Movie Classics	146
Masterpiece Theatre	142
Montel Williams Show	138
Tonight Show with Jay Leno	134
Melrose Place	128
ABC World News Tonight	125

Cars / Trucks

Toyota N93 pickups	659
Mazda MPVs	359
GMC Safaris	316
Imported minivans	307
Toyota Previas	269
Acura Integras	207
Honda Civics	195
Nissan Quests	185
Mercedes-Benzes	183
Lexus ES300s	173

Local dish:
meatloaf, mashed potatoes,
and a side of sushi

SER 15

new empty nests

1.8% of U.S. households

Primary age groups: **45–64, 65+**

Median household income: **$45,100**

Median home value: **$120,100**

Thumbnail Demographics

upscale suburban-fringe couples

single-family housing

predominantly white households

college graduates

white-collar professionals

Politics

Predominant ideology: moderate Independent

1996 presidential vote: Bill Clinton

Key issues: legalizing marijuana, health care reform, tax reform

Sample Neighborhoods

Tucker, Georgia 30084

Haddon Heights, New Jersey 08035

Hatboro, Pennsylvania 19040

Dedham, Massachusetts 02026

Buchanan, New York 10511

When white flight formed the first ring of suburbs in the years following World War II, New Empty Nests was born. Today, these established upper-middle-class neighborhoods are filled with married couples over fifty whose children have flown from the coop. Residents tend to live in aging split-levels and ranch houses surrounded by professional buildings and strip shopping centers. While younger families leapfrog to farther-out subdivisions, New Empty Nest's couples stay in the old neighborhood with thoughts of retirement. "The suburban sprawl has passed us over," says Methodist minister Michael Cash of Tucker, Georgia. "We're the older suburbanites. Some are ready to go out and kick up their heels, and others are clinging to home to care for elderly parents or kids who have moved back."

In Tucker, an Atlanta suburb of 35,000, residents lead a relaxed lifestyle where active fifty-somethings take adult education courses and painting classes, and pursue gardening at high rates. Indeed, the house with the best-trimmed dogwoods and azaleas is noted by a local garden club with an award designed to look like a daisy (lest anything too gaudy detract from the real foliage). And these upscale empty-nesters are interested in finance, having watched their stocks and real estate investments increase in value over the last decade. At Tucker's Rehobeth Baptist Church, the marquee may ad-

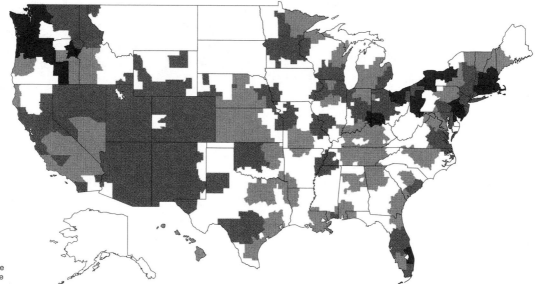

■ High
▨ Above Average
▨ Below Average
☐ Low

pasta machines   low / no-alcohol beer   *Bon Appétit*   *Charlie Rose*   Buick Regals   Marshalls

vertise a two-day seminar with a financial planner. As one local comments, "You see a lot of gray-hairs going into that church at night."

Since many of them are in their peak earning years and no longer caring for children, New Empty Nesters are big on travel and evening entertainment. They're more likely than the general population to eat out, frequenting restaurants such as Red Lobster and International House of Pancakes. They go to college and professional football and basketball games at high rates. For vacations, they'll head to a gambling casino, spa, Caribbean beach, or Sea World — without the kids, thank you very much. At home, they'll gather with friends for parties to play games like Trivial Pursuit and Pictionary — "Fun games that require a little intelligence," as one puts it. These are the Americans who belong to auto clubs and make heavy use of their memberships. "My version of the American Dream is to be debt free so I can travel on my own or visit my family," says Sylvia Daughtry, sixty-four, a retired schoolteacher.

Two-thirds of New Empty Nests residents have gone to college, and their fondness for reading reflects that statistic. They buy hardcover books and magazines like *Vanity Fair, Newsweek,* and *Money* at high rates. They've embraced the computer revolution and subscribe to America Online 30 percent more than average Americans. Their taste in music is eclectic, from gospel to contemporary jazz. Ditto their taste in TV programming, which ranges from bowling shows to *Washington Week in Review.* Their open-mindedness has also made them political swing voters. Self-described Independents, they support a mix of issues, from legalizing marijuana and restricting immigration to gun control and tax reform.

As these neighborhoods continue to empty-nest, it's likely that this cluster will undergo further change. Younger families have already begun to move in as elderly residents depart for retirement developments. U-Haul trucks and "for rent" signs now appear every winter as snowbirds head for warmer climes. At the Tucker Recreation Center, the evening dance programs frequented by middle-aged working women are now being supplemented by gymnastics classes for preschoolers and their at-home mothers. But not everyone in New Empty Nests is looking to pack up and leave the cluster. "We don't want to go to Sun City when we retire," says Riley Deichert, fifty-year-old secretary and exercise instructor at the Tucker Recreation Center. "We have our friends and our family here. We're just as happy to stay put."

PREFERENCES

(Index of 100 = U.S. Average)

Lifestyle / Products

what's hot

pasta machines 226
Marshalls 200
country clubs 161
auto clubs 160
travel insurance 149
adult education courses 146
easy-listening CDs/tapes 142
gambling casinos 137
pianos 136
eating out 134

what's not

auto races 88
no-interest checking 85
watching TV 84
Taco Bell 82
baby furniture 81
motorcycles 80
condoms 80
foreign videos 77
nonfilter cigarettes 57
cross-country skiing 54

Food / Drink

low / no-alcohol beer 174
DoveBars 159
veal 145
low-cal frozen meals 136
Twizzlers 131
Wheaties 131
egg substitute 124
Domino's pizza 124
pretzels 123
fresh fish 117

Magazines / Newspapers

Bon Appétit 171
Vanity Fair 159
First for Women 152
Golf Digest 149
science magazines 140
Newsweek 137
Popular Mechanics 132
American Health 132
Money 124
House Beautiful 122

Television / Radio

Charlie Rose 242
news / talk radio 159
TV bowling 144
Nova 143
Washington Week in Review 138
TV tennis 138
NBC Sportsworld 134
Entertainment This Week 130
Saturday Night Live 127
Academy Awards 125

Cars / Trucks

Dodge Caravans 202
Saturn SWs 169
Subaru SVXs 169
Mercury Sables 167
Buick Regals 167
Ford Tauruses 166
Oldsmobile Cierras 159
Infiniti G20s 159
Buick Rivieras 158
Cadillac Eldorados 157

Status: best-looking yard
in the neighborhood

SER 16

gray power

2.0% of U.S. households

Primary age groups: **55–64, 65 +**

Median household income: **$36,300**

Median home value: **$116,700**

Thumbnail Demographics

affluent married and single retirees in Sunbelt cities

owners of single- and multi-unit housing

predominantly white households

college graduates

white-collar professionals

Politics

Predominant ideology: conservative Republican

1996 presidential vote: Bob Dole

Key issues: reducing size of government, restricting immigration, health care reform

Sample Neighborhoods

Bal Harbour, Miami, Florida 33154

Palm Desert, California 92260

Hilton Head Island, South Carolina 29926

Sarasota, Florida 34242

North Decatur, Georgia 30033

The steady rise of older, healthier Americans in the past two decades has produced one important by-product: the retirement communities of Gray Power. In this satellite-city cluster concentrated in the Sunbelt, affluent seniors live in relative comfort among their peers. Where once elderly Americans anticipated ill health and poverty in their final years, Gray Power offers the prospect of an active retirement for the children of the Depression. Here, residents play golf, take arts and crafts classes, and go gambling at higher-than-average rates. In Sun City, Arizona, golf carts are the favored means of transport. Residents fill their fanny packs with frequent-flier cards and passports for traveling abroad. "People don't sit in a rocking chair and watch the fish play," says Estelle Spiegel, mayor of Bal Harbour, Florida. "They tend to be on the go to stay young and healthy."

With their comfortable pensions supplemented by investments, many Gray Power residents can afford the finer things. In Bal Harbour, an oceanfront retreat of 3,000 — among them political elite like Bob Dole and Robert Strauss — residents go to the pricey Bal Harbour Shops mall, cruising through Tiffany, Cartier, Gucci, Chanel, and Hermès, where a necktie typically costs $125. Prints by Picasso and Warhol hang in one mall gallery. The only residential subdivision, an enclave of ranch homes and minimansions surround-

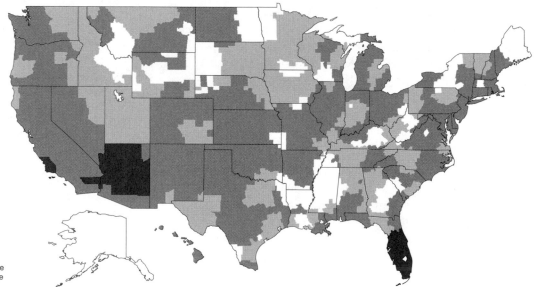

High
Above Average
Below Average
Low

saltwater fishing   bourbon   *House Beautiful*   *Jeopardy*   Cadillac DeVilles   veterans' life

ing a marina, is lined with Jaguars and Mercedes parked near the yachts. Given such valuable possessions, security is a natural concern among Gray Power residents. Bal Harbour, a gated community for fifty years, is accessible only by permission of security guards. "People want to feel safe from crime," says Richard Olsen, president of the Bal Harbour Club, where annual dues run $3,000. "They want to control their own destiny. They don't want to be subject to the whims of politicians."

Inside the homes and condos — ever neat, thanks to maids and cleaning services — Gray Power residents lead quiet lives. Surveys show they watch a lot of television, particularly news, sports, and mysteries. They hit the early-bird specials at restaurants or cook low-fat meals at home, likely with chicken, fish, soup, or cheese. "We take our share of vitamins," notes Ann Gaylon, eighty-three. "We're very health conscious around here." In this lifestyle, people make time for daily exercise, whether it's walking, swimming, or armchair aerobics. (They draw the line at skiing and bowling.) At night, these seniors still have the stamina to attend plays, movies, and basketball games at above-average rates.

Such abundance isn't lost on Gray Power residents, who recognize their good fortune compared to previous generations. When it comes to charity, they give generously to causes and the arts. Politically, these voters are part of the fiscally conservative wing of the Republican Party, in favor of reducing the size of government and cutting funding for schools. But they have some liberal tendencies, taking a laissez-faire approach to gay rights and legalizing marijuana, in part for its medicinal benefits for cancer patients. While Gray Power residents have a high rate for voting, they're not the strident activists who work for political parties. Says Fred Dukler, eighty-eight, "We're past the stage when we're going to argue too loudly about issues."

In Gray Power, it's travel that really grabs their interest. In their Cadillacs and Lincolns, they take to the road to visit family, exotic locations, and sometimes nowhere at all in the case of the gambling cruises popular among seniors. Cluster residents are nearly twice as likely as the general population to stay at hotels like Marriott, Hilton, and Best Western. And despite the old stereotype, they're less likely to engage in sedentary activities like stamp collecting, doing needlepoint, or owning tropical fish. Slowing down is just not on the Gray Power agenda.

PREFERENCES

(Index of 100 = U.S. Average)

Lifestyle / Products

what's hot

saltwater fishing 176
veterans' life insurance 166
attending the theater 157
swimming 145
auto clubs 138
travel agents 136
pipe tobacco 133
golf 129
lottery tickets 124
watching television 119

what's not

bowling 86
family videos 78
stamp collecting 77
three-way calling 74
freshwater fishing 72
chess 66
Victoria's Secret 62
home remodeling 60
cross-country skiing 47
Amway products 35

Food / Drink

bourbon 171
boxed chocolates 163
Light 'n' Lively Kid Yogurt 154
Quaker Puffed Rice 147
liverwurst 140
Wendy's 137
low-fat cottage cheese 136
skim milk 132
vitamins 130
frozen desserts 120

Magazines / Newspapers

House Beautiful 178
Eating Well 165
Golf Magazine 151
New Yorker 142
Travel & Leisure 131
Popular Science 130
business magazines 129
National Geographic 123
McCall's 121
Newsweek 119

Television / Radio

Meet the Press 375
Masterpiece Theatre 289
60 Minutes 176
Nova 170
TV golf 165
easy-listening radio 161
Charles Grodin 153
Chicago Hope 123
Jeopardy 129
Touched by an Angel 106

Cars / Trucks

Cadillac DeVilles 371
Lincoln Continentals 364
Infiniti Q45s 364
Mercury Grand Marquis 341
Lexus LS400s 330
Mercedes-Benzes 275
Lincoln Mark VIIIs 266
Mercury Sables 255
Oldsmobile Auroras 245
Buick Park Avenues 230

Bumper sticker:
"We're Spending Our Children's Inheritance"

SER 17
bohemian mix

1.7% of U.S. households

Primary age groups: **under 24, 25–34**

Median household income: **$33,700**

Median home value: **$135,452**

Thumbnail Demographics

inner-city singles neighborhoods

multi-unit rental housing

ethnically mixed households

college graduates

white-collar professionals

Politics

Predominant ideology: liberal Democrat

1996 presidential vote: Bill Clinton

Key issues: gay rights, legalizing marijuana, defusing
  racial tensions

Sample Neighborhoods

Dupont Circle, Washington, D.C. 20036

Greenwich Village, New York, New York 10014

West Los Angeles, California 90025

Forest Park, Illinois 60130

Broadway, Seattle, Washington 98102

Every Fourth of July, the residents of Dupont Circle in Washington, D.C., raise flags outside their graceful brownstones commemorating the birth of an independent nation. It's not Old Glory they're waving, however, but the rainbow banner celebrating America's gay culture. Dupont Circle is typical of Bohemian Mix, a cluster of inner-city singles neighborhoods representing the most liberal lifestyle type in America. Ever since the sixties, these areas have attracted the beatniks and flower children who made cluster communities like Haight-Ashbury and Greenwich Village capitals of the counterculture. Today, Bohemian Mix features a progressive, multiracial mix of students, executives, writers, and public interest activists. Nearly three-quarters of all Bohemian Mixers are single or divorced, and an estimated third of the populace is gay, continuing the cluster's reputation as a haven for alternative lifestyles. "No one blinks when seeing two men or women holding hands," says Dupont Circle writer Karyn Robinson. "This is a very accepting area."

That openness results in early-adopter consuming patterns among Bohemian Mixers. Residents are quick to try new products — espresso makers, organic pet foods, computer on-line services — and imported goods considered exotic by heartland Americans. Cluster consumers, two-thirds of whom are college educated, prefer imported wine, beer, and cheese to the domestic brands. They

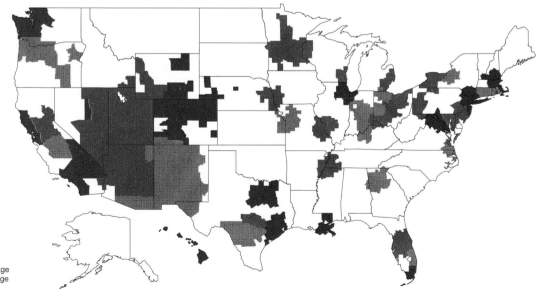

■ High
▨ Above Average
▧ Below Average
□ Low

foreign videos   imported beer   *New York*   *Nightline*   Alfa Romeos   jogging   gourmet coffee beans   G

stay hip to the latest styles and ideas by reading publications like *GQ, Harper's Bazaar,* and *Rolling Stone* at high rates; their favorite TV show is *Nightline.* Other popular shows include *The Simpsons* and *A&E Investigative Reports.* By contrast, Bohemian Mix is a weak market for cheap and cheerful kids' products like Kool-Aid and Kraft Macaroni and Cheese. The apartment-lined streets demand subcompacts because of the lack of parking places, and the locals prefer them to be foreign makes — one more anti-mainstream badge.

With so many single residents under thirty years old, the lifestyle in Bohemian Mix can be described as "the young and the restless." Body-conscious residents enjoy aerobic activities like biking, Rollerblading, and running, in part to balance local passions for alcohol and recreational drugs. Health food is purchased at high rates, and it's not uncommon for cluster restaurants to include an entrée's calorie and cholesterol counts on menus. "Status is having a personal trainer," says Dupont Circle clothing store owner Joe Moriarty. Day and night, residents drift along the sidewalks, cruising, holding hands, and window-shopping the art galleries and leftist bookshops. Many exposed limbs bear at least one tattoo. Virtually every type of alcoholic beverage is consumed at more than twice the national average rate. Condoms and cigarette rolling papers are also purchased at high rates, the rolling papers not destined to enwrap loose tobacco.

Determined to avoid any hint of mainstream conformity, Bohemian Mixers discourage major chains and fast-food restaurants from taking root. "We resist cookie-cutter businesses to preserve our uniqueness," says Dupont Circle resident Deacon Maccubbin, owner of Lambda Rising, the nation's largest chain of gay bookstores. That against-the-grain spirit extends to politics as well. In this, the gayest of all neighborhood types, vigorous activism centers on matters of sex: AIDS research, abortion rights, and gay rights. Politically, Bohemian Mixers are more than twice as likely as average Americans to describe themselves as "very liberal." They're the activist Democrats willing to march in support of politically correct issues like affirmative action, civil rights, and recycling at home. "Someone is always sitting in a fountain to protest something," observes one Dupont Circle resident. If not, they're just window-shopping the galleries, stopping in a bar for a drink, parading in drag, or simply engaging in the most popular pastime in Bohemian Mix: hanging out.

PREFERENCES

(Index of 100 = U.S. Average)

Lifestyle / Products

what's hot

foreign videos 246
jogging 236
Victoria's Secret 217
condoms 193
jazz CDs / tapes 189
espresso makers 189
European travel 188
moviegoing 170
CD players 164
American Express cards 161

what's not

golfing 49
veterans' clubs 47
country music CDs / tapes 46
woodworking 33
power boats 30
hunting 27
gas grills 21
college football 12
stock in own company 15
home-improvement loans 5

Food / Drink

imported beer 201
gourmet coffee beans 191
imported wine 180
brown rice 174
Kellogg's Fruitful Bran 174
olive oil 147
bottled water 146
pita bread 145
low-cal frozen dinners 136
bagels 120

Magazines / Newspapers

New York 440
GQ 340
Esquire 307
Mademoiselle 292
Harper's Bazaar 222
Life 180
Ebony 180
Rolling Stone 167
Time 153
business section 149

Television / Radio

Nightline 270
Homicide 185
contemporary-rock radio 184
America's Most Wanted 162
Melrose Place 157
A&E Investigative Reports 156
Law and Order 151
Simpsons 136
MTV Unplugged 134
60 Minutes 124

Cars / Trucks

Alfa Romeos 277
Volkswagen Cabriolets 234
Audi 90s 228
Saab 900s 212
Mazda RX-7s 201
Infiniti G20s 194
Land Rovers 192
Volkswagen Jettas 183
Mazda 323s 172
Honda CRXs 172

Neighborhood hangout:
gay and lesbian bookshop

SER 18
big fish, small pond

1.9% of U.S. households
Primary age group: **35–54**
Median household income: **$46,000**
Median home value: **$106,400**

Thumbnail Demographics

small-town executive families
single-family housing
predominantly white households
high school graduates, some college
white-collar workers

Politics

Predominant ideology: moderate Republican
1996 presidential vote: Bob Dole
Key issues: supporting capital punishment, welfare reform, eliminating affirmative action

Sample Neighborhoods

Mount Juliet, Tennessee 37122
Kennebunkport, Maine 04046
Kitty Hawk, North Carolina 27949
Danville, New Hampshire 03819
Poulsbo, Washington 98370

"I moved here twenty-five years ago to be a big fish in a small pond. But the pond keeps getting bigger." So says Bill Staggs, a forty-six-year-old pharmacist and entrepreneur in Mount Juliet, Tennessee, a semirural town that is quickly evolving into a middle-class suburb of Nashville. Unlike residents of other American communities getting swallowed by urban sprawl, those in Big Fish, Small Pond mostly support the transformation taking place. The recent arrivals from the city appreciate the virtues of newly built upper-middle-class homes and a less harried way of life. Many new subdivisions have sprung up with $100,000 ranch houses, roomy decks, and above-ground swimming pools. In Mount Juliet, where the population over the past fifteen years has tripled to 9,200, plans for a new mall with a Sears and a JCPenney excite many newcomers. "A community that stays the same," says event planner Betty Stevens, "moves backward."

That view is echoed by many others in Big Fish, Small Pond, with its increasingly white-collar workforce and median income of $46,000. Many residents are businesspeople who tell pollsters they're prodevelopment, tough on crime, and opposed to welfare. They enjoy the trappings of success, belonging to country clubs, traveling to their college football games, and vacationing in the Caribbean at high rates. But the small-town roots of this cluster run deep, and Big Fish, Small Pond residents support the ways of new-

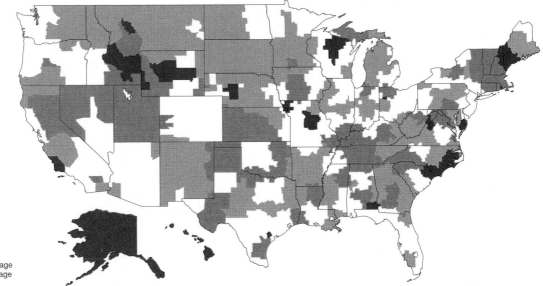

■ High
▨ Above Average
▧ Below Average
□ Low

gas grills   Diet Pepsi Free   *New Woman*   easy-listening radio   GMC Suburbans   power boats

comers only up to a point. Some communities in this cluster are dry, with no opportunity to sip a glass of Merlot at a local restaurant. More common are diners where longtime residents talk of old cars and new homes, and the waitresses welcome all newcomers by asking, "Sweetened or unsweetened?" referring to the iced tea that's served like water.

No, Big Fish, Small Pond is not the rural yuppie haven of the God's Country cluster. Most residents spend their leisure time boating, barbecuing, and playing baseball, and newspaper ads feature products like John Deere five-speed lawn tractors, turkey decoys, and generic sodas like Bubba cola. Status is owning a big bass-fishing boat or one of the new larger houses going up on former pastureland. "People want to move from three bedrooms and two baths to five bedrooms and a family room," says Pastor W. D. Thomason from the Green Hill Baptist Church. "It can get excessive."

With its agrarian roots still strong, Big Fish, Small Pond remains a right-of-center lifestyle in which many residents long for the good old days of homemaking women, one-income families, and traditional gender roles. "A lot of people don't understand what goes on in San Francisco," says Danny Farmer, city manager of Mount Juliet. Around him, the roads are lined with some thirty-five churches of nearly every denomination, except for Jewish, Catholic, and Mormon. A recent editorial in *The Chronicle of Mount Juliet* laments "the removal of prayer and Bible from public schools." Indeed, cluster residents long for a nation without drugs, premarital sex, and gay rights. "In an election between Bill Clinton and anybody else, I'll always choose anybody else," says Randy Travers, a state financial officer. He gave up on commercial TV a long time ago in favor of renting PG and family movies and listening to contemporary Christian music on the radio. "The sex, violence, and bad language turned me off," he says.

Still, Big Fish, Small Pond is not a backward area by most measures. A large percentage of residents have gone to college, and though they may not have graduated, they want diplomas for their children. Many homes have computers and subscribe to magazines like *Financial World* and *U.S. News & World Report*. And there are signs of suburban taste showing up in formerly rural communities like Mount Juliet, from the interactive computer classes at the high school to the morning tennis games played by women at Charlie Daniels' Park. Their game is dreadful, they'll be the first to admit, but like the local lifestyle, it seems to be improving all the time.

PREFERENCES

(Index of 100 = U.S. Average)

Lifestyle / Products

what's hot

country clubs 212
power boats 201
college football games 185
water softeners 174
power tools 171
hot tubs / whirlpools 166
Caribbean travel 161
pianos 149
gas grills 149
car phones 145

what's not

pasta machines 85
Woolworth 84
tennis 84
call forwarding 80
eating out 79
cigar smoking 78
diet pills 77
rap music 66
pro basketball games 43
boxing 19

Food / Drink

Diet Pepsi Free 170
Quaker Puffed Rice 164
pita bread 146
Canadian whiskey 135
low-cal frozen dinners 127
Twinkies 125
canned ham 121
seasoned rice 120
beef 116
canned spaghetti 111

Magazines / Newspapers

New Woman 172
Family Handyman 167
Country Living 153
Colonial Homes 145
PC World 144
science / tech section 136
Guns & Ammo 128
U.S. News & World Report 121
Sports Illustrated 120
Reader's Digest 116

Television / Radio

easy-listening radio 142
Wings 140
TV golf 140
Learning Channel 140
Today Show 129
Daytona 500 126
This Old House 126
Barbara Walters Show 123
Home Improvement 122
Christian-rock radio 109

Cars / Trucks

GMC Suburbans 219
Pontiac Trans Sports vans 193
GMC Safaris 188
Subaru Legacys 181
Buick Rivieras 180
Dodge Vipers 179
Ford Windstars 178
Plymouth Voyagers 169
Volvo 240s 166
Pontiac Bonnevilles 166

Sign of the times:
overcrowded parochial schools

SER 19
greenbelt families

0.9% of U.S. households

Primary age group: **24–44**

Median household income: **$46,700**

Median home value: **$99,700**

Thumbnail Demographics

young upper-middle-class town families

single-family housing

predominantly white households

high school graduates, some college

white-collar professionals

Politics

Predominant ideology: moderate Independent

1996 presidential vote: Ross Perot

Key issues: improving the economy, environmental causes, pro abortion rights

Sample Neighborhoods

Parkville, Missouri 64152

Hyde Park, New York 12538

Yarmouth, Maine 04097

Michigan City, Indiana 46360

Snohomish, Washington 98290

It's a quiet Thursday night in Parkville, Missouri, a Greenbelt Families community north of Kansas City. But at the 850-seat auditorium at Park Hill High School, a noisy crowd has gathered for an annual affair called the Mr. Park Hill Pageant. Part talent show, part beauty pageant, the contest pits male representatives of thirteen school clubs competing in skits, speeches, and formal-wear sashays. The satire is gentle, the crowd polite, and the most disruptive moment comes when two police officers arrive to deal with an errant student who's sneaked a couple of beers in the parking lot. Be cool, the student is told, and the incident is quickly forgotten.

If this tender scene in Greenbelt Families resembles a throwback to the suburban calm of a generation ago, it isn't accidental. "People move here to get away from the contemporary problems of the inner city," says school principal Rudy Papenfuhs. "They want to give their kids a pretty cushy lifestyle." And to a large degree, they've been successful. Greenbelt Families is a cluster of upper-middle-class neighborhoods set in the nation's satellite cities and metro fringes. Two-thirds of the residents have gone to college, half earn more than $50,000 a year, and community life revolves around the children. Parents volunteer at schools and sporting clubs at high rates. Minivans and sport-utility vehicles are must-haves in order to haul multiple kids and all their gear. Sunday is the big shopping day, with Saturdays reserved for attending the kids' games.

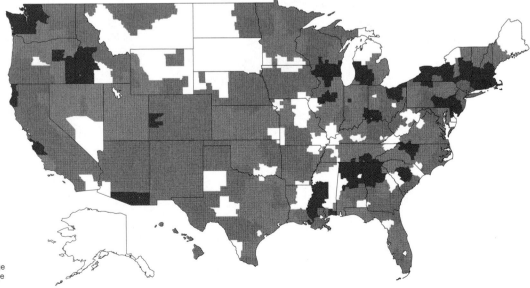

■ High
▦ Above Average
▨ Below Average
□ Low

"We spend the majority of our weekend time with the kids, doing soccer, baseball, and basketball," says Joel Ebbert, a forty-eight-year-old consultant and volunteer soccer coach. "Our focus is on the kids, and we live in an area where people feel the same way."

In these communities, where residents place a premium on education, most homes have up-to-date computers with Internet access. Greenbelt Families visit museums, listen to public radio, and read books all at above-average rates. "These people check out what's on the *New York Times* best-seller list," says librarian Peggy McGinnis. "They want to keep up with the latest trends." Ambivalent about television, viewers here will watch news programs like *Good Morning America* and talk shows like *The Late Show with David Letterman.* In surveys, they have higher rates for subscribing to science and financial magazines. The goal of most parents is to get all their kids into college, and they are heavily invested in the stock market to help pay future tuition bills.

In the marketplace, Greenbelt Families tend to be cost-conscious early adopters. At grocery stores, they're the working couples who buy prepared deli foods but not gourmet takeout. "People don't want to pay top dollar for imported products," explains Frank Muehlbach, owner of the Apple Market in Parkville. Although surveys show that these Americans are fitness freaks who buy treadmills and stationary bikes for their home gyms, they're not so health conscious that they deny themselves pork chops or frozen dinners. And they could care less about reading magazines like *Eating Well, American Health,* and *Cooking Light.* "People used to tear down the doors for SnackWell's low-fat cookies," says Muehlbach, "but it turned out to be just a fad."

Politically, Greenbelt Families tend to be laissez-faire Independents, conservative only on financial issues. "People will listen to Rush Limbaugh as entertainment," one resident says, "but they don't hang their hat on his political views." Young parents will volunteer to save endangered animals but avoid working for political parties. And they'll do almost anything to support educational programs for their children. At the Mr. Park Hill Pageant, audience members saved their loudest applause for the moment when the performing students indicated which college they'd be attending. And while none were Ivy League, most were respectable state universities within an easy commute. As one onlooker observed, "These kids like the area so much they don't want to go far away."

PREFERENCES
(Index of 100 = U.S. Average)

Lifestyle / Products

what's hot

credit cards 179
Amway products 164
Gap 162
computers > $1,000 162
beachgoing 151
downhill skiing 149
camcorders 149
family videos 148
museums 148
stationary bicycles 148

what's not

shocks changed by self 77
sewing 74
power boats 67
pro wrestling 59
pro football games 57
chewing tobacco 40
Price Club 40
chiropractors 20
gospel CDs / tapes 13
spa vacations 7

Food / Drink

imported cheese 186
pasta 151
dry mix salad dressing 149
Kellogg's Pop-Tarts 143
pretzels 142
Domino's pizza 139
frozen dinners 138
olives 129
pork chops 117
steak houses 114

Magazines / Newspapers

PC Magazine 193
Money 171
Popular Science 164
Hot Rod 152
Today 151
Redbook 147
Sports Afield 146
Country Living 143
Consumers Digest 142
TV Guide 126

Television / Radio

Late Show with David Letterman 191
public broadcasting 183
Melrose Place 155
Indianapolis 500 150
adult-contemporary radio 144
Beverly Hills, 90210 139
Bold and the Beautiful 133
Good Morning America 132
Baywatch 132
TV baseball 130

Cars / Trucks

Mercury Capris 220
Ford Windstars 184
Mazda 929s 182
Dodge Ram Wagons 180
Acura Vigors 178
Pontiac Bonnevilles 177
Subaru Legacys 176
Saturns 175
Chevrolet Corvettes 170
Dodges 141

Favorite holiday:
senior prom

SER 20

middleburg managers

1.5% of U.S. households

Primary age group: **55 +**

Median household income: **$37,800**

Median home value: **$94,900**

Thumbnail Demographics

midlevel suburban white-collar couples

single-family housing

predominantly white households

college graduates

professionals, managers

Politics

Predominant ideology: moderate Independent

1996 presidential vote: Bill Clinton

Key issues: increasing military spending, tax reform, legalizing marijuana

Sample Neighborhoods

Lacey, Washington 98512

Hagerstown, Maryland 21742

Dubuque, Iowa 52003

Chapel Hill, North Carolina 27514

Toms River, New Jersey 08753

"This is the suburbs of the suburbs." Political consultant Ken Balsley's observation about his hometown of Lacey, Washington, goes to the heart of Middleburg Managers. Widely scattered throughout the United States, it arose from the migration of city dwellers to midscale satellite cities, with their lower cost of living and more relaxed pace. The residents, overwhelmingly white-collar and college educated, tend to have jobs as business executives, doctors, or lawyers, or be retired military officers. But Middleburg Managers are almost equally divided between older, empty-nesting couples and younger, single, prechild households. Together, these childless Americans have crafted a cushy lifestyle that's heavy on recreation and leisure. In Lacey, a scenic community near Olympia, the neat ramblers and ranches are often flanked by campers, trucks, and RVs. And most housing developments are within a short drive of a golf course. At nearby Panorama City, one of the nation's largest retirement communities, the daily array of cultural programs generates a waiting list as long as a cane.

"Cities used to mean jobs and excitement. Now they mean filth and crime and violence," says Balsley flatly. "Here you can still enjoy a good lifestyle with a nice plot of land, a good house, a feeling of security, and camping and hiking nearby. People come here to escape all of the evils of big-city life."

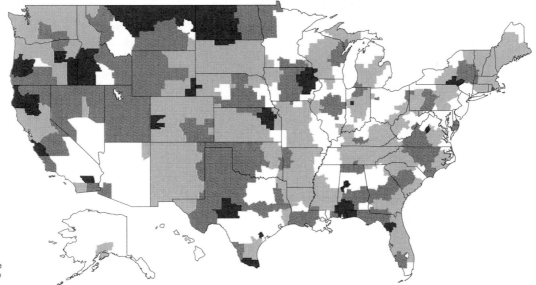

■ High
■ Above Average
■ Below Average
□ Low

The lack of kids to nurture and clothe also means disposable income for travel, country club memberships, and active leisure activities. Middleburg Managers visit ski resorts, gambling casinos, and time-shares at high rates. But they do look for bargains. At Lacey's Capital City Golf Course, the foursomes line up early on Saturday to take advantage of the modest greens fees and teeing charges. "People aren't flashy," notes Russ Olsen, course manager. "You'll see big Dodge trucks, not the BMWs and Mercedes." The educated populace, however, does make this a popular area for joining book clubs, using on-line services, and taking adult education courses. With their fondness for college sports, Middleburg Managers are consummate tailgaters; a game at the old alma mater calls for grilling chicken and steak next to their Olds sedans while sipping Bloody Marys. "There's never enough time to do all the things we want to do," concedes voice teacher Ruth Cowan. "People like to bike and jog and ski. We like to walk on the beach. There's a wealth of things to enjoy."

The age split in Middleburg Managers has a canceling-out effect in the political arena. No candidate in the 1996 election received above-average support in this cluster; the highest percentage of voters identified themselves as Independents. Residents here support liberal causes like abortion rights and marijuana legalization, as well as conservative causes such as school prayer and increased military spending abroad. One issue everyone agrees on is protecting the environment; the still unspoiled scenery of these recently rural areas prompts residents to worry about too much development and the attendant problems of pollution and toxic waste disposal. Many folks are active in community affairs, joining neighborhood homeowners' associations, writing their elected officials, and volunteering for nonpolitical activities. "The AARP is big," says one resident. "Politics is not."

The main fear in Middleburg Managers is that they'll become victims of their success. These uncrowded, bucolic, crime-free nirvanas are rapidly disappearing as newcomers discover them. Some Lacey residents give blunt advice on bumper stickers that read, "Californians Go Home." But as one local observes, "How do you get people to stop wanting what we have?"

PREFERENCES

(Index of 100 = U.S. Average)

Lifestyle / Products

what's hot

college football 250
on-line services 162
fraternal orders 155
domestic travel 152
stamp collecting 146
woodworking 139
golf 139
wholesale clubs 126
book clubs 124
contacting government officials 124

what's not

Home Depot 85
chess 84
disposable lighters 81
pasta machines 80
lottery tickets 77
painting / drawing 76
zoos 76
cross-country skiing 67
Victoria's Secret 65
pro basketball games 31

Food / Drink

Sizzlean 164
decorative icing 141
vodka 138
frozen boneless chicken 135
Kellogg's Special K 133
skim milk 132
bananas 126
beef 123
Wendy's 122
frozen orange juice 120

Magazines / Newspapers

Motor Trend 201
Smithsonian 177
Newsweek 150
Life 149
Popular Science 141
Field & Stream 139
Playboy 131
Popular Mechanics 128
Ladies' Home Journal 126
National Geographic 120

Television / Radio

nostalgia radio 203
Charles Grodin 163
Chicago Hope 145
Live with Regis & Kathie Lee 139
60 Minutes 135
TV college football 133
CNBC 125
Young and the Restless 124
CNN Headline News 122
Today Show 119

Cars / Trucks

Mitsubishi pickups 235
Oldsmobile Auroras 188
GMC C1500 Suburbans 172
Volkswagen Vanagons 168
Buick Park Avenues 167
Cadillac DeVilles 166
Suzukis 164
Mitsubishi Diamantes 163
Mazda 929s 156
Buick LeSabres 141

Cluster motto:
"So much to do, so little time"

SER 21

boomers & babies

1.3% of U.S. households
Primary age group: 25–44
Median household income: **$46,000**
Median home value: **$97,200**

Thumbnail Demographics

young white-collar suburban families
single-family housing
predominantly white and Asian households
college graduates
white-collar professionals

Politics

Predominant ideology: moderate Republican
1996 presidential vote: Bob Dole
Key issues: eliminating affirmative action, restricting
immigration, pro labor unions

Sample Neighborhoods

Thornton, Colorado 80229
Bothell, Washington 98011
Coon Rapids, Minnesota 55433
Midlothian, Virginia 23112
Spring Valley, California 91977

In Thornton, Colorado, they call it the invasion of the stroller people. And their kiddie pools. And their overcrowded classrooms. Thornton, a bedroom suburb northwest of Denver, used to be a quiet community of postwar ramblers and middle-class couples. Then it was discovered by young baby-boom families fed up with the congestion, crime, and gang activity of the city, and now it has the energy of an ant colony. In suburbs like Thornton across the country, an influx of young, upscale families has created Boomers & Babies, a cluster of bustling new subdivisions outside fast-growing metro areas. Over the last decade, such communities have seen their populations soar — Thornton's has doubled to 45,000 — and businesses have struggled to keep up. Boomers & Babies is a cluster where schools are overcrowded, story time at the library is SRO, and parents have to camp out to get their kids into recreation programs. "We used to be known for cow pastures and farmland," says Thornton resident Jim Houston. "Now we're full of young families and new housing developments and chains like Chili's and Applebee's."

Most of the business in Boomers & Babies is geared to early child-rearing families concerned with cost and convenience. In what were rolling wheat fields not five years ago, there are now twenty-four-hour pharmacies, Mexican fast-food restaurants, and mini-marts in every direction. Fifteen years ago, Anita Pacheco started a

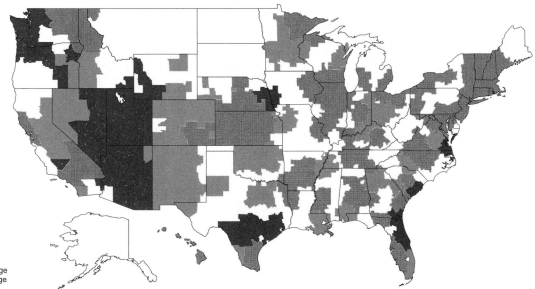

High
Above Average
Below Average
Low

child-care service in her Thornton home that quickly drew ten kids from the neighborhood. Today her setup has moved to an expansive space in a renovated shopping center with a roster of 152 kids, and she's begun talks with a local charter school to offer before- and after-school activities. "All these parents just keep having babies," she marvels. "And the community just keeps growing."

The adults in Boomers & Babies work hard at white-collar jobs during the week, but they give their weekends to their kids. Every third house in Thornton appears to have a camper or trailer in the driveway for weekend getaways. Upper-middle-class incomes allow families to splurge on the latest toys for birthdays and holidays, and surveys show these consumers buy inexpensive computers, video games, and VCRs at high rates. "Everyone has a stack of Disney videos," says one resident.

Boomers & Babies is also a good market for all manner of things related to young adults. That means health clubs are usually busy, with members taking Jazzercise courses or playing racquetball. And anything that has to do with cars is also popular, whether it's car loans, van dealers, or auto supply stores. Residents subscribe at high rates to car and home fix-it magazines, and as one Thornton resident observes, "There are a lot of sidewalk auto mechanics here." Consumers also enjoy bargain shopping at places like Kmart, Sears, and JCPenney; Eddie Bauer and Ann Taylor can skip these communities. On Saturday, adults head to warehouse clubs and local garage sales in search of bargains — that is, when they're not accompanying their kids to soccer fields and swimming pools. "The weekend is when you spend your quality time with your kids," explains Janice Mueller, an accountant and mother of two.

The population shift of city dwellers to clusters like Boomers & Babies reflects more than a desire for bigger yards and cleaner air. It also represents a flight from the ethnically and racially diverse metros by increasingly conservative young people. Political surveys show that these moderate Republicans dislike immigration, welfare, and affirmative action. "Basic conservatism has been growing in recent years," says Thornton councilman Chuck Warner. "A march for gay rights wouldn't get many people out here." Residents also tend to be religious sorts who support the pro-life movement. But mostly they worry about how to protect their kids from assaults on family values — and the more literal assaults of street crimes. Residents may have left the urban lifestyle behind, but they still worry about it every day.

PREFERENCES

(Index of 100 = U.S. Average)

Lifestyle / Products

what's hot

America Online 279
Builder's Square 187
new-car loans 144
call-waiting 144
tropical fish 143
science fiction 141
aerobics 137
softball 136
theme parks 131

what's not

gardens 83
pasta machines 79
stock-rating services 76
classical CDs / tapes 75
home-improvement loans 70
weekly groceries < $60 70
gas chain saws 70
cigars 61
Publishers Clearing House 55
boxing 43

Food / Drink

liquid breakfasts 161
Kool-Aid 157
packaged pasta salad 151
Taco Bell 147
Kellogg's Froot Loops 144
decorative icing 140
frozen boneless chicken 139
children's frozen dinners 129
dry mix salad dressing 125
fast food 105

Magazines / Newspapers

Popular Science 234
Car and Driver 213
Family Handyman 201
Weight Watchers 194
computer magazines 157
Cooking Light 156
Playboy 151
New Woman 142
Newsweek 142
National Geographic 134

Television / Radio

Tonight Show with Jay Leno 187
Martha Stewart Living 170
Christian / faith radio 166
Disney Channel 162
Mad About You 147
X-Files 143
Comedy Central 142
Rush Limbaugh 138
Dateline NBC 132
adult-contemporary radio 128

Cars / Trucks

Isuzu pickups 264
Mitsubishi Galants 204
GMC Safaris 202
Pontiac Firebirds 201
Mazda MPVs 198
Nissan Quests 197
Ford Aerostars 192
Chevrolet Astros 190
Mercury Capris 180
Saturn SCs 179

Status:

the complete Disney video library

SER 22

urban achievers

1.6% of U.S. households

Primary age groups: **25–34, 65+**

Median household income: **$35,600**

Median home value: **$109,900**

Thumbnail Demographics

midlevel urban couples and singles

multi-unit rental housing

ethnically mixed households

college graduates

professionals and managers

Politics

Predominant ideology: liberal Independent

1996 presidential vote: Ross Perot

Key issues: gay rights, defusing racial tensions,
increasing military spending

Sample Neighborhoods

Outer Richmond, San Francisco, California 94121

Hoboken, New Jersey 07030

Reseda, California 91335

Clearwater, Florida 34619

Bitter Lake, Seattle, Washington 98133

Urban Achievers is what American cities are becoming, centers of diverse neighborhoods filled with multi-ethnic groups, young and old residents, single students and older couples. Concentrated in a handful of coastal metros, this cluster reflects the continued significance of port cities for up-and-coming immigrants from Asia and Europe. More than one in six cluster residents are Asian — triple the national average — and about one in five come from other countries. But these folks aren't foreigners just off the boat: They occupy an upper-middle-class world of comfortable midsized apartment buildings, exotic restaurants, and cultural centers that cater to a progressive populace. "It's more interesting to live with a variety of people," explains Linda Fries, an artist from the Outer Richmond section of San Francisco. "I would be bored to death in a monocultural suburban community of any kind."

Outer Richmond is typical of Urban Achievers, a cultural polyglot of locally born whites and second-generation Chinese and Russian immigrants living on streets where the housing stock ranges from subsidized flophouses to ornate $600,000 town homes. The commercial base that caters to these consumers consists of specialty shops, ethnic markets, family restaurants, delis, sushi bars, and taco joints. On weekends, young singles and older couples stroll along the shops, walk their dogs in the many parks, or gather for

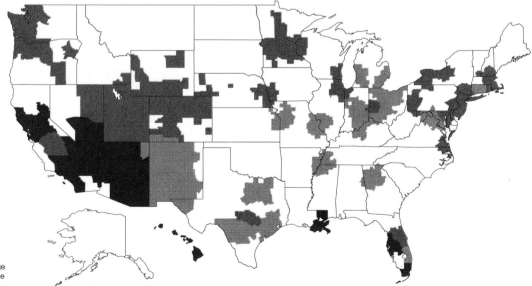

High
Above Average
Below Average
Low

theater   fresh fish   *Esquire*   news radio   Kias   passports   malt liquor   *Popular Photography*

music or arts programs at places like the Richmond Neighborhood Center. At a recent multicultural children's art fair at the center, some seven hundred people arrived for performances by Chinese dancers, Irish step dancers, African American storytellers, mariachi bands, and flamenco dancers. "This is a culturally sophisticated area," says director Patricia Kaussen. "What we try to do here is get people to live together, play together, and get along with each other. The differences are the good parts of the community."

As consumers, Urban Achievers behave like many upper-middle-class metropolitan sophisticates. They surf the Internet, go to movies, eat out, and travel abroad at high rates. With nearly 60 percent having gone to college, residents look for intellectually challenging pursuits, attending the theater, taking adult education classes, going to libraries, and supporting public broadcasting. "If *Fresh Air* with Terry Gross interviews an author, we'll have a run on that person's book," says librarian Blanche Maulet. Because so many people here have gambled on leaving their homelands for America, it's no surprise that casinos and lotteries are popular. But these Americans also maintain their cultural traditions in other ways. In Outer Richmond, many Chinese believe in feng shui, an ancient practice that in one form supposedly wards off evil and improves good fortune through strategic landscaping and interior design. Imported food, newspapers, videos, and CDs are big. And the medical community includes numerous herbalists and acupuncturists who practice in storefront offices. "The lay public is tolerant of alternatives to Western medicine," says pharmacist Alfred Hall. "People feel an advantage to having a choice."

An admittedly liberal group, Urban Achievers are proud of their broad-minded bent, and that value extends to politics. They're one of the most progressive groups in America on issues like gay rights, environmental protection, and racial issues. But they also take a hard-line stand on threats abroad, supporting increased military spending. Voters here don't mind going against the grain, choosing Ross Perot at high rates in the 1996 election. But most residents are more concerned with maintaining their hold on the American Dream. "People here define their dream as stability and a future and preserving a place where the government won't encroach on who you want to be," says Jeff Johnson, pastor of First United Lutheran Church in Outer Richmond. "And they feel they have it. Their fear is that they'll lose it."

PREFERENCES

(Index of 100 = U.S. Average)

Lifestyle / Products

what's hot

theater 170
passports 166
condoms 164
exercise clubs 163
adult education courses 159
on-line services 157
car alarms 156
stamp collecting 155
gambling casinos 142
foreign travel 131

what's not

steak houses 82
golf vacations 80
grocery lists 76
video game systems 70
Victoria's Secret 64
pro football games 62
camcorders 54
gas lawn mowers 47
Amway products 45
cellular phones 38

Food / Drink

Brie cheese 233
malt liquor 207
Cornish hens 155
Taco Bell 137
fresh fish 123
Entenmann's snacks 123
bagels 120
pasta 120
Burger King 120
Kool-Aid 118

Magazines / Newspapers

Esquire 217
Popular Photography 204
Architectural Digest 186
Cosmopolitan 180
Popular Mechanics 173
Life 147
Rolling Stone 142
Popular Science 129
People 128
Consumers Digest 125

Television / Radio

news radio 248
BET 244
Beverly Hills, 90210 222
jazz radio 188
pay-per-view sports 187
Nanny 157
NYPD Blue 157
Nightline 157
General Hospital 153
Wheel of Fortune 133

Cars / Trucks

Kias 217
Volkswagen Corrados 179
Nissan NX1s 172
Alfa Romeos 165
Volkswagen Golfs 162
Toyota 2WD SUs 158
Acura Integras 150
Toyota Corollas 148
Dodge Caravans 142
Volvo 240s 124

Local medical dilemma: pharmacist, herbalist, or acupuncturist?

SER 23

big sky families

1.5% of U.S. households

Primary age group: **35–54**

Median household income: **$45,200**

Median home value: **$98,600**

Thumbnail Demographics

midscale rural families

single-family housing

predominantly white households

high school graduates, some college

blue-collar and farmworkers

Politics

Predominant ideology: moderate Republican

1996 presidential vote: Bob Dole

Key issues: reducing size of government, tax reform, welfare reform

Sample Neighborhoods

Delano, Minnesota 55328

Freeport, Maine 04032

Virginia City, Nevada 89440

Ketchikan, Alaska 99950

Liberty, Missouri 64068

In recent years, Big Sky Families has experienced economic whiplash. First, the disappearance of factory and farming jobs increased local unemployment. Then came the opening of superstores like Target and Wal-Mart, which wrought havoc on their Main Streets, reducing clothing stores and restaurants to boarded-up storefronts and cheap office space. Today, these placid towns in scenic settings have been reborn with the arrival of young families from metro areas. Concentrated in the nation's northern tier from New England to the Rockies, Big Sky Families has become an upper-middle-class lifestyle in rural America, filled with new ranch-house developments surrounding the old town centers.

"I call us a 'third-ring suburb,'" says Lisa Blodgett, chamber of commerce director of Delano, Minnesota, population 2,700, located an hour from Minneapolis. "We were a farming town that's becoming more of a bedroom community — although half the people wouldn't admit it. People here don't want to become any bigger." A stop at the folksy State Bank of Delano proves her point: Every Friday, it serves customers coffee and cookies while they do their banking.

In Big Sky Families, residents enjoy comfortable lifestyles — the median income is $45,200 — derived from well-paying construction and crafts jobs in nearby cities. For leisure, they go off to the woods for hunting, fishing, or "cabining," as one Delano resident de-

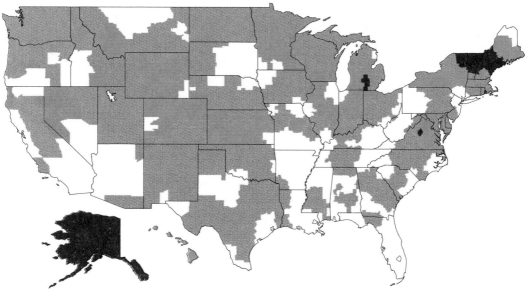

■ High
▨ Above Average
▨ Below Average
□ Low

overnight camping   fresh vegetables   *Outdoor Life   Another World*   Chevrolet Astros   needlepoint

scribes the pastime of hanging out at a lakefront cabin. Surveys show these outdoorsy people have little interest in television, movies, and plays. Among their favorite magazines are *Country Living, Field & Stream,* and *Audubon.* Residents in Big Sky Families are not the farm folks who make homemade meat loaf and potatoes au gratin, nor are they the yuppified consumers who frequent health food stores or sushi restaurants. Pop-Tarts and canned hash do well in this cluster. "We're into fifteen-minute meals," says April Stensgard, a graphic artist. "We'll eat whatever we can throw together in the microwave."

People who move to Big Sky Families communities do so for the old-fashioned amenities unavailable in metro areas. Parents leave their doors unlocked at night. Kids keep their bikes unchained in yards. "Being able to breathe fresh air means a lot," says Edie Taylor, owner of Edie Mae's Eatery in Delano. "People will sit down over a cup of coffee to solve the world's problems." Admittedly, living in these quiet towns means a commercial trade-off: There are no all-night drugstores, and it's a drive to find any sort of ethnic restaurant. But Delano does have a movie theater and a bowling alley, and folks will gather at the local American Legion for a steak fry dinner or pork chop feed. If they want to shop for clothes or specialty items, they'll reach for a mail-order catalog.

In this small-town environment, political views are often divided between longtime residents (conservative) and formerly urban newcomers (liberal). But all Big Sky Families share an antipathy for the symbols of big cities: big government, high taxes, and too much reliance on welfare. "People here like order: mowed lawns, well-kept gardens, and their dogs and children under control," says Delano banker Steve Gilmer, fifty-two. "They respect peace and quiet and neatness." During the 1996 election, they split their vote, giving the edge to Bob Dole because of the "character issue." As one resident more crassly explains, "Clinton has the morals of a goat." But such views aren't out of character in a cluster where residents own guns, support traditional values, and attend church at least once a week. "The old-timers can be clannish," says Joseph Kittock, a forty-nine-year-old farmer. "We tend to look after our own." But that's one reason city dwellers move to Big Sky Families, to be part of a place where neighbors care about each other.

PREFERENCES

(Index of 100 = U.S. Average)

Lifestyle / Products

what's hot

overnight camping 217
needlepoint 175
photography 169
trivia games 167
stereo equipment 165
bus travel 156
freshwater fishing 149
Christian / faith CDs / tapes 149
insect repellent 146
gardens 131

what's not

softball 89
weight lifting 78
college football games 73
electric juicers 72
fraternal orders 71
cigars 69
malt liquor 68
burglar alarms 64
espresso makers 63
on-line shopping 34

Food / Drink

liquid breakfasts 151
imported cheese 146
Kellogg's Pop-Tarts 145
canned hash 140
Diet cola 139
baking chips 138
pudding 128
Stove Top Stuffing 128
frozen orange juice 123
fresh vegetables 112

Magazines / Newspapers

Outdoor Life 212
Country Living 180
Reader's Digest 142
Newsweek 140
Business Week 136
Field & Stream 135
Audubon 131
home / garden section 126
Sports Illustrated 120
People 116

Television / Radio

Another World 221
Full House 207
CNN Sports News 205
country radio 164
Disney Channel 144
Nanny 143
CNN Business News 129
Bob Vila's Home Again 129
Cinemax 126
TV bowling 126

Cars / Trucks

Chevrolet Astros 348
Plymouth Grand Voyagers 347
Subaru Legacys 307
Subaru Loyales 290
GMC Safaris 202
Saab 9000s 194
Ford Econoline Club Wagons 183
Eagle Summits 181
Ford Festivas 161
Oldsmobile Intrigues 150

Conspicuously absent:
suits and ties

SER 24
suburban sprawl

1.8% of U.S. households

Primary age groups: **under 24, 25–34**

Median household income: **$41,000**

Median home value: **$99,900**

Thumbnail Demographics

young midscale suburban couples

owners and renters, single and multi-units

ethnically mixed married couples, some children

college graduates

white-collar workers

Politics

Predominant ideology: moderate Independent

1996 presidential vote: Ross Perot

Key issues: pro abortion rights, saving endangered
  animals, increasing school funding

Sample Neighborhoods

Burnsville, Minnesota 55337

Marlton, New Jersey 08053

Bensalem, Pennsylvania 19020

Burlington, New Jersey 08016

New Castle, Delaware 19720

Suburban Sprawl is an unusual American lifestyle: a multilingual, multi-ethnic cluster found in the heart of suburbia. The schools are decent. The housing is affordable (the median home value is $100,000). And the commute to downtown jobs is convenient. What's striking is the diversity of these middle-class neighborhoods, with above-average concentrations of African Americans, Hispanics, Asians, and foreign-born residents. Suburban Sprawlers have parlayed technical and professional skills into an up-and-coming version of the American Dream, complete with split-foyer homes, trampolines in the yards, and garages filled with adult toys like boats and snowmobiles. These are the large bilingual families who cram their kids into the backs of Toyota Tercels and drive off to a mall or a soccer game. As to any language barrier for the relatively large number of immigrant families, that soon disappears, thanks to ESL (English as a Second Language) classes for children as well as parents. That, and the influence of television shows like *The Simpsons, Friends,* and *Sally Jesse Raphael,* all watched at high rates.

In Burnsville, Minnesota, a bedroom suburb south of Minneapolis developed in the 1970s, life revolves around young families — from the numerous sports leagues to the shopping centers dotted with miniature golf courses, bike shops, and video stores. Residents of Suburban Sprawl generally have their pick of malls; in Burnsville, locals can choose between the Mall of America, with its acres of

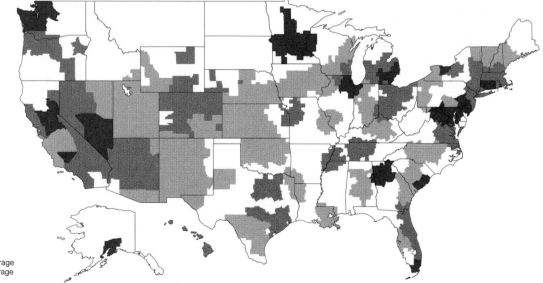

High
Above Average
Below Average
Low

three-way calling   Light 'n' Lively Kid Yogurt   *Motor Trend   Sally Jesse Raphael*   Isuzu Amigos

chain stores and amusement rides, and the Burnsville Center, offering the Disney Store, Gap Kids, and a food court where teenagers talk on cell phones. Younger kids head for the Cinema Café, where they can watch G-rated movies for a dollar. "A couple of clouds, and this place is packed," says theater owner Brian Minette. Weekend nights are for family videos at home. "Our social life revolves around the parents of the kids on our kids' teams," says Gay Dennison, a real estate agent for Edina Realty. "No one goes out on a Saturday night."

Leisure in Suburban Sprawl means active athletics. Every season means a new sport for the kids. Adults jog, ski, skate, play softball, and take aerobics classes, and they take their kids to bowling alleys and college basketball games. Not long out of college, parents still enjoy taking classes in painting, drawing, yoga, and financial planning. Big music fans, residents have eclectic tastes, from rap to easy listening to New Age. In Suburban Sprawl, parents profess to be health-conscious consumers but usually buy whatever's convenient and cheap. Children's frozen dinners, Hostess snack cakes, and Lunchables often find their way into grocery carts. Clothing is bought from bargain basement racks. "If the kids have to have a pair of Nikes, I'll do it," says Sonya Vaurio, a forty-four-year-old Burnsville resident and mother of three. "But price is very important. I only shop sales."

Given this cluster's diverse ethnic mix, it's perhaps no surprise that the political identity of Suburban Sprawl voters is a bit fuzzy. This is one of the few clusters that aligns itself with neither party, and its residents were nearly 50 percent more likely than the general population to have voted for Ross Perot in 1996. In issues surveys, residents tell pollsters that they're pro-choice, pro-church, against further immigration, and in favor of legalizing marijuana — enough contradictions to confuse a Sunday talk-show host. Mostly, these midscale voters are concerned about taxes and the economy, which made Independent candidate Ross Perot so attractive. As Pools & Patios wanna-bes, they one day hope to leave Suburban Sprawl for larger suburban homes a bit farther out in the countryside. "These are generally younger families who are working their way up through their careers," says Burnsville pastor Daniel P. Miller of Eden Baptist Church, a congregation of 150 families that's almost completely turned over in the last eight years. "People want to move here, but they'll move on to advance their careers." It's a sign of upward mobility that Suburban Sprawl residents hold dear — and a value they want to pass on to their children.

PREFERENCES

(Index of 100 = U.S. Average)

Lifestyle / Products

what's hot

three-way calling 182
in-line skating 174
gambling casinos 148
billiards / pool 143
on-line services 141
downhill skiing 141
Radio Shack 138
science fiction 135
bars / nightclubs 134
camera accessories 126

what's not

bus travel 86
cats 81
country music CDs / tapes 80
new-car loans 78
cross-country skiing 75
power tools 74
pipe tobacco 71
Amway products 71
racquetball 68
auto races 55

Food / Drink

Light 'n' Lively Kid Yogurt 243
gin 161
Cornish hens 141
Shake 'n Bake 140
Cap'n Crunch 135
imported cheese 131
Hostess snacks 121
low-cal frozen dinners 118
Kentucky Fried Chicken 109
canned spaghetti 102

Magazines / Newspapers

Motor Trend 195
Smithsonian 161
Essence 160
PC Magazine 148
Muscle & Fitness 146
Time 141
Outdoor Life 133
Inside Sports 133
Good Housekeeping 131
Popular Mechanics 130

Television / Radio

Sally Jesse Raphael 222
Frasier 178
Star Trek: Deep Space Nine 159
Friends 156
Disney Channel 151
HBO 150
NBC News at Sunrise 148
C-Span 146
Law and Order 139
easy-listening radio 135

Cars / Trucks

Isuzu Amigos 196
Hyundai Elantras 188
Toyota Paseos 185
Hyundai Excels 176
Hyundai Coupes 172
Saturns 162
Toyota Tercels 162
Mercury Capris 151
Honda Civics 151
Mazda MX-3s 150

Saturday night date: pizza and G-rated videos with the kids

ine skating   gin   *Smithsonian   Frasier*   Hyundai Elantras   gambling casinos   canned spaghetti

New Eco-topia is the kind of place where baby boomers surf the Net by the heat of a wood-burning stove. In these rural middle-class communities located from New England to the Northern Pacific, a majority of residents are college educated and have enlightened perspectives to match. They attend the theater and take painting classes at above-average rates. They hold New Age values and support recycling, composting, and eating organic foods. Unlike the provincial townspeople skewered by Sherwood Anderson, the worldly residents of New Eco-topia are more likely to subscribe to magazines like *Smithsonian* and the *Atlantic Monthly* than *Sports Afield* and *Guns & Ammo*. These are the citified rustics who buy the latest in composting equipment and don't even mind the chuckles of longtime locals at their hipper-than-thou tastes.

In fact, New Eco-topia may best be described as a mix of granola and grits, given the cluster's blend of educated urban exiles and older farm families. Supermarket surveys show tastes that range from imported cheese and rare wine to Spam and Kool-Aid. When it comes to cars, they purchase sensible Volvos and Hummer trucks at high rates. Politically, this onetime conservative Republican stronghold is now a moderate area because of the influx of more liberal city dwellers. Polls show above-average support for both cutting down the size of government and spending more money to protect endangered animals. In Westminster, Vermont, a small town near the New

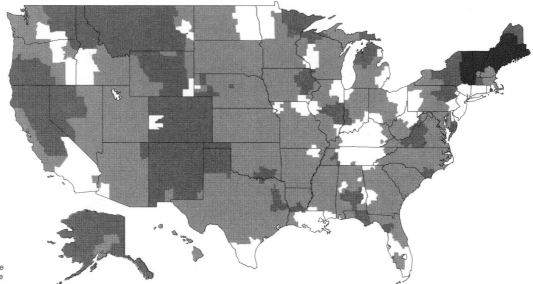

High
Above Average
Below Average
Low

America Online   beef   *Country Living   NBC Nightly News*   Dodge 4x4 pickups   satellite dishes

Hampshire border, those schizophrenic views have created a clash between farm-raised hunters and flatlanders who move in and post "No Hunting" signs. "You see a lot of 'us versus them' in attitudes," says Reverend Pete Hults, a local Congregational minister. And New Eco-topian communities are small enough that many residents get intimately involved in public activities, from charitable causes to political campaigns. Compared to average Americans, these folks write newspaper editors and contact government officials at high rates. "People are active around here," says Westminster native Christopher Barry, forty-seven, who directs a home for troubled youths. "They'll debate anything and everything from national news to what's happening at the local elementary school."

Despite isolated settings at least an hour's drive from the closest metro, the educated New Eco-topians manage to stay abreast of cultural trends. In Westminster, residents go to music programs in Brattleboro, art exhibits at Dartmouth, and the playhouse in Saxtons River. Satellite dishes have sprouted on many homes in New Eco-topia, and people watch above-average amounts of television, catching news programs like *Dateline* as well as fashions on the Home Shopping Network. Computers are de rigueur in this cluster, where residents run their home consulting businesses in long johns and hiking boots; it's not uncommon for people to rely on web sites rather than a morning paper for the latest current events. "We may be removed from the big cities, but we still want to keep in touch with the world," says Joan Smidutz, who runs a continuing-education program for nurses out of her home. "Otherwise, we'd just go brain dead."

For New Eco-topians, the goal is to create a delicate balance between urban awareness and country comfort. "They want a little piece of peace and quiet," says Westminster town manager William O'Connor, "but not too much." Unlike residents of other rural clusters, New Eco-topians exhibit leisure patterns akin to those of metro dwellers who take spa vacations and rack up frequent-flier miles on trips around the country. New Eco-topians have glommed on to the heartland tendency to cook from scratch, but they usually fill their breads with enough wholesome grains to scare away any meat-and-potatoes junkie. These are the consumers who want to surround their back-to-the-land lifestyle with the progressive ideas of downtown college campuses, to have their tofu cake and eat it too. It's no wonder that New Eco-topia is one of the only rural clusters to contribute to public broadcasting, that cultural bridge between highbrow and down-home culture.

PREFERENCES

(Index of 100 = U.S. Average)

Lifestyle / Products

what's hot

America Online 237
satellite dishes 202
furniture refinishing 163
work boots 158
veterans' clubs 149
pasta machines 133
freshwater fishing 129
backpacking / hiking 128
painting / drawing 125
cooking 119

what's not

bars / nightclubs 78
family videos 77
large-screen TVs 73
overdraft protection 71
golf 56
passports 50
jogging 49
call-waiting 47
dry-cleaning 31
7-Elevens 22

Food / Drink

beef 145
imported cheese 143
low-fat sour cream 136
dry mix salad dressing 136
canned hash 134
pasta 126
fresh vegetables 120
oatmeal 119
skim milk 117
salsa 111

Magazines / Newspapers

Country Living 223
Organic Gardening 195
Popular Science 151
Muscle & Fitness 139
Reader's Digest 137
McCall's 129
Travel & Leisure 125
Forbes 123
Playboy 122
Smithsonian 114

Television / Radio

NBC Nightly News 218
As the World Turns 200
Today Show 158
Family Channel 143
public broadcasting 139
Discovery Channel 134
Primetime Live 131
BET 127
Lifetime 126
Chicago Hope 110

Cars / Trucks

Dodge 4 x 4 pickups 586
Hummer trucks 580
Jeep Grand Wagoneers 491
Subarus 426
Saab 9000s 294
Volvo 240s 180
Mitsubishi Expos 167
Mercury Tracers 159
Saturn SWs 148
Ford Aspires 146

Status:
a well-designed
family web site

SER 26
new homesteaders

2.0% of U.S. households

Primary age groups: **35–44, 45–54**

Median household income: **$36,800**

Median home value: **$91,200**

Thumbnail Demographics

young middle-class exurban families

single-family housing

predominantly white households

some college education

white-collar workers

Politics

Predominant ideology: conservative Republican

1996 presidential vote: Bob Dole

Key issues: pro-life movement, family values,
    reducing TV violence

Sample Neighborhoods

West Swanzey, New Hampshire 03469

Oak Ridge, Tennessee 37830

Cody, Wyoming 82414

Charles Town, West Virginia 25414

Asheville, North Carolina 28804

Young middle-class families priced out of suburbia find refuge in New Homesteaders, a collection of small rustic townships whose residents have college educations at above-average rates. With decent jobs in retail, health, and the communications industries, residents earn solid salaries of about $40,000 and plant roots in this patch of exurban real estate, where the median value of ranches and Cape Cods is a below-average $91,200. Many of these homeowners park a camper or power boat in the driveway, take their kids fishing or hunting on the weekend, and often belong to a country club for tennis and golf. In West Swanzey, New Hampshire, a town of 9,000 west of Manchester, kids can play at a new skateboard arena, a bike trail, and two new playgrounds. "There's not much for single people around here," concedes George Nikiforakis, forty-six, owner of Nick's Restaurant, a local seafood house. "But young families feel lucky to be here."

In the marketplace, New Homesteaders behave like many consumers in the early child-rearing phase of their lives. They're big on fast food and grocery stores that feature bulk foods at discounted prices. At Gomarlo's Food & Circus in West Swanzey, the supermarket is arranged to allow shoppers to run in and out in a few minutes. "Everyone is too pressed for time to clip coupons around here," says owner Mike Gomarlo. "They know just what they want and don't

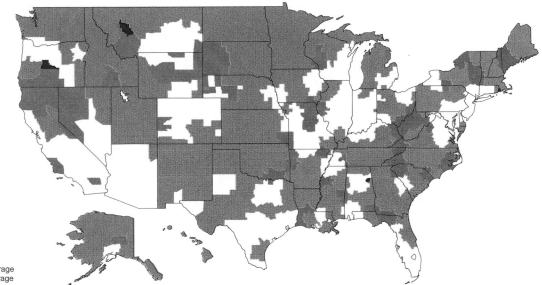

High
Above Average
Below Average
Low

furniture refinishing   peanut butter   *Golf Digest*   *ESPN NFL Primetime*   Jeep Grand Wagoneers

want to spend an extra second shopping." As for their taste in products, the health food revolution has yet to catch on in New Homesteaders. Meals are grabbed out of the microwave and eaten in front of the TV. "We're a bologna-and-potatoes area," says Gomarlo, a fifty-five-year-old second-generation grocer. "We sell fifty pounds of potatoes for five ninety-nine, and we go through pallets of them."

Home is the center of life in New Homesteaders. Halloween is probably the biggest holiday of the year, with elaborate and spooky decorations gracing many homes. By Saturday night, many families just collapse at home with a video. "We're stay-at-home people," one resident observes. Inside, most rooms are filled with TVs, VCRs, or older computers. In this cluster, the TV serves less as entertainment than wallpaper, a constant noise in the background. Every kind of show is "must-see TV": sitcoms, sports, reality-crime, and Jerry Springer and his ilk. Parents read magazines and kids do their homework while Nickelodeon drones away — "None of the sexy and gory stuff," one adult insists. Given the number of children in this exurban setting, it's no surprise that pets are popular. In West Swanzey, the humane society reports families' becoming attached to everything from cats and dogs to rabbits, goats, and potbellied pigs. "The most popular are athletic dogs," says membership coordinator Elizabeth Frenette, "because they can keep up with people who jog and ski and hike."

Maintaining a safe place for children is a paramount concern of parents in New Homesteaders. And that concern extends to politics. Both conservative and Republican, they're unapologetic about wanting to curb pornography and reduce violence on television. They're also among the clusters with the greatest opposition to gay rights, abortion rights, and Bill Clinton. "I'm a typical June Cleaver sort of mother," concedes Sheila Swett, a forty-two-year-old beautician and mother of two preteen boys. "I'm against drugs, drinking, and smoking. And I can see myself getting more conservative and like my parents every day." Their nonstop activities make New Homesteaders relatively apathetic about national and world events beyond their family sphere. In West Swanzey, residents rarely join protest marches unless the issue concerns a development disrupting nearby parkland. "You want to preserve what you have for your kids, for the next generation," says Swett. "You worry about kids hanging out at malls and getting into trouble." The rustic towns where they live, by contrast, are crime free.

PREFERENCES
(Index of 100 = U.S. Average)

Lifestyle / Products
what's hot

furniture refinishing 165

campers 161

soft-rock music 150

downhill skiing 149

boating 146

indoor plants 145

roller-skating 145

religious clubs 138

MasterCards 133

cats 126

what's not

volleyball 84

disposable lighters 80

charitable volunteering 77

chess 72

Adidas 71

HBO 67

cooking 60

TV wrestling 58

jazz radio 57

tractor pulls 18

Food / Drink

butter substitute 145

low-calorie bread 141

Kellogg's All-Bran 134

baking chips 133

domestic wine 129

hot dogs 119

low-cal frozen dinners 117

frozen orange juice 116

peanut butter 111

sausage 105

Magazines / Newspapers

Golf Digest 233

Scientific American 154

Popular Mechanics 150

Star 136

National Geographic 133

sports section 126

health magazines 122

Better Homes and Gardens 117

Family Circle 115

Consumers Digest 115

Television / Radio

ESPN NFL Primetime 804

Jerry Springer Show 194

Mad About You 175

variety radio 171

Beverly Hills, 90210 154

CBS Evening News 140

Home Improvement 140

Rescue 911 139

TV golf 136

TV college football 131

Cars / Trucks

Jeep Grand Wagoneers 216

GMC Sierras 204

Subaru Justys 164

Buick Park Avenues 160

Oldsmobile Auroras 153

Subaru Loyales 153

Buick LeSabres 148

Cadillac DeVilles 146

Lincoln Continentals 141

Mazda 929s 140

Status: a vacation to Disney World

SER 27
boomtown singles

1.2% of U.S. households

Primary age groups: **under 24, 25–34**

Median household income: **$32,000**

Median home value: **$89,300**

Thumbnail Demographics

young middle-income couples and singles

multi-unit renters

predominantly white households

college graduates

white-collar professionals

Politics

Predominant ideology: moderate Republican

1996 presidential vote: Ross Perot

Key issues: reducing government size, balancing
the budget, toxic waste disposal

Sample Neighborhoods

Beaverton, Oregon 97005

Burlington, Vermont 05401

Dover, New Hampshire 03820

Ann Arbor, Michigan 48104

Lynnwood, Washington 98037

A generation ago, young singles moved to the nation's big metro areas to launch new lives and new careers. Today they've taken a detour to Boomtown Singles, a collection of fast-growing satellite cities where there's less crime, fewer crowds, and none of the high costs associated with urban living. In these midsized, midscale communities, residents tend to live in sprawling garden-style apartments, work at high-tech companies, and frequent bars, health clubs, and music stores. You see them in cities like Beaverton, Oregon, just outside of Portland, which is home to dozens of info-tech start-ups. Over the past decade, Beaverton, which describes itself as the center of the "Silicon Forest," has seen its population double to 130,000. "We're growing so fast that we can barely keep up with it," says Robert Enninga, an architect and member of the city's planning commission. "All the available land on our urban boundaries has been snatched up."

With two-thirds of its populace unmarried and 40 percent under thirty-five years old, Boomtown Singles caters to young, active lifestyles. A disproportionate number of residents spend their leisure time engaging in aerobic sports like jogging, Rollerblading, and skiing. In Boomtown Singles, the dating-and-mating dance still revolves around the club scene — whether it's nightclubs or health clubs. "A lot of people will invest three to six hours a week in how

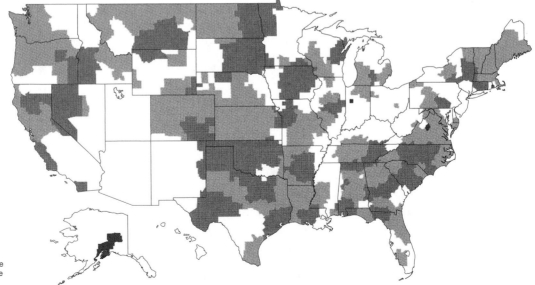

High
Above Average
Below Average
Low

college football games Twizzlers *Inc.* *Comedy Central* Toyota MR2s roller-skating Taco Bell

they look," says Michele Briedé, manager of a Gold's Gym. "They'll come in, work out, and get cologned up before going on a date."

Yet these singles bear little resemblance to the trendier Young Influentials collecting Sharper Image toys. Although they tend to work as white-collar professionals, their relative youth translates to below-median incomes of $32,000, and they carry pagers, not cellular phones. They read *Cosmopolitan,* not *Martha Stewart Living.* At Intel's headquarters, workers enjoy executive parking spots, lunchrooms, and limos. Most employees wear jeans unless a customer is coming to the offices. "It's laid-back in terms of looks but intense in terms of the output," says John Griffiths, an Intel marketing director. And it's no place to find locals sitting down to a home-cooked meal; they live by takeout, fast food, and happy hour grazing. At the Beaverton Town Square, a giant Häagen-Dazs outlet sits near Subway, Ultimate Burrito, and Chicken Bar outlets. The *last* thing cluster residents want to do is eat out more often. "My girlfriends and I are into hors d'oeuvres food," says Alice Fosse, a divorced saleswoman and hospitality director of a ski club. "Our dinner may be deep-fried calamari, mozzarella cheese, and buffalo wings."

A new cluster first identified in the 1990 census, Boomtown Singles reflects a political melding of youthful liberalism with pro-growth economic conservatism. Voter polls show these moderate Republicans want to protect the environment and reduce the size of government. They dislike the hard-core conservatism of Rush Limbaugh and are adamantly opposed to school prayer; they're among the nation's few middle-of-the-road groups that strongly support gay rights and saving endangered animals. At Nike's Beaverton campus, officials have tried to restore the endangered wetlands surrounding its headquarters. Cluster residents pride themselves on their independent streak: Boomtown Singles were nearly twice as likely as other Americans to vote for Ross Perot in 1996. "This is a swing area," says one political observer, "but not an area for activism." Few residents become involved in demonstrations over hot-button issues, in part because so few sink deep roots. And voicing discontent is largely confined to the area just below the trunks of their cars. One of the popular bumper stickers in these areas says simply, "Mean People Suck."

PREFERENCES

(Index of 100 = U.S. Average)

Lifestyle / Products

what's hot

college football games 246

roller-skating 227

education loans 219

hard-rock music 191

furniture refinishing 155

downhill skiing 154

health clubs 153

CD players 138

pagers / beepers 132

bars / nightclubs 128

what's not

vitamins 83

smoking 82

computer books 80

gasoline credit cards 77

financial planners 77

large-screen TVs 74

gambling casinos 69

travel agents 68

foreign videos 20

Price Club 20

Food / Drink

Twizzlers 222

Taco Bell 187

wine coolers 161

Domino's pizza 159

light beer 145

salsa 128

hot dogs 120

regular cola 120

Hamburger Helper 114

pork chops 113

Magazines / Newspapers

Inc. 265

Cosmopolitan 237

Soap Opera Digest 218

bridal magazines 198

Gourmet 182

music magazines 164

sports magazines 146

People 132

Shape 129

New Yorker 125

Television / Radio

Comedy Central 208

Entertainment Tonight 200

Saturday Night Live 168

CBS This Morning 167

MTV 165

Beverly Hills, 90210 159

TV auto racing 148

Days of Our Lives 142

X-Files 130

New York Undercover 121

Cars / Trucks

Toyota MR2s 230

Subaru Justys 193

Mazda MX-6s 175

Suzuki Samurais 173

Mitsubishis 171

Nissan 240SXs 171

Volkswagen Foxes 161

Mazda Navajos 152

Honda CRXs 145

Acura Integras 142

Most common sign:
"Now Hiring"

upstarts & seniors

1.2% of U.S. households

Primary age groups: **under 34, 55 +**

Median household income: **$31,800**

Median home value: **$93,100**

Thumbnail Demographics

middle-income suburban empty-nesters and singles

multi-unit renters

predominantly white households

college graduates

white-collar professionals

Politics

Predominant ideology: moderate Democrat

1996 presidential vote: Bill Clinton

Key issues: tax reform, doctor-assisted suicide,
  gay rights

Sample Neighborhoods

Lakeside, Richmond, Virginia 23228

Woodbine, Nashville, Tennessee 37211

Englewood, Colorado 80110

Milwaukie, Portland, Oregon 97222

South Troost, Kansas City, Missouri 64131

Upstarts & Seniors is one of the more schizophrenic lifestyles, a mix of old and young, singles and widowers, "young marrieds and old codgers," as one resident puts it. Widely scattered throughout the country in older inner-ring suburbs, the cluster is filled with original homeowners who are now empty-nesting and approaching retirement. But a large proportion of the population are newcomers, young singles and couples taking advantage of the affordable housing and easy commute to downtown jobs. "You have older people moving out and younger people moving in," says one real estate broker. What unites them is a middle-class sensibility and an appreciation for an off-the-beaten-track environment between the hip downtown area and the popular suburbs. As one real estate brochure observes in somewhat tortured cadence: "A transient yuppie village it is not."

Research surveys reflect the split personality of Upstarts & Seniors. This is one of the nation's few lifestyles where residents go to both singles bars and museums at high rates, where they support legalizing marijuana as well as banning violent music lyrics. In Lakeside, Virginia, a northwestern suburb of Richmond, the mixed clientele supports pharmacies and fishing stores for the seniors and computer shops and hip clothiers for the Generation X crowd. Longtime mom-and-pop businesses are struggling to survive as national

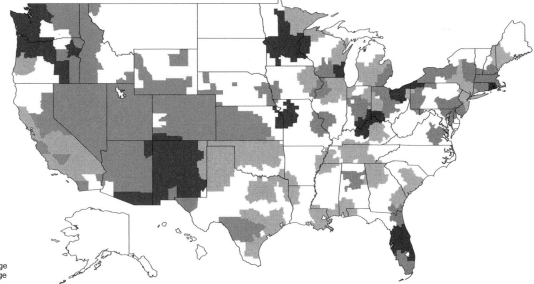

High
Above Average
Below Average
Low

moviegoing   espresso / cappuccino   *Saturday Evening Post*   Bravo   Nissan 300ZXs   college footba

chains like Wal-Mart and Lowe's move in. The midscale economic base supports a ring of fast-food restaurants, 99-cent budget stores, and low-end car dealers. On summer weekends, residents of all ages are seen working in their yards and tinkering with their cars before gathering for barbecues. Some yards are neat and closely trimmed; in others, dented sedans are perched precariously on cinder blocks.

"No one's unfriendly. People get together over a six-pack of beer and whatever sports game is on TV," says Robin Raver, twenty-eight, a Lakeside teacher and massage therapist. Kitty Raver, her fifty-six-year-old aunt and a property manager who lives nearby, sees it differently. "People say hi to each other and are very pleasant," she says, "but they rarely socialize with each other." One of the meeting grounds, both agree, is the Lakeside Pharmacy, with its old-fashioned lunch counter, $2.50 lunch special, and Norman Rockwell prints.

Unlike those of other lifestyles with a high proportion of young people, the residents of Upstarts & Seniors are relatively sedentary. They exhibit relatively low rates for jogging, tennis, and racquetball but have a fondness for reading, watching television, and surfing the Internet. Only one in five have finished college — "Most of us couldn't afford tuition," says one young resident — which makes for relatively little interest in books, foreign films, or magazines other than light reading; the more popular titles range from *Saturday Evening Post* to *Muscle & Fitness*. Gambling on lottery tickets is popular because, as Kitty Raver notes, "everyone has dreams of not having to work anymore." She pauses. "But what's wrong with working? The older generation doesn't mind working for a living, while the younger people are part of the 'gimme generation.'"

That generation gap is seen in political surveys depicting Upstarts & Seniors as a mass of contradictions. Some voters support gay rights, others worry about sexual permissiveness. They do manage to agree on their allegiance to the Democratic Party. "It goes back to the Depression, when the Democrats were the politicians of the people," explains retired barber Ed Garnett. "My father used to say that if the Democrats ran a monkey, people around here would vote for him." But that point of agreement is rare in this cluster, where people share the same quiet streets and affordable bungalows but tend to go their separate ways. "What brings the ages together," says Robin Raver, "is sitting around and yacking."

PREFERENCES

(Index of 100 = U.S. Average)

Lifestyle / Products

what's hot

America Online 331

college football games 311

travel 229

collecting stamps 152

moviegoing 148

golf vacations 145

museums 132

adult education courses 132

bars / nightclubs 125

boating 121

what's not

TV boxing 96

rap music 93

canned spaghetti 86

pipe tobacco 79

children's vitamins 79

country clubs 43

on-line shopping 43

ice hockey games 30

New Age CDs / tapes 0

tractor pulls 0

Food / Drink

espresso / cappuccino 176

whole-bean coffee 158

Domino's pizza 157

domestic wine 156

Kellogg's Special K 149

low-fat sour cream 143

low-cal frozen dinners 133

Nutri bars / snacks 122

pretzels 113

veal 102

Magazines / Newspapers

Saturday Evening Post 263

Inside Sports 257

Travel & Leisure 197

Elle 196

Muscle & Fitness 175

Cooking Light 168

Ladies' Home Journal 161

Cosmopolitan 138

Better Homes and Gardens 138

Money 128

Television / Radio

Bravo 299

Late Night with Conan O'Brien 276

soft-rock radio 198

USA Network movies 188

Chicago Hope 165

NBC Nightly News 154

Murphy Brown 151

Cinemax 145

Good Morning America 130

Oprah Winfrey Show 112

Cars / Trucks

Nissan 300ZXs 144

Isuzu 2WD pickups 141

Suzuki 2WD SUVs 139

Suzukis 135

Toyota Paseos 134

Saturn SLs 132

Saturns 130

Saturn SCs 128

Ford Tempos 121

Buick Skylarks 120

Favorite pastime: hanging out at the drugstore lunch counter

SER 29

new beginnings

1.4% of U.S. households

Primary age groups: **under 24, 25–34**

Median household income: **$31,400**

Median home value: **$93,400**

Thumbnail Demographics

young mobile suburban couples and singles

multi-unit renters

ethnically mixed households

college graduates

white-collar professionals

Politics

Predominant ideology: moderate Republican

1996 presidential vote: Ross Perot

Key issues: gay rights, defusing racial tensions,
     legalizing marijuana

Sample Neighborhoods

Ventura, Orlando, Florida 32822

Redlands, California 92373

Multnomah, Portland, Oregon 97219

Clarkston, Georgia 30021

North Broadway, San Antonio, Texas 78217

In the Ventura section of Orlando, Florida, one apartment complex follows another in a checkerboard of squat, pastel-colored buildings, bisected by swimming pools, tennis courts, and fast-food restaurants. Ventura is a classic New Beginnings community, a magnet for young adults in a state of transition. Concentrated in Sunbelt boomtowns, New Beginnings is filled with young educated singles and couples just starting out on their career paths — or starting over after divorces, layoffs, or company transfers. "People here are either running away from something or running to something," says apartment manager Ann Maynard, who describes her clientele as an assortment of unattached students, teachers, hospital workers, and police officers. "The efficiencies are full of newly divorced men or women trying to get back on their feet. It's often a struggle."

Although 60 percent of New Beginnings residents have gone to college, their living standards are still modest because of their transitional status. The parking lots are lined with older subcompacts such as Sentras, Escorts, Storms, and Tercels. The shopping centers are filled with fast-food restaurants like Taco Bell and Burger King, as well as discount stores such as Payless Shoes, Wal-Mart, and Hair Cuttery. The high concentration of apartment dwellers encourages a do-it-yourself economy, and cluster commu-

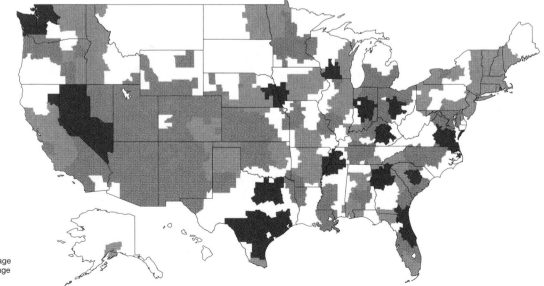

High
Above Average
Below Average
Low

scuba diving   regular cola   *Penthouse*   *People's Court*   Suzuki 2WD SUs   volleyball   brown rice   *Spi*

nities seem to specialize in auto parts shops, hardware stores, self-storage facilities, and laundromats for residents who don't own washers and driers. "You have a lot of people living paycheck to paycheck," says a Ventura construction worker. "It's hard to get very well established here." In New Beginnings, check-cashing establishments are popular for the large number of residents who don't have enough savings to warrant a bank account. The cluster ranks low on financial products ranging from stocks and bonds to money market accounts and IRAs. In Ventura, some video stores even advertise their check-cashing service with flashing window signs like movie marquees.

Given the cluster's disproportionate number of unattached twenty-somethings, it's not surprising that the rhythm of New Beginnings resembles that of a college town. On Saturday nights, locals flock to restaurant chains, sports bars, and movie theaters. In Ventura a popular hangout is the Wing Shack, which specializes in billiards and buffalo wings. Sundays are for sleeping in, going to the swimming pool, doing laundry, and what one resident calls "yard saling" — an activity so common that it warrants a verb. Locals fill their homes with elaborate stereos to listen to contemporary rock and country music, as well as with athletic equipment to keep their young bodies firm. Many living rooms contain mountain bikes as part of a decor that also includes beanbag chairs and milk-crate shelves laden with magazines like *Spin* and *Shape*.

New Beginnings is a transient lifestyle — at Christmas, cluster communities are deserted as residents head home — and the goal of many locals is to establish some permanence in their lives. "All of us are concerned about security: job security, personal security, and relationship security," one resident observes. Politically, this is a swing area, though surprisingly conservative for a neighborhood type filled with young people. The highest percentage of residents describe themselves as Republican, but a large share also voted for Ross Perot in 1996. And voters still support liberal issues like legalizing drugs, behaving more like a young partying crowd than traditional members of the GOP. But New Beginnings usually produces only a low voter turnout, like many transient-filled communities. "People consider their homes only temporary housing," says Ann Maynard of her apartment tenants. In New Beginnings, residents are just passing through.

PREFERENCES

(Index of 100 = U.S. Average)

Lifestyle / Products

what's hot

scuba diving 237
volleyball 208
microwaves 197
power boats 157
weekly groceries
  < $60 157
bars / nightclubs 151
disposable lighters 139
coupons 136
baby furniture 136
answering machines
  128

what's not

auto clubs 82
diet pills 80
pagers / beepers 78
plants 77
gambling casinos 75
sailboats 63
sewing 62
travel agents 59
stair steppers 58
Victoria's Secret 7

Food / Drink

regular cola 165
brown rice 149
frozen dinners 143
ready-to-serve dips
  141
instant grits 140
Pizza Hut 140
light beer 134
Nutri bars / snacks 132
egg substitute 130
Kellogg's Pop-Tarts
  129

Magazines / Newspapers

Penthouse 286
Spin 269
GQ 227
Shape 226
Working Mother 188
American Baby 174
Glamour 174
Guns & Ammo 161
Prevention 145
USA Today 144

Television / Radio

People's Court 209
CBS Morning News 207
Saturday Night Live 179
TV boxing 149
Melrose Place 146
MTV 144
country radio 143
Geraldo 139
Dateline NBC 139
Cops 138

Cars / Trucks

Suzuki 2WD SUs 247
Mitsubishi Eclipses 215
Mercury Capris 200
Hyundai Scoupes 193
Honda Preludes 177
Volkswagen Foxes 177
Mazda Protegés 172
Mitsubishi Mirages 165
Nissan Sentras 155
Isuzu Rodeos 148

Favorite business:
check-cashing video store

SER 30

blue-chip blues

2.2% of U.S. households

Primary age group: **35–64**

Median household income: **$41,700**

Median home value: **$88,700**

Thumbnail Demographics

upscale suburban blue-collar families

single-family housing

predominantly white households

high school graduates, some college

blue- and white-collar workers

Politics

Predominant ideology: moderate Independent

1996 presidential vote: Ross Perot

Key issues: tax reform, defusing racial tensions, school prayer

Sample Neighborhoods

Maple Shade, New Jersey 08052

Redford, Michigan 48239

Tinley Park, Illinois 60477

Grandview, Missouri 64030

Glenside, Pennsylvania 19038

The largest lifestyle in America during the 1980s, Blue-Chip Blues has since shrunk by half following the decline in blue-collar jobs throughout the nation. Today, the cluster is filled with empty-nesting families living in homes that have been likened to the little green Monopoly houses. In these chain-link-fence suburbs built a half-century ago, before neighbors began hiding behind tall stockade fences in newer subdivisions, the streets are often lined with boats and vans, the "company car" for the cluster's many small contractors. On the main street in Maple Shade, New Jersey, a town of 19,000 east of Philadelphia, the businesses include an auto repair shop, two hardware stores, a frozen-custard stand, and an old-fashioned five-and-dime. In the center of town sits a brass-trimmed gazebo donated by residents, who also volunteered their time to build a street-hockey rink and a parking lot at the town softball fields. "It's a blue-collar town, but there are no class divisions," says Carmella Hirnickel, the town librarian. "There's no 'other side of the tracks' around here."

What there are in Blue-Chip Blues communities are middle-class people with working-class values. Residents are more likely than average Americans to work on their cars, trim their shrubbery, and do their own house renovations. "Hechinger's and Home Depot are the two biggest stores in town," says James McComas Jr., who owns an auto detailing shop and two car washes. "Most people

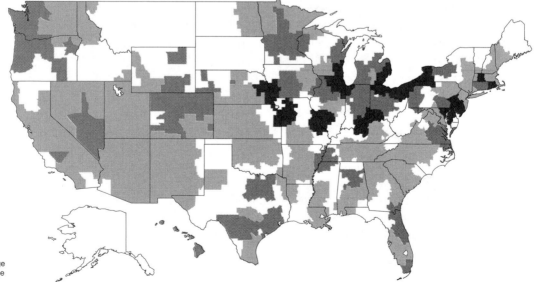

■ High
▨ Above Average
▨ Below Average
□ Low

home renovation Pepsi Free *Golf* *Melrose Place* Ford Tempos lottery tickets Entenmann's snacks

spend their recreation time fixing up their homes." Surveys show Blue-Chip Blues is a sports-crazy cluster, with high rates for attending pro baseball, basketball, and ice hockey games, as well as participating in softball, hockey, and basketball leagues. Swimming is popular in backyard pools, some of which cost more than the homes. And community events are often tied to secular holidays: July Fourth parades, Halloween dances, fall flea markets.

In Blue-Chip Blues areas, most residents have not completed college and don't necessarily see the value in a degree — "as long as the kids can learn a trade and make some money at it," one parent notes. But they do have relatively high rates for subscribing to magazines — especially mainstream publications like *Reader's Digest, Glamour,* and *Sporting News* — as well as joining book clubs. At the Maple Shade library, there are waiting lists to check out best-selling fiction and anything promoted on *Oprah.* "Michael Crichton could put out a book of statistics and it would create a waiting list," says librarian Hirnickel. "People are still reading books about O. J."

Created during the white flight of the postwar years, Blue-Chip Blues is still not the most racially accommodating lifestyle. Maple Shade used to have a Ku Klux Klan chapter, and a visit from a young Martin Luther King prompted a local bartender to meet him brandishing a shotgun. "There's still a strong racist undercurrent," concedes Reverend Joseph Sellers of the Congregational Church of Christ. "You still find hostility toward people who aren't 'our own.'" Politically, Blue-Chip Blues has been called "pragmatically conservative," a cluster of moderate swing voters concerned more about economic issues than anything else. "When people hear about a company announcing layoffs, they all think, 'There but for the grace of God go I,'" says Maple Shade town manager George Haeuber. "A lot of people live from paycheck to paycheck."

Given the economic shift that's transformed the country from a manufacturing to a high-tech economy, the uncertainty expressed in Blue-Chip Blues is understandable. As wealthier Americans have followed new homes, jobs, and malls to farther-out suburbs, these blue-collar residents feel somewhat left behind. And yet they take comfort in their tight-knit neighborhoods, longtime friends, summer block parties, and hearty volunteerism. "There's still a city-stoop mentality among us," says Haeuber. "People are satisfied with the way things are." In these communities, familiarity breeds content.

PREFERENCES

(Index of 100 = U.S. Average)

Lifestyle / Products

what's hot

home renovation	241
lottery tickets	178
zoos	157
pro baseball games	155
gas grills	144
stationary bicycles	142
coupons	136
Mary Kay cosmetics	134
watching TV	131
book clubs	129

what's not

chess	85
freshwater fishing	83
passports	82
Wal-Mart	82
Amway products	81
Medicare / Medicaid	79
chewing tobacco	71
in-home pregnancy tests	67
satellite dishes	62
maids / housekeepers	58

Food / Drink

Pepsi Free	156
Entenmann's snacks	154
fresh cold cuts	140
low-calorie bread	136
pretzels	133
packaged pasta salad	130
Kellogg's Froot Loops	124
canned ham	122
Stove Top Stuffing	121
light beer	121

Magazines / Newspapers

Golf	179
Sporting News	159
Car Craft	158
Audubon	142
American Health	137
Playboy	124
GQ	124
Glamour	121
Reader's Digest	117
Cosmopolitan	117

Television / Radio

Melrose Place	179
Beverly Hills, 90210	161
General Hospital	152
Disney Channel	139
adult-contemporary radio	131
ESPN NFL Primetime	131
progressive-rock radio	130
NYPD Blue	129
Nanny	128
ABC World News Tonight	127

Cars / Trucks

Ford Tempos	228
Chevrolet Berettas	201
Plymouth Sundances	191
Chevrolet Cavaliers	191
Buick Skylarks	184
Plymouth Acclaims	179
Pontiac Sunbirds	174
Ford Aerostars	170
GMC Safaris	150
Mercury trucks	130

Status: wearing the latest shade of Mary Kay nail polish

SER 31

towns & gowns

1.4% of U.S. households

Primary age group: **under 24**

Median household income: **$18,600**

Median home value: **$74,600**

Thumbnail Demographics

college-town singles

10 + unit rental housing

predominantly white and Asian households

college graduates

white-collar and service workers

Politics

Predominant ideology: liberal Independent

1996 presidential vote: Bill Clinton

Key issues: human rights abroad, gay rights, legalizing marijuana

Sample Neighborhoods

Boulder, Colorado 80302

Berkeley, California 94704

Gainesville, Florida 32608

Stillwater, Oklahoma 74075

Bowling Green, Ohio 43402

America's college towns have always been peculiar places, forever young thanks to the annual crop of students who arrive each fall, and often conflicted as locals cope with the latest trends of eighteen-year-olds — from goldfish swallowing to pot smoking to streaking to body piercing. But lately, many college towns have become desired addresses for more than students. Recent graduates now stick around to launch start-up companies, and retirees have begun returning to their alma maters' hometowns to live out their years in places that still hold fond memories.

The result of these crosscurrents is that the college communities of Towns & Gowns are now more upscale and chic than ever before. In Boulder, Colorado, with a population of 100,000 (one-quarter are students at the University of Colorado), almost a third of all residents have no reportable incomes, the older ones living on pensions, the younger ones getting by on their parents' largesse and trust funds. Locals claim that many newcomers are bohemian "trust fund babies" (they drive BMWs and wear Birkenstocks) drawn to an enviable lifestyle that features dramatic mountains nearby, plenty of local nightlife, and a New Age ethic that's prompted local officials to consider banning all cars in town to reduce pollution. "Status used to mean showing up at the farmers' market in town on Saturday," says Karen Mitchell, a lifestyle re-

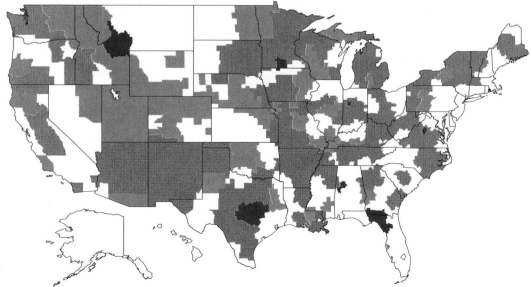

High
Above Average
Below Average
Low

foreign videos   tequila   *Scientific American   Saturday Night Live*   Volkswagen Corrados   volleyball

porter with the Boulder *Daily Camera*. "Now it's running with your personal trainer."

College graduates of decades past would feel right at home in most Towns & Gowns communities. Every summer morning at Boulder's Pearl Street Mall, the hirsute panhandlers show up with bedrolls, guitars, and hangovers from drugs and cheap wine. Their look hasn't changed much since the sixties, nor has the street scene, with its stores selling ice cream, rock music, T-shirts, and crafts. Nearby, disheveled group houses are decorated with weird colors and ratty couches, which are routinely burned on the last day of classes. That tradition may change, however; Boulder's booze-fueled fires of 1997 sparked a three-day riot and millions of dollars in damage.

But Towns & Gowns communities like Boulder are growing up — and turning trendy. Today, shops like Abercrombie & Fitch have moved in near the Gap and Banana Republic. The veggie burger at Dot's Diner now costs $5.50. Residents go to museums at high rates, and their art galleries feature high-quality textiles rather than head-shop posters. They're also interested in low-fat and health foods; one reason for their relatively low index of supermarket products is that shoppers buy tofu, wild oats, and other organic fare that doesn't always appear on marketing surveys. In Boulder, sidewalk hot dog vendors have been replaced by stir-fry stands like Wok in the Park. "This is an extremely fit community, and it rubs off on you," observes Sean Maher, owner of the local Ben & Jerry's shop. "People boast of climbing fourteen-thousand-foot mountains. They'll ask how many fourteeners you've climbed."

With youth comes liberal views, and Towns & Gowns is decidedly Democratic. These voters marched against the Gulf War and in favor of abortion rights. The prevailing permissiveness allows for recreational drugs like marijuana — locals draw the line at hard drugs — and sexual freedom: Condom purchases in Towns & Gowns are among the highest of any cluster in the nation. Residents tend to be environmentalists and routinely are at odds with developers hoping to cash in on the growing population and the gorgeous settings of Towns & Gowns areas. Forget about high-rises in their communities. "You can't stop someone's solar access," declares Anne Fox, an art director and community activist. "Why do you think they call this 'the People's Republic of Boulder'?" So might many Towns & Gowns areas be similarly celebrated.

PREFERENCES

(Index of 100 = U.S. Average)

Lifestyle / Products

what's hot

foreign videos 551
volleyball 269
billiards / pool 221
on-line services 216
rolling papers 209
bars / nightclubs 192
jogging 186
condoms 148
stereo equipment 147
museums 128

what's not

family videos 78
call forwarding 66
coupons 60
Home Depot 58
large-screen TVs 56
dogs 54
dry-cleaning 54
Woolworth 45
premium credit cards 43
sewing 35

Food / Drink

tequila 183
DoveBars 160
Coca-Cola Classic 145
Kellogg's All-Bran 142
pasta salad 141
frozen dinners 136
canned stew 132
frozen boneless chicken 130
skim milk 128
fast food 105

Magazines / Newspapers

Scientific American 215
Cosmopolitan 183
Sports Illustrated 182
Parenting 177
Rolling Stone 175
Self 126
U.S. News & World Report 126
Field & Stream 119
Golf Digest 116
Better Homes and Gardens 113

Television / Radio

Saturday Night Live 247
CNN Sports News 222
Friends 222
progressive-rock radio 217
Another World 196
Face the Nation 164
TV college basketball 161
Star Trek: Deep Space Nine 161
Caroline in the City 153
Oprah Winfrey Show 134

Cars / Trucks

Volkswagen Corrados 220
Mazda 323s 155
Volkswagen Foxes 149
Hyundai Sonatas 141
Subaru Loyales 137
Volkswagen Golfs 131
Mazda 2WD SUs 129
Nissan NX1s 128
Honda Civics 126
Audi 90s 118

Bumper sticker:
"Visualize Whirled Peas"

SER 32
big city blend

1.0% of U.S. households

Primary age group: **25–54**

Median household income: **$35,500**

Median home value: **$89,000**

Thumbnail Demographics

middle-income urban immigrant families

single-unit renters and owners

predominantly Hispanic and Asian households

high school graduates, some college

white- and blue-collar workers

Politics

Predominant ideology: liberal Democrat

1996 presidential vote: Bill Clinton

Key issues: pro immigration, school funding,
    legalizing marijuana

Sample Neighborhoods

Berwyn, Illinois 60402

Mesa, Arizona 85203

Garden Grove, California 92640

Wyandotte, Michigan 48192

Brookhurst Center, Anaheim, California 92804

First came the Czechs and the Swedes. Then came the Italians and the Poles. Now Hispanics, Asians, and other immigrant groups have moved into the urban areas that comprise Big City Blend. Once factory jobs were the lure, but the decline in the nation's smokestack industries has shut down the assembly lines and closed off opportunities to the latest wave of foreign-born residents. Yet still they come, seeking jobs as day laborers, service workers, and management professionals unavailable in their home countries. Today, Big City Blend is a portrait of American diversity, a cluster of middle-class, ethnically mixed neighborhoods where large families live in comfortable bungalows and row houses.

Despite this multinational flavor, Big City Blend is hardly a melting pot. In Berwyn, Illinois, an archetypal cluster community of 45,000, the older European immigrants resent the younger Hispanics who purchase homes and allow several generations of families to live in attic and basement apartments. Czech bakeries stand on the same blocks as Mexican restaurants and German breweries, but the foreign-born consumers stick to their own specialty stores — and have relatively low rates for buying from mainstream grocery chains. The longtime Italian residents make their own sausages and marinara sauces, the Hispanics their own tortillas and salsas, and everyone has a favorite foreign-language newspaper or radio station.

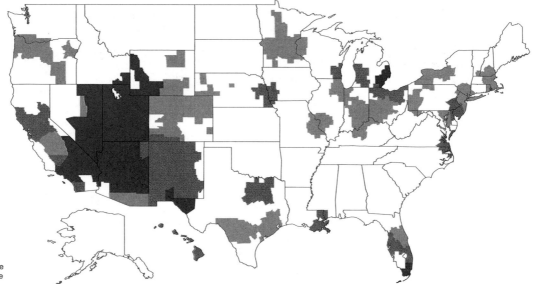

High
Above Average
Below Average
Low

pro football games   decorative icing   *Self*   Spanish radio   Mazda MPVs   7-Eleven   cordials &

At the Italian-American Club, members gather for dinners and dances — like members of any Elks Club — except that their usual fund-raiser is a boccie tournament. But no one talks of leaving the old neighborhood. "Everyone has some bias, but you have to be open-minded to live here," says Eduardo Castaneda, a Mexican émigré and restaurateur. "You can't see color or race."

What unites Big City Blend's ethnic groups are conservative family values, a deep religious streak, and a fierce pride in the hard work it takes to maintain their middle-class lifestyle. "These are not FDR Democrats. They worry over every dollar," says local reporter Eileen Pech. Surveys show that consumers have low rates for owning computers, driving luxury cars, and playing golf; their tendency to belong to country clubs is at zilch. Instead, residents worry about keeping up their property — Home Depot is one of their most popular stores — outdoing their neighbors' gardens, and having their children excel in school. For leisure, they share a fondness for foreign travel, professional sports, theme parks, and gambling. This cluster boasts some of the nation's highest rates for buying lottery tickets, visiting gambling casinos, and frequenting riverboat slot machines. Given that some of these people have risked their lives to come to America, it's no wonder they have such a passion for games of chance.

But life remains a struggle for many of the newest immigrants — illegal and legal. In the two years since Pakistani physicians Rana and Khalid Khan moved with their three children to Berwyn, they've had little contact with other locals. Like many new émigrés, they want their children, ages one to nine, to speak English outside the home to succeed. But they're also worried that they will become too Americanized, watch too many cartoons and "nonsensical" talk shows, forget their native Urdu language, and turn up their noses at traditional vegetable and rice dishes and chapati in favor of hamburgers and pizza. Still, like other Big City Blend residents, they dream not of returning to Pakistan but of moving to a larger house and more affluent neighborhood. And history suggests that this dream of opportunity will continue to lure more immigrants. "This isn't Chernobyl," says restaurateur Castaneda. "The corn is growing. The jobs are around. If the country is open, somebody is going to move in." And likely find his or her way to Big City Blend.

PREFERENCES

(Index of 100 = U.S. Average)

Lifestyle / Products

what's hot

pro football games 204
7-Eleven 157
gambling casinos 156
electric juicers 145
baby furniture 134
U.S. savings bonds 131
adult education courses 124
aerobics 124
pet birds 124
foreign travel 118

what's not

savings accounts 61
auto races 56
Limited 49
volleyball 49
satellite dishes 43
new-wave CDs / tapes 37
cross-country skiing 37
cellular phones 30
college football games 27
country clubs 2

Food / Drink

decorative icing 136
cordials & liqueurs 136
Entenmann's snacks 134
fast-food Mexican 125
Diet Coke 119
pita bread 114
imported cheese 113
bottled water 110
yogurt 107
dry mix salad dressing 102

Magazines / Newspapers

Self 188
Popular Photography 152
Road & Track 148
Muscle & Fitness 138
GQ 137
Sporting News 127
Time 123
Us 121
Cosmopolitan 120
Popular Mechanics 120

Television / Radio

Spanish radio 606
Court TV 273
pay-per-view movies 238
Leeza 194
Rush Limbaugh 148
Cops 147
Learning Channel 145
Disney Channel 142
Melrose Place 141
Wheel of Fortune 137

Cars / Trucks

Mazda MPVs 253
imported minivans 211
GMC Safaris 211
Toyota pickups 176
Toyota Previas 173
Nissan NX1s 160
Ford Aerostars 153
Dodge Ram Wagons 146
Honda Civics 139
Suzukis 135

Travel agency specials:
year-round charters to
Mexico, Italy, Pakistan, and China

SER 33
middle America

1.3% of U.S. households

Primary age group: **25–44**

Median household income: **$37,300**

Median home value: **$74,700**

Thumbnail Demographics

midscale families in midsized towns

single-family housing

predominantly white households

high school graduates

blue-collar workers

Politics

Predominant ideology: moderate Republican

1996 presidential vote: Bob Dole

Key issues: improving the economy, curbing
  pornography, pro labor unions

Sample Neighborhoods

Independence, Missouri 64058

Elkton, Maryland 21921

Lithia Springs, Georgia 30057

Haysville, Kansas 67060

Crete, Illinois 60417

"I Am Blessed." The marquee at the Harmony Heights Baptist Church in Independence, Missouri, offers this plainly optimistic message, though it isn't pegged to any religious holiday. Feeling fortunate just happens to be the prevailing mood in Middle America, a lifestyle near the midrung of the nation's socioeconomic ladder. When politicians and pundits talk about the values of small-town heartland citizenry, they're referring to Middle America. In this cluster, widely scattered throughout the country, residents find comfort in their stable neighborhoods, filled with children of all ages, pets of all species, and a variety of adult toys such as boats, motorcycles, and jet skis. Workers — and most households have two earners — have parlayed high school educations into skilled blue-collar jobs and middle-class incomes. They're the casual folks who frequent fast-food restaurants, enjoy hobbies like bowling and fishing, and spend weekends throwing family barbecues. At My Brother's Place, a bar in Independence, the regulars show up after work to drink seventy-five-cent beers, shoot pool, and take over the karaoke stage. "We're a T-shirt-and-jeans crowd here," says bar owner Brett Barnhart. "It's a comfortable area where you don't have to worry about a roof over your head or where the next meal is coming from."

Yet in some respects, Middle Americans have a tenuous hold on the American Dream. They don't necessarily strive to be wealthy or trendy — "I've never been to Starbucks," one resident proudly re-

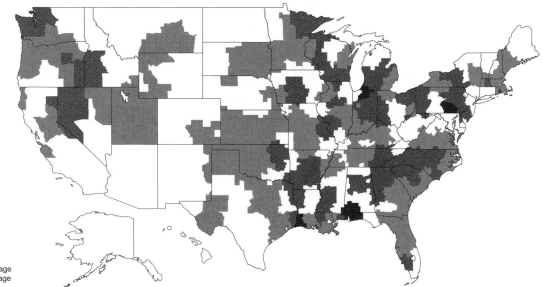

High
Above Average
Below Average
Low

Red Roof Inns   Twinkies   *Parenting*   barbecuing   coupons   Chevrolet Astros   Publisher's Clearing

marks — but they worry about maintaining their living standard and whether their kids will attain their level of comfort. Their older homes — a typical three-bedroom rambler is worth $75,000, about one-third less than the national average — need constant upkeep, and residents are big consumers of home fix-it products and magazines. Enough crime has touched the area that residents fume over the slightest sign of decline — "Kids with tattoos, and cars parked in the yards," as one resident defines it. They borrow heavily to buy new cars and trucks — typically made in Detroit — and pay off multiple loans every month. "What good is money lying in the bank?" asks Walt Berry, foreman of a metal-plating company, expressing a typical view. "You don't know if you'll be here next week, so if you want something, you might as well get it."

At home, Middle Americans pay homage to the past. This is a cluster that enjoys collecting: Hummel figurines, Precious Moments dolls, and grandfather clocks are popular. Most high school boys consider sports trophies the essence of bedroom decor — right up there with pinups from the *Sports Illustrated* swimsuit issue and promotional signs from Coors. Their parents usually have a forty-eight-star flag on a shelf — barely used even when it was purchased forty years ago. "I just like old things," says Independence resident Denise Northcutt, forty, as she runs her fingers across a 1913 hymnal kept on her antique piano. To feed that desire, every Saturday garage sales pop up like weeds. They're like parties with the added benefit of the host's making money while emptying a basement of accumulated junk. "You can go to a garage sale any weekend from spring until fall," says Northcutt, a medical secretary.

In these towns of Little League baseball and bowling leagues, status has nothing to do with money or promotions; it's team successes. "If your child is involved in sports and makes the local paper, it's like being on the cover of the *New York Times,*" says one resident. Unions once were big, and locals disparage those who drive foreign-made cars. But because factory closings have resulted in downsizing so many union shops, many Middle Americans know firsthand the anguish of a pink slip and do charity work at high rates to aid out-of-work neighbors. "Almost everyone has been laid off at one time or another, so they thank God when they're working and can help out," says Father Chuck Tobin, pastor of St. Joseph the Workman Church. "People here know of wealthier areas, but they like it here because of that sense of caring." On balance, Middle America residents are content to be just where they are.

PREFERENCES

(Index of 100 = U.S. Average)

Lifestyle / Products

what's hot

Red Roof Inns 252
Publisher's Clearing House 188
personal loans 173
baby furniture 158
barbecuing 146
coupons 140
JCPenney cards 132
fraternal orders 125
zoos 124
dogs 115

what's not

pagers / beepers 59
dance music 55
backpacking / hiking 52
American Express cards 38
espresso makers 32
foreign videos 30
college football games 10
country clubs 8
tractor pulls 0
shocks changed at garage 0

Food / Drink

Twinkies 158
Shake 'n Bake 144
Kraft Velveeta 140
whole milk 127
Kellogg's Pop-Tarts 125
McDonald's 125
instant mashed potatoes 124
canned ham 123
Coca-Cola Classic 119
peanut butter 113

Magazines / Newspapers

Parenting 195
Better Homes and Gardens 146
Good Housekeeping 142
Hot Rod 138
Cosmopolitan 125
Newsweek 123
People 121
Sports Illustrated 120
Field & Stream 119
Reader's Digest 116

Television / Radio

Bob Vila's Home Again 245
America's Most Wanted 184
Jenny Jones 183
ABC's Wide World of Sports 166
country radio 164
America's Funniest Home Videos 162
ER 158
NBC Nightly News 151
Good Morning America 143
Baywatch 127

Cars / Trucks

Chevrolet Astros 246
Suzuki Samurais 204
Ford pickups 195
Chevrolet cargo vans 182
GMC Safaris 181
Pontiac Firebirds 172
Pontiac Grand Prix 170
Chevrolet Camaros 164
Ford Tempos 160
Plymouth Neons 127

Bumper sticker:
"Eat Your Imports"

SER 34

river city, USA

2.0% of U.S. households

Primary age group: 35–54

Median household income: **$35,700**

Median home value: **$69,700**

Thumbnail Demographics

middle-class rural families

single-family housing

predominantly white households

high school graduates

blue-collar and farmworkers

Politics

Predominant ideology: conservative Republican

1996 presidential vote: Bob Dole

Key issues: pro-life movement, family values,
    curbing pornography

Sample Neighborhoods

Dallas Center, Iowa 50063

Cedar Bluffs, Nebraska 68015

East Helena, Montana 59635

Beulah, North Dakota 58523

New Richmond, Wisconsin 54017

Wholesome is the first word many residents use to describe River City, USA. In these rural middle-class towns dotting the northern tier of the nation, families cultivate an old-fashioned way of life that's changed little from a century ago. The streets are safe enough for youngsters to ride their bikes to schools and parks without fear. Parents sit on porches after dinner, rocking on swings and enjoying the evening. Retirees gather at the local café every morning over a bottomless cup of coffee — no cappuccino, thank you very much. And the entire town shuts down on Friday nights to fill the high school stadium and root for children on the football team or in the school band. If it sounds dull, don't mention that to the folks who live here. In one survey of one hundred activities, their favorite pursuit was "relaxing with spouse and kids."

On first glance, a visitor to River City, USA might think there's not much else to do. In Dallas Center, Iowa, a town of 1,600 in the flat corn and bean fields northwest of Des Moines, there are no traffic lights, no movie theaters; its Main Street has seen better days. The only restaurant closed up after two years. The bowling alley has but six lanes, and a grain silo sits across the road. On Sunday, all the businesses close so residents can attend one of the half dozen churches. "This isn't a suburb," says Christopher Middaugh, forty-one, the owner of Chris' Pizza and Bowl, where an all-you-can-eat lunch costs $3.95. "This town is Mayberry."

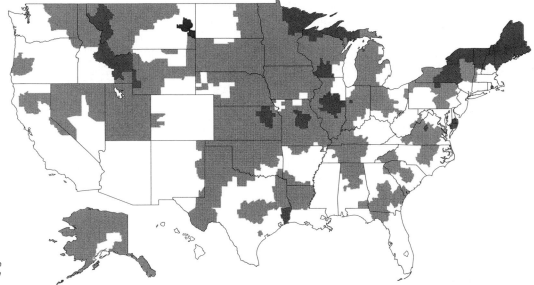

■ High
▨ Above Average
▨ Below Average
□ Low

overnight camping   packaged cold cuts   *Outdoor Life   Guiding Light*   Dodge W350 pickups

But folks here in River City, USA tend to like their small-town ways. "We don't worry about drive-by shootings here," says one. Incomes are stable with blue-collar and farming jobs. The modest cost of housing — the median value is about $69,700 — allows people the extra cash to purchase boats and campers for fishing and hunting. And adults are young enough to play softball, roller-skate, and ski, and enjoy noisy spectator sports like tractor pulls and auto races. In River City, USA people pride themselves on their lack of pretense. They clip coupons from magazines like *Family Circle* and *Ladies' Home Journal,* and do their clothes shopping at discount stores like Wal-Mart, Kmart, and "Tar-*jé*" (the mocking French pronunciation for Target). Few have flashy cars; the most popular nameplates are Ford Festivas, Chevy Luminas, and Subaru Justys. The predominant cuisine is potato-heavy homestyle; at a church supper, couples show up with scalloped potatoes, potato salad, and even chicken and noodles over mashed potatoes. "It's starch city," one Dallas Center local observes. If you want to open a restaurant, you'd better think twice about Continental fare. "There's none of that chicken cacciatore crap around here," says Middaugh, dismissing anything that sounds the slightest bit un-American.

Mostly, River City, USA is about raising kids in a carefree environment, a lifestyle in which many people garden and renovate their homes slowly, one room at a time, by hand. "This is a place where you buy a house and tinker on it for years," says Presbyterian reverend Heather Carver. "It doesn't matter that you do it right away because people come here for the long haul." The TV shows most residents watch are family fare like *Home Improvement* and *Touched by an Angel.* Their favorite magazines are tried-and-true titles that have been around for decades, among them *Good Housekeeping, Country Living,* and *TV Guide.*

Politically conservative, River City, USA voters nonetheless divided their 1996 presidential vote between Bob Dole and Ross Perot, mostly because of the candidates' similar messages about reducing the size of the government. Still, their biggest concern centers on family values, and they back any effort to improve their schools and keep drugs and pornography away from their children. So far, their efforts in these small towns seem to be succeeding. In Dallas Center, the kids are involved in church and school programs — often side by side with their parents. "Around here," says resident Dana Myers, "you know where your kids are."

PREFERENCES

(Index of 100 = U.S. Average)

Lifestyle / Products

what's hot

overnight camping	181
water softeners	154
power tools	141
freshwater fishing	139
power boats	138
work boots	137
adult education courses	134
family videos	133
weekly groceries < $60	132
arts / crafts projects	121

what's not

ATM cards	80
car rentals	76
mysteries	71
beachgoing	70
sailboats	67
theater attendance	62
Price Club	41
Walt Disney World	35
rolling papers	31
classical radio	12

Food / Drink

low-fat cottage cheese	140
regular cola	135
packaged cold cuts	128
Canadian whiskey	122
Pizza Hut	120
instant mashed potatoes	117
pudding	116
beef jerky	116
ready-to-serve dips	113
frozen boneless chicken	113

Magazines / Newspapers

Outdoor Life	199
Weight Watchers	198
Family Circle	155
Prevention	154
American Health	145
Hot Rod	136
Ladies' Home Journal	135
TV Guide	133
Field & Stream	132
Popular Mechanics	129

Television / Radio

Guiding Light	249
Today Show	164
TNN	150
Family Channel	150
country radio	149
Home Improvement	147
CBS Evening News	145
Rescue 911	134
Nanny	119
20 / 20	117

Cars / Trucks

Dodge W350 pickups	344
Ford F350 pickups	260
GMC Sonoma pickups	219
Chevrolet Luminas	174
Chevrolet Sportvans	167
Ford Festivas	166
Subaru Justys	155
GMC Safaris	155
Pontiac Grand Prix	154
Oldsmobile 98s	153

Local vice: weekly poker game that's gone on for twenty years

SER 35
red, white & blues

2.3% of U.S. households

Primary age group: **35–64**

Median household income: **$34,800**

Median home value: **$68,100**

Thumbnail Demographics

small-town middle-class families

single-family housing

predominantly white households

grade school, high school graduates

blue-collar workers

Politics

Predominant ideology: conservative Democrat

1996 presidential vote: Ross Perot

Key issues: family values, militia groups / terrorism,
   tax reform

Sample Neighborhoods

Hiram, Georgia 30141

Gettysburg, Pennsylvania 17325

Angleton, Texas 77515

Chesterton, Indiana 46304

Fort Atkinson, Wisconsin 53538

At the intersection of routes 278 and 92, about a half hour west of Atlanta, stands a commercial sprawl that just ten years ago was woodland. On one side of the street are a Wal-Mart, a McDonald's, and an Eckerd drugstore. On the other are a Kmart, a Kroger, a Waffle House, a Blockbuster Video, and a Checkers. This is Hiram, Georgia, a small (population 1,400) exurban town rapidly morphing into a bedroom suburb. Hiram was once a quaint setting for older brick houses and double-wide mobile homes, but today nearly every cul-de-sac is lined with new split-levels and split-foyers that cost $200,000. And the fast-food eateries have been joined by ethnic restaurants like Happy China and El Jalapeño. At the town hall, next to a water tower built in an earlier era, the concerns are rush-hour traffic and increasing property taxes. "When I came here in 1945, there were no paved roads," marvels Hiram mayor Dewey Pendley, seventy. "Now we've got people moving here from all over the country."

Hiram is classic Red, White & Blues, a middle-class family cluster filled with high school–educated blue-collar workers in manufacturing, milling, and construction jobs. Scattered throughout the Appalachians, the Great Lakes, and the Upper Midwest, the lifestyle is known for its conservative values, and folks hold God and the American flag dear. Voters describe themselves as Perot Democrats,

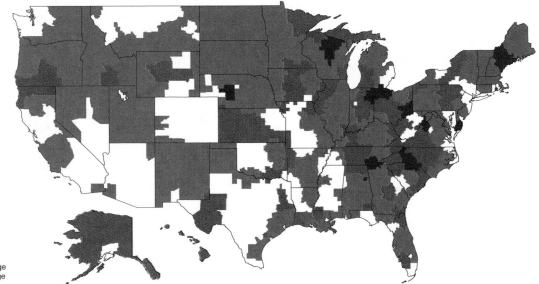

High
Above Average
Below Average
Low

but his appeal was on economic issues, not social concerns. Cluster residents support school prayer, reducing TV violence, and curbing pornography. "People here take pride in their religion," says Larry Eminhizer, a forty-one-year-old assistant principal. "They talk about it more than in other areas." In this lifestyle type, where residents are traditionalists on racial diversity, bigotry is not far below the surface. "There's a reason why you'll only find all-white churches and all-black churches," confides one Hiram native.

Bridging rural and suburban lifestyles, Red, White & Blues reflects consuming patterns from both realms. Residents go fishing and hunting at high rates, as well as bar-hopping and golfing. They pursue athletic activities more often than the general population, whether it's bowling, jogging, and tennis, or attending baseball games, college basketball games, and auto races. "When people get together, the first topic of conversation is always sports," notes one Hiram resident. But when the health-and-fitness revolution hit the nation in the 1980s, Red, White & Blues residents chose to ignore it. People smoke cigarettes and pipes at above-average rates, and they don't seem overly concerned by the relatively large quantities of fast food, sausage, or alcohol they consume. "It's getting to be that you're an outlaw if you're smoking," complains Joyce Smith, a city clerk, shaking her head in disgust. "You can die from anything."

In this quickly changing lifestyle, rural notions are getting caught in exurbia's snowballing expansion. Longtime residents still insist on buying American cars and trucks — preferably muscle cars like Mustangs and Grand Ams — and listening to country music and kick-ass rock and roll. But they celebrate the arrival of Wal-Marts and discount malls into their communities despite the crowds. And they welcome the relatively recent arrival of Pizza Hut, Burger King, and Wendy's. "Everyone wants a Home Depot and a Sizzler out here," says Smith, "so they won't have to drive so far." Carol Rakestraw, a lifelong Hiram resident, loves the small-town ways of her community, where the family has run a liquor store for thirty years and never been robbed. But now when she goes shopping with her friends, they all carry cell phones to alert each other to the best sales. "A lot of people gripe about the changes, but we're happy," says Rakestraw. "We see it as progress." In Red, White & Blues, the arrival of "big box" commerce hasn't shaken their small-town sensibility.

PREFERENCES

(Index of 100 = U.S. Average)

Lifestyle / Products

what's hot

auto races 168
college football games 150
CB radios 147
camera accessories 146
new-car loans 144
needlepoint 143
pro baseball games 137
hunting 126
watching TV 122
pipe tobacco 120

what's not

Visa cards 85
CD players 84
billiards / pool 78
travel agents 62
public broadcasting 64
Quick Lube centers 60
pro football games 48
pagers / beepers 40
airline magazines 36
news radio 17

Food / Drink

instant grits 149
Spam 140
whole milk 127
Burger King 126
doughnuts 124
regular cola 120
pudding 120
sausage 115
frozen pizza 115
Kraft Velveeta 114

Magazines / Newspapers

Field & Stream 191
Forbes 152
Outdoor Life 142
Soap Opera Digest 137
Woman's World 131
motorcycle magazines 130
Road & Track 123
National Enquirer 122
U.S. News & World Report 122
Country Living 121

Television / Radio

Christian / faith radio 166
TV auto racing 142
Rush Limbaugh 139
NBC Nightly News 137
Weather Channel 135
religious / gospel radio 133
Walker, Texas Ranger 131
Guiding Light 130
Lifetime 126
Mad About You 103

Cars / Trucks

Dodge D350 pickups 203
Chevrolet Monte Carlos 176
Pontiac Sunbirds 162
Pontiac Grand Prix 162
GMC Safaris 161
Eagle Talons 161
Chevrolet Luminas 158
Ford Festivas 154
Plymouth Lasers 152
Dodges 140

Cluster cuisine:
Spam and Velveeta

SER 36

starter families

1.6% of U.S. households

Primary age groups: **under 24, 25–34**

Median household income: **$32,200**

Median home value: **$69,300**

Thumbnail Demographics

young middle-class families in second cities

2–9 unit rental housing

ethnically mixed households

high school graduates, some college

blue-collar and service workers

Politics

Predominant ideology: moderate Democrat

1996 presidential vote: Ross Perot

Key issues: child social services, pro-life movement, restricting immigration

Sample Neighborhoods

Fairfield, California 94533

Manchester, New Hampshire 03102

Minot, North Dakota 58703

Pascagoula, Mississippi 39581

Kent, Washington 98032

Starter Families is a nice middle-class lifestyle. Young parents. Lots of children. Decent incomes from stable blue-collar and low-level white-collar jobs. And strong family values where schools and kids come first. What isn't it? A hip destination for yuppies looking for chic boutiques and exotic coffee bars. Rather, Starter Families is the place young marrieds go to buy their first houses ($100,000 for a three-bedroom, two-bath ranch) on streets with other young marrieds and, soon, babies and toddlers, trikes and basketball hoops, soccer practice and bowling parties. "This is a big family area, a blue-jeans community," says Amy Maginnis, a lifestyles editor at the *Daily Republic* in Fairfield, California.

In Fairfield, a satellite city of 87,000 halfway between Sacramento and San Francisco, the Starter Families lifestyle leaps out at you as fast as the skateboarders and Rollerbladers who whiz by. Joni Tuck, a thirty-one-year-old mother of two, lives on a block where six of the ten homes are filled with young children. The cluttered ramblers and modest ranches seem to overflow with Beanie Babies, kid videos, and pictures of children at parties and beaches. Refrigerators are stocked with jumbo-sized tubs of jelly, mayonnaise, fruit punch, and ice cream. "It's cheaper to buy in bulk," explains Tuck, PTA president at Bransford Elementary. In one son's room is a TV, a VCR, and Nintendo. "We use the Nintendo," she says, "when we don't have the time or energy to parent anymore."

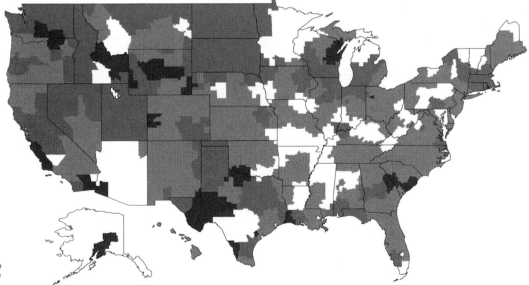

■ High
■ Above Average
■ Below Average
□ Low

sewing bourbon *Petersen's Hunting Baywatch* Mitsubishi pickups camping DoveBars *Sport*

The commercial base of Starter Families, naturally, is child centered. In strip centers are fast-food joints, theme restaurants, skating rinks, and toy stores, but not the more pricey Discovery Zones or Zany Brainys. Yard sales are popular ways to off-load your kids' out-of-favor stuff. In Fairfield, the local *Daily Republic* makes it cheap and easy to advertise yard sales. A three-line ad costs only $3.50, and the paper throws in cardboard signs for free. Saturday means inexpensive entertainment like miniature golf or bowling. "People here demand a deal," says Ken Sousa, owner of the Fairfield Bowling Center, where games cost as little as $1.25 each. "Bowling's a good value for the money."

For clothes shopping, residents head for the many local thrift shops: The center of Fairfield features Goodwill and Salvation Army thrift stores not far from the cleverly named Sak's Thrift Avenue. "Who can afford the Gap?" asks one parent. Holidays are big in Starter Families, an occasion for parties and parades. Fairfield's annual tomato festival is marked with a parade featuring high school bands, dance clubs, and Scout troops. "It's a real Norman Rockwell scene," says editor Maginnis. "People cheer the pooper scooper."

Politically, Starter Families are hard to pin down. They're not strongly affiliated with either party, and they seem to cherry-pick their issues while straddling the partisan fence. They voted for Ross Perot at high rates in 1996 and describe themselves as somewhat liberal. But they also support school prayer, the pro-life movement, and home schooling. On most issues, however, voters rarely become involved unless it concerns their children. These parents have little time for protests, political canvassing, or organized groups. "The only time you see someone picketing is outside his mechanic if he got a bad job done on his car," quips one Fairfield local. In time-use polls, cluster residents concede that the activity they most wish they could spend more time doing is relaxing with their spouses and kids.

Starter Families are mobile areas: Nearly 30 percent of the residents have moved in during the past year, and that's a telling statistic. These Americans don't plan on settling in their neighborhoods forever; this cluster is only the beginning. "We want more space for the kids and more conveniences for us," explains Joni Tuck. "But this is a nice place to start out."

PREFERENCES

(Index of 100 = U.S. Average)

Lifestyle / Products

what's hot

sewing	207
camping	201
science fiction	159
in-home pregnancy tests	154
pro football games	143
video rentals	140
bowling	130
theme parks	126
power tools	126
Kmart	123

what's not

weight lifting	84
religious clubs	84
classical CDs / tapes	78
stationary bicycles	78
frequent-flier miles	78
bus travel	73
pro baseball games	71
nonfilter cigarettes	66
diet pills	41
boxing matches	34

Food / Drink

bourbon	177
DoveBars	151
Twinkies	148
imported cheese	140
children's vitamins	139
Pepsi	137
canned stew	137
frozen dinners	132
hot dogs	124
fast food	107

Magazines / Newspapers

Petersen's Hunting	346
Sport	267
Car and Driver	218
Consumers Digest	169
Working Woman	168
fitness magazines	165
Popular Science	164
Star	153
American Baby	148
Rolling Stone	125

Television / Radio

Baywatch	231
Apollo Comedy Hour	189
Dateline NBC	189
Ricki Lake	166
General Hospital	160
TV auto racing	157
ABC World News Tonight	156
Married . . . with Children	153
MTV	148
America's Funniest Home Videos	145

Cars / Trucks

Mitsubishi pickups	207
Suzukis	203
Mitsubishi Mirages	201
Hyundai Scoupes	183
Hyundai Excels	164
Chevrolet Geo Storms	141
Subaru Justys	138
Mazda 323s	138
Mitsubishi Galants	135
Pontiac Lemanses	133

Status yard ornament:
trampoline

SER 37
old Yankee rows

1.4% of U.S. households

Primary age groups: **25–34, 65 +**

Median household income: **$31,500**

Median home value: **$84,300**

Thumbnail Demographics

empty-nest, middle-class, urban-fringe families

2–9 unit rental housing

predominantly white and Asian households

grade school, high school graduates

white-collar service workers

Politics

Predominant ideology: moderate Democrat

1996 presidential vote: Ross Perot

Key issues: restricting immigration, gun control, defusing racial tensions

Sample Neighborhoods

Everett, Massachusetts 02149

Pawtucket, Rhode Island 02860

Rosebank, Staten Island, New York 10305

Lodi, New Jersey 07644

Parkville, Brooklyn, New York 11204

A half century ago, America boomed with industrial cities built around factory smokestacks and row house neighborhoods teeming with well-paid blue-collar ethnics. But the economic shifts that shut down the factories also left these urban fringe areas down at the heels. Today in Old Yankee Rows, the population is graying, the row houses sagging, and the multigenerational families have given way to singles in search of cheap rental units. Concentrated in New England and the Great Lakes region, Old Yankee Rows is a cluster in transition: a mix of homeowners and renters, twenty-somethings and retirees, as well as multilingual groups of all nationalities. In Everett, Massachusetts, a close-in Boston suburb of 35,000, a community of Italian and Irish families has given way to Hispanics from Brazil and Asians from Vietnam; thirty-six languages are now spoken at local schools. "We're still a blue-collar city with a lot of gray heads," says Carmin Mercadante, chamber of commerce president. "But we're attracting a lot more new people and we're growing."

Like other working-class urban areas, Old Yankee Rows has seen its commercial base follow families to the suburbs. "You can't buy a pair of socks in downtown Everett," says one local, lamenting the loss of clothing and department stores. Left behind are mom-and-pop pizzerias, Asian video stores, and delis where cold cuts and

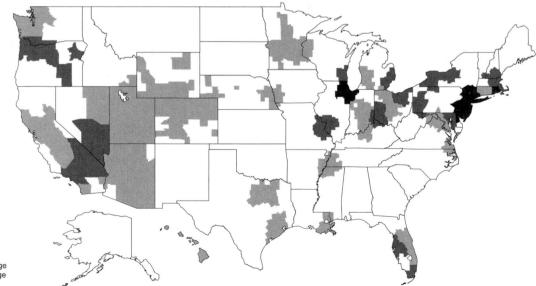

■ High
■ Above Average
■ Below Average
□ Low

religious clubs   imported beer   *Road & Track*   Court TV   Ford Econoline E-350 Cargo Vans   foreign

malt liquor are favorites. Residents typically are home fix-it types who enjoy gardening, woodworking in their homes, and tinkering with their cars; in these urban areas, only a few models are bought at high rates. There's still enough of the working-class culture to make sports like bowling and boxing popular. Residents are more likely to collect lottery tickets than stamps, and are more interested in rooting for pro football teams than college teams (not surprising, given that less than 15 percent of adults possess a college diploma). On a weekend night, the kids cruise the main drag in their jacked-up trucks while their parents get together over family dinners to talk high school sports. "People will go to high school football games even though they don't have kids in school anymore," says Arthur Berardino, an Everett businessman and a high school athletics booster. "They love their sports around here."

Politically, Old Yankee Rows voters have changed from old-line liberals to Ross Perot–backing moderates. They're not the left-wing voters who support gay rights and legalizing pot; as one notes, "We have fewer bleeding hearts than other liberal areas." Because older residents in the cluster are more likely to vote than newer immigrants, Old Yankee Rows tends to back labor unions, oppose affirmative action, and applaud restricting immigration. "The old-timers feel the immigrants get too much," says Berardino. "When our parents came here, they didn't have two nickels to rub together. These new people get a check, food stamps, and a place to live." This sentiment may have deeper roots than economic envy. "Most of these immigrant groups we fought with in one war or another," confides one first-generation Italian American without irony.

In Old Yankee Rows, residents join fraternal organizations at high rates, not just for social activities and charity fund-raisers. For many of these new Americans, groups like the long-standing Italian-American Club and the newer Vietnamese-American Association help members assimilate into the mainstream while preserving their cultural traditions. "Language is a big barrier for these people," says Deborah Abraham, director of the Everett library. "A lot of people get low-level support jobs because they have limited English." But that's not to say that these newcomers stay in entry-level positions. The Everett library has more demand for computer books than any other genre. And city officials talk of building a high-tech "Telecom City" that may turn the blue-collar ethnic neighborhood into a gentrified yuppie haven. In Old Yankee Rows, the factory town lifestyle is being retooled for the information age.

PREFERENCES

(Index of 100 = U.S. Average)

Lifestyle / Products

what's hot

Amway products	200
foreign videos	179
lottery tickets	170
Caribbean travel	163
cigars	147
boxing matches	134
metal polish	130
bowling	127
pro football games	125
vitamins	116

what's not

mail-order shopping	80
backpacking / hiking	79
plants	76
religious clubs	75
stamp collecting	73
sailing	72
chewing tobacco	67
college football games	55
gas chain saws	47
Wal-Mart	40

Food / Drink

imported beer	198
Burger King	152
liverwurst	151
olive oil	149
fresh cold cuts	147
fresh fish	145
Hershey's candy bars	145
yogurt	133
Twinkies	130
low-calorie bread	128

Magazines / Newspapers

Road & Track	164
Gourmet	162
Consumers Digest	133
Car and Driver	132
Health	132
Muscle & Fitness	129
National Enquirer	128
Mademoiselle	128
Woman's Day	123
Barron's	118

Television / Radio

Court TV	271
pay-per-view movies	241
golden-oldies radio	168
HBO	165
TV bowling	153
Oprah Winfrey Show	136
Frasier	134
Law & Order	126
CNN Sports News	124
Touched by an Angel	119

Cars / Trucks

Ford Econoline E-350 Cargo Vans	159
Plymouth Acclaims	129
Dodge Ram wagons	128
Nissan Altimas	128
Plymouth Sundances	115
Toyota Corollas	109
Chevrolet Corsicas	109
Ford Tempos	103
Hyundai Elantras	100
Hyundai Excels	100

Typical resident:
first-generation American
with well-worn bootstraps

SER 38

golden ponds

2.0% of U.S. households

Primary age groups: **55–64, 65 +**

Median household income: **$26,000**

Median home value: **$63,300**

Thumbnail Demographics

retirement-town seniors

single-family housing

predominantly white households

high school graduates

service workers

Politics

Predominant ideology: moderate Democrat

1996 presidential vote: Bob Dole

Key issues: toxic waste disposal, military spending,
improving the economy

Sample Neighborhoods

Boone, Iowa 50036

Branson, Missouri 65615

Rice Lake, Wisconsin 54868

Aberdeen, South Dakota 57401

Gallup, New Mexico 87301

Go to the second floor of the Boone, Iowa, courthouse some week-day afternoon and check out R.S.V.P., the volunteer program for senior citizens. They're knitting a patchwork quilt to raise money for area charities, packaging Christmas ornaments for the homebound, having a pizza lunch before going off to read to local schoolchildren. "Why are we here?" one eighty-year-old asks while pushing a needle through thick green fabric. "We got old. And we got so poor that we couldn't get away." Around her, four women laugh, but the comment is made only partly in jest.

Golden Ponds is mostly a retirement lifestyle: More than half its residents are over fifty years old. One in five is over sixty-five. But unlike those Sunbelt retirement communities of Gray Power, the rustic towns of Golden Ponds are filled with people of all ages. Widely scattered throughout the country, cluster communities are home to plenty of young families living in ranches, cottages, and Victorian gems. In Boone, a town of 12,500 a half hour west of Ames, schools and swing sets dot the streets near four large nursing homes and a handful of pharmacies. The local library holds a sizable collection of large-print books as well as escapist romance novels for women and Westerns for men. A string of fast-food joints caters to teenagers and seniors watching their wallets. On one corner, a gravestone business has opened next to a Subway outlet.

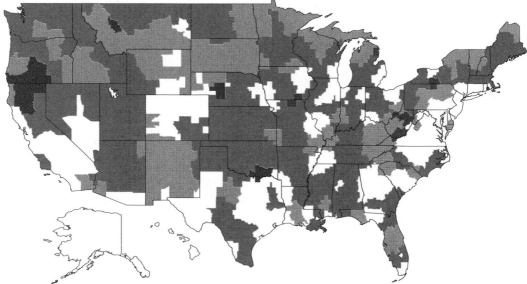

High
Above Average
Below Average
Low

By consumer standards, Golden Ponds is a schizophrenic place, where the midscale tastes in products and services are divided between old and young, working-class and those on fixed incomes. For elderly residents, daily life is a quiet succession of attending church, playing bingo, collecting stamps, and doing crafts projects. At Frames N Things in Boone, residents stop in to frame baptism dresses, pocket watches, old leather booties, and war memorabilia. "They like the homespun look and antiques," says Deborah Weber, the forty-nine-year-old owner. "People are afraid they're going to lose their history." With few movie theaters and playhouses in town, television is the most popular form of entertainment in Golden Ponds, especially daytime soaps and game shows for this early-to-bed populace. "I have to be home at five o'clock to watch *Jeopardy,*" says Theo Anderson, an eighty-one-year-old retired schoolteacher. "It makes me feel smart when I get an answer that they missed."

Marketing surveys also reflect the active lifestyles of younger residents. Roller-skating, volleyball, racquetball, and hunting are all enjoyed at above-average rates in Golden Ponds. Mercury Cougars and Chevy Geo Trackers do well, though the status nameplates are Cadillac and Lincoln. "You won't see any sports cars around here," one local observes. Of course, there are many activities that bridge the age gap. In Boone, if you want to find anyone in the summer, head for one of the weekly band concerts. As in many small-town lifestyles, fraternal clubs like the Moose and the Elks are a big draw for the bingo games, dances, and family dinners. At the Boone Elks Lodge, a big event is Hobo Night, when families dress up as railroad bums and bring cans of soup for a communal dinner and gabfest. "It's a social gathering place," says Ronald Russell, forty-seven, a former exalted ruler of the Elks Lodge. "People talk about sports, the weather, and crops. We joke around and have a good time."

Still, economic concerns weigh heavily in Golden Ponds, where the opening of Wal-Marts threatens many downtown centers. With lower-middle-class incomes — the median is about $26,000 — residents worry about jobs and the survival of their towns. Those concerns translate into a muddled political climate: These working-class Americans describe themselves as moderate Democrats, but they supported the tradition-steeped messages of Bob Dole in the '96 election. "This is still a town where people gather in homes just to visit," says Boone librarian Annamae Reed, sixty-five. "We like to reminisce about the good old days." That's one of the charms of Golden Ponds that never go out of fashion.

PREFERENCES

(Index of 100 = U.S. Average)

Lifestyle / Products

what's hot

fraternal orders 164
Medicare / Medicaid 154
backpacking / hiking 153
stamp collecting 149
water aerobics 149
pet birds 140
religious clubs 138
volleyball 134
bread from scratch 126
watching TV 118

what's not

interest checking 77
trivia games 76
golf vacations 71
moviegoing 71
financial investments 70
easy-listening CDs / tapes 67
pipe tobacco 60
theme parks 56
book clubs 50
on-line services 40

Food / Drink

Sizzlean 189
Quaker Puffed Rice 187
butter substitute 144
miniature chocolates 135
Spam 132
cordials & liqueurs 126
low-fat cottage cheese 125
frozen dinners 123
salsa 120
pudding 117

Magazines / Newspapers

Yankee 179
Family Handyman 144
Sports Afield 134
Reader's Digest 134
gardening magazines 125
Family Circle 120
Good Housekeeping 119
comics section 118
editorial section 115
True Story 114

Television / Radio

Face the Nation 215
48 Hours 178
Live with Regis and Kathie Lee 175
Another World 175
Price Is Right 153
Walker, Texas Ranger 147
Rush Limbaugh 145
CBS Sunday Movie 144
country radio 143
20 / 20 130

Cars / Trucks

GMC Sierra pickups 190
Oldsmobile 98s 174
Chrysler New Yorkers 164
Buick Park Avenues 159
Buick LeSabres 153
Chevy Geo Trackers 153
Oldsmobile 88s 151
Cadillac DeVilles 140
Lincoln Town Cars 131
Mercury Topazes 131

Status: Lincoln Town Car

SER 39

sunset city blues

1.8% of U.S. households

Primary age groups: **55–64, 65 +**

Median household income: **$31,400**

Median home value: **$59,500**

Thumbnail Demographics

empty-nesters in aging industrial cities

single-family housing

predominantly white married couples

high school graduates

blue-collar and service workers

Politics

Predominant ideology: conservative Independent

1996 presidential vote: Bob Dole

Key issues: state of the economy, pro-life movement, gun control

Sample Neighborhoods

Merrillville, Indiana 46410

Battle Creek, Michigan 49014

Wausau, Wisconsin 54403

Hagerstown, Maryland 21740

Williamsport, Pennsylvania 17701

In the Sunset City Blues community of Merrillville, Indiana, a town of 27,000 that bills itself as "a leader in leisure living," few barometers of lifestyle are more telling than the activities at the Lake County Library. Its collections of large-print and World War II books are expanding, the local Association for the Advancement of Retired Persons gathers in its meeting rooms, and the most checked-out books include titles on home repair, financial investing, and health care. With so many recently retired patrons, librarians serve a valuable role in helping residents learn how to maintain their homes, their health, and their financial well-being. "We get people who show up and say, 'I haven't been to a library in twenty years,'" says Merrillville reference librarian Lani Peterson. "But they'll keep coming back when they see how important it is to their lifestyle."

Merrillville is typical of Sunset City Blues, a cluster of midscale urban-fringe neighborhoods where many of the residents are retired or getting close to it. Comfortable in their tight-knit communities settled after World War II, these residents have low mobility rates and express little interest in moving to a mountain cabin or a condo in St. Petersburg. "When my husband said he wanted to retire in Florida, I said, 'Great, I'll come visit you there,'" says Marilyn Miller, fifty-eight, a bookkeeper. Although their children may attend college, Sunset City Blues residents typically haven't gone beyond high school; only 13 percent hold college degrees, contributing to a

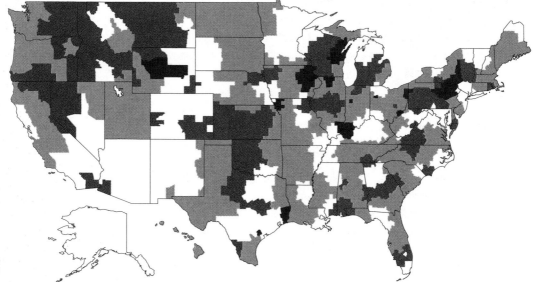

■ High
■ Above Average
▓ Below Average
□ Low

cigars   hot dogs   *Weight Watchers*   *Family Matters*   Buick Centurys   lottery tickets   fast-food fish

mixed employment base of low-level white-collar, blue-collar, and service jobs. These folks have low rates for travel and enjoy spending their time away from work with neighbors for dinner or a card game. "Compared to life in Beverly Hills, this is probably pretty boring," admits Donna Doherty, a sixty-year-old retired nurse. "But we like to get together and talk out here, just sit around, have iced tea, and talk. It's very relaxed."

In Sunset City Blues, life reflects a staid, old-fashioned perspective: The shopping centers feature Wards, JCPenney, and Hickey-Freeman suits; the American Legion advertises a corn boil. At the local McDonald's, retirees fill the booths every Saturday morning to nurse cups of coffee while talking about local politics and high school sports, the men in suspenders and ball caps, the women wearing floral blouses over stretch pants. Cluster residents are big on outdoorsy activities like camping, hunting, and, thanks to the lakes typically near these communities, fishing and boating. But their advancing age also makes for high rates of home-based leisure pursuits. The men are into woodworking fix-it projects, the women like collectibles — Franklin Mint ships a lot of product to this cluster — and together they log many hours in front of their large-screen television sets. In the kitchen, consumers are more interested in the cost of food than nutritional issues — "It's difficult to find health food around here," one Merrillville resident complains — and surveys confirm that Velveeta and cold cuts are much more popular than brown rice and tofu.

Having once been the bedroom suburbs of industrial cities, Sunset City Blues communities have watched their economic fortunes fall with factory closings. The political result is a shift from liberal Democrat to conservative Independent thinkers who've been the swing voters in recent elections. They fret about the economy, having experienced drastic downsizings in the last decade, and they're receptive to middle-class tax-reform proposals from either party. "We worry that our children will not enjoy the lifestyle that we have enjoyed," says Doherty. "Our children are well educated, but the job market doesn't seem to be as good as when we were starting out." There's a general malaise here about the direction the country is moving — more young families and ethnic groups are moving into Sunset City Blues, increasing urban problems and decreasing property values. Cluster residents tell pollsters that they wish they had more time to work on financial investments, the better to maintain a secure retirement.

PREFERENCES

(Index of 100 = U.S. Average)

Lifestyle / Products

what's hot

cigars 202
lottery tickets 143
book clubs 138
bread from scratch 132
bowling 132
woodworking 128
Kmart 126
microwaves 121
pain relievers 120
easy-listening
  CDs / tapes 120

what's not

weight lifting 65
new-wave CDs / tapes 61
foreign travel 54
hot tubs 53
on-line services 52
new imported cars 40
Gap 40
satellite dishes 28
pro basketball games 23
sailboats 15

Food / Drink

hot dogs 154
fast-food fish 151
frozen dinners 145
pasta 140
Nabisco Shredded Wheat 138
packaged cold cuts 133
canned chili 133
Kraft Velveeta 125
steak houses 119
fresh vegetables 117

Magazines / Newspapers

Weight Watchers 171
Family Handyman 169
National Enquirer 150
Star 143
Playboy 143
Saturday Evening Post 139
Car and Driver 136
Field & Stream 131
Ladies' Home Journal 124
Woman's Day 123

Television / Radio

Family Matters 161
Tonight Show with Jay Leno 159
CNBC 159
Frugal Gourmet 157
Nature 153
Family Channel 142
General Hospital 142
Live with Regis and Kathie Lee 142
Oprah Winfrey Show 138
Inside Edition 137

Cars / Trucks

Buick Centurys 149
Chevrolet Geo Trackers 144
Pontiac Sunbirds 139
Oldsmobiles 136
Mazda B3000 pickups 136
Plymouth Acclaims 134
Hyundai Scoupes 131
Oldsmobile 98s 131
Chevrolet Cavaliers 122
Chrysler New Yorkers 122

Living room necessity:
hutch filled with collectible plates,
dolls, and woodland critters

SER 40
military quarters

0.5% of U.S. households

Primary age groups: **under 24, 25–34**

Median household income: **$29,200**

Median home value: **$84,700**

Thumbnail Demographics

Gls and surrounding off-base families

2–9 unit rental housing

ethnically mixed households

high school graduates, some college

white-collar service workers

Politics

Predominant ideology: moderate Republican

1996 presidential vote: Bob Dole

Key issues: more military spending, eliminating
  affirmative action, AIDS education

Sample Neighborhoods

Dover AFB, Delaware 19902

Quantico, Virginia 22134

Camp Lejeune, North Carolina 28542

Homestead AFB, Florida 33039

Fort Sheridan, Illinois 60037

As the name implies, Military Quarters is the lifestyle of Americans who live on and around military bases. Racially integrated and boasting the nation's highest concentration of adults under thirty-five years old, this cluster reflects an unusual slice of Americana, one with its own code of conduct. Neighborhoods are characterized by orderly rows of spotless streets, buzz-cut lawns, and little shrubbery (for security concerns). Most residents live in group quarters or subdivisions where soldiers are assigned to homes or apartments according to rank. At Dover Air Force Base, a cargo facility in Delaware, the lowest-ranking airmen live in small row-house units, sergeants occupy modest three-bedroom split-levels, and the group commanders get more spacious homes with garages. A chain-link fence surrounds the main development of base housing, Eagle Heights, where homes come in any color, so long as it's a washed-out pastel.

"It's like living in a company town where everyone works for one employer," says Larry Palmer, a chief master sergeant at Dover AFB. Not that the enlistees place too much stock in their homes, anyway. Like Palmer, who's lived at six bases since enlisting in 1972, most soldiers pull up stakes every few years for new assignments. The shopping centers in most military towns rarely lack for self-storage companies, truck rental outlets, and discount furniture warehouses.

Despite the $600 hammers and $1,000 toilet seats of military procurement scandals, the residents of Military Quarters live in ma-

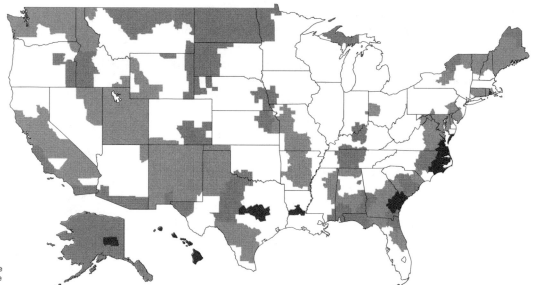

High

Above Average

Below Average

Low

racquetball   cola   *Popular Mechanics*   *Hard Copy*   Pontiac LeManses   nonfilter cigarettes   baby food

terially modest conditions. The median income is only $29,000, and 80 percent of the residents are married, often with young families and little discretionary income. Area strip malls are filled with discount pharmacies and grocery stores that must compete with the tax-free commissary and base exchange (what civilians know as PXs). Fast-food and family restaurants are popular because they can feed a family cheaply. "We have to do a lot of soul searching if we raise a dish a quarter," observes Woody Miller, owner of Captain John's Seafood Restaurant in Dover. Bars are popular in the area, but the rowdiest are off-limits to base personnel. At the Galaxy Inn, soldiers are lured inside with the promise of one-dollar drafts, though, surprisingly, the abundant booze doesn't attract hell-raisers. The boisterous take out their aggression crooning along with the karaoke machine.

With 55 percent of all residents under thirty-five, Military Quarters leads an active life. Jogging, racquetball, and other aerobic exercises are actively pursued because, as one soldier observes, "you have to stay within standards," referring to military guidelines for physical fitness. Locals are frequent travelers who go out on hunting trips almost as often as they fly to Europe for a deployment. With relatively little money invested in their homes, consumers are more inclined to buy collectibles and flashy cars like BMWs, especially when they can get deals by buying them overseas. Residents also exhibit high rates for watching talk shows, sitcoms, and the cable news feeds from CNN. "The TV set is tuned to CNN from the time we wake up to the time we go to bed," says one base secretary, "to keep abreast of what's happening overseas."

Because so many military bases are located in small towns, Military Quarters residents are somewhat isolated from metro sensibilities. Voters describe themselves as "somewhat conservative," though there's not a lot of party loyalty in this cluster; they're twice as likely as average Americans to identify with no political party. Residents are more interested in voting their self-interest: increased military spending, AIDS education, and social services. Their nomadic lifestyle makes for high stress, and in Dover, the St. Andrews Lutheran Church parking lot fills twice a week for Alcoholics Anonymous meetings. Polls show that residents wish they could spend more time pursuing stress-reducing activities like relaxing with friends or family. Admittedly, they know their current community is only a temporary respite until their next assignment — likely another Military Quarters base in another part of the country.

PREFERENCES

(Index of 100 = U.S. Average)

Lifestyle / Products

what's hot

racquetball 506
nonfilter cigarettes 417
Franklin Mint collectibles 301
in-home pregnancy tests 279
jogging 231
new-car loans 210
$300 + software 185
European travel 184
Victoria's Secret 162
freshwater fishing 155

what's not

vitamins 51
pianos 48
Price Club 44
burglar alarms 42
classical CDs / tapes 37
college football games 32
cats 31
ice hockey games 0
pagers / beepers 0

Food / Drink

cola 290
baby food 271
canned chili 178
children's frozen dinners 175
Kentucky Fried Chicken 171
Burger King 163
domestic beer 158
packaged cold cuts 154
chewing gum 139
Spam 137

Magazines / Newspapers

Popular Mechanics 267
Playboy 251
Muscle & Fitness 233
Parenting 233
Field & Stream 227
Guns & Ammo 216
Us 196
Sports Illustrated 171
Essence 141
Time 115

Television / Radio

Hard Copy 417
Ricki Lake 230
X-Files 216
Dateline NBC 207
Baywatch 190
Simpsons 189
Cops 180
CNN Headline News 178
Star Trek: Deep Space Nine 165
TV basketball 164

Cars / Trucks

Pontiac LeManses 1270
Suzukis 910
Mitsubishi Mirages 805
Volkswagen Foxes 565
Mazda 323s 535
Mitsubishi pickups 532
Hyundais 514
Isuzu pickups 503
BMW 318s 499
Volvo 940s 297

Restaurant scene:
your choice of fast food

mobility blues

1.6% of U.S. households

Primary age groups: **under 24, 25–34**

Median household income: **$30,900**

Median home value: **$70,400**

Thumbnail Demographics

young working-class married couples and single parents

multi-unit rental housing

ethnically mixed households

high school graduates, some college

blue-collar and service workers

Politics

Predominant ideology: moderate conservative

1996 presidential vote: Ross Perot

Key issues: tax reform, capital punishment,
restricting immigration

Sample Neighborhoods

Olathe, Kansas 66061

Bristol, Pennsylvania 19007

Gresham, Oregon 97030

Highland Springs, Virginia 23075

Port Orchard, Washington 98366

For first-time visitors to Olathe, Kansas, the single-story shop on the busy street corner invariably causes double takes: Its red-and-white sign offers customers auto repair and country crafts. In rural hamlets across America, such commercial pairings are commonplace. But its presence in an inner-ring suburb says much about Mobility Blues, a diverse lifestyle whose populace is predominantly young, ethnically mixed, and often on the move. Once a stable area of middle-class families who knew each other, today it's known as a fixer-upper community with a high proportion of mobile single-parent families and recent Hispanic immigrants. Its residential neighborhoods are well within range of small factory noise and industrial odors. In Olathe, the flood of newcomers has meant crowded garden-style apartments, classroom trailers at the schools, and dilapidated single-family homes undergoing major renovations. "It's a mixed area, but they're all down-home people," says Chuck Kurtz, forty-six, an editor at the *Olathe Daily News.* "They're not out to impress anybody. They're just trying to survive day by day."

No one's particularly wealthy in Mobility Blues, but residents do manage to live decently by stretching lower-middle-class incomes. They have high rates for attending professional sports games and enjoy the usually urban pursuits of billiards and boxing. They're regular gamblers who go to casinos and bingo parlors, and to liquor

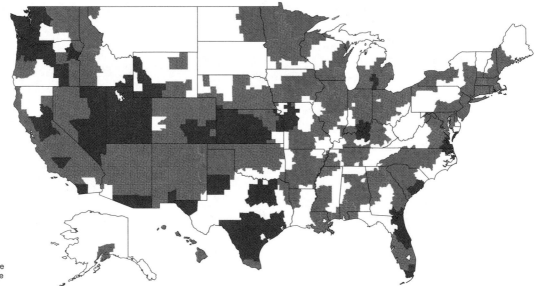

High
Above Average
Below Average
Low

pro basketball games   RC Cola   *Baby Talk*   Spanish radio   Montgomery Ward   Canadian whiskey

stores to play the daily lottery. With their high school educations and low-level white- and blue-collar jobs, these are not the Americans who belong to country clubs, take adult education courses, or own vacation homes. But they do read a wide assortment of magazines at above-average rates: from *Ebony* and *Audubon* to *Car Craft* and *Vogue.* Indeed, the residents of Mobility Blues tend to be homebodies who tell pollsters they wish they could spend more time doing household chores and watching television; most of their top-rated programs are sports or talk shows. They're into cooking, but, as one local notes, "that tofu stuff isn't big around here." If they go shopping, it's to seek out bargains at stores like Montgomery Ward, Price Club, and Home Depot. In one attitude survey the desire to keep up with fashion came in dead last among their priorities.

During political elections, the transient nature of Mobility Blues has a depressing effect on voter turnout. Many residents don't feel connected to the political process. "We don't vote," says Shannon Hackleman, a thirty-year-old married day care provider. "I've just never wanted to. And my husband's almost forty-four and he's never voted either. Our main priority is paying our bills." The highest percentage of residents are conservative, but their apathy doesn't endear them to the Republican Party. Just about the only political issues that cause these residents to raise an eyebrow are restricting immigration and eliminating affirmative action. In 1996, most of those who did bother to vote backed Ross Perot.

Whether Mobility Blues will resurrect itself as a comfortable bedroom community is uncertain. At the veterans' clubs and fraternal orders that are so popular in the cluster, longtime residents talk about the changes wrought by the younger newcomers — and not all for the better. In Olathe, there are worries about the increasing number of teenagers involved in drugs, committing acts of vandalism, and turning up their car stereos as they cruise the narrow streets. "The old-timers feel that the newcomers don't respect them," says one resident, "and they're afraid of the way the kids dress in gangster clothes." But as long as the younger families are attracted to the relatively inexpensive housing — the median home value is $70,400 — such culture clashes are inevitable in Mobility Blues. "This is the kind of community you get with a big transient population," says editor Kurtz. If that means selling tune-ups and teddy bears under the same roof, so be it.

PREFERENCES

(Index of 100 = U.S. Average)

Lifestyle / Products

what's hot

pro basketball games 258

Montgomery Ward 163

condoms 160

Motel 6 152

disability insurance 145

Home Depot 138

sewing 131

gambling casinos 125

stair steppers 121

furniture refinishing 114

what's not

boating 73

stamp collecting 71

Limited 64

hunting 63

camcorders 62

CB radios 61

Christian / faith music CDs / tapes 60

money market funds 51

travel insurance 39

college football games 38

Food / Drink

RC Cola 151

Canadian whiskey 139

Taco Bell 135

whole milk 134

baby food 126

Cap'n Crunch 114

doughnuts 110

Mexican food 109

pasta 108

canned chili 104

Magazines / Newspapers

Baby Talk 241

Ebony 197

Sunset 196

Car Craft 174

Life 151

Cosmopolitan 151

Prevention 135

Family Handyman 127

National Enquirer 126

People 125

Television / Radio

Spanish radio 378

Cinemax 233

Comic Strip Live 146

Tonight Show with Jay Leno 136

Inside Edition 133

CBS Sports Sunday 128

Nickelodeon 127

Simpsons 121

Geraldo 119

Melrose Place 110

Cars / Trucks

Kias 281

Suzukis 187

Hyundai Elantras 163

Hyundai Excels 160

Toyota Tercels 152

Nissan Sentras 150

Mitsubishi Mirages 147

Toyota Paseos 137

Chevrolet Geo Metros 136

Ford Aspires 130

Local hangout:
Home Depot

SER 42
gray collars

2.1% of U.S. households

Primary age groups: **55–64, 65 +**

Median household income: **$31,400**

Median home value: **$62,400**

Thumbnail Demographics

aging couples in inner suburbs

single-family housing

ethnically mixed households

high school graduates

blue-collar and service workers

Politics

Predominant ideology: liberal Democrat

1996 presidential vote: Bill Clinton

Key issues: environmental programs, health care reform, defusing racial tensions

Sample Neighborhoods

Assumption, Houston, Texas 77037

South St. Paul, Minnesota 55075

Pittston, Pennsylvania 18642

Kenosha, Wisconsin 53140

Opa Locka, Florida 33055

Back in the 1970s and early '80s, many of America's factory towns hit the skids. Factories were closing. Residents were pulling up stakes for out-of-town job opportunities. Foreigners were taking over the steel and automobile industries, costing Americans more than a million jobs. Across the Rust Belt, liquidation sale notices blew down deserted streets like tumbleweeds in a ghost town.

Slowly, painfully, many of these areas have come back from the brink. Gray Collars reflects these communities' rising fortunes; it is a cluster of working-class inner suburbs filled with older couples who never left and young migrants hoping to cash in on the industrial renaissance. Gray-collar employees — a mix of service workers, clerks, and low-level management types — are hardworking, low-key, and family-centered men and women. They live in modest three-bedroom ranch houses with carports that typically hold pick-ups, boats, and campers. They travel little, but when they do, it's to nearby campgrounds, theme parks, or beaches; their favorite motel is a Red Roof Inn. "It's a plain lifestyle," says Ramona Garbs, secretary at the Fonville Middle School in the Assumption section of Houston, Texas. "People just want a decent house for their kids to grow up in."

Leisure activities in Gray Collars tend to follow traditional gender roles: The men go to auto races, the women buy romance nov-

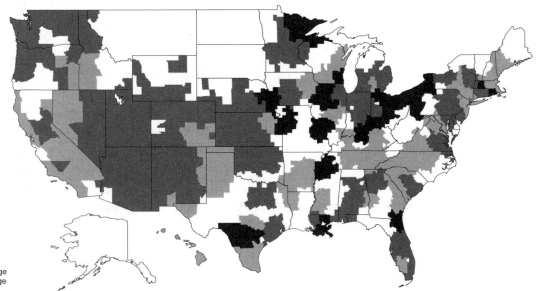

■ High
■ Above Average
■ Below Average
□ Low

Builder's Square   Twinkies   motorcycle magazines   Movie Channel   Ford Tempos   lottery tickets

els, and everyone goes to bowling leagues and dance clubs at high rates. Residents enjoy eating out, but it's usually at fast-food franchises like Pizza Hut, Burger King, or Wendy's. At home, most refrigerators are well stocked with cold cuts and beer. When residents sit down in front of the television, they tend to tune in a range of sitcoms and family programming, from *The Nanny* and *Martin* to *Touched by an Angel.* In Assumption, a gritty area where the ethnic makeup has shifted from Eastern European to Central American, many residents spend their free time working on their cars and homes. "If you can build anything, or repair something, that's the best thing in the world," says Henry Novak, a local Czech-born retiree. "People look down on those who don't keep up their homes."

With their tight budgets, Gray Collars are the kinds of consumers who clip coupons and take out home-improvement loans at high rates. Assumption's commercial district is filled with thrift stores, pawn shops, laundromats, storage businesses, and auto parts stores, and residents frequent Wal-Marts and Builder's Squares. The churches are important in this area for the spiritual and social foundations they provide. Gray Collars have high rates for belonging to religious clubs and charitable volunteering. In Assumption, even the men who frequent the local cantinas to drink and gamble show up for church on Sunday. When the Assumption Catholic Church underwent a renovation, some sixty people showed up to help, chatting with each other in English and Spanish. "The volunteer activities break down barriers of suspicion between ethnic groups," says Father Italo Dell'Oro. "People think, 'They work like us. They love the church in the same way.'"

Politically, Gray Collars is a mixed bag. Voters are conservative enough to support school prayer and curbing pornography. But they also remain big backers of labor unions and environmental reform — traditional liberal causes. "The unions are falling apart, but we still believe in them," says one metal lather in Assumption. Gray Collars complain about jobs lost to NAFTA; in these patriotic, economically shaky areas, residents drive American cars and trucks as an expression of support for their fellow workers. But they're also worried about changes to their neighborhoods that could mean a replay from the past: crime on the rise and property values on the decline. Years into the high-tech revolution, Gray Collars residents still long for the days when American manufacturing was king.

PREFERENCES

(Index of 100 = U.S. Average)

Lifestyle / Products

what's hot

Builder's Square	191
lottery tickets	169
auto races	140
six-month CDs	134
theme parks	133
menthol cigarettes	130
needlepoint	129
bowling	122
caller I.D.	121
romance novels	119

what's not

zoos	77
traveler's checks	76
photography	71
veterans' clubs	69
golf	69
museums	68
Mary Kay cosmetics	62
tennis	42
country clubs	24
Price Club	13

Food / Drink

Twinkies	160
fresh cold cuts	136
fast food	134
frozen dinners	130
low / no-alcohol beer	129
Godfathers Pizza	130
Pepsi Free	126
Nabisco Shredded Wheat	126
Wendy's	125
canned spaghetti	124

Magazines / Newspapers

motorcycle magazines	181
Parenting	177
Cooking Light	167
Hot Rod	166
Ebony	159
American Health	142
McCall's	141
Seventeen	140
House Beautiful	133
National Enquirer	130

Television / Radio

Movie Channel	183
New York Undercover	175
Rolanda	153
Meet the Press	144
Good Morning America	139
TV wrestling	137
Tonight Show with Jay Leno	136
America's Funniest Home Videos	134
Nanny	131
Law & Order	117

Cars / Trucks

Ford Tempos	213
Chevrolet Astros	195
Mercury Topazes	166
Buick Skylarks	162
Plymouth Acclaims	157
Plymouth Sundances	150
Dodge Spirits	149
Dodge Shadows	147
Chevrolet Sportvans	145
Pontiac Sunbirds	144

Status: any college's decal on a car's rear window

shotguns & pickups

1.7% of U.S. households

Primary age group: **35–54**

Median household income: **$33,300**

Median home value: **$58,400**

Thumbnail Demographics

rural blue-collar families

single-family housing

predominantly white households

high school educations

blue-collar workers

Politics

Predominant ideology: conservative Republican

1996 presidential vote: Ross Perot

Key issues: family values, restricting immigration, school prayer

Sample Neighborhoods

Lynchburg, Tennessee 37352

Iron Station, North Carolina 28080

Bethel, Pennsylvania 19507

Dallas, Georgia 30132

Hager City, Wisconsin 54014

There's only one stoplight, no building towers more than two stories, and the high school senior class tops out at seventy-five kids. That's the skinny on Lynchburg, Tennessee (population 700), a typical Shotguns & Pickups community. In these drowsy rural towns, where residents rarely lock their doors and often hang deer antlers in their bedrooms, life looks like a page out of a century-old scrapbook. Men hunt, women can vegetables, and children tend to chickens in backyard pens. "This is slow-paced living out here," says Clayton Knight, assistant manager of the Lynchburg Hardware and General Store. "People will get what they want in a store and then go over to the courthouse to talk and whittle a while."

To outsiders, Shotguns & Pickups is an insular world where family ties often count more than education. Only one in ten students earn college diplomas, partly because most local jobs don't require one and partly because most parents don't possess one. "A lot of people think that if it's good enough for your daddy, it's good enough for you," says Randall Fanning, a thirty-eight-year-old worker at the Jack Daniel's Distillery, the largest employer in Lynchburg. (Fanning estimates that he's related to about 10 percent of the 350 plant workers.) This attitude breeds a parochialism that's played out in media preferences; Shotguns & Pickups residents boast relatively little interest in newspapers, newsweeklies, and TV news shows. The more popular publications feature outdoor leisure

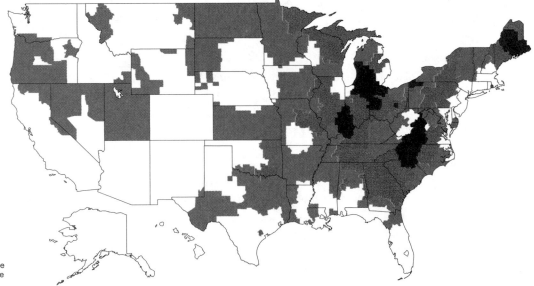

■ High
▓ Above Average
▒ Below Average
□ Low

chewing tobacco Spam *Woman's World Bold and the Beautiful* Dodge 3500 pickups tractor pulls

activities like fishing and gardening. At the library, women check out cookbooks and best-selling fiction, and the men take home fix-it books and Civil War histories. When the Lynchburg library had the opportunity to get connected to the Internet, about half the townspeople resisted. "Out here, change occurs over people kicking and screaming," observes librarian Sara Hope. "A classic line is 'It's always been done that way.'"

Indeed, progress comes slowly to Shotguns & Pickups towns. It's not unusual to find adults who've never flown in an airplane, never seen a first-run movie, never sniffed the cloying aromas of a trendy French bistro. Residents still sew their own bedroom quilts and fill their freezers with fish and game from hunting trips. If they want to splurge, they'll travel many miles for a movie, country music show, or pro wrestling match. On Saturday nights, teenagers still park at the courthouse square, smoking cigarettes and sneaking beers, as they did in the fifties.

The goals of these cluster residents were not unknown to their agrarian ancestors: raising respectful children, producing well-tended gardens, keeping a few cattle for extra money. Much of the housing stock is old, and property is frequently passed down from generation to generation. "If you've got a house with more than two bathrooms, you're doing well," notes one resident. By contrast, residents frequently have new pickups worth almost as much as their homes. Given the modest housing, a polished muscle car becomes a form of rolling status for tearing over the hilly Shotguns & Pickups back roads. "If you see someone in a big Buick or a Lincoln Town Car," says one Lynchburg resident, "you know they're in high cotton."

Old-fashioned family values run deep in this politically conservative cluster, where Lynchburg residents can still watch election returns on a chalkboard at the courthouse. Politicians rarely raise liberal issues like gay and abortion rights. Gun control is a foreign concept. "I'm not voting for Clinton, or her husband either," one local quipped during the 1996 campaign, when Ross Perot received many votes in the cluster. Residents regard government as an intrusive conglomerate of corrupt politicians, unnecessary regulations, and high taxes — 55 percent of the price of a bottle of Jack Daniel's whiskey goes to pay federal taxes. "Around here, you elect people on what they're not going to do," says Roger Brashears, a Jack Daniel's spokesman. In a fast-paced society moving forward, the residents of Shotguns & Pickups like to drive with an eye on the rearview mirror, trying to preserve the rural lifestyle of the past.

PREFERENCES
(Index of 100 = U.S. Average)

Lifestyle / Products

what's hot

chewing tobacco 265
tractor pulls 240
auto races 197
woodworking 175
hunting 172
freshwater fishing 163
camera accessories 156
sewing 156
power boats 153
veterans' clubs 148

what's not

bowling 45
foreign videos 42
foreign travel 38
gambling casinos 36
chess 36
exercise at clubs 34
college basketball games 27
spa vacations 13
Price Club 15
on-line services 0

Food / Drink

Spam 163
Diet-Rite cola 154
grits 153
pasta 140
Kraft Velveeta 134
canned stew 131
butter substitute 129
Cap'n Crunch 126
hot dogs 124
canned spaghetti 123

Magazines / Newspapers

Woman's World 231
Bassmaster 216
Modern Bride 197
Guns & Ammo 183
Country Living 182
Motor Trend 159
Ladies' Home Journal 154
Sports Afield 154
Family Circle 148
Hot Rod 140

Television / Radio

Bold and the Beautiful 267
Young and the Restless 212
CBS This Morning 191
Family Feud 187
Rush Limbaugh 182
CBS Sports Saturday 181
Price Is Right 174
Baywatch 168
country radio 156
Geraldo 158

Cars / Trucks

Dodge 3500 pickups 251
Chevrolet 4 x 4 pickups 246
Dodge 4 x 4 pickups 232
Ford 4 x 4 pickups 224
Pontiac Sunbirds 177
Chevrolet Berettas 176
GMC Safaris 163
Chevrolet Astros 160
Oldsmobile 98s 154
Dodge Spirits 153

Status: new four-wheel-drive truck with CD player and gun rack

SER 44
Latino America

1.3% of U.S. households

Primary age groups: **under 24, 25–34**

Median household income: **$30,100**

Median home value: **$110,100**

Thumbnail Demographics

Hispanic middle-class families

2–9 unit rental housing

predominantly Hispanic households

grade school, high school graduates

blue-collar and service workers

Politics

Predominant ideology: liberal Democrat

1996 presidential vote: Bill Clinton

Key issues: gun control, public education funding,
defusing racial tensions

Sample Neighborhoods

Virgil Village, Los Angeles, California 90039

Hudson City, Jersey City, New Jersey 07307

Cicero, Illinois 60650

Colton, California 92324

Ridgewood, Flushing, New York 11385

"This is an immigrant gateway community," declares Geoff Saldivar, a thirty-five-year-old community activist in the Virgil Village section of Los Angeles. He's not kidding. With the nation's highest proportion of foreign-born residents — sixty languages are spoken in Virgil Village — Latino America is a multi-ethnic lifestyle where Spanish is more common than English and consumers shop at mom-and-pop *mercados* rather than national supermarket chains. Concentrated in only a handful of cities like New York, Chicago, and Los Angeles, Latino America is filled with young families with middle-class incomes, though not the status that goes with it due to modest educations and the sheer size of their large families. Many residents live in cramped apartments with windows crisscrossed with bars to discourage break-ins. One in four adults hasn't finished the eighth grade and only 10 percent have a college diploma. "A lot of people don't even think about college," says architect Christopher Covault. "They just want enough money to buy the simplest things for their family."

With only 15 percent of adults working as professionals, most residents know their blue-collar and service positions are jobs, not careers. Accordingly, leisure time means a lot to Latino Americans, and watching TV is their most popular activity. Cluster residents buy big-screen TVs and watch nearly a hundred programs at above-average rates, especially soap operas and talk shows; *Ricki Lake* and *Jerry Springer* are favorites among the disproportionate num-

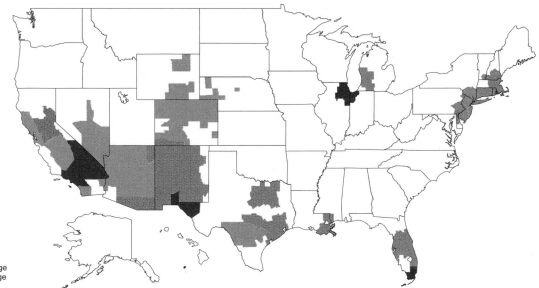

- ■ High
- ▨ Above Average
- ▨ Below Average
- □ Low

boxing matches   *Baby Talk*   Spanish radio   Toyota Tercels   dance music CDs / tapes   avocados

ber of women at home during the day. "It helps me learn English," explains Maura Garcia, a recent immigrant from El Salvador. But the close quarters also encourage adults to go out at night, to pool halls, dance clubs, and bars. At the Smog Cutter's Bar, a dingy Virgil Village hole-in-the-wall lit year-round by Christmas lights, neighbors of various ethnicities show up nightly to shoot pool or sing with the karaoke machine.

"There's a lot of melting pot going on," says community activist Saldivar. "No one thinks twice about interracial dating and marriage. Here, the diversity is appreciated."

In these densely packed neighborhoods, the street scene is often vibrant and sometimes dangerous. Residents tell pollsters they worry about crime, support gun control, and look to the church as a source of stability; burglar alarms are purchased at high rates. Neighborhoods like Virgil Village are also known as havens for drugs and gangs, and it's taken a concerted effort by active residents to clean up the graffiti on neighborhood buildings. One project organized teenagers to paint colorful murals to discourage gangs from "tagging." Another tried to reclaim a trash-strewn vacant lot for a soccer field. Politically, this is a liberal Democratic cluster, but voters typically feel disenfranchised and go to the polls at a low rate. Many look to community activists to deal with issues involving immigration, taxes, and social justice. "The big issues in the community are economic, not political," says Virgil Village librarian Arthur Pond. "They take out books on how to learn computers and fix their cars."

Their large families and midscale incomes make for tight budgets when Latino Americans go shopping. Surveys show they spend a lot on weekly groceries, though few foodstuffs are bought at above-average rates (admittedly, such research doesn't always pick up purchases from street vendors or ethnic markets). If someone owns a car, it's likely an imported subcompact — and often an old clunker kept running thanks to the numerous auto supply dealers. In this cluster, residents frequent corner stores like 7-Eleven and discount chains such as Montgomery Ward and Marshalls as well as more upscale retailers such as the Gap and even Saks Fifth Avenue for the status of designer clothes. When they travel abroad, it's often to the country of their origins, though they rarely stay long. "We miss our relatives, sometimes too much," says Gilda Zavala, forty-two, an apartment manager born in Guatemala. "But everything is easier here. And there's more of a future for my kids." For many, Latino America is a gateway cluster to the future.

PREFERENCES

(Index of 100 = U.S. Average)

Lifestyle / Products

what's hot

boxing matches 443
dance music
  CDs / tapes 194
pagers / beepers 156
Marshalls 145
foreign videos 134
auto races 128
chess 120
passports 118
weekly groceries
  $150 + 118
7-Eleven 113

what's not

Kentucky Fried Chicken
  62
barbecuing 57
stair steppers 54
campers 45
sewing 44
softball 43
work boots 43
lottery tickets 40
easy-listening music
  37
nonfilter cigarettes 36

Food / Drink

Shakey's 310
avocados 230
tequila 204
canned ham 140
pita bread 115
boxed chocolates 114
brown rice 113
beef jerky 113
Coca-Cola Classic 108
chewing gum 105

Magazines / Newspapers

Baby Talk 384
Cosmopolitan 228
Muscle & Fitness 188
True Story 166
Playboy 160
National Geographic
  Traveler 139
Self 138
People 124
National Enquirer 121
Seventeen 112

Television / Radio

Spanish radio 992
All My Children 333
Late Night with Conan
  O'Brien 298
Touched by an Angel
  193
Movie Channel 191
Married with Children
  173
Comedy Central 171
Rescue 911 162
Baywatch 161
Court TV 156

Cars / Trucks

Kias 238
GMC Safaris 180
Toyota N81 pickups 151
Mazda MPVs 151
Toyota Tercels 149
Toyota Corollas 139
Mitsubishi Monteros
  138
Toyota Previas 130
Honda Civics 118
Nissan Sentras 118

First language: Spanish

SER 45

agri-business

1.7% of U.S. households

Primary age groups: **45–54, 55–64, 65 +**

Median household income: **$32,300**

Median home value: **$63,800**

Thumbnail Demographics

rural farm-town and ranch families

single-family housing

predominantly white households

grade school, high school graduates

farmworkers

Politics

Predominant ideology: conservative Republican

1996 presidential vote: Bob Dole

Key issues: family values, restricting immigration, reducing size of government

Sample Neighborhoods

Nicollet, Minnesota 56074

Deer Isle, Maine 04627

Fort Dodge, Kansas 67843

Menomonie, Wisconsin 54751

Kersey, Colorado 80644

America was once a land of small rural communities, and it still is in Agri-Business. Although the towns in the cluster are still small — a couple of main streets with several dozen businesses — there's nothing modest about the size of the homesteads. These are sprawling farms, heavily capitalized and equipped, where residents raise grain and livestock, relying on combines and chemicals to handle the toughest chores. Their sturdy brick homes often sit amid neat barns and grain silos, and above-average purchases of cars, satellite dishes, pianos, and camcorders bespeak a comfortable rural lifestyle. On a summer Saturday in Nicollet, Minnesota, population 795, the farmers are just as likely to be sunburned from a round of golf as a stint in a cornfield.

Concentrated in the heartland of the Upper Midwest and Northwest, Agri-Business communities are filled with large families, countless animals, and rustic lifestyles. There's rarely a police officer in town and crime is infrequent. "If you see juvenile crime, you just grab the kids and take them to their parents," one resident notes. Among these rural Americans, hunting and fishing remain prime leisure activities, and dens often are graced with bear skins and deer antlers; living rooms feature ornate glass-and-mahogany hutches that hold shotguns. Given the sparse landscape, residents pursue social activities through clubs: They have a higher-than-average rate

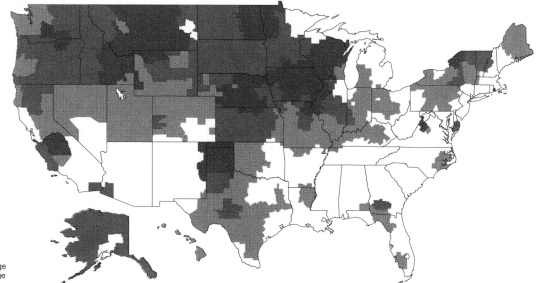

■ High
■ Above Average
■ Below Average
□ Low

hunting   baking chips   *Audubon*   Disney Channel   Chevy K3500 pickups   gas chain saws   skim milk

for belonging to church groups, fraternal organizations, and veterans' clubs. In Nicollet, the center of community life is the Nicollet Conservation Club, where the most ardent hunters compete in duck- and goose-calling contests. Every month, some 700 people gather for a pork chop fry, lining up for two hours to have dinner with friends and neighbors — few minding the wait as they drink cocktails and chat in line. "Everyone gets to know their neighbors," says Fred Froehlich, forty-seven, a rural postal carrier and director of the club. "In the cities, people don't want to get involved. Here, everyone gets involved."

Although Agri-Business boasts a job base involved in forestry, fishing, ranching, and mining, the rhythm of the community is tied to agriculture. Status is expressed in the size and newness of your farm machinery, like a tractor with four-wheel drive or a Caterpillar truck. Mornings find many residents passing through the local coffee shop, attempting to solve the world's problems in an hour. Shopping involves at least a thirty-minute drive to larger towns, and many residents have never heard of Starbucks. "We drink coffee, not espresso," explains a resident. Agri-Business is still a place of tradition, where the women bake bread from scratch and the men hunt game that ends up on the table. "It's not a trendy place," says Bruce Schmidt, owner of a meat market known for its steaks, pork chops, and sausage. "No one says, 'I've got to see the latest movie.' They'll get around to it when it comes out on video."

Like other rural communities, Agri-Business tends to be politically conservative, down on big government, welfare programs, and taxes, but in favor of privacy rights, gun ownership, and capital punishment. "At work, we toast each other every time they fry someone in prison," says one farmer. Rush Limbaugh is popular here, picked up on kitchen and combine radios. Newspapers are viewed as suspect for their leftist leanings, and residents have little tolerance for pacifists. "This is a patriotic community," says farmer Ronald Rudenick, fifty-seven, drawing on a Marlboro. "A lot of veterans live in this part of the country." Agri-Business voters save their vehemence for environmentalists — "the tree huggers who spend their dollars on attorneys" — and those opposed to hunters and the National Rifle Association. "Every law seems to be for the criminals and against the law-abiding citizens," Fred Froehlich says disgustedly. In Agri-Business, people just want to be left alone.

PREFERENCES

(Index of 100 = U.S. Average)

Lifestyle / Products

what's hot

hunting 211
gas chain saws 210
insect repellent 175
dogs 171
bread from scratch 158
pianos 149
book clubs 143
auto races 138
family videos 137
vitamins 130

what's not

bowling 83
zoos 80
car alarms 67
stamp collecting 64
backpacking / hiking 59
Limited 57
keeping up with fashion 53
Domino's pizza 50
dance music CDs / tapes 30
airline magazines 17

Food / Drink

baking chips 174
skim milk 160
canned stew 153
Diet Pepsi 145
low-fat cottage cheese 143
Cheerios 136
Kraft Velveeta 133
cooked ham 132
frozen orange juice 128
beef 115

Magazines / Newspapers

Audubon 229
Outdoor Life 224
Sporting News 173
GQ 172
gardening magazines 154
Field & Stream 137
Muscle & Fitness 133
Sunset 126
Reader's Digest 120
McCall's 114

Television / Radio

Disney Channel 210
Tonight Show with Jay Leno 179
Days of Our Lives 172
ABC Wide World of Sports 166
TNN 166
Wheel of Fortune 154
Home Improvement 147
Discovery Channel 142
48 Hours 139
Family Matters 122

Cars / Trucks

Chevy K3500 pickups 428
Ford F-250 pickups 402
GMC 4WD pickups 258
Dodge Dakota pickups 241
Suzuki Swifts 186
Oldsmobile 98s 172
Buick Park Avenues 169
Plymouth Sundances 142
Buick LeSabres 139
Pontiac Grand Prix 130

Favorite holiday:
hunting season

mid-city mix

1.3% of U.S. households

Primary age group: **under 24, 25–44**

Median household income: **$31,400**

Median home value: **$65,700**

Thumbnail Demographics

African American families and singles

2–9 unit renters and owners

predominantly African American solo parents and married couples

high school graduates, some college

service and white-collar workers

Politics

Predominant ideology: liberal Democrat

1996 presidential vote: Bill Clinton

Key issues: AIDS education, pro labor unions, defusing racial tensions

Sample Neighborhoods

Brightwood Park, Washington, D.C. 20011

East Orange, New Jersey 07017

Dorchester, Massachusetts 02124

Compton, California 90221

Auburn Park, Chicago, Illinois 60620

Mid-City Mix stands at an urban crossroads: a cluster of middle-class, predominantly African American neighborhoods trying to preserve their family values against the pressures of drugs and violence. Located in older cities throughout the Northeast and Great Lakes regions, Mid-City Mix typically fringes an urban core with well-kept streets, aging row houses, and squat apartment buildings, the tiny yards trimmed and decorated with flowers. Many residents are well educated — 40 percent have gone to college — and hold decent jobs as teachers, craftspeople, and service workers. But the commercial base is modest. Liquor stores, hair salons, and convenience stores predominate. And it's not uncommon to see a clutch of street people in an alley, passing a bottle of fortified wine. Violent crime plagues the cluster's neighborhoods, the sound of gunfire erupting routinely in Mid-City Mix.

But an underlying pride separates this lifestyle type from America's more downscale urban districts. Most of the households are headed by working couples and single mothers aspiring to improve their children's lives. They decorate their homes, valued at an average of $65,700, with awards from high school and college. In the evening, they sit on front porches to chat with neighbors or watch children play on the sidewalk. "This is a good neighborhood but for some bad elements always luring away our kids," says Carolyn Robinson, a forty-seven-year-old resident of the Brightwood Park

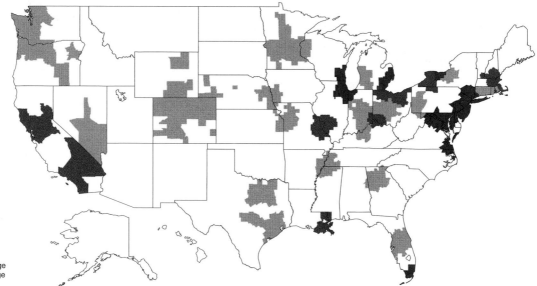

■ High
▨ Above Average
▨ Below Average
□ Low

bus travel   fresh fish   *Essence*   BET   Hyundai Elantras   R & B CDs / tapes   malt liquor   *Ebony*

section of Washington, D.C. "It's harder to do the right thing than the wrong thing."

It's also harder to maintain a middle-class lifestyle when most retail chains and supermarkets have abandoned these urban areas for the suburbs. To shop for anything other than staples, Mid-City Mixers usually carry their multiple credit cards to suburban malls, destined for Macy's and Eddie Bauer as well as Woolworth. Back in their neighborhoods, residents make do at carry-outs and mom-and-pop markets where, as one shopper puts it, "they sell more beer and cigarettes than meat and potatoes." The streets are lined with older cars — boxy American sedans as well as cheap imports such as Nissan Sentras and Toyota Corollas. When it comes to leisure, Mid-City Mixers watch more television, listen to more gospel music, and go to more movies than average Americans. Their social life centers on the many local churches, from the ornate buildings of established denominations to storefront chapels for splintered sects. Every Sunday, the sidewalks come alive with families dressed in their finest going to church.

"We have two worlds around here," says Dr. Alpha Estes Brown, minister of Brightwood Park United Methodist Church. "One is of stable, healthy families where parents work, go to church, and lead mainstream lives. The other is of marginal people who don't have much and are involved in criminal activity. Depending on what happens, we can go up or down in the future."

Mid-City Mix is a classic transitional neighborhood type: Once residents achieve middle-class status, many tend to move to the suburbs to escape the noise and congestion of the city. In their place arrive poorer immigrants from South America and the Caribbean islands. In Brightwood Park, the highlight of the social calendar is the Caribbean Street Festival, when recent immigrants parade through the streets in colorful sequined costumes, waving rum cocktails to the beat of reggae bands. Most of the time, however, there's an uneasy truce between the longtime African American residents and these newcomers, especially among the immigrant shopkeepers who operate the local stores — sometimes from behind bulletproof glass. In surveys, cluster residents tell pollsters one of their biggest concerns is defusing racial tensions. "People don't complain about racial problems because they have to survive the best way they can," says hairstylist Vera Winfield. "They strive for harmony. They're just not there yet."

PREFERENCES

(Index of 100 = U.S. Average)

Lifestyle / Products

what's hot

bus travel 337

R & B CDs / tapes 311

three-way calling 246

Woolworth 203

money orders 171

pro basketball games 168

Lord & Taylor 160

unions 153

boxing matches 143

Adidas 139

what's not

science fiction 67

Publishers Clearing House 57

aerobics 54

cats 51

satellite dishes 28

Mary Kay cosmetics 27

ice-cream restaurants 26

chewing tobacco 22

power boating 19

woodworking 11

Food / Drink

Cherry Coke 271

malt liquor 198

pancake restaurants 182

Kentucky Fried Chicken 147

frozen desserts 141

canned chili 134

salt substitute 132

Kellogg's Corn Flakes 131

Kool-Aid 130

fresh fish 113

Magazines / Newspapers

Essence 792

Ebony 541

Sport 355

Baby Talk 313

Stereo Review 291

GQ 281

Vogue 257

Business Week 219

American Health 209

Star 199

Television / Radio

BET 635

urban-contemporary radio 500

Living Single 490

Montel Williams Show 371

Charlie Rose 285

Homicide 219

America's Most Wanted 207

Young and the Restless 155

Married . . . with Children 153

Law & Order 141

Cars / Trucks

Hyundai Elantras 285

Pontiac LeManses 226

Ford Econoline Club Wagons 162

Plymouth Acclaims 159

Plymouth Sundances 151

Chevrolet Corsicas 150

Toyota Corollas 146

Mercury Tracers 145

Dodge Colts 137

Oldsmobile Achievas 119

Typical billboard:
"Just Say No to Drugs"

SER 47

blue highways

2.2% of U.S. households

Primary age group: **35–54**

Median household income: **$27,000**

Median home value: **$56,700**

Thumbnail Demographics

lower-middle-class farm families

single-family and mobile-home housing

predominantly white households

grade school, high school graduates

blue-collar and farmworkers

Politics

Predominant ideology: conservative Republican

1996 presidential vote: Bob Dole

Key issues: welfare reform, family values,
    restricting immigration

Sample Neighborhoods

Horse Shoe Run, West Virginia 26769

Interlochen, Michigan 49643

Moab, Utah 84532

Hopkinsville, Tennessee 42240

San Ysidro, New Mexico 87053

On maps, blue highways are often two-lane roads that wind through remote stretches of mountains, deserts, and lake country. Among lifestyle types, Blue Highways is a collection of small, isolated communities, rarely with more than several hundred people spread across a rural landscape. There are no distinguishable towns, no stoplights, supermarkets, or movie theaters. Neighbors live a quarter mile from each other. In places like Horse Shoe Run, West Virginia, locals make do with a single church (billed as "The Littlest Church in the Lower 48 States"), a craft shop, a grocery store jammed in someone's home, and a campground store that doubles as restaurant, video rental, and game room. Phone calls are all long-distance. Many of the local schools closed years ago. Families drive sixty miles to do their serious food and clothing shopping. "Every time we want to do something, it's a long drive," notes one resident.

But the people who live in Blue Highways say they like the unspoiled scenery, their close relationship with nature, and the crime-free setting for raising children. "It helps if you're a down-home person who likes the quiet," says Edith Cowger, owner of the Silver Lake Park café and campground. Churches serve as social centers for Wednesday night Bible groups and Sunday box socials. In these areas with a lot of logging, you see plenty of ads for Homelite chain saws. The service stations and tiny storefronts that serve as grocers tend to stock canned meat and beer, condiments and soda. Almost

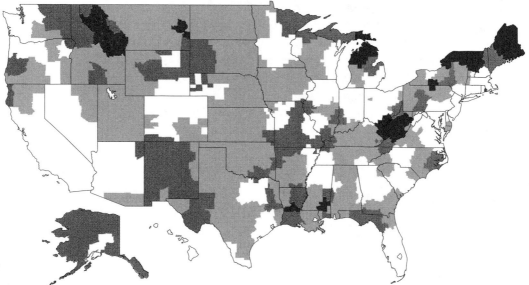

High
Above Average
Below Average
Low

hunting   country radio   *Sally Jesse Raphael*   Ford pickups   satellite dishes   Hamburger Helper   *Field*

every house has a garden for fresh vegetables that are later canned for winter; most locals either hunt or fish to fill basement freezers. "We've probably got enough food on hand for ninety days," says Betty Bolyard, a farmer with three freezers and two refrigerators full of meat and vegetables. "You won't find any takeout menus around here." A popular pastime is coon hunting, which occurs near midnight and involves a hunting dog treeing a raccoon by headlamp. "A big night is going out for ice cream," says dairy farmer Carl Bachtel, thirty-five. "We do a lot of family stuff here."

But the isolation of Blue Highways also makes it difficult for young people, who tend to leave to find decent jobs. Those who remain typically earn lower-middle-class incomes from farming, logging, or mining jobs. "Status is making enough money to pay the bills," one resident observes. The housing stock is a mix of older clapboard houses, brick Cape Cods, and mobile homes; Blue Highways communities are too far from city centers to make them attractive to subdivision developers. Nevertheless, people here worry about the disappearance of their rural way of life. Voters complain about government regulations that depress farm prices and estate taxes that make it difficult to pass on farms to children. "We're the only people in America who buy retail and sell wholesale, and everyone else tells us what they'll pay us," says farmer Edward Lipscomb, sixty-three. Mostly, these self-described conservatives resent where they believe their tax dollars go: not to farmers but to city welfare recipients and politicians. Despite the bitterness, cluster residents consider themselves patriotic, the first to stand and sing the anthem at a baseball game, the ones who insist on buying American. "An American product is always better than one that's foreign made," explains vegetable farmer Dayton Bolyard. "It sounds selfish, but I know we're the greatest nation in the world," adds Carl Bachtel. "There are things in this country that need to be taken care of before we go across the pond."

Like other rural lifestyles, Blue Highways is dotted with satellite dishes to pull in the TV shows that are the chief form of entertainment. Residents also tune in to country music and read women's magazines at high rates. Travel rates are low here; cows need milking twice a day, and residents make do with picnics and short drives for holidays. "There's not much pleasure activities," says one local. Yet for all the hard work and deprivation, few adults talk about leaving Blue Highways. "Once this way of life gets in your blood," says one farmer, "it's hard to get out."

PREFERENCES

(Index of 100 = U.S. Average)

Lifestyle / Products

what's hot

hunting	248
satellite dishes	175
work boots	165
needlepoint	155
watching TV	146
campers	138
Medicare / Medicaid	136
Mary Kay cosmetics	132
electric blankets	129
35-mm cameras	119

what's not

adult education courses	85
stair steppers	76
fraternal orders	69
tennis	65
bars / nightclubs	63
hot tubs	62
interest checking	62
ATM cards	58
condoms	50
Woolworth	32

Food / Drink

Spam	249
Hamburger Helper	178
canned stew	161
baby food	152
Tab	142
sausage	139
ready-to-serve dip	136
whole milk	128
energy drinks	123
fresh vegetables	114

Magazines / Newspapers

Sport	224
Field & Stream	161
automotive magazines	144
Star	143
Country Living	138
Playboy	133
Woman's Day	132
gardening magazines	126
Reader's Digest	125
Prevention	111

Television / Radio

Sally Jesse Raphael	313
CBS This Morning	250
Meet the Press	236
Another World	215
Price Is Right	183
country radio	176
Rescue 911	174
Cinemax	162
Walker, Texas Ranger	154
Nature	144

Cars / Trucks

Ford pickups	261
Chevrolet pickups	229
GMC Sierras	214
Plymouth Sundances	156
Dodge Shadows	147
Ford Aspires	141
Subaru Imprezas	139
Chevrolet Monte Carlos	126
Ford Tempos	121
Pontiac Grand Prix	115

Household necessity:
freezer stocked with deer
meat and homegrown veggies

SER 48
rustic elders

1.9% of U.S. households

Primary age groups: **45–64, 65 +**

Median household income: **$25,200**

Median home value: **$49,900**

Thumbnail Demographics

low-income older rural couples

single-family housing

predominantly white households

grade school, high school graduates

blue-collar and service workers

Politics

Predominant ideology: conservative Democrat

1996 presidential vote: Bob Dole

Key issues: family values, school prayer, welfare reform

Sample Neighborhoods

Green Bank, West Virginia 24944

Berkeley Springs, West Virginia 25411

Rimrock, Arizona 86335

Princeton, Kentucky 42445

Cumberland, Wisconsin 54829

Rustic Elders, as one resident puts it, was a quiet country lifestyle long before country became cool in American culture. Its remote rural communities are scattered throughout the nation, but especially in the heartland of the Great Plains states. Its housing stock consists of older wood-framed houses and mobile homes typically on large, acre-plus-sized lots. And its labor force is blue-collar, in large measure because the younger people with ambition have left for colleges and jobs in cities far away. Today, Rustic Elders is the third-oldest lifestyle type in America, with half the residents over fifty-five years old and many of them retired. "Most people here are piddlers, working in the garden or doing carpentry or ceramics," says Melba Fitzgerald, who owns a restaurant in Green Bank, West Virginia. The local newspaper, the *Pocahantas County Times,* even prints obituaries on the front page. Everyone knows that who died is the real news in these parts.

In the tucked-away villages of Rustic Elders, there are few businesses other than a general store or crafts shop. But most residents appreciate a way of life far removed from the metropolitan mainstream and have a fondness for the sound of chain saws rather than leaf blowers. These residents hunt, fish, and attend tractor pulls at nearly double the average national rate. They chew tobacco at high rates, in part because their jobs in paper mills and tannery plants forbid smoking. Most dens have a cabinet filled with shotguns rather

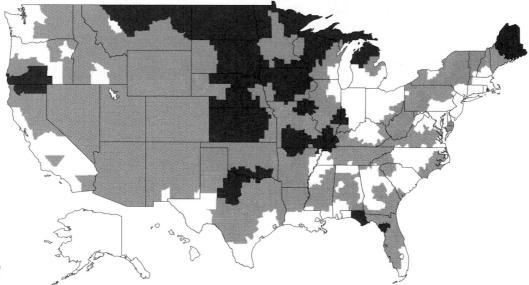

High
Above Average
Below Average
Low

power boats   canned ham   *Family Handyman*   *Price Is Right*   Dodge 3500 pickups   chewing

than computer equipment. According to surveys, Rustic Elders show virtually no interest in Net surfing, in-line skating, or visiting a spa for a vacation. Living often an hour from the closest movie theater or supermarket, these Americans learn to live with the long drive for shopping and entertainment, bothered only by the hours it may take to reach a hospital. "At our age," says retired schoolteacher Harold Crist, "that can be dangerous."

Cars play a major role in Rustic Elders, as they do in many rural clusters with hand-me-down houses, as indicators of status and the focus of leisure activities. Fans of auto racing will argue the greatness of Dale Earnhardt or Jeff Gordon with as much passion as any city kid will discuss the NBA's Michael Jordan or Shaquille O'Neal. In Green Bank, one resident living along a narrow mountain road has tacked up a homemade sign that reads, "Dale Earnhardt Blvd." Most driveways hold dusty pickups alongside large sedans that can handle the rugged country roads. And gun racks are a standard feature on most trucks, gun control being a hated concept here. "They'd have a heckuva time wrestling these old guns from these hillbillies," says one resident.

With their location in rustic areas, residents are outdoorsy people who walk and garden at high rates and often can their harvests for meals throughout the year. Restaurants feature not ethnic cuisines but down-home cooking heavy with meat, potatoes, and all varieties of beans. Few homemakers pay much mind to health food or low-cholesterol diets. As one resident observes, "People around here say, 'My grandfather lived to ninety-two and ate eggs every day, so why shouldn't I?'" At night, there's little opportunity to go out to a show or a movie; in Green Bank, the closest movie theater is sixty miles away. Instead, Rustic Elders tune in to cable and satellite TV shows. "On Saturday night we watch TV and go to bed," says Betty Mullenax, who works at her son-in-law's general store. "There's not much to do around here."

In Rustic Elders, conservative values are a given. Bob Dole was their natural presidential choice in 1996. In polls, voters speak of returning prayer to the schools and reforming the welfare system that, they feel, has depleted city life in America. Local churches are more than places of worship; they provide the social life for many residents. But most Rustic Elders find ways to entertain themselves on their own. "People come here because they like to hunt and fish," says Eddie Mullenax, Betty's semiretired husband. "But we stay because it's quiet, it's country, and that's the way we like it."

PREFERENCES

(Index of 100 = U.S. Average)

Lifestyle / Products

what's hot

hunting	198
chewing tobacco	163
in-home purchases	142
veterans' clubs	142
attending church	136
woodworking	133
bargain shopping	131
power boats	131
freshwater fishing	120
auto races	115

what's not

call-waiting	37
dry-cleaning	35
Public Broadcasting	33
tennis	31
New Age CDs / tapes	26
ice hockey games	25
sailing	21
foreign videos	15
on-line services	2
spa vacations	0

Food / Drink

low-fat cottage cheese	196
beef	133
Kraft Velveeta	127
Wheaties	124
canned ham	121
frozen pizza	119
Shake 'n Bake	116
baking chips	114
dry mix salad dressing	113
frozen orange juice	110

Magazines / Newspapers

Family Handyman	168
Outdoor Life	155
4 Wheel & Off Road	135
Woman's World	134
Country Living	133
Saturday Evening Post	127
Reader's Digest	127
McCall's	124
Bassmaster	116
Soap Opera Digest	110

Television / Radio

Price Is Right	186
country radio	184
Young and the Restless	162
Dateline NBC	160
Wheel of Fortune	160
Leeza	145
Family Channel	137
48 Hours	137
Oprah Winfrey Show	131
Touched by an Angel	122

Cars / Trucks

Dodge 3500 pickups	327
Chevrolet K3500 pickups	277
Ford F-150 4WD pickups	266
Oldsmobile 98s	198
Buick LeSabres	163
Ford Crown Victorias	154
Buicks	144
Chevrolet Luminas	140
Mercury Topazes	139
Ford Tempos	136

Bumper sticker:
"Don't Laugh. It's Paid For"

SER 49
smalltown downtown

1.9% of U.S. households

Primary age groups: **under 24, 25–34, 65 +**

Median household income: **$21,500**

Median home value: **$57,600**

Thumbnail Demographics

older singles and young families

multi-unit rental housing

predominantly white and Hispanic households

high school graduates, some college

blue- and white-collar workers

Politics

Predominant ideology: moderate Democrat

1996 presidential vote: Bill Clinton

Key issues: legalizing marijuana, saving endangered
   animals, pro-life movement

Sample Neighborhoods

Vancouver, Washington 98661

Zanesville, Ohio 43701

Joplin, Missouri 64802

Hoffman Heights, Aurora, Colorado 80011

Hollywood, Salem, Oregon 97303

Passersby who stumble on these scruffy downtown neighborhoods may think there's nothing much to these dead-end areas that thrived decades ago. But the residents of Smalltown Downtown, typically located on the fringe of major metros, believe otherwise. Today, these onetime industrial patches are gentrifying, their aging retirees now joined by young singles and solo-parent families attracted to cheap apartments — nearly two-thirds of residents rent — in an urban setting. In Vancouver, Washington, just over the Columbia River from Portland, longtime residents have watched the area decline from a once-bustling shipyard center to a quiet, downscale community dotted with thrift shops and used-book stores. "Some of the houses are begging for a new coat of paint, and some lawns are overgrown," observes Farley Maxwell, a former minister and YMCA director. "But people feel secure here. They've raised their kids and paid off their mortgages, and they don't want to think of their area as a has-been."

Geographically centered in the western states, Smalltown Downtown neighborhoods often appear near city colleges and appeal to students and recent grads starting their first jobs. The median income is low, just $21,500, but the cost of living is low as well, with the median home value only $57,600. Because its population comes from the two ends of the age spectrum, consuming patterns

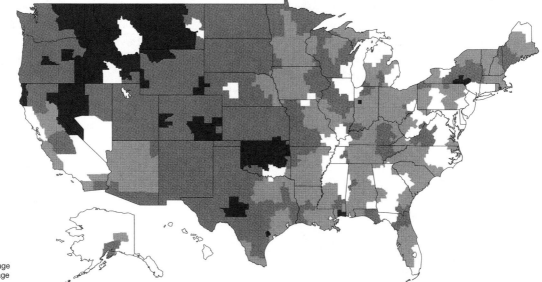

■ High
▨ Above Average
▧ Below Average
□ Low

book clubs   Wheaties   *Car Craft*   *General Hospital*   Suzuki Swifts   lottery tickets   Kentucky Fried

in Smalltown Downtown are disjointed. Residents are more likely than average Americans to enjoy fraternal orders, woodworking, and magazines like *Sunset* (the older ones), as well as rap music, weight lifting, and *Shape* (the younger ones). Both groups share a fondness for fast food, adult education classes, and gambling, especially lottery tickets. And there's a clusterwide passion for TV talk shows and daytime soap operas. In contrast, few residents of any age travel abroad, own power boats, or go to movies and plays. You see elderly residents watching their neighbors' children from stoops and park benches. In this cluster, filled with small cafés, bars, and used-furniture shops, meals and parties are usually informal; microwavable entrées are especially popular for the young and the old. "People who come here with a closet full of cocktail dresses won't have any place to go," says Karen Ciocia, executive director of the Downtown Vancouver Association, a business group. "I've been to weddings where people show up in tennis togs."

Politically, Smalltown Downtown leans left of center. Voters describe themselves as "somewhat liberal" supporters of legalizing marijuana, gay rights, and endangered animals. Yet there's also a disproportionate number of residents identified as conservative who support tax reform, the pro-life movement, and balancing the budget. When the city proposed a $55 million bond for a new library — the first in forty-five years — voters turned it down on fiscal and moral grounds. "Some people don't approve of our collection," says librarian Sharon Hammer, noting that their branches include works by Madonna and Judy Blume. "They think we're purveyors of pornography."

Many longtime Smalltown Downtown residents worry that such ills may upset their delicate balance. Their neighborhoods are hardly immune from the problems of street crime, panhandling, and economic decline. "You have to worry when the biggest business in the center of town is a liquidator," observes Farley Maxwell. Still, for all these problems, Smalltown Downtowners show an optimistic streak unusual for many struggling downtown residents, donating money and volunteering for charitable causes at relatively high rates. "We don't necessarily have wealth, but we give because we're convinced it's a good thing for families," says Agnes Alexander, a seventy-nine-year-old widow, matter-of-factly. It's a view that residents hope will help revitalize their neighborhoods and recapture some of their former glory.

PREFERENCES

(Index of 100 = U.S. Average)

Lifestyle / Products

what's hot

book clubs 180
lottery tickets 164
woodworking 160
bars / nightclubs 152
fraternal orders 151
pro baseball games 148
microwaves 142
country music
  CDs / tapes 135
adult education courses
  129
weight lifting 125

what's not

exercising 87
gasoline credit cards 72
motorcycles 68
power tools 65
Victoria's Secret 64
religious clubs 57
dance music
  CDs / tapes 51
business trips 48
chewing tobacco 46
classical radio 0

Food / Drink

Wheaties 169
Kentucky Fried Chicken
  167
regular cola 134
canned hash 130
Hostess snacks 117
children's vitamins 116
ready-to-serve dips
  115
packaged cold cuts
  114
Hamburger Helper 110
pudding 107

Magazines / Newspapers

Car Craft 305
Ebony 165
music magazines 165
Working Mother 147
science magazines 146
Playboy 144
Shape 129
Life 125
Road & Track 121
Guns & Ammo 119

Television / Radio

General Hospital 173
Rush Limbaugh 169
Nick at Nite 166
Face the Nation 159
Country Music TV 153
Star Trek: Deep Space
  Nine 151
CNN Sports News 142
X-Files 136
NBC Nightly News 126
20 / 20 116

Cars / Trucks

Suzuki Swifts 182
Kia trucks 175
Isuzu pickups 144
Mazda pickups 139
Isuzu Amigos 125
Plymouth Sundances
  124
Dodge Shadows 116
Suzuki 2WD SUs 110
Hyundai Excels 108
Ford Aspires 104

Local scene:
Main Street thrift stores

cken *Rush Limbaugh* canned hash woodworking regular cola music magazines *X-Files*

SER 50
rural industria
1.6% of U.S. households
Primary age groups: **under 24, 24–34**
Median household income: **$26,000**
Median home value: **$53,700**

Thumbnail Demographics
low-income blue-collar families
single-family housing
predominantly white and Hispanic households
grade school, high school graduates
blue-collar and service workers

Politics
Predominant ideology: conservative Independent
1996 presidential vote: Ross Perot
Key issues: restricting immigration, family values,
    health care reform

Sample Neighborhoods
Milton, Pennsylvania 17847
Chillicothe, Ohio 45601
Bentonville, Arkansas 72712
Wabash, Indiana 46992
International Falls, Minnesota 56649

The growth of railroads and the trucking industry allowed American factories to push out to smaller towns over the last century. But recent years have watched the downsizing of many of these towns as factories closed and the trains began passing them by. Today, Rural Industria barely survives as the most industrial of town lifestyles, a collection of mill towns in rural settings populated by young blue-collar families. Educational achievement is relatively limited — only 8 percent of residents have college degrees — and cluster incomes are low, in the mid-$20,000 range. Worse, the vagaries of the job market make these working-class towns anxious places, their residents fretting over job security and their ability to pay the bills. "Every month, we worry about layoffs," says Ed Nelson, mayor of Milton, Pennsylvania (population 7,500). "There's just no way of knowing when they're coming."

In Rural Industria, many of the aging towns face crumbling infrastructures and dwindling commercial districts. Residents tend to live in older pre-1940s homes that are valued at 50 percent below the U.S. average and require constant upkeep. "The prevailing style is American Bastard Architecture," says one resident. "It's an amalgamation of Victorian, craftsman, and Queen Anne — you name it." Distant malls have hurt the cluster's Main Streets, wiping out clothing and hardware stores. Most residents clip coupons and admit a

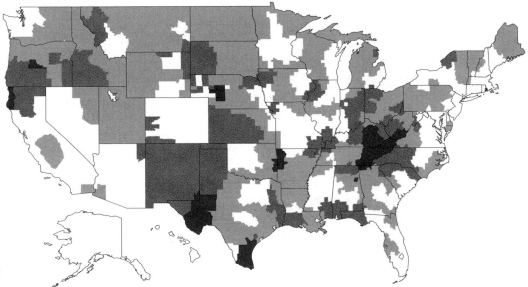

High
Above Average
Below Average
Low

cross-country skiing   children's vitamins   *Parenting*   *Cops*   Dodge 3500 pickups   satellite dishes

passion for bargain shopping. "We usually end up at Wal-Mart," says construction worker John Dietrick, thirty-four. "We don't pay to buy junk, but we can't afford the best." Despite their lower-middle-class status, residents do buy adult toys like snowmobiles, satellite dishes, and four-wheel-drive trucks — preferably with add-ons like roll bars and fog lights. "It's a factory mentality," says Bill Raup, owner of an antiques shop, of Milton's consumers. "They buy the biggest, brightest, and shiniest thing they see on their TV set."

The rural settings of Rural Industria make the towns conducive to outdoor leisure activities. A high proportion of adults engages in activities like fishing, camping, and hunting. In Milton, the schools close down the day after Thanksgiving to allow family deer-hunting trips. The group mentality among residents of factory towns — known as "belongers" in psychographic terms — also encourages team sports like bowling, football, and baseball. In Milton, the bowling lanes are jammed, and more than five hundred children play Little League baseball. "Group sports are big around here," says Little League president Charlene Stahlnecker, forty. "People know each other as friends and coworkers in the plants. So they feel a real kinship with each other." A big night out is a trip to the local dinner theater, but most of the socializing is centered on young families. Women, most of whom work outside the home, tell pollsters they wish they could spend more time cooking and relaxing with their families. In Rural Industria, holiday celebrations like Christmas, the Fourth of July, and Halloween are major civic affairs. In Milton, the streets are blocked for a parade of costumed youngsters a full week before trick-or-treating begins.

But while Rural Industria residents take their families seriously, they appear less concerned about traditional party politics. They show low interest in either political party and voted for Ross Perot in 1996. Mostly, they espouse a cultural conservatism, worried about pocketbook issues as well as societal threats to their children. "Times are getting worse," one cluster resident comments. "And we need more people who care about their families." In Milton, the Baptists shake their heads at the line of cars headed for the flea market located near their church parking lot on Sundays. But as long as money remains the cluster's major concern, no one foresees that pattern changing. "Everywhere you look," says Mayor Nelson, "people are striving just to keep their heads above water."

PREFERENCES

(Index of 100 = U.S. Average)

Lifestyle / Products

what's hot

cross-country skiing 195

satellite dishes 167

college football games 153

watching TV 150

hunting 148

camping 145

tropical fish 140

diet pills 140

veterans' clubs 135

sewing 131

what's not

bus travel 72

exercise clubs 70

dance music CDs / tapes 68

theater 63

Builder's Square 62

pay-per-view movies 62

Woolworth 57

car phones 46

America Online 18

imported beer 0

Food / Drink

children's vitamins 167

Sizzlean 155

regular cola 142

Domino's pizza 140

Kellogg's Froot Loops 132

Kraft Macaroni and Cheese 130

Mexican food 129

Kellogg's Pop-Tarts 126

peanut butter 110

fast food 106

Magazines / Newspapers

Parenting 194

Field & Stream 183

Hot Rod 167

Family Circle 141

gardening magazines 129

comics section 127

editorial section 124

Woman's Day 122

Reader's Digest 119

Family Handyman 115

Television / Radio

Cops 199

Rescue 911 197

religious / gospel radio 183

Bold and the Beautiful 180

Melrose Place 175

country radio 166

Family Channel 164

CBS Evening News 144

Unsolved Mysteries 141

Married . . . with Children 134

Cars / Trucks

Dodge 3500 pickups 213

Chevrolet C3500 pickups 181

Mercury Topazes 155

Ford Aspires 150

Plymouth Sundances 149

Dodge Shadows 144

Chevrolet Camaros 142

Pontiac Sunbirds 141

Dodge Colts 138

Suzuki Swifts 131

Bumper sticker:
"I Shot Bambie"

SER 51

single city blues

1.7% of U.S. households

Primary age groups: **under 24, 25-34, 65 +**

Median household income: **$19,600**

Median home value: **$54,500**

Thumbnail Demographics

lower-middle-class urban singles

multi-unit rental housing

ethnically mixed singles and single parents

grade school, high school graduates

service workers

Politics

Predominant ideology: liberal Democrat

1996 presidential vote: Bill Clinton

Key issues: gay rights, pro labor unions,
    legalizing marijuana

Sample Neighborhoods

Southeast Portland, Portland, Oregon 97214

Capitol Hill, Denver, Colorado 80218

Lake Street, Minneapolis, Minnesota 55408

Pioneer Square, Seattle, Washington 98104

Daytons Bluff, St. Paul, Minnesota 55106

Single City Blues seems to be an aberration, a time-warp haven for aging hippies, political leftists, and community activists. But it's home for 4.3 million Americans who still wear overalls, sing protest songs, and paint their rooms with psychedelic motifs. Concentrated in a dozen large cities around the country, these urban neighborhoods are characterized by scruffy streets, secondhand stores, and funky cafés. In Single City Blues, the rents are cheap, the food co-ops plentiful, and the mood tolerant. The men wear ponytails, the women pierce their noses, and everyone seems to be a vegetarian or an activist for some leftist cause. In the Southeast section of Portland, Oregon, locals recently tried to legalize marijuana and create a "hemp zone" where residents could grow and smoke pot without penalty. Though the initiative failed, pot remains the recreational drug of choice at area parties and dinners; more rolling papers are sold in this cluster than in any other.

Young, downscale, and transient, Single City Blues doesn't aspire to trendy fashions, status cars, and yuppie values. They belong to organic-food-buying clubs, filling their kitchens with jars of oats, grains, and beans. They shop for secondhand clothes and color their hair shades that nature never intended. Many live in apartment buildings or odd homes carved into multi-unit housing, decorating them with that icon of white-trash chic, the pink flamingo. Yet they

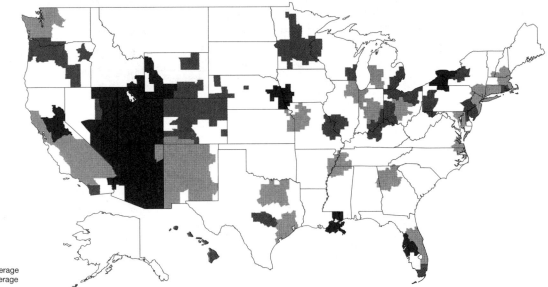

■ High
■ Above Average
■ Below Average
□ Low

rolling papers   frozen chicken   *Esquire*   Showtime   used Acuras   ice hockey games   rum   *Self*

also have an appreciation for art and history, and they go to museums and art galleries at high rates. Few cars are bought new; those used vehicles that are purchased tend to be modest-sized imports or models that extol the virtues of safety and low gas mileage. "This is not an up-and-coming place, and people are happy about that," says café owner Anne Hughes, who drives a beat-up Dodge Dart. "People around here just want to get along and get by." Mostly they get along on bicycles and in hiking boots.

Residents in Single City Blues tend to be educated beyond their socioeconomic status, and in some ways they've dropped out of the rat race that pushes Americans toward higher incomes and greater acquisitions. It's not uncommon to find homes without a television set, a microwave, or a CD player. Status, such as it is, is the level of vegetarianism you've attained: vegan, fruitatarian, macrobiotic, or some combination thereof. For entertainment, residents head to bars, (art) movie houses, and local cafés, like Portland's Café Lena, a Parisian-style joint with brightly painted tables and walls plastered with photos of Bob Dylan, Jimi Hendrix, and Allen Ginsberg. In homes, media tastes lean toward public broadcasting, quirky sitcoms, and nature shows on cable. With so many homeowners renovating the ramshackle housing stock, it's no wonder that residents are also big fans of *This Old House* and *The New Yankee Workshop*.

Politically, Single City Blues residents are often to the left of liberal. During the last election, "Nader for President" placards sprouted on front lawns. One of the more common bumper stickers was "Dole for Pineapple." These unmarried voters support gay rights, abortion rights, and ecological issues, and they have a high degree of political activism. At block parties, bearded men haul out their old Gibsons to sing protest songs. On bedroom walls, you'll see a photo of a nude whose gender is ambiguous. In Single City Blues, one of the biggest holidays of the year is the National Night Out, when residents patrol the streets to discourage criminal activity. While they pride themselves on tolerating fringe behavior, they work together to fight drug dealing (the hard stuff), prostitution, and robbery. "Problems bring a community together," explains Andy Eisman, a bearded thirty-nine-year-old civic activist from Southeast Portland. "I don't want to live in a place where people shy away from someone who needs help." He and his neighbors think it's cool to live in Single City Blues.

PREFERENCES

(Index of 100 = U.S. Average)

Lifestyle / Products

what's hot

rolling papers 362
ice hockey games 357
chess 228
foreign videos 234
book clubs 191
billiards / pool 163
museums 155
weight lifting 149
Price Club 143
bars / nightclubs 134

what's not

baby food 84
steak houses 83
JCPenney cards 74
Franklin Mint collectibles 71
gardens 68
auto races 61
dogs 60
stair steppers 59
frequent-flier miles 55
new-car loans 54

Food / Drink

domestic beer 204
rum 199
avocados 160
bottled water 144
Entenmann's snacks 125
Cornish hens 124
instant mashed potatoes 115
frozen boneless chicken 107
canned stew 107
Diet Coke 107

Magazines / Newspapers

Esquire 224
Self 216
Spin 198
Star 179
fitness magazines 171
Sporting News 170
Sunset 148
Prevention 132
Family Circle 131
New York 128

Television / Radio

Showtime 230
E! Cable 188
Bob Vila's Home Again 188
news radio 187
Comedy Central 183
MTV 168
48 Hours 135
Cops 130
Martin 129
Simpsons 118

Cars / Trucks

Acuras* 185
Cadillacs* 141
Volvos* 137
Mitsubishis* 115
Land Rover Defenders 115
Suzuki Samurais 107
Buicks* 104
Mercurys* 104
Ford Tempos 98
Ford Aerostars 91

Reflects ownership, not new car purchases, which are relatively low.

Dress code:
thrift-shop chic

SER 52

hometown retired

1.3% of U.S. households

Primary age groups: **55–64, 65 +**

Median household income: **$18,800**

Median home value: **$57,200**

Thumbnail Demographics

low-income older couples and singles

multi-unit rental housing

predominantly white households

grade school, high school graduates

service workers

Politics

Predominant ideology: conservative Democrat

1996 presidential vote: Bill Clinton

Key issues: militia groups, defusing racial tensions, pro-life movement

Sample Neighborhoods

Cumberland, Maryland 21502

Scranton, Pennsylvania 18504

Guyandotte, Huntington, West Virginia 25702

Woodbine, Tennessee 37211

Easton, Pennsylvania 18042

"People call this area 'the old folks' home,'" one Cumberland, Maryland, retiree recently observed. The same could be said for much of Hometown Retired, the nation's oldest cluster, with fully half of all residents over sixty years old. Concentrated in Appalachia and central Florida, these senior-citizen communities are not home to the affluent retired Americans who tread country-club golf courses or take package tours abroad. Most are lower-middle-class people struggling to make ends meet on social security and modest pensions. They've typically grown up in these once-thriving industrial towns only to see their factories close, their children leave for jobs in other towns, and their friends die off. In old railroad towns like Cumberland, with a population of 25,000, downscale seniors fill aging apartment buildings, spending their days watching television or playing cards, bingo, and dominoes. "There's no young people around here. The jobs are all gone," says Garfield Beckward, sixty-seven, a retired baker living on disability. "This is just a retiring town."

With a median income of only $18,800 annually, Hometown Retired has some of the nation's lowest rates for buying food, consumer electronics, and automobiles. Marketing surveys barely register any purchases of cellular phones, pasta machines, hot tubs, or computers; the percentage of residents who belong to an on-line

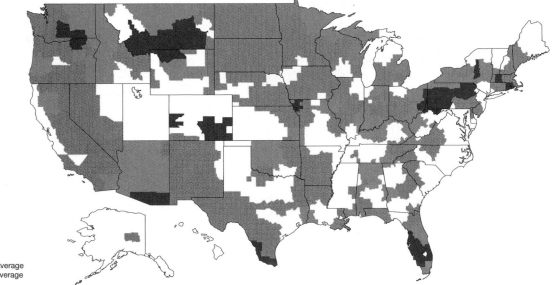

■ High
▓ Above Average
▒ Below Average
□ Low

bus travel   billiards / pool   *Nightline*   frozen dinners   Medicare / Medicaid   Kellogg's All-Bran

service is zero. Residents, nearly 40 percent of whom are unmarried, do buy large quantities of single-serving soup and frozen dinners, as well as cereal, cold cuts, and low-alcohol beer. And they take their television seriously, many springing for more than $300 to buy a TV set — a big-ticket item in this cluster — on which they watch soaps and game shows at high rates. Media polls find that these viewers spend more hours in front of a TV than almost any other cluster, especially during daytime hours.

But because these working-class residents grew up during the Depression, they learned to get by on relatively little most of their lives, and so their modest retirement doesn't reflect a marked decline in their standard of living. The shopping centers feature discount stores like Rent America, Payless Shoes, and G. C. Murphy, where the chili platter lunch special costs $1.69. Compared to the general population, residents are more likely to sign up for adult education classes in subjects like woodworking, crafts, and cooking. Hometown Retired is filled with churches, senior centers, and fraternal organizations — "the animal clubs," in the local vernacular, referring to groups like the Elks and the Moose — that provide residents with recreation and companionship. At Cumberland's senior citizen center, residents show up every day for the two-dollar lunches and afternoon bingo — a dime a round for five cards.

Compared to other Americans, Hometown Retired's residents tend to be among the nation's most vulnerable to economic downturns and sudden changes in their health. In political surveys, residents articulate numerous concerns, from cuts in Medicare and Social Security to crime and inflation. Having lived through the Depression and having never achieved tangible affluence, they worry about slipping below the poverty line. "Status around here is having a secure retirement with good health benefits," says Reverend Edward Chapman of the Emmanuel Episcopal Church. But that's beyond the grasp of many Hometown Retirees. Although these seniors describe themselves as conservative, they retain enough of their blue-collar roots to identify with the Democratic Party, and they handed Bill Clinton one-third more votes than average Americans did in 1996. Still, there's an element of apathy among these voters, who express disenchantment with the political process. "It doesn't matter who you pick," says Walter Hite, a seventy-eight-year-old retired construction worker. "At my age, I can't help too many people, and nine out of ten times, nobody is going to help me."

PREFERENCES

(Index of 100 = U.S. Average)

Lifestyle / Products

what's hot

bus travel	244
Medicare / Medicaid	188
Woolworth	173
weekly groceries < $60	154
needlepoint	140
tropical fish	134
billiards / pool	133
menthol cigarettes	132
$300 + TV sets	127
religious clubs	120

what's not

environmental causes	65
Domino's pizza	55
dancing	50
Price Club	48
new-car loans	48
hunting	38
American Express cards	31
country clubs	27
Mary Kay cosmetics	18
pagers / beepers	0

Food / Drink

Shakey's	192
Kellogg's All-Bran	191
low / no-alcohol beer	168
pasta salad	154
fast-food fish	130
Pepsi Free	126
cooked ham	120
gelatin desserts	119
frozen dinners	118
liverwurst	114

Magazines / Newspapers

Discover	181
Star	165
Parade	159
House Beautiful	159
American Health	156
Saturday Evening Post	140
Prevention	129
Ladies' Home Journal	125
Reader's Digest	123
editorial section	118

Television / Radio

Nightline	231
Sally Jesse Raphael	218
TV bowling	204
Price Is Right	188
Matlock	183
Inside Edition	158
Meet the Press	158
America's Funniest Home Videos	144
General Hospital	137
TV horse racing	130

Cars / Trucks

Suzuki Samurais	153
Buick Centurys	144
Chevrolet Geo Trackers	138
Chrysler LeBarons	135
Oldsmobile Cierras	131
Mercury Grand Marquis	126
Plymouth Acclaims	124
Dodge Spirits	118
Chevrolet Cavaliers	114
Isuzu pickups	111

Favorite sport: bingo

r Sally Jesse Raphael Buick Centurys Woolworth low / no-alcohol beer *Parade* TV bowling

SER 53
back country folks

1.8% of U.S. households

Primary age groups: **45–64, 65 +**

Median household income: **$25,600**

Median home value: **$44,600**

Thumbnail Demographics

remote rural / town families

single-family and mobile housing

predominantly white households

high school educations

blue-collar and farmworkers

Politics

Predominant ideology: moderate Republican

1996 presidential vote: Bob Dole

Key issues: school prayer, family values,
    pro environmental programs

Sample Neighborhoods

Waynesboro, Tennessee 38485

Breezewood, Pennsylvania 15533

Heflin, Alabama 36264

Homer, Georgia 30547

Vanleer, Tennessee 37181

Standing in a rolling green pasture in rural Waynesboro, Tennessee, thirty-year-old Valerie Nutt admires the one hundred head of cattle grazing contentedly at sunset. Rustling trees on one side of the field softly compete with the sound of a bubbling creek on the other. "It's so peaceful, it feels like heaven here," she says. "We really believe the best things in life are free."

That sentiment is echoed throughout Back Country Folks, a collection of isolated farm communities centered in the eastern United States from Pennsylvania to Arkansas. In Waynesboro, there are no traffic lights, no fast-food chains, no movie theaters, bowling alleys, or malls. Residents appreciate a simpler lifestyle in which they don't lock their doors. Getting together with friends means playing cards or going horseback riding. These outdoorsy folks enjoy fishing, hunting, and boating at high rates, and among their favorite magazines are *Field & Stream* and *Country Living*. On Saturday night, the teens who aren't playing baseball at the city park cruise the town square in their shiny pickups, their boom-box sound systems blasting country or — heavens — rap music. They park only to smoke cigarettes and drink beer. "There isn't much else to do," says Virginia Hunt, sixty-six, a lifelong resident and director of the town's chamber of commerce. The closest cinema is forty miles away.

Back Country Folks isn't economic heaven. At $25,600, the me-

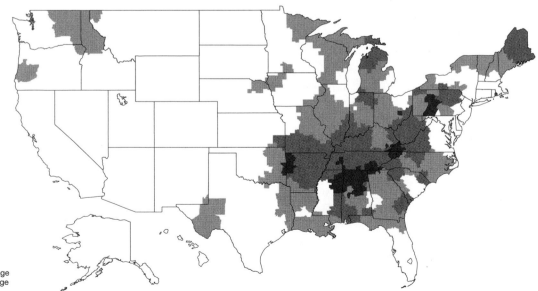

High
Above Average
Below Average
Low

satellite dishes   Spam   *Sports Afield*   Daytona 500   Nissan 4 x 4 trucks   hunting   canned stew

dian income is 25 percent below the national midpoint; one in four families live in mobile homes, and too many of the cluster's rural towns contain boarded-up factories, motels, and drive-ins. Part of the problem is low educational achievement; 20 percent of residents never finished high school, and as Waynesboro librarian Katherine Morris reports, "Sports are bigger than smarts out here. My kids are in the band and they hate it because they're considered geeks. I told my husband we should have taught them how to hit a ball rather than how to read and sing and dance." Repeated efforts to start a PTA at the high school have failed because of parental apathy. When Morris tried to get local commissioners to approve matching federal funds for a new library, "their view was 'We don't need no library.'" It took three votes before they finally approved the measure.

Life in Back Country Folks is a throwback to an earlier era, when farming dominated the American landscape. In homes, art features scenes of horses or hunting dogs. Status is having a "double-wide" or even a "triple-wide" trailer, with an add-on porch and arched roof to give the appearance of a cathedral ceiling. In their bedrooms, couples will put up shotgun racks, some romantically decorated with hearts and flowers, reflecting the integral role guns play in the area. Danny Brown, a forty-two-year-old lumber foreman in the cluster community of Collinwood, Tennessee, enjoys a close bond with his eleven-year-old daughter thanks to their regular Friday night activity: going raccoon hunting by flashlight.

Outside of family-based activities, the church is the center of community life in Back Country Folks. Indeed, the cluster's concentration in the nation's Bible Belt results in high rates for church membership, Bible reading, and Christian rock. Besides places to worship, churches offer community suppers, camping trips, and drama productions. Politically, that background helps explain this lifestyle's conservative streak. As one resident explains his distaste for the Democratic platform in 1996, "We don't much like that homosexual deal and that abortion deal." And though everyone talks tough on crime in Back Country Folks, as one resident observes, "Most of the crimes here are the kind where someone breaks in and steals your weed eater." Local politicians typically run on the same platform year after year, which can be summed up in four words: "I won't raise taxes." Opinion polls show that these salt-of-the-earth people care little about financial investments, fashion, or gourmet cooking. "We don't like to put on airs," one resident declares. "We like being common people."

PREFERENCES

(Index of 100 = U.S. Average)

Lifestyle / Products

what's hot

satellite dishes	259
hunting	257
chain saws	191
camping	182
boating	166
microwaves	161
college football games	160
water filters	146
romance novels	138
bread from scratch	118

what's not

bars / nightclubs	60
on-line services	55
country clubs	51
fine jewelry	45
pro football games	45
theater	24
mutual funds	17
frequent-flier miles	13
sailing	0
pagers / beepers	0

Food / Drink

Spam	205
canned stew	170
Kool-Aid	159
decorative icing	154
Hamburger Helper	150
Kraft Macaroni and Cheese	127
frozen pizza	125
fresh vegetables	124
instant mashed potatoes	116
pork chops	112

Magazines / Newspapers

Sports Afield	254
Country Living	188
True Story	183
4 Wheel & Off Road	165
Home Mechanix	164
Woman's Day	126
Popular Science	125
Popular Mechanics	124
Discover	124
McCall's	123

Television / Radio

Daytona 500	203
Price Is Right	195
Young and the Restless	170
TV wrestling	164
NBC News at Sunrise	157
Jerry Springer Show	144
20 / 20	137
Family Channel	136
Unsolved Mysteries	124
Christian / faith radio	120

Cars / Trucks

Nissan 4 x 4 trucks	287
Ford F-150 pickups	257
Chevrolet S10 pickups	237
Dodge D150 pickups	197
Chevrolet Monte Carlos	181
Ford Festivas	146
Chevrolet Berettas	132
Ford Crown Victorias	126
Eagle Talons	125
Chevrolet Camaros	124

Status: triple-wide trailer with a cathedral ceiling

SER 54

norma rae-ville

1.4% of U.S. households

Primary age groups: **under 24, 65 +**

Median household income: **$19,400**

Median home value: **$45,900**

Thumbnail Demographics

biracial mill towns

single-unit owners and renters

singles and solo parent families

grade school, high school graduates

blue-collar and service workers

Politics

Predominant ideology: moderate Democrat

1996 presidential vote: Bill Clinton

Key issues: school prayer, health care reform, reducing
  TV violence

Sample Neighborhoods

Monroe, Georgia 30655

Pine Bluff, Arkansas 71601

Natchez, Mississippi 39120

Selma, Alabama 36702

Vidalia, Georgia 30474

Norma Rae-ville earned its name from the movie featuring Sally Field as a union organizer at a textile mill. But this lifestyle of racially mixed Southern mill towns is undergoing change. Foreign competition has shut many of the mills, and more and more residents now work in white-collar jobs an hour's commute away. The metropolitan sprawl has begun encroaching on Norma Rae-ville and has created even more diversity: white and black, rich and poor, city dwellers and country folk. Monroe, Georgia, a once-sleepy small town, has been transformed as the Kuppenheimer plant and the Duckwood clothing factory closed down and urban exiles from Atlanta moved in, bringing with them traffic, new restaurant chains, and drug problems. "We're still a mill town, but we're rapidly becoming a bedroom suburb," says Marvin Sorrells, a superior court judge in Monroe. "Our biggest problem used to be moonshine. Now it's crack cocaine."

With its small-town roots, Norma Rae-ville still has an unhurried pace and old-fashioned tastes. Residents fish, hunt, and attend tractor pulls at above-average rates. Many of the towns are too small to support a movie theater or a bowling alley, so young residents go to the bars and fast-food joints to hang out. Fast cars are part of this down-home picture, and muscle cars and trucks are big in these towns, in part to compensate for a relatively downscale housing stock (median home value: $45,900). "We're not modern people,"

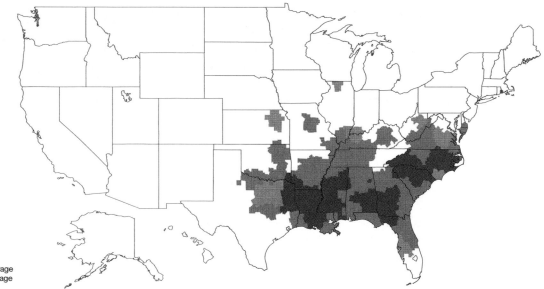

High
Above Average
Below Average
Low

tractor pulls   instant grits   *Ebony*   *Rolanda*   Nissan 2WD pickups   romance novels   bourbon   *Sport*

says Charles Sanders, a third-generation furniture store owner, noting that most of his customers prefer eighteenth-century traditional and country styles. "People do business over a handshake, bringing up 'how my grandfather knew your grandfather.'"

For all its charms, Norma Rae-ville has always been something of an educational backwater. One in five residents haven't finished the eighth grade and less than 10 percent hold college diplomas. "Kids feel they have to go out and make money as soon as possible," explains one resident. And Norma Rae-ville remains a segregated society where blacks and whites live an uneasy truce, frequenting their own bars, clubs, and churches. "The doors are always open," says Monroe librarian Shan Taylor, "but they go to their churches and we go to ours." Surveys show high cluster membership in country clubs and attendance at boxing matches, but it's clear which racial groups are going where. In Monroe, even the American Legions are segregated, black members meeting in a dilapidated building and struggling to collect dues. "Everything appears smooth on the outside, but if you look inside, you can see it's not fair," says Herman Robertson, commander of the black chapter. "It just seems like the rich are getting richer and the poor are getting poorer."

Beyond the racial divide, these days the more powerful factor affecting Norma Rae-ville is the influx of city dwellers, bringing with them shops that sell health food and computer modems not far from the feed store and the barbecue joints. "The tastes are changing," says one resident, "more classical than country music." The shift is playing out in the political arena as well, bringing a more moderate cast to the traditionally conservative electorate. Norma Rae's sentiments notwithstanding, cluster residents are less likely than average Americans to support labor unions. "Unions mean high wages for employees but trouble for companies trying to make a profit," explains one Monroe businessman. On other issues, local voters tend to express the values of old-time religion, supporting school prayer and family values, opposing gay rights and abortion rights. In these homes, pictures of Billy Graham hang in living rooms and Wednesday night is often reserved for church suppers.

"We're the traditionals," says Andy Reynolds, co-owner of a florist shop and men's clothing boutique. "We like the antiques and family recipes. When people get married, they like their grandmother's bible. We like to pass things down." But in Norma Rae-ville, the lessons are changing, and no one is certain what will be passed down in the future.

PREFERENCES

(Index of 100 = U.S. Average)

Lifestyle / Products

what's hot

tractor pulls 370
satellite dishes 275
cigars 259
hunting 153
homeowners insurance
  < $50K 147
country clubs 142
Victoria's Secret 133
Christian / faith music
  CDs / tapes 120
power boats 113
romance novels 112

what's not

cats 80
fraternal orders 70
country music
  CDs / tapes 69
pro football games 64
gardens 60
boxing matches 58
science fiction 43
Gap 43
motorcycles 37
sewing 36

Food / Drink

instant grits 376
bourbon 180
children's frozen
  dinners 170
whole milk 144
packaged cold cuts
  137
egg substitute 125
canned spaghetti 123
sausage 120
doughnuts 115
fast food 113

Magazines / Newspapers

Ebony 486
Sport 386
Soap Opera Digest 360
Baby Talk 252
American Health 239
National Enquirer 219
Guns & Ammo 215
GQ 194
McCall's 177
Popular Mechanics 150

Television / Radio

Rolanda 510
CBS This Morning 436
New York Undercover
  342
urban-contemporary
  radio 255
TV wrestling 204
Days of Our Lives 204
Price Is Right 203
48 Hours 197
*Married . . . with
  Children* 144
HBO 135

Cars / Trucks

Nissan 2WD pickups
  233
Hyundai Elantras 228
Mazda 929s 217
Mitsubishi Galants 207
GMC 2WD pickups 207
Dodge Colts 202
Mitsubishi Mirages 184
Buick Roadmasters 180
Hyundai Scoupes 174
Cadillac Fleetwoods 170

Favorite furnishings:
family heirlooms

wrestling   Dodge Colts   cigars   children's frozen dinners   *Soap Opera Digest*   country clubs

SER 55
scrub pine flats

1.5% of U.S. households

Primary age groups: **55–64, 65 +**

Median household income: **$21,600**

Median home value: **$44,600**

Thumbnail Demographics

older racially mixed blue-collar families

single-family and mobile-home housing

racially mixed families and single parents

grade school, high school graduates

blue-collar and farmworkers

Politics

Predominant ideology: liberal Democrat

1996 presidential vote: Bill Clinton

Key issues: school prayer, reducing TV violence,
     pro education funding

Sample Neighborhoods

Louisa, Virginia 23093

Mound Bayou, Mississippi 38762

Union Point, Georgia 30669

Moundville, Alabama 35474

Holly Springs, Mississippi 38634

When the town of Louisa, Virginia, opened a new middle school, residents divided over the proposal to name the school after the area's first African American elected to Congress. Town officials settled on the neutral name of Louisa County Middle School, but the debate was typical of Scrub Pine Flats, a racially mixed cluster that's the most geographically cohesive lifestyle in the nation: It is found across the Old South from the James to the Mississippi Rivers. At one time, this area was mostly agrarian, home to the nation's tobacco and peanut belts, where big landowners and bankers ran sleepy rural towns. But many of the farms have disappeared, eaten up by retirement communities, small factories, and subdivisions from which professionals commute over an hour to big-city jobs. "We now have as many lawyers as farmers in town," says Danny Patton, a forty-five-year-old forester from Louisa. "Most of the farmers have jobs elsewhere and do their farming as a hobby."

In the business districts of Scrub Pine Flats, hardware and feed stores have been joined by cellular phone shops and fast-food restaurants. But this is still a downscale area, where the median income is less than $22,000 annually. At diners decorated with deer antlers, men wear Caterpillar caps while eating their sausage-and-egg breakfasts and drive away in pickup trucks with fishing gear tucked behind the seats. The commercial base in Louisa is iffy: Furniture shops offer layaway plans, and the boarded-up Safeway

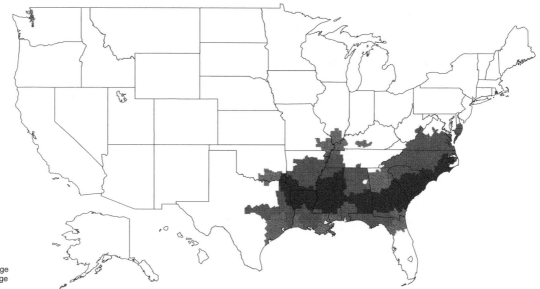

High
Above Average
Below Average
Low

gospel CDs / tapes   pasta salad   *Hunting*   *Rolanda*   Ford F-350 pickups   freshwater fishing

means residents must travel elsewhere for groceries, their wads of cents-off coupons firmly stuffed in pocketbooks. At home, many residents bake bread, can vegetables, and catch fish to store in their deep-freezers. There's little pressure to save for a bigger house, a flashier car, or designer clothing. Without bowling alleys or movie theaters nearby, entertainment in Scrub Pine Flats is a home-cooked meal with friends or watching TV with family. Many residents take pride in never having eaten a TV dinner.

With a population that's 49 percent African American, Scrub Pine Flats has a high index for media targeted to whites and blacks. Lola Richardson, a fifty-two-year-old African American assistant principal, reads *Ebony* and *Jet* as well as *Redbook* and *Elle*. On TV, game shows and talk shows like *Oprah* and *Rolanda* are especially popular among black viewers; Country Music TV is preferred by whites. Given the proximity of the two races living in a Southern setting, strained relations are not uncommon. Blacks and whites go to different Baptist and Catholic churches, and, as Louisa County administrator William Porter puts it, "we make conflict avoidance an art form." When a bond issue was floated to pay for a new swimming pool, some whites quietly opposed it for fear of racial mixing. "Folks around here don't like a lot of changes," says Richardson, who attended a segregated school as a youngster. But community spirit overshadows ethnic differences on Friday nights, when everyone gathers for basketball and football games at the high school.

Politically, this is an FDR-Democratic area, where self-described liberals are concerned about TV violence and want prayer back in the schools. "The working man can earn more money voting for a Democrat than a Republican," one farmer explains. There's a strong religious streak in the cluster that comes from the agriculturally based economy, where having a successful year depends so much on divine forces. "When you're paying high taxes on land, interest on farm equipment, and seventy dollars a bushel for seed corn, suppose it doesn't rain?" asks Ned Terrell, a seventy-two-year-old farmer who milks 130 dairy cows. "You have to put your lives in the Lord's hands that the weather will provide." But trust only goes so far in Scrub Pine Flats. Whereas residents used to keep their cars and homes unlocked, the influx of newcomers has altered that attitude. Many homes now have security-company stickers on their windows, and the disappearance of civility bothers longtime residents. "You still wave to everybody," remarks farmer and insurance agent Charles Rosson, "but only three in ten wave back."

PREFERENCES

(Index of 100 = U.S. Average)

Lifestyle / Products

what's hot

gospel CDs / tapes 325
truck / tractor pulls 210
weekly groceries < $60 199
Medicare / Medicaid 190
chewing tobacco 182
satellite dishes 157
dealer financing 154
Wal-Mart 149
electric blankets 147
freshwater fishing 123

what's not

college basketball games 61
gardens 54
needlepoint 50
moviegoing 48
call-waiting 46
classical CDs / tapes 32
fraternal orders 30
campers 24
stamp collecting 16
furniture refinishing 8

Food / Drink

instant grits 370
whole milk 208
Kentucky Fried Chicken 169
Coca-Cola Classic 159
Spam 145
domestic beer 139
pasta salad 130
fresh vegetables 125
pork chops 121
canned stew 116

Magazines / Newspapers

Ebony 285
Southern Living 266
Sports Afield 196
True Story 188
Hunting 171
McCall's 143
Redbook 137
National Enquirer 126
Field & Stream 120
Good Housekeeping 119

Television / Radio

Rolanda 379
Jenny Jones 296
BET 288
Country Music TV 241
Martin 219
New York Undercover 215
Meet the Press 210
Cinemax 204
Young and the Restless 199
Silk Stalkings (USA) 152

Cars / Trucks

Ford F-350 pickups 253
Mitsubishi pickups 232
Dodge D350 pickups 228
Nissan pickups 192
Hyundai Elantras 182
Mitsubishi Mirages 176
Ford Crown Victorias 164
Hyundai Scoupes 162
Dodge Colts 151
Oldsmobile 98s 136

Still politically correct:
displaying Southern
Civil War memorabilia

SER 56
mines & mills

2.0% of U.S. households

Primary age groups: **55–64, 65 +**

Median household income: **$19,600**

Median home value: **$41,000**

Thumbnail Demographics

older families and singles, mine and mill towns

owners and renters, single-unit housing

predominantly white households

grade school, high school graduates

blue-collar and service workers

Politics

Predominant ideology: conservative Democrat

1996 presidential vote: Bill Clinton

Key issues: health care reform, restricting immigration, school prayer

Sample Neighborhoods

Ottumwa, Iowa 52501

Hannibal, Missouri 63401

Harlan, Kentucky 40831

Oil City, Pennsylvania 16301

McMinnville, Tennessee 37110

Lifestyles can shift according to economic winds. In Mines & Mills, global competition, NAFTA, and the rise of America's high-tech industry have all wrought havoc on once-thriving mining and manufacturing towns. Today, the cluster's median income is under $20,000, most adults are retired (younger people having fled for better jobs), and the company towns are shadows of their former selves.

Ottumwa, Iowa, is a classic Mines & Mills story. The boom years ended with the closing of the Merrell meat-packing plant and the downsizing of the John Deere factory. In recent years, the population has dropped from 36,000 to 24,000, and downtown businesses have locked their doors, leaving pawnshops and coin launderettes in their wake. Despite the neat rambler homes, now valued at a song for only $41,000, Ottumwa has taken on a gritty, depressed air, and its residents fear further downsizing. On the south side of town, the liveliest action takes place at bars like the Tap Room, the Keg, and the River Bend. At a city auction at the Ottumwa Coliseum, where you can buy anything from hunting bows and bicycles to weed whackers, most of the bidding starts at under ten dollars. When the local rock station offers a giveaway promotion, the grand prize is a Harley-Davidson motorcycle.

"It's depressing now because people remember the way it used

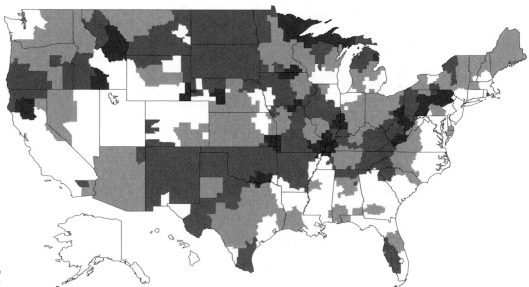

- ■ High
- ■ Above Average
- ▨ Below Average
- □ Low

auto races   fraternal orders   motorcycle magazines   *As the World Turns*   Mercury Topazes

to be," says Jeanne Dillon, a server at Canteen Lunch in the Alley, an Ottumwa landmark diner. "What we need are jobs."

Typically set in scenic rural areas, Mines & Mills stands out for its leisure activities. Residents go fishing, hunting, and camping at high rates, and take their children and grandchildren to state fairs every summer. On Saturdays, the men work on rebuilding old cars. "A lot are old craftsmen, so they're used to making precise stuff," explains barber Rick McFarland. For shopping, women drive to mall stores like JCPenney and to Wal-Mart, looking for products with "Made in the U.S.A." labels. "This is a union town," says Charles (Rex) Ford, seventy-four, a retired construction worker. "People like to support our country rather than another country." In these downscale communities, residents see relatively few movies because of the high cost, but they will splurge on a trip to Burger King and the occasional NASCAR auto race. "This is a Chevy town, not a Cadillac town," says a financial planner. "My clients aren't traders. They're conservative people who invest in mutual funds."

In Mines & Mills, residents tend to be conservative and Democratic, viewing the GOP as the party of the rich. In the 1996 election, voters backed Bill Clinton as a moderating force in the party. The issues that most concerned them were the state of the economy, restricting immigration, and revitalizing labor unions. Today, there's a traditional religious streak that finds residents backing school prayer and the reduction of sex and violence on TV. Their favorite shows are not the racy twenty-something sitcoms but the golden oldies and nature shows found on Nickelodeon and the Discovery Channel. Urbane comedies like *Frasier* and *Mad About You* fare poorly among these cluster viewers. "I'd rather watch a herd of elephants chasing each other than half-naked people chasing each other," says Joe Leinhauser, sixty-nine, a retired John Deere engineer from Ottumwa. "We wouldn't miss Lawrence Welk on Saturday night for the world. You don't have to worry about swear words."

Mines & Mills residents have more important things to worry about, though, like how they can revitalize their communities with new industries and new businesses. "Too many guys in their early forties worry that their jobs won't last until they retire," says one Ottumwa resident. And in this cluster, where people are risk averse, the biggest gamble is moving away from these old company towns.

PREFERENCES
(Index of 100 = U.S. Average)

Lifestyle / Products

what's hot

roller-skating 185
Medicare / Medicaid 166
auto races 147
fraternal orders 142
smoking 136
hunting 134
Christian / faith music CDs / tapes 133
Wal-Mart 132
in-home purchases 127
lottery tickets 117

what's not

stereo equipment 79
moviegoing 68
ATM cards 54
softball 48
diet pills 47
needlepoint 45
foreign travel 43
gambling casinos 37
Price Club 34
racquetball 0

Food / Drink

ready-to-serve dip 185
hot dogs 159
frozen dinners 158
low-fat cottage cheese 153
domestic beer 144
cooked ham 126
Cap'n Crunch 125
Stove Top Stuffing 124
canned spaghetti 121
doughnuts 120

Magazines / Newspapers

motorcycle magazines 194
fishing / hunting magazines 163
Country Living 145
Woman's Day 140
TV Guide 140
gardening magazines 132
Home Mechanix 130
Family Circle 126
American Health 119
National Enquirer 116

Television / Radio

As the World Turns 186
TV wrestling 184
Country Music TV 176
Cops 168
Primetime Live 157
America's Funniest Home Videos 156
Family Channel 144
CNN Sports News 142
Walker, Texas Ranger 141
Discovery Channel 111

Cars / Trucks

Mercury Topazes 185
Chevy S10 pickups 168
Ford F-150 pickups 162
Plymouth Sundances 157
GMC Sierra pickups 149
Pontiac Sunbirds 145
Dodge Shadows 136
Buick Centurys 133
Pontiac Grand Prix 132
Ford Tempos 132

Status:
new Harley-Davidson hog

edicare / Medicaid   hot dogs   fishing / hunting magazines   TV wrestling   Chevy S10 pickups

SER 57

grain belt

2.0% of U.S. households

Primary age groups: **45–54, 55–64, 65 +**

Median household income: **$22,600**

Median home value: **$41,900**

Thumbnail Demographics

married farm owners and tenants

single-family housing

predominantly white and Hispanic households

grade school, high school graduates

farming, mining, and ranching workers

Politics

Predominant ideology: conservative Republican

1996 presidential vote: Bob Dole

Key issues: pro-life movement, improving the economy,
  reducing government size

Sample Neighborhoods

Matheson, Colorado 80830

Linneus, Missouri 64653

Long Prairie, Minnesota 56347

Ridgeland, Wisconsin 54763

Holly, Colorado 81047

About a hundred miles southeast of Denver, in Colorado's High Plains, sit dozens of tiny farm communities originally settled by rugged homesteaders more than a century ago. The locales thrived for many years, until giant ranching corporations came in, took over the farms, and sent the families packing. Matheson, Colorado, is typical of these communities. During its heyday in the 1940s, the town had a bank, a school, several blacksmith shops and grocery stores, a movie theater, a billiards parlor, and even a dance hall. But when competition from the big agricultural companies became too great, the families who raised wheat and cattle sold off their land. Today, barely eighty people live in Matheson, which is less a town than a wide spot on a desolate road. The only operating businesses are an antiques store, an auto body shop, and a post office. The brick school and Catholic church serve as storage sheds for grain. The big storage silos by the train depot are rusted and empty. And most of the surrounding farmhouses and barns are boarded up and leaning oddly from the dry winds.

"We're considered a ghost town," says Matheson retiree Dorothy King. "There's nothing here to keep people from moving away."

This is the setting for many Grain Belt communities, a cluster of aging farmers and small-town retirees — half the residents are over fifty-two — who remain rooted to the land they work. They often live amid gravel streets and empty buildings, relying on bigger towns

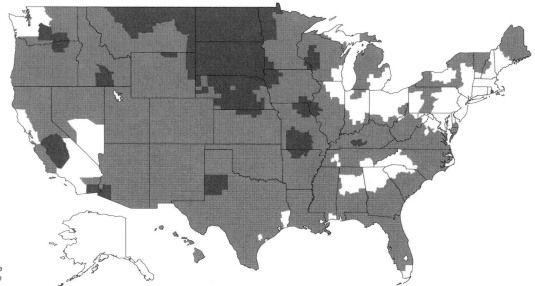

High
Above Average
Below Average
Low

hunting   Post Grape-Nuts   *Popular Mechanics*   Country Music TV   Chevy K3500 pickups   Motel 6   Kr

fifteen or fifty miles away for groceries, gas, and entertainment. Many residents have satellite dishes, but more often these traditionalists watch little TV news because they feel removed from the shootings and stabbings that make up so much of the nightly newscasts. "We don't really care that much for the big city," says Donald Ashcraft, a fifty-seven-year-old farmer from Matheson. "There's too much crime and traffic, and it's too fast. We're happy out here in the country, not having to fight the crowds."

Even in the most isolated Grain Belt villages, residents believe they have plenty going for them. The wide-open spaces have a primal beauty, and in places like Matheson, mountains can be seen fifty miles away. Kids can still ride bikes through the streets, play in creeks, and build tree houses. As in other rural clusters, hunting and fishing are popular, as well as sewing and canning vegetables. "Basically, we entertain ourselves," says postmistress Peg McElwain. "We fish, go to anniversary parties, baseball games, and school things. You learn that you don't have to be entertained all the time."

By heritage and inclination, Grain Belt is conservative country. In public-opinion polls, adults support school prayer, family values, and curbing pornography. They're critical of how big government regulates loans, price controls, and farming policies. "Households have to have two workers because one works for the family, the other for the government," says seventy-eight-year-old Gladys Atwater, scowling. Mostly, though, residents describe themselves as God-fearing sorts and tell pollsters the activity they'd most like to spend more time doing is attending church. "You have to be religious to be on the farm," explains Verl McElwain, a cattle and wheat farmer. "You're at the mercy of the 'Man Upstairs' for rain and sun."

Despite the great open plains of Grain Belt, residents stay connected to mainstream culture through their cars, phones, and satellite dishes. And, lately, young families from cities an hour away have begun arriving, with their mobile homes, computers, and theories about home schooling. Although Grain Belt has yet to experience a real revival, attitudes have begun to change, and longtime locals are a bit more inclined to lock their doors when going on vacation — something unheard of a decade ago. "It's true we're more cautious," says farmer McElwain. "But when you live in the country, you have to trust your neighbor. If your car breaks down, you know someone will stop and help you."

PREFERENCES

(Index of 100 = U.S. Average)

Lifestyle / Products

what's hot

Motel 6	284
hunting	202
woodworking	195
sewing	184
freshwater fishing	169
camping	159
science fiction	158
fraternal orders	143
stamp collecting	136
auto races	129

what's not

stereo equipment	80
museums	72
billiards / pool	63
Builder's Square	60
dealer financing	59
weight lifting	54
financial investments	42
auto races	31
Marshalls	13
pay-per-view movies	3

Food / Drink

Post Grape-Nuts	218
Kraft Velveeta	165
tequila	158
Pizza Hut	142
frozen pizza	129
pasta	126
oatmeal	127
beef jerky	122
gelatin desserts	118
Mexican food	117

Magazines / Newspapers

Popular Mechanics	187
Field & Stream	173
Saturday Evening Post	162
Guns & Ammo	162
Redbook	157
Country Living	133
Organic Gardening	123
food / cooking section	122
U.S. News & World Report	119
Golf Digest	118

Television / Radio

Country Music TV	199
CBS Evening News	190
Nova	177
Price Is Right	168
Walker, Texas Ranger	164
Touched by an Angel	157
Larry King Live	148
Travel Channel	147
Another World	141
Tonight Show with Jay Leno	137

Cars / Trucks

Chevy K3500 pickups	402
Dodge 2500 pickups	274
Ford 4WD pickups	272
GMC Sierra pickups	244
Mazda 4WD pickups	178
Oldsmobile 98s	176
Isuzu pickups	160
Buick Park Avenues	154
Chrysler New Yorkers	124
Suzukis	124

Financial credo: Pay in cash; credit cards are the devil's friends

SER 58

hard scrabble

2.0% of U.S. households

Primary age groups: **55–64, 65 +**

Median household income: **$17,400**

Median home value: **$37,800**

Thumbnail Demographics

older families in poor, isolated areas

single-family housing

predominantly white households

grade school education

blue-collar and farmworkers

Politics

Predominant ideology: moderate Democrat

1996 presidential vote: Bill Clinton

Key issues: family values, school prayer,
   restricting immigration

Sample Neighborhoods

Richwood, West Virginia 26261

Tombstone, Arizona 85638

Powhatan, West Virginia 24877

Albany, Kentucky 42602

Erin, Tennessee 37061

The nation's poorest rural communities comprise Hard Scrabble, a cluster of isolated settlements from Appalachia to the Dakota Badlands. Here, the unemployment is high, the housing stock is aged, and many of the residents are retirees living on meager fixed incomes. "We qualify for any kind of assistance program you can name," says Jay Comstock, editor of the *Nicholas County News Leader* in the cluster community of Richwood, West Virginia. "The obituaries are the most popular feature in the newspaper." Richwood was once a thriving industrial town, but most of its coal mines and wood manufacturing plants have closed up and left the business district vacant, the housing stock depressed. Three-quarters of the elementary school students receive free lunches. No one can remember the last time a house sold for more than $100,000. A buyer could get a three-bedroom rambler on a hilly street for $15,000 — furnished. "We could stand a good payroll or two," one Richwood resident observed. "As soon as something's expensive, we can't afford it."

Hard Scrabble communities tend to be economically poor but rich in scenery. There's always talk of expanding the economic base to lure tourists to the isolated beauty of these areas. Residents fish, hike, and camp at high rates, not to mention more exotic pursuits like chasing bees or hunting squirrel. They have learned to make do with the limited opportunities of their isolated communities. They

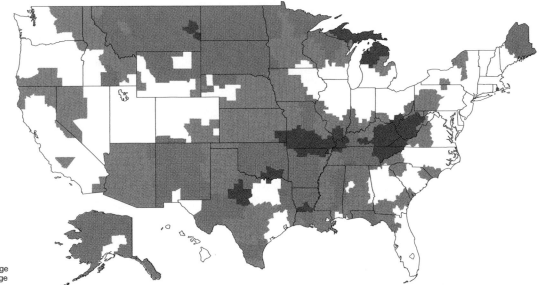

High
Above Average
Below Average
Low

chewing tobacco   canned stew   *Bassmaster*   *Another World*   Chevrolet S10 pickups   tractor pulls

play bingo at the American Legion and watch their kids play high school sports. The chief form of entertainment is television, especially programs on the Nashville Network or the Family Channel. A status car is a midsized sedan like a Chevy Cavalier or a Ford Crown Victoria; there are no foreign luxury cars in Hard Scrabble, thank you very much. A big night out is attending a NASCAR auto race, with the chance to cheer on the rivalry between veteran Dale Earnhardt and upstart Jeff Gordon. It's a point of pride to have a fast car — but not just any fast car in this buy-American lifestyle. Says one Richwood local, "If someone drove up in a Mercedes, everyone would know it was rented or borrowed."

The poor, rural residents of Hard Scrabble provide a formula for moderate Democratic politics. "People would elect a rattlesnake if it were a Democrat," one cluster voter notes, adding that Republicans are "the party of the rich." Churches play a prominent role in local communities, not just as a reflection of the importance of faith to residents but for the social activities afforded by church suppers and Bible study groups. Residents support school prayer and oppose gay rights. "When Ellen [DeGeneres] came out of the closet, there wasn't a ripple in Richwood," Jay Comstock notes. "Around here, people believe in every word in the Bible." Diversity is still an uncommon notion in Hard Scrabble, where nine out of ten residents are white. But while prejudice is a given, health care isn't for this elderly population. With long drives to the closest hospitals, residents worry about serious illnesses and tell pollsters they're concerned about the cost and quality of health care. This is still a landscape where dirt roads are common, and many residents grew up without indoor plumbing and access to health information. "I usually say I live in the middle of nowhere, and I'm not being facetious," remarks Rand Bailey, Richwood's postmaster. "Every time we go shopping, it takes an hour just to get to a store."

The one issue that divides Hard Scrabble residents is protecting the environment. These outdoor-minded Americans support saving endangered animals and worry that runoff from farm pesticides and coal mine tailings are polluting their fishing streams. But these economically depressed areas also need jobs. "When it comes down to employment," says teacher Becky O'Dell, "environmental protection usually takes a backseat."

PREFERENCES

(Index of 100 = U.S. Average)

Lifestyle / Products

what's hot

chewing tobacco	388
tractor pulls	285
satellite dishes	258
auto races	206
hunting	188
sewing	171
Wal-Mart	161
freshwater fishing	156
veterans' clubs	154
Medicare / Medicaid	150

what's not

foreign travel	26
ice hockey games	24
electric coffee grinders	23
health clubs	21
fax machines	20
jazz	15
on-line services	15
pagers / beepers	11
Marshalls	10
tennis vacations	7

Food / Drink

canned stew	196
Spam	186
Kool-Aid	157
cola	153
cooked ham	140
Hostess snacks	140
instant mashed potatoes	139
hot dogs	138
Kellogg's Pop-Tarts	135
bourbon	130

Magazines / Newspapers

Bassmaster	284
Sports Afield	231
Organic Gardening	201
Guns & Ammo	174
Field & Stream	161
Woman's World	140
National Enquirer	138
Country Living	123
Hot Rod	123
Star	112

Television / Radio

Another World	328
Country Music TV	288
NBC News at Sunrise	261
Wild America	223
TNN	179
Family Channel	172
The 700 Club	170
Price Is Right	168
country radio	156
Cops	154

Cars / Trucks

Chevrolet S10 pickups	303
Ford F-150 pickups	268
GMC Sierra 3500 pickups	266
Dodge Shadows	147
Plymouth Sundances	146
Ford Aspires	138
Toyota Tacomas	136
Ford Crown Victorias	120
Chevrolet Cavaliers	118
Chevrolet Camaros	112

Bumper sticker:
"My Kid Beat Up Your Honor Student"

SER 59

family scramble

2.0% of U.S. households

Primary age groups: **under 24, 25–34**

Median household income: **$19,400**

Median home value: **$41,700**

Thumbnail Demographics

low-income urban Hispanic families

2–9 unit rental housing

predominantly Hispanic and white households

grade school, high school graduates

blue-collar and service workers

Politics

Predominant ideology: moderate Independent

1996 presidential vote: Bill Clinton

Key issues: pro labor unions, restricting immigration, welfare reform

Sample Neighborhoods

Cloverleaf, Houston, Texas 77015

Stockyards, Denver, Colorado 80216

Calumet City, Illinois 60409

Packers, Kansas City, Kansas 66105

Roy Royall, Houston, Texas 77093

Young Hispanic families who've already spent some years in the U.S. often make their way to Family Scramble, a cluster of downscale city neighborhoods concentrated in the Southwest. These are Americans with little money — the median income is $19,400 — and even less education; the cluster is ranked last in the percentage of residents with college diplomas, a meager 5 percent. Workers get by with jobs in transportation, construction, and service industries, but advancement is difficult. "People here face economic prejudice," says Fidel Vergara, a Baptist pastor in the Cloverleaf community that borders Houston, Texas. "They can't get the loans to start businesses. And they can get jobs, but not the ones at the top. Sometimes opportunities don't knock on the door."

Cloverleaf is a classic example of this struggling Family Scramble lifestyle. Outsiders see the neighborhoods as poverty stricken, with working outhouses, trailer homes perched on cinder blocks, and dilapidated shotgun shacks surrounded by junked cars. The corner markets have floor-to-ceiling bars on the doors and windows. Signs on streetlights offer homes for sale at prices below those of many cars. Trucks prowl the streets with Tex-Mex music blaring from radios, and children as young as ten join gangs, sometimes using bicycles as getaway vehicles after committing petty crimes. "It's been poor here a long time, the third or fourth generation of poverty," says Lois Killough, principal of Cloverleaf Elementary,

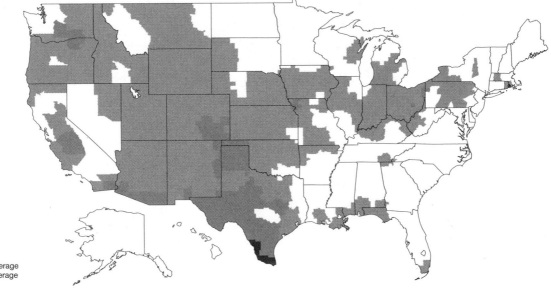

High
Above Average
Below Average
Low

shocks changed by self   canned chili   *Car and Driver*   *New York Undercover*   Suzuki Swifts   bowling

where 93 percent of her 1,020 students receive free or reduced-cost lunches. "We've got people who live in the back of pickups."

Despite these harsh realities, Family Scramble residents haven't succumbed to despair. In homes where Spanish is the first language, parents treat their children with video rentals, pets, and frequent trips out for fast food. For nightlife, the men are more likely than average Americans to go to auto races, pool halls, and tractor pulls. Women enjoy bingo. Many families participate in anti-gang activities sponsored by schools and churches, the centers of community life in this cluster. Religious icons hang on walls in homes; some create little shrines in a corner of a room. And TV is popular, especially reality-based shows like *Unsolved Mysteries* and Spanish *novellas.* "The *novellas* reflect our values and attitudes," says Pastor Vergara. "The English soaps with their mansions don't look like the homes where we live."

In the marketplace, Family Scramble consumers are big on bargain hunting, favoring Wal-Marts and Sam's Clubs. "We buy what's economical," says one, "not the brand names." Few cars are bought new, and used vehicles are kept running by weekend tinkering — "shade-tree mechanics," in the local vernacular. Supermarket surveys show families eat both Mexican and American fare, with rice, chili, beef, and baby food all bought at above-average rates. A splurge means going out to Taco Bell or McDonald's.

Family Scramble is no place to build a political base, according to surveys. Most residents are apathetic and some don't have green cards, let alone citizenship. Locals describe themselves as Independents who support family values, child social services, and welfare reform. But they're not so far removed from welfare rolls that they don't know firsthand of those who abuse the system. "We take pride in our jobs — whatever they are," says Barbara Solis, a bus driver. "Welfare's okay for the people who really need it, but it gets abused." What Family Scramble citizens want, says Realtor Frank Nadolney, is "a piece of the rock. A lot just want to own a piece of dirt in this country. They'll put up a manufactured house, and it's home."

Still, there's more to life than a double-wide on American soil, and many Family Scramble residents work at improving their lot. "People think this is a bad neighborhood, but it's changing," says Hector Parra, a Cloverleaf carpenter who works with a Neighborhood Watch group and whose fifteen-year-old daughter would like to be a lawyer. "It's still not that safe at night, but you can walk to the store now without waiting for somebody to jump you."

PREFERENCES

(Index of 100 = U.S. Average)

Lifestyle / Products

what's hot

shocks changed by self 179
tractor pulls 163
microwaves 162
auto races 157
homeowners insurance < $50k 156
cigarettes 141
bowling 133
pasta machines 131
pet birds 122
weekly groceries < $60 120

what's not

moviegoing 80
photography 77
weight lifting 75
veterans' clubs 74
softball 69
Visa cards 62
metal polish 59
IRAs / Keoghs 53
college football games 44
chewing tobacco 32

Food / Drink

Sizzlean 220
RC Cola 215
Hostess snacks 161
malt liquor 156
beef jerky 156
baby food 149
children's frozen dinners 142
Taco Bell 138
canned chili 128
packaged cold cuts 125

Magazines / Newspapers

Car and Driver 302
Popular Mechanics 173
GQ 171
Parenting 161
Sports Illustrated 142
Glamour 136
Playboy 132
TV Guide 123
Time 120
Soap Opera Digest 119

Television / Radio

New York Undercover 313
Loving 286
Jenny Jones 278
Price Is Right 232
Law & Order 216
Unsolved Mysteries 212
Comic Strip Live 207
Walker, Texas Ranger 183
Nickelodeon 175
Spanish radio 164

Cars / Trucks

Suzuki Swifts 156
Plymouth Sundances 137
Ford Tempos 117
Chevrolet pickups 117
Dodge pickups 110
Kia trucks 108
Chevrolet Corsicas 107
Hyundai Excels 105
Ford Aspires 103
Chevrolet Berettas 100

Frequent purchase:
money orders bound for Mexico

SER 60

Hispanic mix

1.4% of U.S. households

Primary age groups: **under 24, 25–34**

Median household income: **$17,600**

Median home value: **$59,800**

Thumbnail Demographics

urban Hispanic singles and families

multi-unit rental housing

predominantly Hispanic households

grade school, high school graduates

blue-collar and service workers

Politics

Predominant ideology: liberal Democrat

1996 presidential vote: Bill Clinton

Key issues: pro affirmative action, gun control, child
social services

Sample Neighborhoods

Atwater Village, Los Angeles, California 90029

South El Paso, Texas 79901

Highlands, Denver, Colorado 80211

Soundview, Bronx, New York 10472

Wyckoff Heights, Brooklyn, New York 11237

In the Los Angeles neighborhood of Atwater Village, the American Dream lives on streets where a family of four rents a one-bedroom apartment with a sloping floor and the children find safety from rival gangs at a busy rec center supervised by protective eyes. At night, the recent Hispanic immigrants cringe as gang members engage in shootouts over drug deals gone sour. By day, they meet at building-supply yards in search of a day's labor. The local language is Spanish, from church services to signs on apartment buildings reading "Se Renta" ("For Rent"). Every Saturday, yard sales spring up in vacant lots, offering newcomers old clothes hanging on rusted fences: a faded shirt for a quarter, a colorful cotton dress for a buck.

This is Hispanic Mix, a collection of Latino barrios found in some of the poorest sections of New York, Miami, Chicago, and cities in the Southwest. Filled with young, child-rearing families, it's the cluster with the highest percentage of new immigrants and the second-highest concentration of foreign-born residents. The vast majority of adults work as laborers or service workers, and one-third of them haven't finished the eighth grade. Although the poverty is frightening by middle-class standards, many Hispanic Mix residents have come from Third World countries and find the lifestyle an improvement over their past. At the very least, they have the promise of something better.

"It's a tough area," says Sophia Pina-Cartez, a recreation center

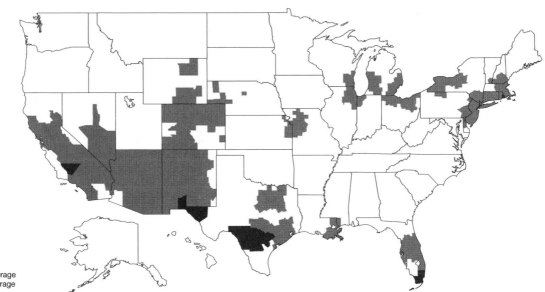

High
Above Average
Below Average
Low

boxing matches individual chocolates *Baby Talk* Spanish radio Ford Econoline Club Wagons

director in Atwater Village. "There's a vicious cycle of poverty, drugs, and gangs that leaves some of the families split. Half want to get out of here and half don't. Because it's a Hispanic community, many feel comfortable here."

With a $17,600 median income, barely above the poverty level, Hispanic Mix consumers rank low on most surveys of products, services, and activities. The Polk Company reports that only a handful of new car models, like the Kia and the Toyota Tercel, are bought at above-average rates. Residents invest in no financial products above the norm other than coins. "Status is just trying to keep the wolf from the door," says Barbara Lass, a community activist. "A lot of people are just hanging on." Despite the ghetto conditions, the cluster lifestyle isn't totally bleak. There's pride in Atwater Village, seen in the rituals of women sweeping the sidewalks every morning and men washing their rehabbed subcompacts every Saturday. Homemakers like Marisela Uribe, a thirty-year-old émigré from Mexico, insist that their children not wear the baggy jeans and ripped sweatshirts favored by gang members; indeed, cluster shoppers go to the Gap and Montgomery Ward for new clothes.

For nightlife, Hispanic Mix residents head to a handful of entertainment spots at high rates, among them dance clubs, basketball games, boxing matches, and video arcades. Where Hispanic Mix residents do excel is in consumption of media: Their fondness for rap and, especially, Spanish music is off the charts. Beyond their foreign-language publications, they also buy baby, car, and TV magazines more often than the general population. They're big TV fans, watching all manner of soaps, game shows, gritty cop shows, and *novellas*. "When I watch TV, I'm trying to pick up English," says Uribe, who works as a domestic.

Although voting rates are low in Hispanic Mix, residents do identify themselves as liberal Democrats. They tend to favor affirmative action, gay rights, and saving endangered animals. But as is the case in many immigrant-filled clusters, these residents also have a conservative streak, telling pollsters that they support family values, school prayer, and curbing pornography. On issues regarding English-first and immigration measures, there's surprising ambivalence. "I don't think this country can afford everyone who wants to come here," says Gabino Gutierrez, a Mexican American who manages a pizzeria. "I will never forget my home country, but I'm also concerned with my life right here." In Hispanic Mix, that life progresses one day at a time.

PREFERENCES

(Index of 100 = U.S. Average)

Lifestyle / Products

what's hot

boxing matches	556
bus travel	292
pro basketball games	230
Gap	196
Adidas	171
three-way calling	136
charitable volunteering	122
dance music CDs / tapes	121
regular cigarettes	116
life-insurance loans	108

what's not

Limited	67
passports	66
moviegoing	64
hardcover books	61
Home Depot	53
gardens	50
jazz CDs / tapes	48
billards	47
Walt Disney World	28
overdraft protection	19

Food / Drink

individual chocolates	332
avocados	174
Domino's pizza	162
domestic beer	156
children's vitamins	136
decorative icing	128
brown rice	124
veal	118
salsa	118
energy drinks	115

Magazines / Newspapers

Baby Talk	288
Health	219
Vogue	203
Essence	199
Seventeen	178
automotive magazines	127
Home	121
GQ	118
National Enquirer	117
TV Guide	114

Television / Radio

Spanish radio	1559
Martin	350
Entertainment Tonight	296
X-Files	252
New York Undercover	251
urban-contemporary radio	242
Ricki Lake	229
All My Children	222
VH1	217
Married . . . with Children	151

Cars / Trucks

Ford Econoline Club Wagons	122
Kias	111
Toyota 2WD SUVs	109
Toyota Tercels	105
Nissan 2WD SUVs	95
Suzuki 2WD SUVs	91
Mitsubishi Monteros	93
Mazda MPVs	85
Ferraris	83
Toyota Corollas	80

Status: finishing high school and getting a job

SER 61

inner cities

2.1% of U.S. households

Primary age groups: **under 24, 25–44**

Median household income: **$15,000**

Median home value: **$40,400**

Thumbnail Demographics

inner-city, single-parent families and singles

multi-unit rental housing

predominantly African American households

grade school, high school graduates

blue-collar and service workers

Politics

Predominant ideology: liberal Democrat

1996 presidential vote: Bill Clinton

Key issues: public school funding, AIDS education, defusing racial tensions

Sample Neighborhoods

Morrisania, South Bronx, New York 10456

Roxbury, Massachusetts 02119

West Newark, New Jersey 07103

Westvern, Los Angeles, California 90062

Sunny Slope, Kansas City, Missouri 64110

The poorest of urban lifestyles, Inner Cities suffers its share of bad karma. High unemployment, low educational levels, and a high percentage of residents on public assistance combine to create a desolate economic landscape. Family life is challenged by the fact that seven in ten households with children are headed by a single parent, and the median income is below the poverty line. Those striving to make it must often cross economic and racial divides; eight out of ten households are African American. The reputation of Inner Cities has been traditionally the worst of any cluster: a desolate place with high levels of crime, drugs, prostitution, and homeless people. In the South Bronx, New York, home of the largest public housing project in the nation, residents in the late '70s and early '80s figured the best solution was simply to burn it down.

But a funny thing has happened to Inner Cities communities like the South Bronx: They're undergoing a renaissance. Federal and state funds have enabled private developers to build and renovate formerly dilapidated apartments and homes. New legislation is pushing welfare recipients into the workforce and the wage-earning class; the Morrisania Public Library in the South Bronx now keeps one hundred sets of GED preparation materials for people trying to earn a high school diploma, and the newspaper "Help Wanted" section must be kept behind the reference desk so that no one walks away with it. A $29 million 10,000-square-foot shopping center is coming

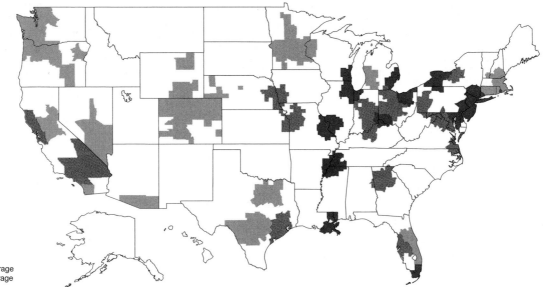

High
Above Average
Below Average
Low

bargain shopping   malt liquor   *Jet*   BET   Hyundai Elantras   moviegoing   Kentucky Fried Chicken

in, on the heels of a new pharmacy and bank. Even vacant lots have been refurbished with gazebos, picnic benches, and greenery.

Today, Inner Cities is no longer the nation's poorest neighborhood type, and the lifestyle is improving. On a Saturday, residents go shopping nearby (dollar bargain stores are typical) or out to eat (mom-and-pop fast-food joints are the norm). Churches and schools offer programs for children, from Scouting to choral singing. Telephone-pole flyers advertise bands at discos and boxing matches: Inner Cities is one of the top clusters for both pursuits. But the chief form of entertainment hasn't changed in neighborhoods where cramped apartments are the norm. "People still sit on their stoops to talk to each other," says Ralph Porter, president of the Mid Bronx Desperadoes, a community housing group, "only now they don't have to watch their backs."

Much of the media in Inner Cities is geared to its African American audience. Magazines like *Jet, Essence,* and *Ebony* are big. At the local record stores, gospel and rhythm and blues garner most of the buyers' interest. Residents watch TV at high rates, especially the talk shows of Montel Williams, Rolanda, and Oprah Winfrey. Because African Americans log three times as many minutes on the phone as whites, telephone services like call-waiting and beepers are popular to keep residents connected. "You go to a party and everyone has a beeper," says José (Ruby) Aristides-Rubiera, manager of Leonardo's Record Shop, which sells CDs and beepers. "People want to keep in touch."

Politically Democratic, Inner Cities voters tell pollsters they're less interested in national issues than the quality-of-life concerns of a poor neighborhood: the safety of their children, the drugs on the corner, keeping their jobs. "People worry about getting by today, never mind tomorrow," says Steve Papaioanou, owner of the Blue Pearl Pizzeria. "When people get their welfare checks on the first and the fifteenth of the month, we're packed." Yet the cluster also has a disproportionate number of people involved in charitable volunteering. "We're poor but proud," explains Marcella Brown, sixty-two, a resident and community board member in the South Bronx. "We feel we couldn't do anything without the help of God." That religious brand of self-help has borne fruit. Community meetings that once drew a dozen people now attract 250, and drugs and homelessness have abated. "People like myself used to feel threatened living here, and we don't anymore," says Brown, a widow who raised eight children. "We're not completely back yet, but we're getting there."

PREFERENCES
(Index of 100 = U.S. Average)

Lifestyle / Products

what's hot

menthol cigarettes	249
moviegoing	152
7-Eleven	149
rolling papers	144
weekly groceries < $60	138
bargain shopping	135
pagers / beepers	130
dancing	120
lottery tickets	117
baby furniture	114

what's not

Taco Bell	79
dry-cleaning	75
volleyball	69
museums	68
barbecuing	67
coupons	61
sewing	57
power tools	52
credit cards	46
Price Club	22

Food / Drink

malt liquor	299
Kentucky Fried Chicken	175
children's vitamins	153
Pepsi	134
fresh fish	122
frozen dinners	120
Kellogg's Corn Flakes	119
doughnuts	115
Pizza Hut	105
pasta	103

Magazines / Newspapers

Jet	933
Sesame Street Parents	326
Soap Opera Digest	262
Sporting News	237
Esquire	207
Spin	184
Muscle & Fitness	181
Life	175
Star	173
Parenting	161

Television / Radio

BET	798
New York Undercover	573
Cosby	509
Beverly Hills, 90210	322
Montel Williams Show	268
Showtime	251
Hangin' with Mr. Cooper	235
Baywatch	225
Oprah Winfrey Show	214
jazz radio	198

Cars / Trucks

Hyundai Elantras	213
Ford Econoline Club Wagons	162
Hyundai Sonatas	158
Chrysler Sebrings	128
Suzuki 2WD SUVs	120
Dodge Spirits	115
Plymouth Acclaims	114
Hyundai Excels	111
Chevrolet Corsicas	108
Plymouth Neons	99

Cluster fashion statement:
wearing a beeper

SER 62
southside city

2.0% of U.S. households

Primary age group: **mixed**

Median household income: **$15,800**

Median home value: **$40,700**

Thumbnail Demographics

poor African American singles in second-tier cities

2–9 unit rental housing

predominantly African American single parents
  and singles

grade school, high school graduates

blue-collar and service workers

Politics

Predominant ideology: liberal Democrat

1996 presidential vote: Bill Clinton

Key issues: defusing racial tensions, public education
  funding, AIDS education

Sample Neighborhoods

Downtown Petersburg, Virginia 23803

Greenville, Mississippi 38701

East Saint Louis, Illinois 62204

Opa-Locka, Florida 33054

Rome, Georgia 30161

This is ground zero, the bottom rung of the nation's socioeconomic ladder: Southside City. The median income is below the poverty line. Much of the housing consists of dilapidated shacks and cinder-block-and-tin-roof dwellings, most worth less than $40,000. Unlike the big-city ghettos that most Americans associate with the face of poverty, Southside City is concentrated in second-tier cities throughout the Southeastern states that lack the private investment necessary to spark a renaissance. Only 7 percent of the predominantly African American residents hold a college diploma, and high schools face endemic problems associated with poor, single-parent families, teenage pregnancy, and a high dropout rate. At elementary schools in Petersburg, Virginia, the goal isn't to excel but merely to bring kids above the fiftieth percentile.

The poverty of Southside City didn't happen overnight. In Petersburg (population 38,000), busing in the 1970s prompted white flight that emptied the city of middle-income residents, businesses, and stable housing prices. Welfare programs increased and began to draw poor people from throughout central Virginia. "The city became a dumping ground for less fortunate people," says banker William Patton. "We became a depressed city." Today, much of the housing stock is more than seventy-five years old and the worse for wear, with peeling walls and sagging roofs. On some streets, for every occupied home, one is boarded up. A downtown shopping

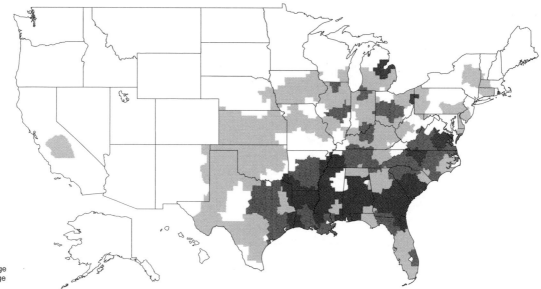

High
Above Average
Below Average
Low

three-way calling   pro wrestling   *Ebony*   urban-contemporary radio   Hyundai Elantras   gospel

strip now includes a pawnshop, a wig store (ninety-nine-cent braids), a Family Dollar Store, and a used-furniture shop. Merchants vie for customers with local drug dealers.

"Petersburg has the strongest drug base for any city of its size in the country," declares Marilynn Sheppard, a pharmacist who also runs the local Western Union outlet. Too many of those customers, she says, are drug dealers transferring cash to contacts in Jamaica.

For residents, living in Southside City can be a desolate experience. All the movie theaters, dance clubs, and white-tablecloth restaurants have long since left the area. Residents tell pollsters they wish they could spend more time keeping up with fashion. As record store clerk Marie Parham observes, "We're behind on a lot of things. The kids have nothing to do and nowhere to go." Consumers make do with corner grocers, carryouts, hair salons, and the occasional record shop. Television is the chief form of entertainment, especially sitcoms and talk shows like *Jerry Springer.* "People are happy to watch someone who's worse off than they are," says Yvette Robinson, a thirty-seven-year-old rural-development specialist. "TV helps them transcend their situation."

Southside citizens are heavy users of phone services like call-waiting and caller ID, especially single mothers, for whom phones are like a lifeline, keeping them in touch with friends and making sure their loved ones are safe. Record stores are also popular, selling rap, rhythm and blues, and gospel music at high rates. "Gospel sends a positive message to people," explains Parham, thirty-eight, of Crockett's Records & Tapes. "But a lot of people are into hip-hop because they like the beat and don't listen to the words."

Politically, Southside City is one of the most liberal clusters in America, though low voter turnout dilutes their power at the polls. Residents are all for increasing funding for public schools, child social services, and environmental programs. But apathy is palpable in communities like Petersburg, where residents complain of difficulties finding enough people to join a march honoring Dr. Martin Luther King. For all this depressing news, residents aren't completely pessimistic about the future. In Petersburg, local business leaders are trying to spur gentrification with renovated housing and antique shops. In every cluster community, activists like Yvette Robinson are joining committees to reduce teen pregnancy, mentor at-risk students, and plan for a better future. "We're a dying city, but we're trying to come back," says a hopeful Robinson. "We're hanging in there, and we will come back."

PREFERENCES

(Index of 100 = U.S. Average)

Lifestyle / Products

what's hot

three-way calling 304

gospel music
CDs / tapes 230

college basketball
games 193

weekly groceries < $60
163

pro wrestling matches
168

diet pills 154

attending church 139

cooking 126

karate / martial arts
111

Holiday Inn 111

what's not

vitamins 77

voting 75

35-mm cameras 71

coupons 72

mail-order shopping 67

campers 22

gas grills 24

new-wave CDs / tapes
10

woodworking 6

tractor pulls 0

Food / Drink

instant grits 227

whole milk 171

domestic beer 139

baby food 148

Pepsi 134

Kentucky Fried Chicken
134

sausage 126

canned chili 124

Spam 123

pork chops 123

Magazines / Newspapers

Ebony 401

Baby Talk 258

Esquire 239

Soap Opera Digest 203

fitness magazines 170

bridal magazines 148

Stereo Review 137

Star 133

Us 130

Glamour 125

Television / Radio

urban-contemporary
radio 1103

Cosby 361

religious / gospel radio
354

The Wayans Bros. 306

Hangin' with Mr. Cooper
216

Living Single 244

Good Morning America
207

Jerry Springer Show
196

Court TV 188

Showtime 159

Cars / Trucks

Hyundai Elantras 296

Mitsubishi Mirages 233

Hyundai Sonatas 210

Hyundai Accents 193

Suzuki 2WD SUVs 191

Mitsubishi Galants 165

Cadillac Fleetwoods 139

Suzuki Swifts 137

Mazda Protegés 126

Mazda 929s 123

American Dream:
winning the lottery

Determining Your Cluster

If you live in the United States, you can determine any neighborhood's PRIZM cluster makeup by visiting the Claritas site on the World Wide Web called "You Are Where You Live." Simply log on to the Web and go to http://yawyl.claritas.com/ and key in the appropriate zip code. Then check chapter 7 for detailed portraits of the typical lifestyle of each cluster — the food, the drink, the magazines and TV shows, the leisure activities and daily concerns.

APPENDIX THE **UNIVERSAL PRINCIPLES** OF **CLUSTERING**
in the clustered world, ten rules to live by

1 *People and Birds of a Feather Flock Together.*

Clusters are based on the observable sociological phenomenon that people tend to live with others like themselves, sharing similar demographics, lifestyles, and values. Surveys show that the hip singles in America's Bohemian Mix lifestyle have more in common with their counterparts in England's Studio Singles cluster than with working-class neighborhoods down the street. Both groups tend to buy imported food, hang out at bars and coffee shops, and dislike fast-food chains. Plans for the arrival of a new McDonald's generally spark noisy protests.

2 *The Mass Market Is Dead.*

In today's clustered world, there are so many niche audiences that cable channels can devote round-the-clock programming to science fiction, comedy, or equestrian sports. Shoppers who used to buy all their groceries in a supermarket can dash into a gas station mini-mart, load up at warehouse clubs, or buy designer coffee beans at a specialty chain like Starbucks. In Britain, you can buy beer at cinemas. In Spain, 7-Elevens sell hard liquor, bulk olives in barrels, and fresh-baked pies. In today's marketplace, a hole-in-the-wall store in the Inner Cities community of the South Bronx may sell rap tapes, rent pagers, offer international long-distance phone service, and have a video arcade on the premises.

3 *There's Little Connection Between Income and Lifestyle.*

Time was that what you earned had a great influence on how you lived. But even those who earn the same amount of money may choose among myriad lifestyles today. With a household income of

$40,000, you may be a middle-class white-collar family of the Suburban Sprawl group, driving an Acura, watching MTV, and carrying a wallet full of credit cards to the shopping mall. Or you may live in a blue-collar Blue-Chip Blues cluster, drinking domestic rather than imported beer and filling your basement with camping equipment rather than computer software.

4 *The Super-Rich Live Differently from the Rest of Us — But Not from Each Other.*

F. Scott Fitzgerald had it right when he wrote that the well-to-do live in a world removed from the rest of us. But the corollary to his observation is that although the rich live differently from the masses, they live very much like other rich people in other countries. In clusters like Blue Blood Estates (U.S.), Canadian Establishment (Canada), and Clever Capitalists (Great Britain), residents live in sprawling mansions, drive luxury imports, belong to nearby country clubs, and support a strong service economy. In what might be called domestic outsourcing, they hire outsiders to do everything from cooking and gardening to interior decorating and child care. Status is the reputation of your child's play group.

5 *Culture Does Not Honor Political Boundaries.*

Every tourist knows that people are different from one nation to the next. But thanks to the marvels of telecommunication and multinational companies, you can watch *Baywatch* across Europe, find Barbie dolls even in the elusive Japanese market, and get your Big Mac hot almost anywhere from New Jersey to Japan. Through thick and thin, Sara Lee and Weight Watchers are contributing to universal lifestyles, and teenagers around the world strive to look as bored and gaunt as models from Levi's and the Gap.

6 *Everyone Collects Something.*

Whether it's Elvis plates in America's Shotguns & Pickups cluster or antique furnishings in Spain's Classic Bourgeoisie Neighborhoods, people in every lifestyle have a penchant for collectibles. The real reason, according to Bill Raup, who makes ceramic miniatures of houses in his Rural Industria community of Milton, Pennsylvania, is the chance to be an authority. "Everyone wants to be an expert, and you are an expert with your own collection," he explains from his cluttered shop, called Landmark Antiques. "All the memories are your own. You don't need anyone else to appreciate them." If we are born alone and we die alone, we all spend the time in between collecting something that at least we alone value.

7 *Everybody Complains About Junk Mail, But Nobody Does Anything About It.*

With clusters allowing marketers to better target their products and services, many consumers view the inundation of junk mail and telemarketing pitches as an invasion of privacy. Don't just complain. If you really hate direct-marketing come-ons, stop buying by catalog, limit the personal information you include on warranty cards and credit applications, and contact the Direct Marketing Association to request that your name be removed from marketing lists (DMA, Mail Preference Service, P.O. Box 9008, Farmingdale, NY 11735; or DMA, Telephone Preference Service, P.O. Box 9014, Farmingdale, NY 11735). Better yet, move to the countryside, where you're less likely to be hassled by marketing pitches.

8 *No Home Is Complete Without a Trophy.*

No matter how meager the accomplishment, almost everyone in every cluster has some kind of trophy or award on display. In a Single City Blues bedroom, a master's degree hangs prominently on a wall decorated with tie-dyed macramé. A welfare mother from Inner Cities covers a windowsill with her four sons' trophies in baseball, football, math, and school attendance. In Cumberland, Maryland, Walter Hite's Hometown Retired apartment features his prized possession atop a TV set: a foot-high trophy from a horseshoe-pitching contest the year before. He won it when he was eighty years old.

9 *There's Always an Exception That Proves the Rule.*

The late billionaire Sam Walton used to live in a backwater Arkansas town classified Golden Ponds. There's a gay couple renting a house in a Kids & Cul-de-Sacs community. Mechanics earning less than $20,000 a year live in Blue Blood Estates. And you think you can't possibly be like your next-door neighbors (they've got such awful taste). It's a knee-jerk reaction, but census demographics, marketing research, and public opinion polls indicate otherwise: You really are more like your neighbor than someone from the other side of town. And just because you can point to a local anomaly like Sam Walton doesn't mean the system is flawed. You and your neighbor may seem dissimilar on the surface, but dig deeper (like in your pantries and upbringing) and you're likely to find you have much in common.

10 *Every Community Has a Historian.*

No matter how small the dot on the map, every community typically has someone who can explain how the area became what it is today. You can call that person the block mayor, an old-timer, even just a busybody, but he or she knows who lived where over the last century, which businesses have come and gone, and what it was like in the 1940s on a Saturday night. God should reserve a special place in heaven for these individuals. They hold the world's institutional memory and pass on how their communities' lifestyles evolved in the clustered world.

RESOURCES

The geodemographic information used in this book was provided by the following companies:

■ Claritas Inc., 1525 Wilson Boulevard, Suite 1000, Arlington, Virginia 22209 USA. (800) 234-5973. Web site: www.claritas.com

■ Compusearch Micromarketing Data & Systems, 330 Front Street West, Suite 1100, Toronto, Ontario M5V 3B7 Canada. (416) 348-9180. Web site: www.bpmsi.com

■ Experian Micromarketing, Talbot House, Talbot Street, Nottingham NG1 5HF United Kingdom. (44) 115 941 0888. Web site: www.experian.com

The survey data included in this book came from the following sources:

■ Mediamark Research Inc., 708 Third Avenue, New York, New York 10017 USA. (800) 310-3305. Web site: www.mediamark.com

■ NFO Research, Inc., 2700 Oregon Road, Northwood, Ohio 43619 USA. (419) 666-8800. Web site: www.nfor.com

■ The Polk Company, 26955 Northwestern Highway, Southfield, Michigan 48034 USA. (248) 728-7000. Web site: www.polk.com

■ Simmons Market Research Bureau, 309 West 49th Street, New York, New York 10019 USA. (212) 373-8900.

■ U.S. Bureau of the Census, Population Division, Washington, D.C. 20233 USA. (301) 457-2422. Web site: www.census.gov

ACKNOWLEDGMENTS

This book could not have been written without the help of many people, and I am sincerely grateful to all of them.

First, I want to thank Christine Zylbert, whose incomparable editing graces every page of the book. For fifteen years as the editor of my writing projects, she has been the one who makes me look better than I am with her wit, intelligence, and sensitivity.

Thanks go to everyone at Claritas for their many contributions to *The Clustered World,* which draws heavily on their PRIZM cluster system and Compass marketing software: Kathy Dugan, for her friendship and energy championing the book; Dave Miller, for his insights into the PRIZM clusters and his guidance divining my computerized itinerary for the U.S. research; Kevin Lourens, for his technical wizardry and assistance bringing to life the Compass software; Brent Roderick, for mapping the cluster neighborhoods I visited; Mike Cevarr, for providing critical information about the PRIZM clusters; Nancy Deck, for her warm support throughout this project; and Jay Ulrich, Ed Walker, and Deborah Helman, for their valuable technical help in developing cluster profiles and maps. I am also thankful to other Claritas staffers who shared their expertise with me in countless ways: Rose Bacon, Mike Mancini, Fran Laura, Richard Worden, Ken Hodges, Alan Wong, Ron Cohen, Geneen Roby, Soraya Chemaly, Andy Paul, Eddie Pickle, Larry Disney, Mike Madigan, Keith Satter, Michael Mosley, Sandy Watson, Heather Oles, and Blair Zucker.

My thanks also go to a number of staffers at Compusearch who had a hand in chronicling Canada's lifestyles with data, maps, and commentary: R. Bruce Carroll, Jan Kestle, Rupen Seoni, Wendy Correoso, Elena Bozzelli, Nicole Frechette, Martin Dalpé, and Steve

Rayner. I am particularly indebted to geodemographer Tony Lea for his seasoned wisdom and his gracious help throughout the project.

I want to thank all the Experian staffers in London and Nottingham, England, for their expertise and courtesy in helping me research the British and Global MOSAIC systems, their cluster lifestyles, and their client projects. I am especially grateful for all the time and effort extended on my behalf by Richard Webber and Andrea McDonald. In addition, I want to thank everyone at Experian MOSAIC Iberia in Madrid for their hospitality in helping arrange interviews, an interpreter, and a tour of neighborhoods representing the Spanish MOSAIC clusters. I am especially indebted to David Monsó and Ernst Verbeek for serving as guides through the lifestyles of Spain, and Regina Werum for her assistance with consuming patterns in Germany.

Over the years, many people have provided me with the opportunity to write about a wide range of contemporary issues that found their way into the pages of this book: thank you, Don Collier and Melanie Mumper-Dickerson at NFO Research, Inc.; Randy Rieland at Discovery Online; Jack Limpert at *Washingtonian;* George Hackett, Nancy Cooper, and Paul O'Donnell at *Newsweek;* Cullen Murphy and Allan Reeder at *The Atlantic Monthly;* Lewis Lord at *U.S. News & World Report;* and Myrna Blyth, Pamela Guthrie O'Brien, and Shana Aborn at *Ladies' Home Journal.*

I want to thank journalist Jessica Sandham for her survey research and editing contribution on this and many other projects; Gar Willoughby for his research and fieldwork in Washington and Montreal; Barbara Morgenstern, for being a thoughtful editor as well as my sister; and Jonathan Robbin, the father of geodemography and the one who started me on this journey. I'd be remiss if I didn't thank my super agent, Elaine Markson, for all her encouragement and assistance in innumerable ways; Catherine Crawford, the editor at Little, Brown who acquired the book; Betsy Uhrig, the copyeditor who polished the manuscript with a deft touch; and Sarah Burnes, who saw the book through to publication with energy, skill, and care.

Thanks, of course, go to my family and friends for their support as well as their beds and breakfasts: Ellen and Gary Franks; Barbara and Paul Lusman, as well as Joel, Debbie, and Rebecca Lusman; Sheila and Lee Mondshein; Phil and Roxy Stanger; Peter and Jan Stanger; Bruce Duffy; Steve and Barbara Fennell; Alan Green; Louis and Eva Greenspan; Allan Mandell; Liz and Wayne Michel; Joanne Ostrow, Liz Shane and baby Anna; Rudy Papenfuhs; Michael Vezo;

Lorraine Rose and Joel Kaplan; Steve Sack; Judy and Luis Salgado; and Ted Salins. A special thanks to Jim O'Neill, the world's best travel agent, at Travelogue; and Moses Mongo, political analyst and Diamond Cab driver. Also a heartfelt expression of appreciation to Sidney Weiss, my father and friend, whose curiosity and generosity of spirit taught me how to talk to strangers.

I am most thankful to my wife, Phyllis Stanger, and our children, Elizabeth and Jonathan, for their steadfast love, support, and understanding during my weeks on the road and the months holed up in my office. These words won't make up for all the time I was away, but at least I can put into print how much I cherish them and their tolerance of my writing life.

Finally, thanks go out to the hundreds of people who agreed to be interviewed for this book, who opened their kitchens and bedrooms to my prying eyes and questions, and who did so graciously and without reticence. *The Clustered World* could not exist without them, and for their trust and warmheartedess, I am sincerely grateful.

INDEX